The **Sounds** of
Chinese

This accessible textbook provides a clear introduction to the sounds of Standard
Chinese, designed for English-speaking students with no prior knowledge of
linguistics. It explains from scratch the fundamentals of articulatory phonetics (the
study of how speech sounds are produced) and phonology (the study of sound
systems), and clearly applies them to the phonetic and phonological properties of
Chinese. Topics covered include consonants, vowels, syllable structure, tone, stress,
intonation, loanwords, and different varieties of Standard Chinese. Clear
comparisons with English sounds are given wherever relevant, along with practical
pronunciation advice. All the sounds described are demonstrated by native speakers
on the audio CD (included) and over fifty graded exercises are provided, encouraging
students to put their knowledge into practice. Building a solid understanding of how
Chinese sounds work, this text will be invaluable to students of Chinese wishing to
improve their pronunciation, their teachers, and students of Chinese linguistics.

YEN-HWEI LIN is Professor of Linguistics at Michigan State University. She has
published widely on Chinese phonology and several other areas of phonology,
including syllable structure, feature theory, and segmental phonology. She is editor of
Special Issue on Phonetics and Phonology (Language and Linguistics 5.4, 2004) and
Proceedings of the Fifteenth North American Conference on Chinese Linguistics (2004),
and is currently writing a book on Chinese segmental phonology.

The **Sounds** of
Chinese

Yen-Hwei Lin

CAMBRIDGE
UNIVERSITY PRESS

CAMBRIDGE UNIVERSITY PRESS
Cambridge, New York, Melbourne, Madrid, Cape Town, Singapore, São Paulo
São Paulo, Delhi, Mexico City

Cambridge University Press
The Edinburgh Building, Cambridge CB2 8RU, UK

Published in the United States of America by Cambridge University Press, New York

www.cambridge.org
Information on this title: www.cambridge.org/9780521603980

First published 2007
3rd printing 2012

Printed at Print on Demand, World Wide, UK

A catalogue record for this publication is available from the British Library

Library of Congress Cataloguing in Publication data
Lin, Yen-Hwei.
The Sounds of Chinese / Yen-Hwei Lin.
    p.   cm.
Includes bibliographical references and index.
ISBN 978-0-521-60398-0 (pbk.)
1. Chinese language–phonetics.   2. Chinese language–phonology.   3. Chinese
language–Textbooks for foreign speakers–English.   I. Title.
PL1205.L56   2007
495.1′15 – dc22   2007006788

ISBN 978-0-521-60398-0 Paperback

Contents

Figures and tables

Figures

Tables

Preface

This book provides an introduction to Standard Chinese phonetics and phonology, designed for English-speaking students and readers with no prior knowledge of linguistics. The intended readers include students learning Chinese as a foreign language, undergraduate and beginning graduate students majoring in Chinese language and/or Chinese linguistics, Chinese language teachers, and anyone who is interested in learning more about the sounds of Standard Chinese. As a textbook, it can be used for an introductory course in Chinese phonetics and phonology, for the phonetics and phonology parts of a Chinese linguistics or Chinese grammar course, for Chinese language teacher training courses/workshops, or as a supplementary text for a Chinese language course. The book can also serve for independent study or as a reference book for anyone who wants to improve their Standard Chinese pronunciation or to obtain general knowledge of Chinese phonetics and phonology.

After the introductory chapter which provides background information regarding the Chinese language, its linguistic characteristics, its writing system, and phonetics and phonology, the book covers: (i) the phonetics of consonants, vowels, and tone (how they are produced) in chapters 2–4; (ii) syllable structure (how sequences of sounds are organized) in chapter 5; (iii) the phonological system (how and why a sound changes its pronunciation in what context) in chapters 7–9; (iv) the interaction of tone with stress and intonation in chapter 10; (v) loanword adaptation (how English sounds are adapted into Chinese sounds) in chapter 11; (vi) dialectal variation in Standard Chinese in chapter 12; and (vii) a comparison between the *pīnyīn* romanization spelling system and phonetic transcription in chapter 6.

The appendices provide information about the symbols used for phonetic transcription, a set of tables listing all possible Chinese syllables with *pīnyīn* spelling and corresponding phonetic transcription, and Internet resources. There are also over fifty graded exercises, suggestions for further reading, and a glossary of technical terms. The terms are in small capitals in the text when they first appear and also when they reappear in a different chapter or in appropriate contexts as a reminder. *The Sounds of Chinese CD* included with this book demonstrates the sounds and examples in the text and some exercises. In the book, a headphone icon is placed before the sets of examples that can be found on the CD.

I have tried to cover both the phonetic and phonological aspects evenly with sufficient details since the practical purpose of improving pronunciation involves learning both how an individual sound is produced (the phonetic aspect) and how and why a sound must or may be pronounced differently in a particular context (the phonological aspect). Needless to say, the comprehensive coverage also makes this volume useful as a textbook and a reference book for Chinese phonetics and phonology. Many phenomena discussed in the book have multiple analyses in the literature. My choice for a particular analysis over others is partly determined by the ease of presenting the idea to readers with no prior linguistics background and partly influenced by personal preference based on my own research. For those who want to know different views from what is presented or to go beyond the basics, I have included suggestions for further reading.

Although it took a little longer than I expected to complete this book, I have thoroughly enjoyed working on the project. I want to thank Helen Barton of Cambridge University Press, who suggested the idea for this book to me and provided helpful suggestions on the draft chapters, an anonymous reader, my production editor Liz Davey of Cambridge University Press, and my copy-editor, Adrian Stenton. I acknowledge the permission to reprint the International Phonetic Alphabet granted by the International Phonetic Association (http://www.arts.gla.ac.uk/IPA/ipa.html), and a Research Enhancement Grant for Visiting Professor granted by City University of Hong Kong from May 6 to June 5 in 2005. I am grateful to Eric Zee and Wai-Sum Lee for their answers to several specific questions I had about Chinese phonetics. Thanks also go to Joseph Jue Wang and Hsiao-ping Wang for recording the sounds and examples for *The Sounds of Chinese CD*.

Yen-Hwei Lin

1 Introduction

Chinese is the native language of the *Han* people, who form the largest ethnic group in China with over 90 percent of the total population. The Chinese language consists of seven mutually unintelligible dialect families, each of which contains many dialects and the largest of which is the Mandarin dialect family. In the broad sense, the word *Chinese* refers to all varieties of the language spoken by the *Han* people. In the narrow sense, Chinese or Mandarin is also used to mean Standard Chinese or Standard Mandarin, the official language of mainland China and Taiwan. Since there are major differences in the sound systems among the major dialect groups (cf. §12.1), this book will mainly focus on the sounds of Standard Chinese.

This introductory chapter has three goals. First, it provides basic background about the Chinese language in general and Standard Chinese in particular (§§1.1–1.4). Second, it presents a brief introduction to phonetics and phonology to set the foundation for the discussion of the subsequent chapters (§1.5). Third, it gives an overview of the topics and organization of the book.

1.1 The Chinese language family

The Chinese language family is genetically classified as a major branch of the Sino-Tibetan language family. The different varieties of Chinese can be grouped into seven dialect families, each of which consists of many dialects. The Mandarin dialects (or the northern dialects), spoken by more than 70 percent of Chinese speakers in the northern and southwest regions of China, can be further divided into four subfamilies: northern, northwestern, southwestern, and Lower Yangzi. The Beijing (or Peking) dialect, which forms the basis of Standard Chinese, is the best-known Mandarin dialect. The Wu dialects are spoken by more than 8 percent of Chinese speakers in the coastal area around Shanghai and Zhejiang Province. In Guangdong and Guangxi Provinces and in Hong Kong, the Yue dialects are spoken by 5 percent of Chinese speakers. Cantonese is a Yue dialect spoken in and around the city of Guangzhou (or Canton) and Hong Kong, as well as many traditional overseas Chinese communities. The speakers of each of the remaining four dialect families constitute less than 5 percent of the Chinese-speaking population. The Min dialects, consisting of northern Min and southern Min subfamilies, are spoken in Fujian Province, Taiwan, and some coastal areas of southern China. The Min dialect spoken in Taiwan, which is a variety of southern Min, is often called Taiwanese. The Hakka dialects are found near the borders of Guangdong, Fujian, and Jiangxi Provinces and widely scattered in other parts of China from Sichuan Province to Taiwan. Finally, the Xiang dialects are spoken in Hunan Province and the Gan dialects in Jiangxi Province.[1]

The different varieties of Chinese are traditionally referred to as *regional dialects* (*fāngyán* 'regional speech') although the different dialect families and even some dialects within the same family are mutually unintelligible and could be considered different languages. For example, we can think of Mandarin and Cantonese as two different languages of the Chinese language family, just as Portuguese and Italian are two different languages of the Romance language family. In fact, some linguistics scholars prefer the term *Chinese languages* for those mutually unintelligible varieties. However, the tradition persists partly because all these varieties of Chinese share the same written language and a long tradition of political, economic, and cultural unity. For the moment, let us follow the tradition and refer to different varieties of Chinese as dialects and this issue will be discussed again in §12.1.

1.2 Standard Chinese

Standard Chinese (henceforth SC) is called *Pǔtōnghuà* 'common speech' in China, *Guóyǔ* 'national language' in Taiwan, and *Huáyǔ* 'Chinese language' in Singapore. Other English terms for SC include Standard Mandarin, Mandarin Chinese, or Mandarin. As the official language of China and Taiwan, SC is used in school and universities and serves all official functions. On national radio and television broadcasts, SC is the language used, but on regional stations, local dialects may be used in addition to SC.

In the early twentieth century, the standard pronunciation of SC was established and promoted by the Republic of China as *Guóyǔ* 'national language.' After 1949, when the People's Republic of China was founded, SC was renamed as *Pǔtōnghuà* 'common speech' and defined as 'the common language of China,

---

[1] This classification of Chinese dialects is based on Li and Thompson (1981:3) and Ramsey (1989:87). For a map of Chinese dialects, see Li and Thompson (1981:4), Ramsey (1989: Figure 6), Lyovin (1997: Map VIII), and the websites in Appendix C.

based on the northern dialects, with the Peking phonological system as its norm of pronunciation' (Norman 1988: 135).[2] The lexical and grammatical expressions of SC are based more broadly on the northern Mandarin dialects but exclude specific local expressions including those used in the Beijing dialect. Although the pronunciation of SC is based on the phonology of the Beijing dialect, this does not mean the two have identical phonological and phonetic systems. For example, RHOTACIZED vowels (§8.2 and §3.4.5) are much more common in the Beijing dialect than in SC.

Although SC is taught in school and used in broadcasts, in reality the pronunciation of SC speakers is by no means uniform. What is considered to be the standard accent of SC tolerates a range of slightly different pronunciations. This phenomenon is common for any so-called standard language; for example, what is considered to be standard English in North America also covers a range of slightly different accents. In addition, there are different norms of SC in China, Taiwan, and Singapore, just as there are different norms of standard English in different English-speaking countries or regions. For example, in Taiwan and Singapore, the use of NEUTRAL TONE and rhotacized vowels is much less common than that in mainland China (see §12.2). The development of different norms of SC is mainly due to socio-political separation and the influence of the local dialects.

SC is generally associated with good education, authority, and formality, but educated people and government officials do not necessarily have the prescribed pronunciation of SC. Most Chinese learn to speak SC only after they have acquired their regional dialects and may learn from schoolteachers who do not have correct SC pronunciation themselves. In general, local dialects are used with family members and sometimes in public places, whereas SC is used more in schools and in workplaces (Chen 1999:54–5). In addition, many Chinese speakers regard SC simply as a practical tool of communication and often retain their local accents when speaking SC, especially within their local communities. Since there are so many different regional dialects, there are as many dialect-accented SCs or local SCs. More discussion of different varieties of SC will be given in §§12.2–12.3.

1.3 Tone, syllable, morpheme, and word

Chinese is a TONE language, a language in which changes in the PITCH of the voice can be used to denote differences in word meaning. We can think of tone as a third type of speech element in addition to consonants and vowels.

---

[2] For more details on the history of the establishment and promotion of standard spoken and written Chinese, see Chen (1999).

English makes use of consonants and vowels to form different words: *bad* and *pad* differ in one consonant and have different meanings; *bed* and *bad* have different vowels and also have different meanings. In addition to consonants and vowels, Chinese also uses tone to differentiate word meaning.

The examples in (1) from SC illustrate that in words with identical consonant and vowel combination, differences in tone are used to signal differences in meaning. The pitch value in the third column is based on a scale of 1 to 5, with 5 indicating the highest pitch and 1 the lowest (Chao 1930, 1968:26). In SC, the five levels of pitch distinguish four tones. For example, for the word 'hemp', the pitch starts in the middle of the pitch range (pitch level 3) and moves higher to pitch level 5. Traditionally, for ease of reference, the four tones are labeled as tone 1 to tone 4, as shown in the 'tone number' column (see also §4.2.1, example (7)). In the *pīnyīn* romanization system of SC (see §1.4 below), the tonal mark is placed on the vowel. It is important to note that, as a third type of speech element, tone is not an inherent feature of a vowel but can be viewed as a property of the whole SYLLABLE (see §4.1.3).

(1) Four tones in SC

C+V	TONE/PITCH PATTERN	PITCH VALUE	TONE NUMBER	*PĪNYĪN*	MEANING
ma	high level	55	tone 1	*mā*	'mother'
ma	high rising	35	tone 2	*má*	'hemp'
ma	low falling-rising	214	tone 3	*mǎ*	'horse'
ma	high falling	51	tone 4	*mà*	'to scold'

C = consonant   V = vowel

In general, each Chinese syllable bears a tone. A syllable is a PROSODIC UNIT for carrying tone and STRESS. For example, in English, the word *system* has two syllables, *sys* and *tem*, with the first syllable as the STRESSED SYLLABLE. A Chinese word like *xuéxiào* 'school' has two syllables and two tones, a high rising tone (tone 2) on the first syllable *xué* and a high falling tone (tone 4) on the second syllable *xiào*. Chapters 4 and 9 will have further discussion of SC tone.

Chinese is typically classified as an analytic or isolating language in which each MORPHEME is usually a word. A morpheme is the smallest meaningful unit in a language. For example, in English, the word *uncontrollable* is formed by three morphemes: the word *control* is followed by the SUFFIX *able* and preceded by the PREFIX *un*. A free morpheme like *control* can stand alone as an independent word. On the other hand, an AFFIX (a prefix or a suffix) is a bound morpheme that must be attached to a STEM (i.e. a morpheme to which an affix is added). AFFIXATION is the general process of adding an affix to a stem. Specifically, SUFFIXATION is the process of adding a suffix after a stem and PREFIXATION is the process of adding a prefix before a stem. Unlike English and many other languages, Chinese has very few prefixes and suffixes to form a complex word. On the other hand, modern Chinese has a great number of compound words similar to such compounds as *street light* and *wool sweater* in English. For example, *jiēdēng* 'street light' consists of two morphemes: *jiē* 'street' and *dēng* 'light', and *máoyī* 'wool sweater' can be decomposed to *máo* 'hair, wool' and *yī* 'clothing'.[3]

Chinese is also often referred to as a MONOSYLLABIC language, which means that almost all words contain only one syllable. In English there are a great number of POLYSYLLABIC words. Whether or not Chinese words are monosyllabic depends on how a *word* is defined in Chinese, but to reach a consensus on such a definition has proved to be unexpectedly difficult in Chinese, partly because of the general lack of AFFIXATION in Chinese word formation.[4] The term *zì* 'character' refers to a graph in the Chinese writing system (see §1.4 below) that corresponds to a morpheme and is one syllable in length. If each Chinese character is equivalent to a word, then Chinese words are indeed monosyllabic. However, if a word is defined as an independent basic unit for forming sentences, polysyllabic forms such as *xuéxiào* 'school' and *rúguǒ* 'if' should be considered single words although they consist of two syllables and they are written with two characters. The characterization of Chinese as being monosyllabic fits much better with classical Chinese where over 90 percent of words are monosyllabic. In modern Chinese, however, 95 percent of morphemes are monosyllabic,[5] but about half or more than half of the words are polysyllabic and consist of more than one morpheme (cf. Chen 1999:138–9).

To summarize, in modern Chinese, each syllable generally bears a tone, most morphemes are monosyllabic, and words may consist of one or more morphemes and hence may be monosyllabic or polysyllabic.

1.4 Chinese characters, romanization, and pronunciation

Chinese has a logographic writing system in which each character represents a morpheme, whereas an alphabetic writing system as used in English employs

---

[3] In fact, *yī* is not usually used as a single word; it is combined with *fú* 'clothes' to yield *yīfu* 'clothes'. Some non-affix morphemes in modern Chinese have to be combined with other morphemes to form independent words. For more information about Chinese morphemes and words, see Li and Thompson (1981: chapters 2 and 3) and Packard (2000).

[4] See Duanmu (2000: chapter 5) and Packard (2000) for more details.

[5] Polysyllabic morphemes include words such as *húdié* 'butterfly' and most transliterated loanwords, such as *niǔyuē* 'New York'.

a character (or letter) or combination of characters to represent the speech sounds. As mentioned above, each Chinese character is one syllable in length and the majority of Chinese morphemes are monosyllabic. Since a morpheme is the smallest meaningful linguistic unit, each Chinese character expresses some meaning. This does not mean there is no way to get a hint of pronunciation from the characters. In fact, over 90 percent of Chinese characters consist of one subcomponent denoting meaning and another denoting the pronunciation (Chen 1999:141). In (2a–c), all three characters are pronounced with the same consonant and vowel combination.

(2)

	CHARACTER	C+V	TONE	MEANING	*PĪNYĪN*
a.	马	ma	214	'horse'	*mǎ*
b.	妈	ma	55	'mother'	*mā*
c.	蚂	ma	214	'ant'	*mǎ*
d.	女			'female'	*nǚ*
e.	虫			'insect'	*chóng*

The character in (2a) is used in (2bc) to denote the pronunciation of the consonant and the vowel but not the meaning. That is, all three characters in (2a–c) share the same component 马 and are pronounced with the same consonant and vowel combination [ma], but the meaning of 'horse' for 马 has nothing to do with 'mother' (2b) or 'ant' (2c). The subcomponent at the left side of (2b) means 'female' and that of (2c) means 'insect', as illustrated in (2de). The left-side subcomponents in (2bc) do not denote possible pronunciation but do contribute to the meaning: 'mother' is female and 'ant' is a kind of insect. Although most Chinese characters contain a subcomponent to signal possible pronunciation, there is still a relatively high degree of arbitrariness between a written character and its actual pronunciation.[6]

    The Chinese writing system as a well-developed system was established roughly in the fourteenth century BC and since then has undergone several major stages of development. The total number of Chinese characters is now around 56,000 but the number of most common characters are 2,500 and a college graduate is expected to recognize at least 3,500 characters (Chen 1999:136). The high number and complexity of Chinese characters and the difficulty of

---

[6] However, see DeFrancis (1984) for a different view and for more discussion of the nature of Chinese characters. See also Chen (1999: chapter 8) for the basic features and history of the Chinese writing system.

learning them were often regarded as obstacles to achieving a high literacy rate and modernization. Simplification of the writing system thus became an issue during the first half of the twentieth century. In 1956 the People's Republic of China promulgated the Scheme of Simplified Chinese Characters and since then this new set of simplified characters has been used in China. However, the traditional characters are still used in Taiwan and many traditional overseas Chinese communities. Throughout this book, when Chinese characters are provided in examples, the simplified characters are adopted.

The romanization systems designed to indicate the pronunciation of Chinese characters were first developed by Western missionaries in China. The first phonographic writing of Chinese promoted by the government was *zhùyīn zìmǔ* 'sound denoting letters' or *zhùyīn fúhào* 'sound denoting symbols', which was used as a tool to teach and annotate the pronunciation of characters before 1958 in China and has been in continuous use in Taiwan. In this system, the roman alphabet is not adopted and instead a set of simple characters is used; for example, ㄇ represents the sound [m] and ㄞ the vowel sequence [ai]. In contrast, *hànyǔ pīnyīn* 'Chinese sound spelling' or simply *pīnyīn* 'sound spelling', which replaced *zhùyīn zìmǔ* after 1958 in the People's Republic of China, adopts the roman alphabet. The *pīnyīn* system, which has become the standard transcription system of Chinese words, has been taught in school in China, is the most popular romanization system taught in school outside China, and is used as the input system in Chinese word processing on computers. Before *pīnyīn* became commonly in use, the Wade-Giles romanization system, which was created by Sir Thomas Wade and modified by Herbert A. Giles in his *Chinese–English dictionary*, published in 1912, served as the standard transcription system in scholarly works in English (Norman 1988:173). A less commonly used system is the Yale system, which was developed from the *Dictionary of Spoken Chinese* issued by the War Department in the United States in 1945 (Norman 1988:174–5). In Taiwan there is an official romanization scheme for the transliteration of Chinese proper names, which is similar but not identical to *pīnyīn*; however, many people continue to use the Wade-Giles system or base the transliteration on the pronunciation of the local dialects.[7] In this book, we use only the *pīnyīn* system.

However, the *pīnyīn* system is not really a phonetic transcription system. In fact, no romanization or alphabetic systems provide a perfect match between an alphabetic letter and the actual pronunciation. For example, in English, the

---

[7] For more details on the system of *zhùyīn fúhào* and the official romanization system in Taiwan, see Chen (1999:181 and 190). For a comparison of the Wade-Giles system, the Yale system, and *pīnyīn*, see the Internet resources in Appendix C.

letter *i* is pronounced differently in *live* and *life*, and in *pīnyīn* the letter *i* is also pronounced differently in *sī* 'silk' and *jīa* 'home'. To accurately transcribe pronunciation, we have to use a phonetic transcription system such as the INTERNATIONAL PHONETIC ALPHABET (IPA). The IPA is the standard transcription system used by linguists to represent the sounds of all human languages. Since in this system each attested human language sound is represented by a unique phonetic symbol, it becomes possible to transcribe and describe phonetically different sounds that are not differentiated by orthography or romanization systems. In chapter 6, we will see a systematic comparison between *pīnyīn* and the IPA transcriptions of SC sounds.

1.5 Phonetics and phonology

Linguistics is the scientific study of human language that investigates: (i) what the structure of language is and in what aspects languages are similar and different; (ii) how language is acquired and processed and how language works in the human cognitive system (psycholinguistics); (iii) how the brain functions in language production, perception, and processing (neurolingusitics); (iv) how language is used in different societies and speech contexts (sociolinguistics); (v) how language changes over time (historical linguistics); and (vi) how the knowledge derived from linguistic studies is applied to other areas such as language teaching, speech disorders, and computer science (applied linguistics). Different aspects of language structure are studied by different subfields of linguistics. PHONETICS studies speech sounds: how they are produced and classified, what their physical properties are, and how they are perceived. PHONOLOGY examines the sound system of language: how speech sounds are organized to form a system for encoding linguistic information. MORPHOLOGY is the study of word formation: how words are constructed out of smaller meaningful units (i.e. morphemes); SYNTAX is the study of sentence structure; semantics is the study of meaning; and pragmatics the study of meaning in context, i.e. how the meaning and interpretation of a word or sentence depends on the context in which it is used. The linguistic grammar, then, is the combination of all these different aspects of language structure. It is important to note that a linguistic grammar *describes* the language that speakers actually use, and, unlike traditional grammar books, does not *prescribe* what a correct grammar should be. To know more about what linguistics is, see the suggested introductory linguistics textbooks given in Further Reading.

In this book we study the phonetics and phonology of SC. The following subsections provide a brief introduction to phonetics and phonology to set the stage for the discussion and more advanced topics in the remaining chapters.

1.5.1 Phonetics

Phonetics consists of three areas of inquiry. ARTICULATORY PHONET-
ICS describes how speech sounds are produced and how sounds are classified
according to their articulatory properties. ACOUSTIC PHONETICS examines the physical properties of speech sounds such as duration, frequency, and
intensity; PERCEPTUAL PHONETICS (or auditory phonetics) is the study
of the perception of speech sounds. In the discussion of SC phonetics, this
book focuses on articulatory phonetics with supplementary information from
acoustic and perceptual phonetics.

Speech sounds are produced by modifying the airstream. Most speech sounds
are made when the air from the lungs is pushed through the larynx and the
oral and nasal cavities. Sounds created in this way are said to use the pulmonic egressive airstream mechanism.[8] Different speech sounds are produced
by modifying this airstream at different points along the pathway of the airflow
(see Figure 2.2 in §2.1.2).

The air coming from the lungs may be modified at the larynx (sometimes
called the voicebox), which is located at the top of the trachea (or windpipe)
and houses the vocal folds. The front of the larynx (Adam's apple) protrudes
slightly at the front of the throat. This is the first point where the flow of the
airstream can be modified. The VOCAL FOLDS are folds of muscle that can
close together or move apart; the opening between the vocal folds is called the
GLOTTIS. When the vocal folds are held close together and made to vibrate by
the air pushed repeatedly through the vocal folds, a VOICED sound is produced;
on the other hand, when the vocal folds are open and the air flows through the
glottis freely, a VOICELESS sound is produced. For example, in English, [z] in
zip is a voiced sound and [s] in *sip* is a voiceless sound. To help detect if a sound
is voiced or voiceless, put your fingers lightly on your throat (close to where
the Adam's apple is) and say [z] for a few seconds and [s] for a few seconds
and then say [zzzzssssszzzzssss]. You should be able to feel vibration inside the
larynx when you produce [z] but no such vibration when you say [s]. You can
use the same method to find out what other sounds in English are voiced and
voiceless. For example, [v] in *vine*, [m] in *man*, [l] in *life*, and all vowels are
voiced sounds; the first sounds in *five*, *she*, and *thing* are voiceless sounds.[9]

Another important component of human physiology for speech production
is the VOCAL TRACT above the larynx (supralaryngeal vocal tract), which

---

[8] Other airstream mechanisms are possible for some less common sounds (Ladefoged 2001: chapter
6). SC and English, like most languages, use only the pulmonic airstream mechanism.

[9] Note that this voicing test does not work well for the voiced–voiceless pairs of sounds such as
[b]–[p], [d]–[t], and [g]–[k]. See §2.1.1.

includes the pharynx (the passage connecting the larynx and the oral cavity in the mouth), the oral cavity in the mouth and the nasal cavity within the nose. The flow of air can be modified at various locations in the vocal tract to produce different sounds. For example, to produce a [b] sound as in *bay*, we obstruct the airstream temporarily by closing the lips, and to produce a [d] sound in *day*, we obstruct the airstream by placing the tongue tip or tongue blade (the frontmost part of the tongue) at the back of the upper teeth or the ALVEOLAR RIDGE (the protruding bony area behind the upper teeth). The different points at which obstruction can be made are the PLACES OF ARTICULATION. The flow of air can also be modified with different degrees of obstruction. The different ways in which a sound is modified are the different MANNERS OF ARTICULATION. Compared to consonants, vowels have relatively free flow of air through the vocal tract. Among consonants, a sound like [d] makes a complete obstruction of the airstream whereas a sound like [z], which has the same place of articulation as [d], has a narrow opening between the raised tongue and the alveolar ridge to let the air squeeze through the narrow channel. A consonant like [d] is called a STOP because the airstream is completely obstructed and a consonant like [z] is called a FRICATIVE because the air pushed through the narrow channel produces friction noise. In chapters 3 and 4, we discuss how consonants and vowels are made and classified according to the status of the vocal folds, the place of articulation, and the manner of articulation.

When a sound is produced, the flow of air is converted to sound waves that can be transmitted through the air for the listener to perceive. The vibration rate of the vocal folds determines the FUNDAMENTAL FREQUENCY of a sound wave. If the vocal folds complete each cycle of vibration 100 times in a second, then the fundamental frequency is 100 Hz. A high tone has higher pitch and higher frequency and a low tone has lower pitch and lower frequency. A rising tone then has a pitch pattern of change from a lower pitch to a higher pitch. The phonetic properties of different tones in SC is discussed in chapter 4.

Each speech sound has its own set of acoustic properties so that the listener can distinguish one sound from another. The various modifications of the airstream in speech production create different patterns of sound waves. That is, the source of a sound wave produced by the lungs and the vocal folds is modified in different ways in the vocal tract to yield different acoustic characteristics (different patterns of sound waves) for different sounds. The human speech production system is similar to a musical instrument: a musical instrument also has a source of sound (e.g. the air blown across a flute's mouth hole) and produces different musical notes by modifying the sound in different ways in the instrument's resonant chamber (e.g. by closing and opening the different holes on the body of the flute). The vocal tract acts like the resonant chamber in a musical instrument to highlight different frequencies of the source sound wave to produce different patterns of sound waves that are perceived as different sounds. We can see the acoustic differences that characterize different sounds on a spectrogram. Spectrograms are graphs that encode three aspects of the acoustic properties of speech sounds: duration, frequency, and the amount of acoustic energy (intensity and loudness). Since this introductory book focuses on articulatory phonetics, suggested readings for phonetics in general and acoustic phonetics in particular can be found in Further Reading.

To summarize, phonetics studies what the possible speech sounds are, how these sounds are produced and perceived, and what their physical acoustic properties are.

1.5.2 Phonology

Phonology investigates how speech sounds are organized in a particular language and in what aspects the sounds systems of various languages are similar and different. Even when the same sounds occur in two or more languages, each language may organize its sound inventory differently and these same sounds may function and behave differently in each language's sound system.

The first task of a phonological study is to determine the sound inventory of a language: which sounds can affect the meaning of words and which sounds are predictable based on the contexts in which they occur. For example, in English /b/ and /p/ are DISTINCTIVE (or CONTRASTIVE) sounds called PHONEMES that can differentiate word meaning: *bet* and *pet* differ in only one sound, /b/ versus /p/, and have different meanings. Such pairs of words that differ in only one sound and have different meanings are called MINIMAL PAIRS, which are used to determine the distinctive sounds in a language. Phonemes are abstract phonological units, which are represented with slashes, e.g. /b/ and /p/, whereas phonetic sounds are transcribed using square brackets, e.g. [b] and [p]. The phonetic sound (i.e. what is actually pronounced) associated with a phoneme is the PHONETIC REALIZATION of the phoneme, e.g. the [b] sound is the phonetic realization of the phoneme /b/ in English. You can think of a phoneme as an abstract representation stored in our mental grammar and its phonetic realization as the actual sound we produce.

However, a phoneme often has more than one possible phonetic realization. For example, in English there are two types of /p/ sounds: a [p] sound after

[s] as in *spot* and a [pʰ] sound at syllable initial position as in *pot*. If you put your palm in front of your mouth when producing the syllable initial [pʰ] sound in *pot*, you can feel a puff of air on your palm; on the other hand, no or little puff of air is produced when the [p] in *spot* is made. The kind of sound with a puff of air is called an ASPIRATED sound and is represented in IPA with a superscript [h] as in [pʰ]. In English, then, the two sounds [pʰ] and [p] have different distributions (different contexts in which they occur): [pʰ] occurs in syllable initial position[10] and [p] occurs after [s]. If you pronounce [pʰ] instead of [p] in the word *spot*, the meaning of the word does not change, although the pronunciation would be considered non-standard or showing a foreign accent. Non-distinctive sounds such as [pʰ] and [p] are ALLOPHONES of the same phoneme /p/: they are in COMPLEMENTARY DISTRIBUTION (i.e. occur in mutually exclusive contexts) and they do not serve to distinguish word meaning. Therefore, in English, /b/ and /p/ are separate phonemes or phonologically distinctive sounds, but [pʰ] and [p] are not. The phonetic realization of the phoneme /b/ is [b] but there are two phonetic realizations of the phoneme /p/ and each of the two sounds occurs in specific contexts that do not overlap. In contrast, /pʰ/ and /p/ in SC function as two separate phonemes: the minimal pair [pan] *bàn* 办 'to do' and [pʰan] *pàn* 判 'to sentence' differ only in one sound, [pʰ] versus [p], and have different meanings. (The letter *b* in *pīnyīn* is actually a [p] sound and SC does not have a /b/ phoneme.) As the diagram in (3) illustrates, English has two phonemes /b/ and /p/ and /p/ has two phonetic realizations [p] and [pʰ], whereas in SC /p/ and /pʰ/ are two separate phonemes. We have seen that the same pair of sounds can be distinctive in one language but non-distinctive in another. The sound inventory of a language, then, includes a set of distinctive sounds that constitute the phoneme inventory and a set of non-distinctive sounds (allophones) whose distribution is systematic and predictable. The sound inventory of SC will be discussed in chapters 2 and 3.

		English		SC	
(3)					
Phoneme		/b/	/p/	/p/	/pʰ/
		|	∧	|	|
Phonetic realization/ allophone		[b]	[p] [pʰ]	[p]	[pʰ]

---

[10] Aspirated consonants in American English do not always occur in an UNSTRESSED SYLLABLE, so a more accurate description should be that an aspirated consonant occurs either in initial position in a STRESSED SYLLABLE or in a word-initial unstressed syllable.

The second task of a phonological study is to determine how sounds are sequenced and organized in a language. Just as there are rules on how words are put together to form sentences, there are rules on how sounds are put in sequence to form morphemes and words in a language. For example, in English the consonant cluster [pl] can be used at the beginning of a word or syllable but no words or syllables can begin with [lp]; in SC, neither consonant cluster is permissible. In English, it is possible to have at most three consonants in word or syllable initial position; however, in such a consonant cluster, the first consonant must be the sound /s/ and the second consonant must be a /t/, /p/, or /k/, e.g. *stride*, *sprite*, and *squeeze*. In comparison, SC does not allow such consonant clusters in word or syllable initial position. Sequences of sounds are also organized into syllables and a sequence of sounds may belong to the same syllable or two different syllables. For example, as shown in (4a), in the DISYLLABIC word *standard*, the [n] of the [nd] cluster is part of the first syllable but [d] is part of the second syllable; on the other hand, in the disyllabic word *employ*, the [m] of the [mpl] cluster belongs to the first syllable but both [p] and [l] belong to the second syllable. A syllable has its internal structure, as illustrated in (4b). Within each syllable, the consonants before the vowel are in ONSET, the consonants after the vowel are in CODA, the vowel is the NUCLEUS, and the RIME consists of the nucleus and the coda. What sounds can be put together and in what order in a word and how sounds are organized into syllables are governed by a set of linguistic principles, and phonology analyzes the organization of sound sequences to discover these principles. How sounds are organized in SC will be discussed in chapter 5.

(4)   Syllable structure

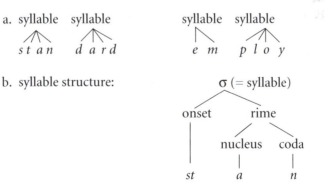

The third task of a phonological study is to examine how a sound changes its phonetic properties depending on context, and to discover the rules and principles that govern such changes. As discussed above, some phonemes may have more than one phonetic realization. For the example of English /p/, we can say that English has a rule: /p/ is realized as [pʰ] syllable initially. This same rule applies also to the /t/ and /k/ phonemes: /t/ is realized as [tʰ] and /k/ as [kʰ] in the same context, e.g. *top* and *cop*, but they remain unaspirated [t] and [k] respectively after [s], e.g. *stop* and *scold*. We can then have one unified rule: voiceless stops become aspirated in syllable initial position. In the phonological analysis of a language, we seek to present a system of rules and principles that can explain how and why these context-sensitive phonetic changes and variations occur. In chapters 7–9, we examine the phonological rule system of SC.

To summarize, phonology studies: (i) which sounds are phonemes and which are allophones in a language's sound inventory; (ii) how sounds are put in a sequence to form a word and how they are organized into syllables; and (iii) how sounds vary in their phonetic properties depending on different linguistic contexts. On a broader scale, phonology is also concerned with the universal phonological properties and principles shared by all languages and how languages may differ in their phonological systems.

1.5.3 Phonetics versus phonology

As we have seen in the discussion above, the two areas of inquiry, phonetics and phonology, are distinct but intricately intertwined. Phonetics is concerned with the concrete physical aspects of speech sounds, i.e. their production, perception, and acoustic properties. On the other hand, phonology, which is usually defined as the study of sound systems, is not a study of speech sounds per se; rather, it is concerned with the representation and organization of sounds and sound-related processes in our cognitive system, and hence can be viewed as some sort of abstract mental grammar. However, the boundary between the two areas is not entirely clear-cut. To better understand many phonological patterns and issues requires taking phonetics into consideration, and to conduct any phonetic study of language also requires phonological knowledge.

1.6 The organization of this book

As an introduction to SC phonetics and phonology, this book covers the phonetics of consonants, vowels, and tone (chapters 2–4) and the phonological system (chapters 5, 7–9). In addition, we discuss the interaction of tone, stress, and intonation (chapter 10), the adaptation of English sounds in SC loanwords (chapter 11), different varieties of SC (chapter 12), and the comparison between *pīnyīn* and phonetic transcription (chapter 6).

Chapters 2 and 3 are concerned with the classification and phonetic characteristics of SC consonants and vowels respectively. Each chapter introduces articulatory phonetic properties first and moves to a detailed discussion of SC sounds. Practical advice for pronunciation is provided for those sounds that are absent in English. Similar content and organization are followed in chapter 4 on the classification and phonetic properties of SC tones.

Chapter 5 introduces the notion of syllable structure and examines how SC sounds are organized into syllables and what combinations of sound sequences and what syllable types are permissible. With the knowledge of syllable structure and the phonetic representation of sounds and tones, a systematic comparison between *pīnyīn* and phonetic representations is then provided in chapter 6.

Chapters 7 and 8 are concerned with segmental phonology, i.e. the phonology of consonants and vowels. In chapter 7, after the introduction of the basic notions of phonological analysis, we discuss the phonological status of SC sounds (phonemes versus allophones) and the PHONOLOGICAL PROCESSES that affect the actual pronunciation of a sound in different linguistic contexts. Chapter 8 discusses processes motivated by syllable structure and how the sounds in a word change when the suffix *r* is added. Since *r*-suffixation is much more prevalent in the Beijing dialect than in SC, the data will be based on the Beijing dialect.

Chapters 9 and 10 deal with SUPRASEGMENTAL PROPERTIES that span more than one sound. In chapter 9, we study how and when a tone is changed to a different tone in a tonal sequence, and the phonetic realization of the neutral tone in different tonal contexts. Chapter 10 provides an overview of stress and intonation and their interaction with tone in SC.

The knowledge of the phonetics and phonology of SC helps us understand why the sounds of foreign words are adapted in certain ways. A loanword has to conform to the phonetic and phonological systems of the borrowing language in order to be a regular part of the vocabulary, and chapter 11 showcases the application of the phonetics and phonology of SC in loanword adaptation.

The final chapter classifies different varieties of SC and compares Taiwan SC and Taiwanese-accented SC with SC to demonstrate how a different norm of SC and a locally accented SC can deviate from the prescribed SC (or textbook SC).

The appendices provide supplementary resources such as information about the IPA, the complete list of SC syllables in *pīnyīn* and corresponding phonetic transcriptions, and Internet resources. Suggestions for further reading are provided for readers who would like to go beyond this introductory book and study more on Chinese phonetics and phonology in particular and linguistics, phonetics, and phonology in general. A glossary is also provided for quick reference on technical terms, and the CD included with the book demonstrates the SC sounds and examples.

EXERCISES

1 Decide if each of the following statements is true or false. For each false statement, provide the correction.

   a. The phonology of Standard Chinese is based on the Beijing dialect, which belongs to the Mandarin dialect group.
   b. All Chinese dialects are more or less mutually intelligible.
   c. Standard Chinese tolerates a range of slightly different accents.
   d. Chinese is a tone language and English is a stress language.
   e. Chinese tone is PHONEMIC in that it can differentiate word meaning.
   f. There are four phonemic tones in Standard Chinese.
   g. The Chinese writing system is alphabetic.
   h. *Pīnyīn* is a phonetic transcription system.
   i. In general, each written Chinese character is one SYLLABLE long.
   j. Most Chinese morphemes are MONOSYLLABIC but many Chinese words are POLYSYLLABIC.
   k. The MORPHEME is the smallest meaningful unit used in word formation processes.
   l. MORPHOLOGY studies how words are put together to form a sentence.
   m. SYNTAX studies the meanings of words and sentences.
   n. PHONETICS studies how sounds are organized into an abstract system.
   o. PHONOLOGY is a study of the physics of language sounds.
   p. In Chinese, an ASPIRATED STOP like [pʰ] and a plain stop without aspiration [p] are ALLOPHONES of the same PHONEME in COMPLEMENTARY DISTRIBUTION.

2 Decide if each of the following statements better falls into the realm of phonetics or phonology.

   a. In English, the PHONEME /t/ is pronounced as [t] in *stop* but as an aspirated stop [tʰ] in *top*.
   b. The sound [m] as in *map* is produced by bringing the two lips together to block the airstream in the mouth but allowing the airstream to escape from the nasal cavity.

c. In Chinese, it is not possible to have three consonants at the beginning of a syllable or a word.

d. Chinese has five vowel phonemes and twenty-three consonant phonemes.

e. The word *sister* is a DISYLLABIC word.

f. The pitch of the high rising tone (tone 2) in SC starts in the mid-range pitch level and rises toward the high end.

g. A STRESSED SYLLABLE can be longer in duration, higher in pitch, and/or has higher intensity (or louder).

h. In English [s] as in *sea* is a VOICELESS consonant and [z] as in *zoo* is a VOICED consonant. A voiced sound is made by vibration of the closed VOCAL FOLDS.

i. In English /s/ and /z/ are separate phonemes because they can differentiate meaning as evidenced in the MINIMAL PAIR *sip* and *zip*.

j. English has a rule that changes the voiceless stops /p/, /t/, and /k/ to ASPIRATED ones in syllable initial position.

3 Provide a MINIMAL PAIR test for each pair of the following English sounds to prove that each pair of sounds are separate PHONEMES in English. Be reminded that orthographic letters often do not correspond to actual pronunciation and minimal pairs are based on pronunciation not on letters.

Example: /s/ /z/

The consonants /s/ and /z/ are separate phonemes in English because there is a minimal pair like *sip* and *zip*. These two words form a minimal pair for /s/ and /z/ because they have identical pronunciation except /s/ versus /z/ and have different meanings.

a. /f/ /v/   b. /k/ /g/   c. /r/ /l/   d. /n/ /m/

4 Consider the following minimal pairs from SC, in which each pair of words have different meanings but differ only in one consonant, one vowel, or one tone in pronunciation. For each MINIMAL PAIR, identify which pair of sounds or tones are proved to be PHONEMIC by the minimal pair test. For each word, the *pīnyīn* of the word in italic is followed by the phonetic transcription in square brackets and the tone is labeled with the tone number for convenience (see (1) in §1.3).

Example 1: *nǐ*   [ni]tone 3   'you'
            lǐ   [li]tone 3   'inside'

This minimal pair shows that /n/ and /l/ are phonemic consonants in SC.

Example 2:   *mā*   [ma]tone 1   'mother'
              mǎ   [ma]tone 3   'horse'

This minimal pair shows that tone 1 (a high level tone) and tone 3 (a low falling-rising tone) are phonemic tones in SC.

a. *mà*   [ma]tone 4   'to scold'   *nà*   [na]tone 4   'that'
b. *ná*   [na]tone 2   'to take'   *nà*   [na]tone 4   'that'
c. *fǎ*   [fa]tone 3   'hair'   *sǎ*   [sa]tone 3   'to scatter'
d. *mǐ*   [mi]tone 3   'rice'   *mǎ*   [ma]tone 3   'horse'

2 Consonants

In this chapter, we study the phonetic properties of SC consonants and how they are classified. We start with how consonants are produced and what articulatory properties are associated with each type of consonant (§2.1). Whenever appropriate, American English consonants are used for reference and comparison. In §2.2, the consonants of SC are discussed in detail and practical advice on pronunciation is provided. The final section (§2.3) summarizes the main points of the chapter.

2.1 The production and classification of consonants

Consonants and vowels constitute the first major division of speech sounds. When we produce a vowel, the air flows through the vocal tract with ease; in contrast, when we produce a consonant, the airflow is obstructed to various degrees depending on the types of consonants.

The major differences among consonants involve: (i) whether or not a consonant is VOICED or VOICELESS; (ii) where within the vocal tract the CONSTRICTION to impede the airflow is made (PLACE OF ARTICULATION); and (iii) how and to what degree the airflow is obstructed (MANNER OF ARTICULATION). Some consonants are also differentiated by being ASPIRATED or unaspirated. In what follows, we discuss those phonetic properties relevant to SC and English consonants.

2.1.1 The state of the glottis: voiced and voiceless sounds

Vowels are voiced sounds, but consonants can be either VOICED or VOICELESS. Recall from §1.5.1 that the VOCAL FOLDS are folds of muscle located inside the larynx that can come closer together or move apart. A voiced sound is produced when the vocal folds are held close together and the air from the

19

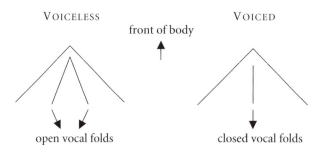

Figure 2.1.   A schema of the states of the glottis.

lungs is pushed through the GLOTTIS (the opening between the vocal folds), making the vocal folds vibrate. When the vocal folds are held apart, the air from the lungs can go through the glottis with relative ease and a voiceless sound is produced. The glottis therefore takes on different shapes or different states in voiced and voiceless sounds. Figure 2.1 schematizes the different positions of the vocal folds and the resulting different states of the glottis for voiced and voiceless sounds.[1] We can see that the vocal folds are pulled apart in voiceless sounds, whereas in voiced sounds, the vocal folds are pulled close together.

The front of the larynx that houses the vocal folds protrudes slightly at the front of the throat (Adam's apple). To find out if a sound is voiced or voiceless, you can put your fingers lightly on your throat close to where the Adam's apple is. You should be able to feel vibration inside the larynx when you produce a voiced sound and you should not feel any vibration when you produce a voiceless sound. For example, for a word like *zoo*, you should feel the vibration for the whole word because the consonant [z] and the vowel are both voiced. Say [z] and prolong it for a few seconds; you should feel the vibration by your fingers on the throat. Then say [s], the consonant in *see*, and prolong it for a few seconds; no vibrations should be detected. Alternate a prolonged [z] with a prolonged [s] to produce [zzzzzzssssssszzzzzzsssss]; you should feel that vibration occurs during the production of [z] but not during the production of [s]. Note that this voicing test does not work as well for voiced STOPS such as [b], [d], and [g] because you can easily feel the vibration only when the air is moving outward as in this case for [z] and vowels. When a stop is made, the airflow is completely blocked (§1.5.1, §2.1.4.1), making it impossible to feel the vibration of the vocal folds. However, at the point when a stop is opened up to let the air out, there is a very short period of time that some weak vibration might be detected by this voicing test (§2.1.4.1).

---

[1] Some languages also make use of other glottal states, such as murmur and creaky voice. For a brief introduction to other states of the glottis, see Ladefoged (2001:122–5).

The English examples in (1) show pairs of sounds like [z] and [s] that are different only by being voiced versus voiceless. That is, each pair has exactly the same place and manner of articulation but differ only in voicing. In (2), we see other voiced consonants in English that do not have voiceless counterparts. Note that in English the voiced consonants in word initial position, as in *bee*, *deed*, *geese*, are often only partially voiced or even DEVOICED (i.e. changing from voiced to voiceless). In contrast, in French and Spanish, the voiced [b], [d], [g] sounds in word initial position are fully voiced.

(1) Voiced and voiceless consonant pairs in English

VOICELESS		VOICED	
IPA	EXAMPLE	IPA	EXAMPLE
[s]	*see*	[z]	*zoo*
[f]	*fee*	[v]	*vine*
[θ]	*think*	[ð]	*that*
[ʃ]	*she*	[ʒ]	*azure*
[tʃ]	*church*	[dʒ]	*judge*
[p]	*spot*	[b]	*about*
[t]	*stop*	[d]	*reduce*
[k]	*sky*	[g]	*ago*

(2) English voiced consonants with no voiceless counterparts

[m]	*me*	[n]	*noon*	[ŋ]	*sing*
[l]	*live*	[ɹ]	*road*		
[j]	*yes*	[w]	*way*		

In comparison, SC does not have contrasting pairs of voiced and voiceless consonants like those in (1). SC has the voiced consonants in (3) (examples shown in *pīnyīn*). The voiced sounds [w], [j], and [ɥ] are often considered to be vowels rather than consonants in SC. These sounds are GLIDES (SEMI-VOWELS) that have vowel-like articulation but function like consonants. The differences between true consonants, glides, and vowels will be discussed in §3.2.

(3) SC voiced consonants

IPA	EXAMPLE		IPA	EXAMPLE	
[m]	*mǎi*	'to buy'	[w]	*wǎn*	'evening, late'
[n]	*nán*	'difficult'	[j]	*yǒu*	'to have'
[ŋ]	*bāng*	'to help'	[ɥ]	*yuè*	'moon, month'
[l]	*lái*	'to come'	[ɹ]	*ròu*	'meat'

SC consonants other than those in (3) are all voiceless. The sounds represented by the letters *b, d, g* in *pīnyīn* are in fact voiceless [p], [t], [k]. The sounds represented by the letters *p, t, k* in *pīnyīn* are also voiceless, but they are ASPIRATED. If you put your palm in front of your mouth and say *pan, tan,* and *can,* you should feel a puff of air coming out because the initial consonant sounds in these English words are aspirated (§1.5.2). An aspirated sound is transcribed with a superscript [h], e.g. [pʰ], [tʰ], [kʰ]. SC voiceless consonants are either aspirated or unaspirated. We will discuss aspirated and unaspirated consonants later in §2.1.5.

2.1.2 The vocal organs

When we produce speech sounds, we make use of organs in the VOCAL TRACT. As mentioned in §1.5.1, the vocal tract, located above the larynx, covers the pharynx (the passage between the larynx and the oral cavity), the oral cavity (or the oral tract), and the nasal cavity (or the nasal tract). The parts of the vocal tract that are used in producing speech sounds are called ARTICULATORS. Figure 2.2 shows the mid-sagittal section of the vocal tract and the articulators.

Let us explore first the articulators on the upper surface of the oral tract. The upper lip and the upper teeth need no explanation. Behind the upper teeth, you can feel with your tip of the tongue a small protruded rugged bony structure. This is the ALVEOLAR RIDGE. Now use your tongue tip to probe the front part of the roof of the mouth, and you should also feel a smoother bony structure. This is called the HARD PALATE. The back of the alveolar ridge before the hard palate is called the POST-ALVEOLAR region. To probe further back beyond the hard palate, you can either curl the tongue up or use a fingertip to reach the softer back part of the upper side of the mouth. This is the VELUM, or the SOFT PALATE. At the end of the velum is the uvula. The area between the velum and the larynx is the pharynx. These passive articulators on the upper surface of the vocal tract serve as the targets toward which other articulators move during sound production.

The velum can be raised to press against the back wall of the pharynx to prevent air from going through the nose. A sound made without any airflow through the nose is called an ORAL sound, and most sounds are oral sounds. When the soft palate is lowered away from the back wall of the pharynx, as in Figure 2.2, there is an air passage going into the nasal cavity. A NASAL sound is made with the lowered velum, allowing air to go through the nose. For example, [m], [n], and [ŋ] in (2) and (3) above are nasal sounds.

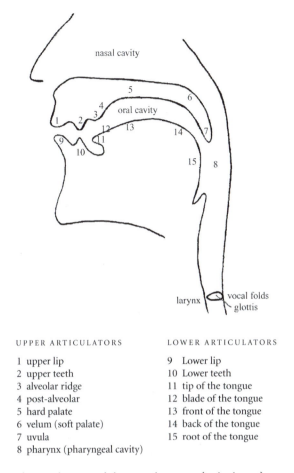

UPPER ARTICULATORS	LOWER ARTICULATORS
1 upper lip	9 Lower lip
2 upper teeth	10 Lower teeth
3 alveolar ridge	11 tip of the tongue
4 post-alveolar	12 blade of the tongue
5 hard palate	13 front of the tongue
6 velum (soft palate)	14 back of the tongue
7 uvula	15 root of the tongue
8 pharynx (pharyngeal cavity)	

Figure 2.2.   The vocal tract and the speech organs (articulators).

The articulators on the lower surface of the vocal tract include the lower lip, the lower teeth, and different parts of the tongue. The frontmost parts of the tongue are the tip and the blade, which are highly mobile in articulation. The body of the tongue consists of the front and the back of the tongue. When the tongue is at rest, the front of the tongue lies underneath the hard palate, the back of the tongue is below the velum. The root of the tongue is opposite to the back wall of the pharynx. The active articulators on the lower surface of the vocal tract, especially the various parts of the tongue, move toward the passive articulators on the upper surface during sound production.

Most consonants are made by moving an active articulator on the lower surface of the vocal tract from its neutral resting position toward an articulatory target on the upper or rear surface of the vocal tract. For example, to produce

[z] and [s] in English, the tip or blade of the tongue is moved very close to the alveolar ridge, leaving only a very narrow opening between the two articulators. In what follows, we study how the articulators are used in producing different consonants.

2.1.3 Place of articulation

Consonants are produced by obstructing the airstream through the vocal tract in some way. The location at which articulators form a CONSTRICTION in the vocal tract to obstruct the airstream is the PLACE OF ARTICULATION. Most languages make use of three primary articulators for the production of consonants: the lips, the tongue tip and blade, and the body of the tongue. Speech sounds using the lips have LABIAL articulation, those using the tip or blade of the tongue have CORONAL articulation, and those using the body of the tongue have DORSAL articulation. There are more specific subcategories within each of these three types of articulations (§§2.1.3.1–2.1.3.3) and some sounds involve more than one of these articulations (§2.1.3.4).

2.1.3.1 Labial: bilabial and labiodental

In English and in SC, there are two types of labial sounds: BILABIAL and LABIODENTAL. A bilabial sound is made with both lips. Say the words *pay*, *bay*, and *may*, and note that both lips come together in the first sound of each of these words. A labiodental sound is made with the lower lip raised to touch the upper front teeth. The first consonants in *fine* and *vine* are labiodental sounds. In (4) and (5) we see examples of bilabial and labiodental sounds in English and SC. Figure 2.3 illustrates the difference between the two types of labial sounds.

(4) Bilabials

IPA	SC EXAMPLES		ENGLISH EXAMPLES
[m]	*mǐ*	'rice'	*me*
[p]	*bái*	'white'	*spy*
[pʰ]	*pí*	'skin'	*peak*
[b]			*about*

(5) Labiodental

IPA	SC EXAMPLES		ENGLISH EXAMPLES
[f]	*fàn*	'rice'	*fine*
[v]			*vine*

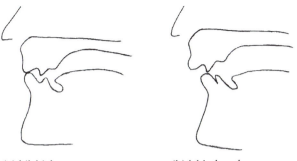

(a) bilabial   (b) labiodental

Figure 2.3.   The articulation of labials.

2.1.3.2 Coronal: dental, alveolar, and post-alveolar

Dental and alveolar

When a sound is made with a tongue tip or blade and the teeth, it is a DENTAL sound. Say the words *thin* and *this* and note how you produce the first consonant for each of these two words. For many speakers of American English, the tongue tip is slightly protruded between the upper and lower teeth. Such a dental sound is called an INTERDENTAL. Many speakers of British English place the tongue tip behind the upper front teeth for the dental consonants (Ladefoged 2001:6). The IPA symbol for the voiceless interdental sound as in *thin* is [θ] and for the voiced interdental as in *this* is [ð]. SC does not have these interdentals.

(6) English (inter)dental and alveolar consonants

VOICELESS		VOICED		VOICED	
IPA	EXAMPLE	IPA	EXAMPLE	IPA	EXAMPLE
[θ]	*thin*	[ð]	*this*		
[t]	*stop*	[d]	*adopt*	[n]	*night*
[tʰ]	*top*			[l]	*life*
[s]	*sip*	[z]	*zip*	[ɹ]	*ripe*

When a sound is made with a tongue tip or blade and the alveolar ridge, it is an ALVEOLAR sound. Some English speakers use the tongue tip and some others use the tongue blade. The first consonants in *nip, tip, dip, sip, zip, lip,* and *rip* are alveolars.

Now compare the *n* sound in *ten* and *tenth*. For most speakers, the nasal [n] in *ten* is made on the alveolar ridge and the one in *tenth* is made with the tongue tip or blade touching the upper front teeth, which can be transcribed as [n̪] with a DIACRITIC beneath the main symbol to indicate dental articulation. A diacritic is a small mark that can be added to a symbol to show more precise information of the phonetic quality of the sound. For many SC speakers, the *n* sound in SC is more like a dental than an alveolar. In languages that do not distinguish dental and alveolar sounds as separate PHONEMES (i.e. DISTINCTIVE sounds that can differentiate word meaning in a language as introduced in §1.5.2), the IPA symbols such as [t], [tʰ], [n], [s], and [l] are used for both dental and alveolar sounds. The type of transcription that uses a simple set of symbols without recording all of the phonetic details is called a BROAD PHONETIC TRANSCRIPTION. In contrast, a NARROW PHONETIC TRANSCRIPTION encodes more phonetic details by using special symbols or diacritics. How broad or narrow a transcription is chosen depends on the purpose of the transcription. For example, to compare detailed phonetic differences between different dialects or between the accents of different speakers, a narrow transcription is often called for. This book uses both types of transcriptions. Relatively broad transcriptions are used for those sounds that exhibit much speaker variation or have highly consistent or detailed phonetic information that I have decided not to encode for the sake of typographical simplicity. For example, a dental sound in SC is broadly transcribed without the diacritic indicating dental articulation. On the other hand, in order to provide enough phonetic details for studying the phonetics and phonology of SC, narrow transcriptions are used for most of the sounds that can be derived by the RULE system in chapters 7–9 and for dialect/accent comparison (chapter 12).

In SC, [t], [tʰ], [n], and [l] can be dentals made with the tongue tip/blade on or close to the upper front teeth or they can be alveolars. The sounds for *z, c,* and *s* in *pīnyīn* are mostly dentals with the tongue tip/blade on or close to the lower front teeth or the upper front teeth. Some speakers may also make use of the front part of the alveolar ridge (cf. Ladefoged and Maddieson 1996:151–2; Lee and Zee 2003). Since these sounds do not have very exact constriction location, they have been variably classified as dentals or alveolars or both. In general, these SC sounds are made more forward than their English counterparts, so in this book we follow Chao (1968) and Duanmu (2000:27) in calling all of these SC sounds dentals, examples of which are given in (7).

🎧 (7) SC dental sounds

VOICELESS		VOICELESS		VOICED	
IPA	EXAMPLE	IPA	EXAMPLE	IPA	EXAMPLE
[t]	*dà* 'big'	[ts]	*zǎo* 'early'	[n]	*nǐ* 'you'
[tʰ]	*tā* 'he'	[tsʰ]	*cāi* 'guess'	[l]	*lái* 'to come'
		[s]	*sān* 'three'		

Post-alveolar

When a sound is made with the tongue tip or blade and the back of the alveolar ridge, it is a POST-ALVEOLAR sound. Post-alveolars made with the tongue tip are APICAL post-alveolars and those made with the tongue blade are LAM- INAL post-alveolars or PALATO-ALVEOLARS.

Say the word *she* and during the consonant production, your tongue blade is raised behind the back of the alveolar ridge, i.e. the post-alveolar region between the alveolar ridge and the hard palate. This consonant is called a laminal post-alveolar or a palato-alveolar. When a palato-alveolar is produced, the tip of the tongue may be down behind the lower front teeth or up near the alveolar ridge. One way to better feel the place of articulation is to hold the consonant position and take in a breath through the mouth. The incoming air cools the articulators that form the constriction. Now say the consonant for *she* and hold the tongue position while breathing inward through the mouth. You should feel the incoming cool air on the blade of the tongue and the back part of the alveolar ridge. Now try the same with the consonant [s] for *see* and you can feel that the incoming air cools the tongue tip or blade and the alveolar ridge. In (8), we see examples of palato-alveolars from English. The first voiceless/voiced pair differ from the second pair in terms of MANNER OF ARTICULATION, to be discussed in §2.1.4.

(8) Palato-alveolars (laminal post-alveolars) in English

VOICELESS		VOICED	
IPA	EXAMPLE	IPA	EXAMPLE
[ʃ]	*sh*ow	[ʒ]	plea*s*ure
[tʃ]	*ch*ip	[dʒ]	*j*eep

Consider now apical post-alveolars. Say the words *ride, road*, and *rain* and pay attention to the position of your tongue tip when you produce the first consonant, transcribed as [ɹ], in each of these words. Many speakers have an alveolar sound but others have an apical post-alveolar made with the tongue tip raised up to the post-alveolar region. Some English speakers also have an apical post-alveolar sound for the *r* at the ends of words such as *tire, air*, and *hour*. SC has four apical post-alveolar sounds as in (9).

🎧 (9) Apical post-alveolar sounds in SC

Voiceless		Voiced	
IPA	Example	IPA	Example
[tʂ]	*zh*è 'this'		
[tʂʰ]	*ch*ē 'car'		
[ʂ]	*sh*é 'snake'	[ɻ]	*r*è 'hot'

These sounds are traditionally referred to as RETROFLEX sounds, which is one major characteristic of SC speakers from Beijing. A retroflex sound is made by curling the tongue tip upward and backward and using the underside of the tongue tip to make a constriction at the post-alveolar region. However, for these Beijing speakers, it is the upper surface of the tongue tip rather than the under surface of the tongue tip that forms the constriction at the post-alveolar region (Lee and Zee 2003, Zee 2003a). That is, these SC 'retroflex' sounds are not the typical types of retroflex sounds that make use of the underside of the tongue tip as those in the Dravidian languages of southern India. In this book I use apical post-alveolars for these SC sounds and we will have more discussion on them in §2.2.4.

To pronounce the apical post-alveolar, move your tongue tip very close to the post-alveolar region, and do not raise the front part of the tongue. To feel the difference between the palato-alveolar [ʃ] and the apical post-alveolar [ʂ], hold the consonant position in each case and inhale the air through the mouth. For the palato-alveolar, you may feel that the cool air flows through the tongue blade and even a portion of the front part of the tongue. For the apical post-alveolar, the cool air is more limited to the tongue tip/blade region.

In the IPA system, the symbol [ɹ] is used for a dental, alveolar or post-alveolar RHOTIC sound (*r*-sound). Although the [ɹ] sound in SC and that in English are similar, there are a couple of differences. We have mentioned earlier that English [ɹ] can be alveolar or post-alveolar, but SC [ɹ] is an apical post-alveolar. The more obvious difference is that most English speakers pronounce [ɹ] with lip-rounding (Ladefoged 2001:55). Say *read* and *lead* and if you notice some lip movement when pronouncing *read* but no such movement when pronouncing *lead*, then you have lip-rounding for [ɹ]. In SC, there is no lip-rounding for [ɹ] unless it is followed by a sound with lip-rounding, such as [w].

Summary

There are three types of coronals: dentals, alveolars, and post-alveolars. As illustrated in Figure 2.4, a dental sound can be an interdental with the tongue tip between the teeth or a plain dental with the tongue tip/blade right behind the teeth. The post-alveolars can be further divided into apical post-alveolars and laminal post-alveolars (palato-alveolars).

Figure 2.5 illustrates the alveolar [s] and the palato-alveolar [ʃ] in English and the apical post-alveolar [ʂ] in SC. You can see that in [s] the tongue tip/blade is close to the alveolar ridge while in [ʃ] the tongue blade is mostly behind the alveolar ridge. In [ʂ] it is the tongue tip that is raised behind the alveolar ridge. Note that the blade and front part of the tongue are raised in [ʃ] but not in [ʂ].

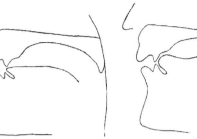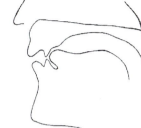

(a) interdental [θ] in English   (b) dental [s] in SC

Figure 2.4.   The articulation of dentals.

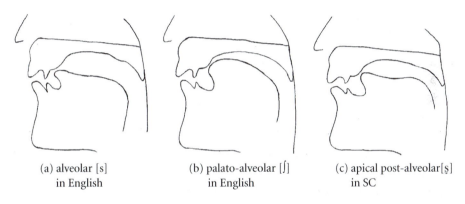

(a) alveolar [s]   (b) palato-alveolar [ʃ]   (c) apical post-alveolar [ʂ]
    in English   in English   in SC

Figure 2.5.   The articulation of alveolars and post-alveolars.

2.1.3.3 Dorsal: velar

When the articulation of a consonant involves the back of the tongue and the velum, it is a **velar** sound. Say the words *back*, *bag*, and *bang* and pay attention to the consonant at the end of each of these words. Your tongue tip/blade is down and the back of the tongue is raised to touch the velum. Figure 2.6 shows the tongue position of a velar consonant such as [k] or [g]. Examples of SC and English velars are given in (10).

(10) Velars in SC and English

    a. Voiceless
        IPA SC example   English example
        [k] *gěi* 'to give'   *sky*
        [kʰ] *kàn* 'to look'   *key*
        [x] *hēi* 'black'

b. VOICED
IPA SC EXAMPLE   ENGLISH EXAMPLE
[g]   *again*
[ŋ] *tīng* 'to listen'   *hang*

Figure 2.6.   The articulation of velar stops.

As we can see in (10), SC does not have the voiced [g] and English does not have the voiceless velar sound [x], which corresponds to the letter *h* in *pīnyīn*. The voiceless velar sound occurs in several languages, for example *Bach* [bax] in German. In English, the [h] sound is not a velar but a GLOTTAL sound with constriction at the glottis by bringing the vocal folds closer without causing vibration (Carr 1999:9). Ladefoged (2001:56) suggested that [h] in English can be considered a voiceless counterpart of the surrounding vowels.

2.1.3.4 Labiovelar and palatal

The [w] sound in English *wide* and SC *wài* 'outside' is a LABIOVELAR sound because it brings the lips closer for lip-rounding and the back of the tongue also approaches the velum. In other words, this sound has both labial and dorsal articulations.

The [j] sound for the first consonants in English *yes* and SC *yě* 'also' is a PALATAL sound made by raising the front part of the tongue toward the hard palate with the tongue tip down behind the lower front teeth. Depending on different analyses and theories, a palatal sound either has a dorsal articulation or involves both coronal and dorsal articulations. For the purposes of this introductory book, we assume that a palatal is classified as both a coronal and dorsal (Keating 1988, 1991; cf. Clements and Hume 1995). In SC [ɥ], the first sound spelled as *yu* in *yuè* 'moon, month' is a [j]-like sound with lip-rounding and it can be classified as a labial-palatal sound (see §3.2 for details).

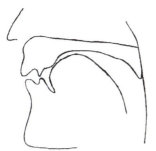

Figure 2.7.   The articulation of alveolo-palatals: alveolo-palatal [ɕ] in SC.

SC has three additional palatal sounds, as the examples in (11) show, all of which are voiceless. Figure 2.7 illustrates the alveolo-palatal [ɕ] in SC.

(11) SC voiceless alveolo-palatals

IPA   [tɕ]   [tɕʰ]   [ɕ]
EXAMPLE   *jiào* 'to call'   *qiáo* 'bridge'   *xiǎo* 'small'

More precisely, these are ALVEOLO-PALATALS that involve both the post-alveolar and palatal regions and both the blade and front of the tongue. An alveolo-palatal in SC combines a post-alveolar sound with the front of the tongue raised closer toward the hard palate. In Figure 2.7, the blade and the front of the tongue are both raised high. See §2.2.5 for more on SC alveolo-palatals.

2.1.4 Manner of articulation

The articulators can form the CONSTRICTION in the vocal tract in different ways by varying the degree of obstruction of the airstream. How the articulators form the constriction is the manner of articulation. The articulators may completely block off the airstream temporarily, narrow the air passage considerably to cause friction, or simply approach each other. All or some of these *manners of articulation* can be applied to most *places of articulation*.

2.1.4.1 Stops: oral stops and nasal stops

If the articulators involved have complete closure so that the airstream cannot escape through the mouth, then a STOP is articulated. There are two major types of stops: oral stops and nasal stops.

An oral stop (or PLOSIVE) is formed by the complete blockage of the airstream both through the oral cavity and through the nasal cavity. In addition

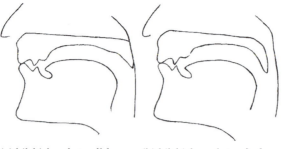

(a) bilabial oral stop [b]   (b) bilabial nasal stop [m]

Figure 2.8.   The articulation of oral and nasal stops.

to the closure in the oral cavity, the velum is raised to press against the back wall of the pharynx so that the air passage to the nasal cavity is blocked off. Since the air within the oral cavity has no outlet to vent, the air pressure will build up. When the articulators move apart, the previously trapped air will be released with a small burst or explosive sound.

Say the bilabial consonant of the word *bay* and hold the consonant position. Note that the lips completely block the airstream from escaping from the oral cavity. There is no way to vent the air through the nose either. Now move the lips apart to release the air; there is usually a little burst at the release. Try the same for the avleolar stop of *day*; you should note that the tongue tip or blade touches the alveolar ridge and the air is confined behind the alveolar ridge. When the tongue tip or blade is moved away from the alveolar ridge, the air rushes out of the oral cavity with a burst of sound. In the case of the velar stop as in *guy*, the articulatory closure is formed by the back of the tongue and the velum (see Figure 2.6 in §2.1.3.3 for a velar stop).

A nasal stop is produced if the airstream is blocked in the oral cavity but the velum is lowered down away from the back wall of the pharynx so that the air can go through the nasal cavity. In Figure 2.8 we can see the diagrams for the articulation of a bilabial oral stop [b] and a bilabial nasal stop [m] and note the difference in the position of the velum.

We can see that for both [b] and [m], the lips are closed. However, for the articulation of a bilabial oral stop [b], the velum is raised to block off the nasal cavity, whereas there is an air passage leading to the nasal cavity for [m] because the velum is lowered to move away from the back wall of the pharynx.

Now say the bilabial nasal stop [m] as in *may* by keeping the lips closed, and you should be able to continue the sound as long as your breath allows. This is because the airstream can go through the nasal cavity. Try the same for the alveolar nasal stop [n] as in *no*, and the velar nasal stop [ŋ] as in the last consonant of *sing*. In contrast, if the articulators are closed when producing an oral stop [b], [d], or [g] there is no way to hear any sound. To make or hear the sound, the articulators must come apart to let the air out. In (12) and (13), we see the classification of oral and nasal stops and examples from SC and English. Although both oral and nasal stops are classified as stops, the term STOP usually refers to an oral stop and the term NASAL is used to refer to a nasal stop. I follow this convention here. Stops can be voiced or voiceless but nasals are typically voiced.

(12) Stops and nasals

		Bilabial	Dental/Alveolar	Velar
Stop	voiced	b	d	g
	voiceless unaspirated	p	t	k
	voiceless aspirated	p^h	t^h	k^h
Nasal	voiced	m	n	ŋ

(13) Stops and nasals in SC and English

IPA	SC EXAMPLE		ENGLISH EXAMPLE
[b]			*abound*
[d]			*adult*
[g]			*ago*
[p]	*bēi*	'cup'	*spent*
[t]	*dì*	'floor, earth'	*still*
[k]	*gǎi*	'to change'	*sky*
[p^h]	*pán*	'dish'	*pan*
[t^h]	*tán*	'to talk'	*tan*
[k^h]	*kāi*	'to open'	*kite*
[m]	*máo*	'hair'	*mouse*
[n]	*nǎi*	'milk'	*night*
[ŋ]	*bīng*	'ice'	*being*

2.1.4.2 Fricatives

Instead of having a complete closure, two articulators can be brought very close together but do not completely block the airstream by leaving a very small narrow gap for the air to escape. Because the articulators are so close together, turbulent airflow and friction is created when the air is pushed through the narrow opening. Sounds using this mechanism of articulation are referred to as FRICATIVES. Since the air can escape from the oral cavity, we can produce a fricative continuously. For example, you can say [s] for as long as your breath can hold and then you can also hear clearly the hissing friction.

Fricatives may be articulated at any place of articulation. For each place of articulation, the articulators involved must come close enough to cause friction when the air squeezes through the narrow channel. For example, to articulate an apical post-alveolar fricative [ʂ] in SC, the tip of the tongue comes very close to the post-alveolar region without completely blocking the outgoing airstream (see Figure 2.5c in §2.1.3.2). In (14) and (15), we see the places of articulation for the fricatives in English and SC and examples of fricatives.

(14) English fricatives

	labiodental	(inter)dental	alveolar	palato-alveolar
voiceless	f	θ	s	ʃ
voiced	v	ð	z	ʒ

IPA	Example	IPA	Example
[f]	*fine*	[v]	*vine*
[θ]	*thought*	[ð]	*though*
[s]	*soon*	[z]	*zoom*
[ʃ]	*show*	[ʒ]	*pleasure*

(15) SC fricatives

	labiodental	dental	apical post-alveolar	alveolo-palatal	velar
voiceless	f	s	ʂ	ç	x

IPA	Example			IPA	Example		
[f]	*fēi*	'to fly'		[s]	*suān*	'sour'	
[ʂ]	*shǒu*	'hand'		[ç]	*xī*	'west'	
[x]	*hǎo*	'good'					

2.1.4.3 Affricates

An AFFRICATE is a sound that combines a stop and a fricative that have the same place of articulation. Consider the first consonant of the word *cheese*, which is a palato-alveolar affricate [tʃ]. It is like a stop because there is a temporary complete closure, but it is also like a fricative because there is friction when the air escapes. Compare this affricate with a stop like [t] as in *team*. You should notice that for [t] there is no friction when the articulators are separated to let the air out.

The articulation of a stop has a CLOSURE phase and a RELEASE phase. The closure phase is when the articulators have complete closure to block the airstream, and the release phase starts when the closure is released by moving the articulators apart so that the air can escape through the vocal tract. The difference between a stop and an affricate is that the release phase of a stop is a quick and open release with the articulators pulling quickly apart, whereas the release phase of an affricate is a slow fricative release with the articulators slowly moving first a little apart in a fricative-like position before they are completely apart. That is why a stop does not have the friction we find in an affricate during the release phase.

English has two affricates as shown in (16). In (17), we see three pairs of voiceless affricates in SC. For example, an apical post-alveolar affricate is made by forming a complete closure between the tongue tip and the post-alveolar region and releasing into a post-alveolar fricative.

(16) Affricates in English

PHONETIC DESCRIPTION	IPA	EXAMPLE
Voiceless palato-alveolar affricate	[tʃ]	*choose*
Voiced palato-alveolar affricate	[dʒ]	*juice*

(17) Voiceless affricates in SC

	dental	apical post-alveolar	alveolo-palatal
unaspirated	ts	tʂ	tɕ
aspirated	tsʰ	tʂʰ	tɕʰ

IPA	Example		IPA	Example	
[ts]	*zài*	'at'	[tsʰ]	*cài*	'vegetable'
[tʂ]	*zhè*	'this'	[tʂʰ]	*chē*	'car'
[tɕ]	*jī*	'chicken'	[tɕʰ]	*qī*	'seven'

2.1.4.4 Approximants

We have seen that the highest degree of constriction is complete closure and that sounds made with this type of constriction are stops. The lesser extreme of constriction is the close approximation of articulators to cause friction, and sounds made with this type of constriction are fricatives. We have the least degree of constriction when the articulators approach each other but do not come close enough to cause friction. Sounds made with this type of constriction are APPROXIMANTS. Examples of approximants in English and SC are given in (18) and (19). Notice that there are two alveolar approximants [ɹ] and [l] in English, the difference of which is the topic of the next subsection.

(18) English approximants

PHONETIC DESCRIPTION	IPA	EXAMPLE
voiced labiovelar approximant	[w]	*wide*
voiced alveolar approximant	[l]	*life*
voiced alveolar approximant	[ɹ]	*ride*
voiced palatal approximant	[j]	*yard*

(19) SC approximants

PHONETIC DESCRIPTION	IPA	EXAMPLE	
voiced labiovelar approximant	[w]	*wǎn*	'bowl'
voiced alveolar approximant	[l]	*lán*	'blue'
voiced post-alveolar approximant	[ɹ]	*ròu*	'meat'
voiced palatal approximant	[j]	*yáng*	'sheep'
voiced labial-palatal approximant	[ɥ]	*yuè*	'moon, month'

2.1.4.5 The lateral [l]

The voiced alveolar approximant [l] is a LATERAL sound. A lateral is made with complete closure along the center of the vocal tract but with incomplete closure between one or both sides of the tongue and the upper surface of the oral tract. To produce [l] as in *lie*, there is complete closure of the blade of the tongue against the center of the alveolar ridge; however, the sides of the tongue and the alveolar ridge have incomplete closure and no friction is created. Say [l] and note that you can prolong the sound, so this is not a stop despite the complete closure at the center of the alveolar ridge. The reason that you can prolong the [l] sound is because the air can flow through between the sides of the tongue and alveolar ridge. Say [l] again, and hold the tongue position while you breathe inward. You should feel that the tongue feels cooler on the side. Do the same for [ɹ] and see if you can feel the difference in where the air flows. For laterals, the air flows past the sides of the tongue. In contrast, if the air flows past the central line of the tongue as in [ɹ], we have a C E N T R A L sound. Both SC and English, and many other languages, have only one lateral sound, [l], and it can therefore be simply referred to as voiced alveolar lateral. All other sounds in SC and English are central.

2.1.5 Voice onset time: aspirated and unaspirated consonants

A S P I R A T I O N is an [h]-like sound between the end of a voiceless stop, frica- tive, or affricate and the start of vocal fold vibration in an adjacent voiced sound, usually a vowel. The time between the moment the consonant closure or constriction is released and the beginning of voicing of the adjacent voiced sound is called the V O I C E O N S E T T I M E, usually abbreviated as V O T.

(a) voiceless unaspirated stop [p]: short VOT

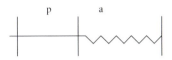

(b) voiceless aspirated stop [pʰ]: long VOT

Figure 2.9.   VOT for voiceless unaspirated and aspirated stops.

   In the diagrams in Figure 2.9, the vertical lines indicate the start and end of the production of the consonant and the vowel, and the straight horizontal line indicates the lack of vibration of the vocal folds (i.e. voicelessness) and the wavy part of the horizontal line indicates vibration of the vocal folds (i.e voicing). As the diagram in Figure 2.9a illustrates, the end or release of a voiceless unaspirated stop is shortly followed by vocal fold vibration of the following vowel. A very short VOT is not perceived as having aspiration. In contrast, in Figure 2.9b, when a voiceless aspirated stop ends or is released, there is an obvious delay in time before the vowel and vocal folds vibration starts. A long VOT like this is perceived as having aspiration.[2]

---

[2] For our purposes, this simple difference of long versus short VOT should suffice. Languages may differ in how short and how long the VOT may be for their voiceless aspirated and unaspirated consonants. For a voiceless aspirated consonant, the VOT value (the time length of the voicing delay) may be around 60 ms (milliseconds). For a voiceless unaspirated consonant, the VOT value can be around 20 ms. A voiced consonant has a negative VOT value because it starts voicing before the release of the closure. For more details, see Ladefoged (2001:125–31).

Recall from §1.5.2 that in English, voiceless aspirated stops occur only in syllable initial position whereas voiceless unaspirated stops occur after [s], as shown in (20). You can either put your palm or hang a thin facial tissue before your mouth when pronouncing these words. Pay attention to how a puff of air is felt in your palm or how the tissue is blown when aspirated stops are produced.

(20) English aspirated and unaspirated stops in different contexts

Syllable initial position		After [s]	
IPA	Example	IPA	Example
[pʰ]	*pan*	[p]	*span*
[tʰ]	*tan*	[t]	*stand*
[kʰ]	*can*	[k]	*scan*

SC has six pairs of aspirated and unaspirated stops and affricates occurring in the same contexts: all in syllable initial position. In (21) we see the classification of these sounds and examples.

(21) SC unaspirated and aspirated stops and affricates

	voiceless stop		voiceless affricates	
	unaspirated	aspirated	unaspirated	aspirated
bilabial	p	pʰ		
dental	t	tʰ	ts	tsʰ
post-alveolar			tʂ	tʂʰ
alveolo-palatal			tɕ	tɕʰ
velar	k	kʰ		

IPA	Example		IPA	Example	
[p]	*bāo*	'to fold'	[pʰ]	*pǎo*	'to run'
[t]	*dàn*	'egg'	[tʰ]	*tàn*	'charcoal'
[k]	*gān*	'dry'	[kʰ]	*kào*	'to depend'
[ts]	*zǎo*	'early'	[tsʰ]	*cǎo*	'grass'
[tʂ]	*zhǎo*	'to find'	[tʂʰ]	*chǎo*	'noisy'
[tɕ]	*jiǎo*	'foot'	[tɕʰ]	*qiāo*	'to knock'

2.1.6 Summary and phonetic description

Consonants are articulated with obstruction of the airstream in the vocal tract to various degrees and in different ways and can be classified according to their

manners of articulation. Consonants also form constrictions in different locations within the vocal tract and can be classified by their places of articulation.
Stops, fricatives, and affricates as a group of sounds are called OBSTRUENTS
because of the greater degree of constriction. Nasals and approximants as a
group are also called SONORANTS because the air can flow out through either
the oral or nasal cavity without friction. Sonorants, like vowels, are normally
voiced, but obstruents can be voiced or voiceless and voiceless obstruents can
be aspirated or unaspirated. Non-nasal sonorants, i.e. approximants, can be
further divided into LIQUIDS and GLIDES. Liquids are [ɹ] and the lateral [l],
and glides are [j], [w], and [ɥ].

We can now uniquely describe and classify each consonant phonetically by
the following factors:

(22) Phonetic description

    1. STATE OF THE GLOTTIS: voiced or voiceless
    2. VOT: aspirated or unaspirated
    3. PLACE OF ARTICULATION:
       bilabial, labiodental, dental, alveolar, palato-alveolar (laminal
       post-alveolar), apical post-alveolar, alveolo-palatal, palatal, velar,
       or glottal
    4. CENTRAL OR LATERAL ARTICULATION
    5. ORAL OR NASAL SOUNDS
    6. MANNER OF ARTICULATION:
       stop, fricative, affricate, approximant

To give a phonetic description of a sound, follow the order given in (22). If
a term is normal or irrelevant to a sound or applies to most sounds, it can be
omitted. For example, since most sounds are central and oral, we can specify
only lateral and nasal sounds, and other sounds unspecified with lateral or nasal
are assumed to be central and oral. Since, in most languages, aspiration is relevant only to voiceless stops and affricates, the terms aspirated and unaspirated
can be omitted for other sounds. If a language does not distinguish between
apical and laminal post-alveolars, such as SC, the terms apical and laminal
become optional. If a more specific term is used, then the more general term is
optional. For example, if the term glide is used for an approximant, the term
approximant can be omitted. Examples of the phonetic descriptions of some
SC consonants are given in (23). The terms in parentheses indicate those that
are omitted or optional.

Table 2.1 Chart of English consonants.
Whenever there are two symbols under the same place of articulation, the one on the left is voiceless and the one on the right is voiced. The cells that contain voiceless sounds are shaded.

	bilabial	labio-dental	(inter)dental	alveolar	palato-alveolar	palatal	velar	glottal
stop	p b			t d			k g	
nasal	m			n			ŋ	
fricative		f v	θ ð	s z	ʃ ʒ			h
affricate					tʃ dʒ			
(central) approximant	w			ɹ		j	w	(h)
lateral (approximant)				l				

(23) Sample examples of phonetic description of SC consonants

IPA   PHONETIC DESCRIPTION
[t]   voiceless unaspirated dental (central) (oral) stop
[m]   voiced bilabial (central) nasal (stop)
[s̺]   voiceless (apical) post-alveolar (central) (oral) fricative
[tɕʰ]   voiceless aspirated alveolo-palatal (central) (oral) affricate
[x]   voiceless velar (central) (oral) fricative
[l]   voiced dental lateral (oral) (approximant)
[ɹ]   voiced (apical) post-alveolar (central) (oral) approximant
[w]   voiced labiovelar (central) (oral) glide (approximant)

In Tables 2.1 and 2.2 we see the complete charts of consonants in English and SC. Note that the aspirated stops in English are allophonic variants of the corresponding unaspirated stops in a specific context (§1.5.2 and §2.1.5) and are not listed. The labiovelar [w] shows up in two cells under bilabial and velar, and the same applies to SC labial-palatal [ɥ], which appears in two cells under bilabial and palatal (§2.1.3.4). Depending on different analyses, the glottal [h] in English can be classified as a fricative or a glide (approximant).

2.2 Consonants in SC

This section covers the following aspects of SC consonants: (i) the phonetic properties; (ii) phonemic versus allophonic status; and (iii) the context in which

Table 2.2 Chart of SC consonants.
When there are two symbols under the same place of articulation, the one on the left is voiceless unaspirated and the one on the right is voiceless aspirated. Nasals and approximants are all voiced. The cells that contain voiceless unaspirated sounds are shaded.

	bilabial	labio-dental	dental	post-alveolar	alveolo-palatal	palatal	velar
stop	p pʰ		t tʰ				k kʰ
fricative		f	s	ʂ	ɕ		x
affricate			ts tsʰ	tʂ tʂʰ	tɕ tɕʰ		
nasal	m		n				ŋ
(central) approximant	w ɥ			ɻ		j ɥ	w
lateral (approximant)			l				

a consonant or a group of consonants occurs. Practical advice to learners of SC is provided and special attention will be given to those consonants that are absent in English. You may want to consult Table 2.2 during the following discussion.

2.2.1 Stops, nasals, and the lateral

Stops, nasals, and the lateral in SC are generally easy for learners of SC to pronounce, but there are some differences between SC and English regarding these sounds.

First, as mentioned earlier in §2.1.3.2, SC [t], [tʰ], [n], and [l] can be dentals or alveolars or both depending on the speaker. If you regularly pronounce these sounds as alveolars, you may also want to practice placing the tip or blade of your tongue either on the upper front teeth or slightly behind the upper front teeth before the alveolar ridge for a dental articulation.

Second, aspirated and unaspirated stops are separate phonemes in SC but allophones in English. Let us review what we mentioned earlier in §1.5.2. In SC each pair of aspirated and unaspirated stops are separate PHONEMES (DIS-TINCTIVE or CONTRASTIVE sounds) since there are MINIMAL PAIRS for them, as given in (24). The examples in (24) provide full phonetic transcription for each word and the pitch value for each tone is given as a subscript (see §1.3

and §4.1.4). Each pair of words have the same tone and the same vowels but differ only in the consonants. We can see that a change of aspiration leads to a change in word meaning, so aspirated and unaspirated stops in SC are distinctive. Note also that these stops in SC can only occur in syllable initial position.

(24) Minimal pairs for aspirated and unaspirated stops in SC

	PHONEME	EXAMPLE		
		PHONETIC TRANSCRIPTION	PĪNYĪN	GLOSS
a.	/p/	[pa]$_{51}$	bà	'father'
	/pʰ/	[pʰa]$_{51}$	pà	'to fear'
b.	/t/	[ti]$_{35}$	dí	'flute'
	/tʰ/	[tʰi]$_{35}$	tí	'to lift'
c.	/k/	[kou]$_{214}$	gǒu	'dog'
	/kʰ/	[kʰou]$_{214}$	kǒu	'mouth'

In contrast, the aspirated and unaspirated stops in English are non-distinctive because they are ALLOPHONES appearing in COMPLEMENTARY DISTRIBUTION (i.e. mutually exclusive contexts): aspirated stops in syllable initial position and unaspirated stops after [s]. For example, the voiceless aspirated and unaspirated bilabial stops in English are allophones of the same phoneme /p/. If you use aspirated stops after [s], as some non-native speakers of English do, the word meaning does not change, although the pronunciation sounds non-standard. Recall from §1.5.2 that phonemes are abstract mental units and each phoneme has one or more phonetic realizations. Allophones are those phonetic variants of the same phoneme and the distribution of allophones is systematic and predictable. The diagram in (25) illustrates the differences in phonological status of SC and English voicelelss aspirated and unaspirated bilabial stops (cf. (3) in §1.5.2). In SC they are phonologically different at the mental abstract level and maintain the same difference phonetically in actual articulation whereas in English they are phonetic variants or allophones (i.e. different pronunciations) of the same phonological unit in different contexts.

(25)

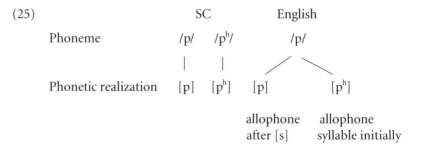

Since the voiceless unaspirated stops occur only syllable initially and they are spelled as *b*, *d*, and *g* in *pīnyīn*, learners of SC may mispronounce them as voiced stops. However, because word initial voiced stops in English are usually devoiced, the mispronunciation may not be a pervasive problem for English-speaking learners. The strategy to keep in mind is that those *b*, *d*, and *g* letters in *pīnyīn* should be pronounced as unaspirated [p], [t], and [k], respectively, like those stops after [s] in English.

Third, the nasals and the lateral in SC, as in English, are also separate phonemes, as shown by the minimal pairs in (26). Each of these pair differs in only one consonant in the same position of the word. Note that the lateral and the nasal [m] can occur only in syllable initial position. In syllable final position, only [n] and [ŋ] are allowed. That is, all these consonants, with the exception of [ŋ], can start a syllable but only the alveolar and velar nasals can end a syllable. The alveolar nasal [n] is the only one that can occur in both syllable initial and syllable final positions.

(26) Minimal pairs for nasals and the lateral

	PHONEME	EXAMPLE PHONETIC TRANSCRIPTION	*PĪNYĪN*	GLOSS
a.	/l/	$[\text{la}]_{51}$	*là*	'spicy'
	/n/	$[\text{na}]_{51}$	*nà*	'that'
b.	/n/	$[\text{nai}]_{214}$	*nǎi*	'milk'
	/m/	$[\text{mai}]_{214}$	*mǎi*	'to buy'
c.	/n/	$[\text{mən}]_{35}$	*mén*	'door'
	/ŋ/	$[\text{məŋ}]_{35}$	*méng*	'to cover'

2.2.2 Labiodental and velar fricatives

The labiodental and velar fricatives are also phonemes in SC, as the minimal pair in (27) show, and both occur only in syllable initial position.

(27) Minimal pair for labiodental and velar fricatives

PHONEME	EXAMPLE PHONETIC TRANSCRIPTION	*PĪNYĪN*	GLOSS
/f/	$[\text{fei}]_{55}$	*fēi*	'to fly'
/x/	$[\text{xei}]_{55}$	*hēi*	'black'

The pronunciation of [f] is pretty much the same as that in English. Since the voiceless velar fricative [x] is spelled as *h* in *pīnyīn*, English speakers tend to pronounce the SC [x] as the glottal [h] in English. To pronounce a velar fricative, try the velar stop [k] first and move the back of the tongue slightly down to make a fricative. Keep repeating [k] and along the way try to lower the back of the tongue a little bit from the velum to get the velar fricative. Note, however, that the phonetic realization of /x/ can vary between [x] and a glottal sound like [h] for some SC speakers.

2.2.3 Dental affricates and fricative

The dental affricates and fricative, [ts], [ts], and [s], may be articulated with the tip of the tongue closer to the lower front teeth or to the upper front teeth. It is important to note that the upper and lower teeth are very close to each other when these consonants are pronounced, so the tip of the tongue may also end up in the middle of the front teeth between the upper and lower teeth. One strategy to help learners of SC to pronounce these consonants is to: (i) make sure that the upper and lower front teeth are very close; and (ii) place the tongue tip right behind the front teeth, either the lower or the upper ones. Now follow the strategy and practice the pronunciation of the three dental consonants in the examples in (28). Note that these consonants can occur only in syllable initial position.

(28) SC dental affricates and fricative

Phonetic description	IPA	Example	
voiceless unaspirated dental affricate	ts	$[tsai]_{51}$	*zài* 'again'
voiceless aspirated dental affricate	ts^h	$[ts^hai]_{51}$	*cài* 'vegetable'
voiceless dental fricative	s	$[sai]_{51}$	*sài* 'to compete'

If you still find it difficult to produce the correct pronunciation, you may also try the second strategy. The $[ts^h]$ affricate in SC sounds similar to *ts* in *cats*. The differences are that in English, *ts* is a two-consonant sequence and can not appear in syllable initial position; on the other hand, in SC $[ts^h]$ is a dental affricate that is allowed only in syllable initial position. Start with *ts* in *cats*, and if possible move the tongue tip close to the front teeth and make sure you have aspiration. And now see if you can add the vowel [ai] after [ts] to pronounce [ts^{h}ai]. The unaspirated [ts] affricate in SC also sound similar to *ds* [dz] in *seeds*, but do make sure not to pronounce [ts] as a voiced sound. You can try *ds* in *seeds*, then make sure it is voiceless and dental, and then add the vowel [ai] to pronounce [tsai]. For [s], it is easier: start with an [s] in English and move the tongue tip a little forward behind the front teeth (Figure 2.4b in §2.1.3.2).

2.2.4 Post-alveolar consonants

The post-alveolar consonants in SC, [tʂ], [tʂ^h], [ʂ], and [ɹ], are often quite difficult for English speakers to master, as they are for Chinese speakers whose native dialects do not have these consonants. Chao (1948, 1968) describes these sounds as RETROFLEXES, which are apical post-alveolars in which the tongue tip is curled upward and backward and make use of the underside of the tongue tip to touch or approach the post-alveolar region (§2.1.3.2). Following this tradition, many teachers of SC teach students to pronounce these sounds as retroflexes. However, recent phonetic studies have shown that these post-alveolars are not retroflexes in the normal sense in the speech of the speakers of the Beijing dialect, on which the pronunciation of SC is based. For example, Lee and Zee (2003) and Zee (2003a) maintain that it is the upper side, not the underside, of the tongue tip that is used to approach the back of the alveolar ridge. For a more narrow transcription, these sounds can be transcribed with a diacritic dot beneath the symbols (e.g. [tʂ̣], [ʂ̣], [ɹ̣]) as seen in Ladefoged and Maddieson (1996:151 and 164). In this book, I continue to use the IPA retroflex symbols partly because of tradition and partly because of typographical convenience.

The major difference between dental [ts], [ts^h], and [s] versus post-alveolar [tʂ], [tʂ^h], and [ʂ] respectively, is that the tip of the tongue is behind the front teeth in the former but behind the alveolar ridge in the latter. Assuming that you have mastered the dental affricates and fricative discussed in the previous subsection, one strategy to help you learn the pronunciation of SC post-alveolar affricates and fricative is to first pronounce [ts], [ts^h], and [s] and then move the tongue tip from behind the front teeth to the back of the alveolar ridge for [tʂ], [tʂ^h], and [ʂ] respectively. To compare the dental [s] and the post-alveolar [ʂ], see Figure 2.4b and Figure 2.5c in §2.1.3.2.

The post-alveolar approximant [ɹ] in SC sounds similar to the [ɹ] in English, but the English version can be alveolar or post-alveolar or can even be made with the tongue tip down and a bunched tongue body (Ladefoged and Maddeison 1996:233–6). In addition, many English speakers have lip-rounding when producing [ɹ] (§2.1.4.4). In the articulation of SC [ɹ], raise the tongue tip toward the back of the alveolar ridge, do not have lip-rounding (unless it is followed by a [w] or [u]), and make sure it is voiced with vibrating vocal folds. Now see if you can pronounce the examples in (29).

(29) SC post-alveolar consonants

Phonetic description	IPA		Example
voiceless unaspirated post-alveolar affricate	tʂ	[tʂɑŋ]$_{51}$	*zhàng* '(water, price) to rise'
voiceless aspirated post-alveolar affricate	tʂʰ	[tʂʰɑŋ]$_{51}$	*chàng* 'to sing'
voiceless post-alveolar fricative	ʂ	[ʂɑŋ]$_{51}$	*shàng* 'up, top, above'
voiced post-alveolar approximant	ɹ	[ɹɑŋ]$_{51}$	*ràng* 'to let, to yield'

I stated earlier that these SC post-alveolars are apical sounds. Ladefoged and Maddieson (1996:150–3) claim that SC post-alveolar affricates and fricative are not APICAL but LAMINAL post-alveolars; that is, the blade rather than the tip of the tongue is used. This then raises a question: what distinguishes [ʂ] in SC from [ʃ] in English if both are laminal post-alveolars? In English [ʃ], the front part of the tongue is slightly raised toward the hard palate, but in SC [ʂ] the front of the tongue is flat (Figure 2.5c in §2.1.3.2).

For the practical purpose of learning the pronunciation of SC post-alveolars, it is easier to manipulate the tip of the tongue. If you produce [ʃ] first and hold the tongue position, you may be able to notice that the front of the tongue is slightly raised too. Once you are in the [ʃ] tongue position, raise your tongue tip up to the post-alveolar position, then the bunch of the front of the tongue in [ʃ] can be flattened to SC [ʂ]. In this book, I continue to follow tradition and Lee and Zee (2003) and Zee (2003a) in classifying SC post-alveolars as apical sounds.

The post-alveolars all occur in syllable initial position, but under some circumstances the voiced post-alveolar approximant [ɹ] can also take up syllable final position, e.g. *èr* [əɹ]$_{51}$ 'two'. Some linguists believe that phonetically there is no consonant in this word and some claim that this [ɹ] is a vowel rather than a consonant. We will discuss RHOTACIZED vowels (*r*-colored vowel) in §3.1.5 and §3.4.5.

Since many Chinese dialects do not have these post-alveolar consonants, many speakers and learners of SC replace them with dental or alveolar consonants: [ts], [tsʰ], [s], and [z] (see §12.2). (Note that the approximant [ɹ] tends to become a voiced fricative.) Some of these speakers make no distinction between the dentals and post-alveolars; that is, all four post-alveolars are made with dental articulations. Some other speakers make some degree of distinction between the two series of consonants by pronouncing the post-alveolars as alveolars so that they are somewhat different from the dentals. In either case, the absence of post-alveolars can lead to ambiguity or confusion; for example, *shan* [ʂan]₅₅ 'mountain' and *san* [san]₅₅ 'three' would sound the same or very similar.

2.2.5 Alveolo-palatal consonants

The alveolo-palatal consonants, [tɕ], [tɕʰ], and [ɕ], which are spelled as *j, q,* and *x* respectively in *pīnyīn*, can occur only in syllable initial position followed by the vowel [i] (as in [ni]₂₁₄ *nǐ* 'you'), the glide [j] (as in [je]₂₁₄ *yě* 'also'), the vowel [y] (as in [ly]₅₁ *lǜ* 'green'), and the glide [ɥ] (as in [ɥe]₅₁ *yuè* 'moon, month'). As we will see in §3.4.1, these vowels/glides are classified as high and front vowels/glides that make use of the front part of the tongue.

According to Ladefoged and Maddieson (1996:150–3), SC alveolo-palatals are more precisely PALATALIZED post-alveolars. PALATALIZATION is a kind of SECONDARY ARTICULATION that can be simultaneously added to the primary articulation of a consonant. In this case, in addition to the primary place of articulation, i.e. post-alveolar, the front of the tongue is also raised toward the hard palate at the same time with an approximant-like constriction, i.e. a [j]-like constriction.

One important difference between the post-alveolar (palato-alveolar) [ʃ] and the avleolo-palatal [ɕ] is that in [ɕ] the blade and the front of the tongue are raised higher than in [ʃ] (cf. Figure 2.5b in §2.1.3.2 and Figure 2.7 in §2.1.3.4). Therefore, one strategy to help you learn the pronunciation of SC alveolo-palatals is to start with English post-alveolar (palato-alveolar) fricative [ʃ] as in *she* [ʃi]. Notice that for many English speakers, there is some degree of lip-rounding for [ʃ]. Now pronounce [ʃ] in *she* first, hold the articulators/tongue position while intentionally spreading your lips, and then add the vowel. If you do this correctly, instead of pronouncing *she*, you will produce something similar to [ɕi] *xī* 'west' in SC. You can also try to intentionally spread your lips when pronouncing [dʒ] as in *jeep* and [tʃ] as in *cheese*, and you can get pretty close to [tɕ] and [tɕʰ] respectively as long as you make sure that [tɕ] is voiceless and [tɕʰ] is aspirated. Now practice the pronunciations of the first

two examples for each alveolo-palatal in (30), where the consonant is followed
by [i] or [j]. Remember to have spread lips throughout for both the consonant
and the vowel.

(30) SC alveolo-palatal consonants

Phonetic description	IPA	Example		
voiceless unaspirated alveolo-palatal affricate	tɕ	[tɕi]$_{55}$	jī	'chicken'
		[tɕje]$_{35}$	jié	'holiday, festival'
		[tɕy]$_{55}$	jū	'residence'
		[tɕɥe]$_{35}$	jué	'stubborn'
voiceless aspirated alveolo-palatal affricate	tɕʰ	[tɕʰi]$_{55}$	qī	'seven'
		[tɕʰje]$_{35}$	qié	'eggplant'
		[tɕʰy]$_{55}$	qū	'district'
		[tɕʰɥe]$_{35}$	qué	'cripple, lame'
voiceless alveolo-palatal fricative	ɕ	[ɕi]$_{55}$	xī	'west'
		[ɕje]$_{35}$	xié	'shoes'
		[ɕy]$_{55}$	xū	'beard'
		[ɕɥe]$_{35}$	xué	'to study, to learn'

When SC alveolo-palatals are followed by [y] or [ɥ], lip-rounding occurs
because the vowel and glide have lip-rounding (§2.1.3.4 and §3.4.1). In the
third and fourth examples for each consonant in (30), where the consonants
are followed [y] and [ɥ], you may find that [tɕ], [tɕʰ], and [ɕ] sound similar to
[dʒ] (as in *juice*), [tʃ] (as in *choose*), and [ʃ] (as in *shoes*) respectively. Of course,
SC alveolo-palatals and English palato-alveolars are not the same. In SC, the
front part of the tongue is raised higher and closer to the hard palate. The
strategy suggested here is just for a practical starting point. Practice carefully
by listening to and imitating pronunciations on the CD or by having a SC
speaker's or your teacher's feedback to help you achieve refinement toward
correct SC pronunciations.

One interesting fact about SC alveolo-palatals is that they are in COM-
PLEMENTARY DISTRIBUTION with three sets of consonants: the dental
affricates/fricative, the post-alveolar affricates/fricative, and the velars. That
is, the alveolo-palatals never occur in the same contexts as these three sets of
consonants, as shown in (31). It can be claimed that SC alveolo-palatals are
not independent phonemes but allophones that occur only before high front
vowels/glides. The problem, however, is that it is unclear which set of phonemes

they are allophones of. In (32), we see two common views in the literature.[3] For our purposes, and without getting into the details of controversy and arguments, let us tentatively adopt the view in (32a) (see also Duanmu 2000 and §7.2.1).

(31) a. [tɕ]   [tɕʰ]   [ɕ]   occur only before [i]/[j] and [y]/[ɥ]
     b. [ts]   [tsʰ]   [s]   never occur before [i]/[j] and [y]/[ɥ]
     c. [tʂ]   [tʂ]   [ʂ]   never occur before [i]/[j] and [y]/[ɥ]
     d. [k]   [kʰ]   [x]   never occur before [i]/[j] and [y]/[ɥ]

(32) a. phonemes   /ts/   /tsʰ/   /s/

         allophones [ts]   [tɕ]   [tsʰ]   [tɕʰ]   [s]   [ɕ]

     b. phonemes   /k/   /kʰ/   /x/

         allophones [k]   [tɕ]   [kʰ]   [tɕʰ]   [x]   [ɕ]

2.2.6 Glides

The three GLIDES (SEMI-VOWELS) in SC, [j], [w], and [ɥ], sound like the vowels [i], [u], and [y] respectively, are spelled with vowel letters in *pīnyīn*, and have often been treated as vowels in the literature of Chinese phonetics and phonology. In SC the glides and their corresponding vowels are in complementary distribution: glides occur only in syllable onset position or before the syllable nuclear position and vowels occur in syllable nuclear position. We can say that glides are not phonemes in SC but phonetic variants of their corresponding vowels in syllable onset position. We will have further discussion on glides in §§3.2 and 3.4.1.

2.2.7 SC consonant phonemes

Table 2.3 summarizes the consonant phoneme inventory in SC. If you compare this table with Table 2.2, you can see that glides and alveolo-palatals are removed because they can be treated as allophones that occur in predictable contexts and are therefore not accorded phonemic status.

---

[3] There is also the suggestion that alveolo-palatals can be treated as distinctive phonemes in SC since there is no compelling phonological evidence in choosing one set of phonemes over the other. See Cheng (1973: chapter 5) for discussion.

Table 2.3 Consonant Phonemes in SC.
When there are two symbols under the same place of articulation, the one on the left is voiceless unaspirated and the one on the right is voiceless aspirated. Nasals and approximants are all voiced. The cells that contain voiceless unaspirated sounds are shaded.

	bilabial	labio-dental	dental		post-alveolar		velar	
stop	p pʰ		t	tʰ			k	kʰ
fricative		f	s		ʂ		x	
affricate			ts	tsʰ	tʂ	tʂʰ		
nasal	m		n				ŋ	
(central) approximant					ɻ			
lateral (approximant)			l					

2.3 Summary

In this chapter, we have studied the phonetic features used for describing and classifying SC and English consonants.

- A consonant can be either VOICED or VOICELESS (§2.1.1), and either ASPIRATED or unaspirated (§2.1.5).
- Consonants also have different PLACES OF ARTICULATION (§2.1.3) and MANNERS OF ARTICULATION (§2.1.4).
- SC and English consonants have been compared for their similarities and differences in phonetic properties (§2.1; Tables 2.1–2.2 in §2.1.6).
- SC has six oral stops, three of which are voiceless aspirated and three voiceless unaspirated. The places of articulation of the six oral stops and the three nasal stops include BILABIAL, DENTAL, and VELAR (Table 2.2 in §2.1.6; §2.2.1).
- SC has five FRICATIVES: LABIODENTAL, DENTAL, POST-ALVEOLAR, ALVEOLO-PALATAL, and VELAR (Table 2.2 in §2.1.6; §§2.2.2–2.2.5).
- SC has three pairs of voiceless aspirated and voiceless unaspirated AFFRICATES that differ in place of articulation: DENTAL, POST-ALVEOLAR, and ALVEOLO-PALATAL (Table 2.2 in §2.1.6; §§2.2.3–2.2.5).

- The three ALVEOLO-PALATALS can occur only before a specific set of vowels/glides and can be considered ALLOPHONES of the dental affricates/fricative (§2.2.5 and §5.3; cf. §7.2.1).
- SC APPROXIMANTS include a LATERAL, a POST-ALVEOLAR [ɹ], and three GLIDES (Table 2.2 in §2.1.6; §§2.1.4.4–2.1.4.5; §2.2.1; §2.2.4). The glides can be treated as allophones of the corresponding vowels (§2.2.6).
- With a detailed discussion of SC consonants (§2.2), we have come to the conclusion that SC has 19 consonant PHONEMES (Table 2.3 in §2.2.7). The PHONETIC REALIZATIONS (or phonetic variants) of these phonemes, i.e. actual phonetic pronunciations of these phonemes, are governed by phonological and phonetic rules to be discussed in chapters 7 and 8.

EXERCISES

1   For each of the following English words, identify if the boldfaced consonant is voiced, voiceless unaspirated, or voiceless aspirated and write down the IPA symbol for the consonant.

	VOICED, VOICELESS UNASPIRATED, OR VOICELESS ASPIRATED?	IPA SYMBOL
man	voiced	[m]
a. *star*		
b. *ago*		
c. *pattern*		
d. *name*		
e. *juice*		
f. *lay*		
g. *face*		

2   For each of the following English words, identify the place and manner of articulation of the boldfaced consonant and provide the IPA symbol for the consonant.

	PLACE/MANNER OF ARTICULATION	IPA SYMBOL
man	bilabial nasal stop	[m]
a. *city*		
b. *thin*		
c. *vine*		
d. *rose*		

    e. **ch**in

    f. **b**oat

    g. **t**oast

    h. **sh**oes

    i. si**ng**

3 For each of the following phonetic descriptions of SC consonants, provide the IPA symbol.

PHONETIC DESCRIPTION	IPA SYMBOL
voiced bilabial nasal stop	[m]
a. voiceless unaspirated dental oral stop	
b. voiceless aspirated velar stop	
c. voiceless dental fricative	
d. voiced velar nasal stop	
e. voiceless labiodental fricative	
f. voiceless velar fricative	
g. voiceless alveolo-palatal fricative	
h. voiceless post-alveolar fricative	
i. voiceless aspirated post-alveolar affricate	
j. voiceless unaspirated dental affricate	
k. voiceless aspirated alveolo-palatal affricate	
l. voiced post-alveolar approximant	
m. voiced dental/alveolar lateral	

4 For each of the following SC consonants, provide the phonetic description.

IPA	PĪNYĪN/GLOSS		PHONETIC DESCRIPTION
[m]	*mǎi*	'to buy'	voiced bilabial nasal stop
a. [t]	*dōng*	'east'	
b. [ɕ]	*xī*	'west'	
c. [kʰ]	*kǔ*	'bitter'	
d. [ŋ]	*tīng*	'listen'	
e. [tsʰ]	*cóng*	'from'	
f. [tʂ]	*zhǐ*	'paper'	
g. [tɕ]	*jī*	'chicken'	
h. [ɹ]	*rè*	'hot'	
i. [ʂ]	*shí*	'ten'	

5 Each of the following pairs of consonants differ only in one phonetic property such as voicing, aspiration, and place or manner of articulation. Identify the difference for each pair.

Examples:

[p] and [b]:	voicing: voiceless versus voiced
[p] and [pʰ]:	aspiration: unaspirated versus aspirated
[b] and [m]:	manner of articulation: oral versus nasal
[p] and [t]:	place of articulation: bilabial versus dental/alveolar

a. [n] and [ŋ]   b. [t] and [tʰ]

c. [f] and [v]   d. [ts] and [s]

e. [ʂ] and [ɕ]   f. [tsʰ] and [tɕʰ]

g. [tʂ] and [tʂʰ]   h. [k] and [x]

6 Each of the following groups of SC consonants have some phonetic properties in common. Choose the most precise and complete description of the shared properties for each group of consonants.

Example: [p, t, k]

(i) voiceless unaspirated oral stop (ii) oral stop (iii) fricative

The answer is (i) since all three consonants are voiceless unaspirated and they are all oral stops.

a. [pʰ, tʰ, kʰ]

(i) stop (ii) voiceless aspirated oral stop (iii) fricative (iv) affricate

b. [k, kʰ, x, ŋ]

(i) fricative (ii) stop (iii) velar (iv) velar stop

c. [f, s, ʂ, ɕ, x]

(i) fricative (ii) stop (iii) coronal fricative (iv) affricate

d. [ts, tʂ, tɕ, tsʰ, tʂʰ, tɕʰ]

(i) fricative (ii) stop (iii) affricate (iv) dental affricate

e. [m, n, ŋ]

(i) bilabial nasal (ii) nasal stop (iii) approximant (iv) velar nasal

f. [j, w, ɥ]

(i) glide or semi-vowel (ii) labial (iii) liquid (iv) labiovelar

g. [l, ɹ, j, w, ɥ]

(i) liquid (ii) fricative (iii) coronal approximant (iv) approximant

h. [f, m, p, pʰ]

(i) bilabial (ii) labiodental (iii) labial (iv) labial stop

7 Describe the position and action of the articulators during the production of each of the following SC consonants.

Example: [t]

The SC consonant [t] is produced: (i) with the vocal folds open without vibration (i.e. voiceless); (ii) with little time delay between the release of the consonant and the start of voicing (i.e. unaspirated); (iii) with the tongue tip or blade forming a complete closure behind the teeth or before the alveolar ridge (i.e. dental stop); and (iv) with the velum (soft palate) raised to prevent the air from escaping to the nasal cavity (i.e. oral).

a. [pʰ]   b. [ŋ]   c. [s]
d. [ts]   e. [l]   f. [ʂ]
g. [x]   h. [ɕ]   i. [ɹ]

🎧 8   Performance exercise

Practice the pronunciation of SC consonants and glides by learning to pronounce the following pairs or groups of words that differ in only one consonant. The phonetic transcription with a subscripted pitch value for the tone (see (1) in §1.3, §4.1.1, §4.1.4) is shown first and the second and third lines provide the *pīnyīn* and meaning respectively. Since we have not studied SC vowels and tones, you may want to listen to *The Sounds of Chinese CD* or ask your teacher or a SC speaker to help with your practice.

a. oral stops

$[pan]_{51}$	$[p^han]_{51}$	$[tan]_{51}$	$[t^han]_{51}$	$[kan]_{51}$	$[k^han]_{51}$
bàn	*pàn*	*dàn*	*tàn*	*gàn*	*kàn*
'to do'	'to sentence'	'but'	'coal'	'to do'	'to see'

b. syllable initial nasal stops and lateral

$[man]_{51}$	$[nan]_{51}$	$[lan]_{51}$
màn	*nàn*	*làn*
'slow'	'disaster'	'rotten'

c. syllable final nasal stops

$[kən]_{55}$	$[kəŋ]_{55}$
gēn	*gēng*
'root'	'to cultivate'

d. velars

$[kwa]_{55}$	$[k^hwa]_{55}$	$[xwa]_{55}$
guā	*kuā*	*huā*
'melon'	'to boast'	'flower'

e. labiodental, dental, post-alveolar, and velar fricatives

[fan]$_{51}$ [san]$_{51}$ [ʂan]$_{51}$ [xan]$_{51}$
fàn   *sàn*   *shàn*   *hàn*
'rice'   'to scatter'   'fan'   'drought'

f. dental/post-alveolar affricates and fricatives and post-alveolar approximant

[tsou]$_{51}$ [tsʰou]$_{51}$ [sou]$_{51}$
zòu   *còu*   *sòu*
'to beat'   'put together'   'cough'

[tʂou]$_{51}$ [tʂʰou]$_{51}$ [ʂou]$_{51}$ [ɻou]$_{51}$
zhòu   *chòu*   *shòu*   *ròu*
'wrinkle'   'foul smell'   'beast'   'meat'

g. alveolo-palatals

[tɕja]$_{55}$ [tɕʰja]$_{55}$ [ɕja]$_{55}$
jiā   *qiā*   *xiā*
'home'   'to pinch'   'shrimp'

h. glides

[je]$_{51}$ [ɥe]$_{51}$ [ja]$_{55}$ [wa]$_{55}$
yè   *yuè*   *yā*   *wā*
'leaf'   'moon'   'duck'   'frog'

3 Vowels and glides

In this chapter, we study the phonetic properties of SC vowels and GLIDES (semi-vowels) and how they are classified. We start with how vowels are produced, and what IPA symbols and what features are associated with each type of vowel (§3.1). Whenever appropriate, American English vowels are used for reference and comparison. We then introduce glides, which sound like vowels but function like consonants in SYLLABLE structure (§3.2), and DIPHTHONGS, which combine two vowels within a single syllable (§3.3). In §3.4, SC's vowels and glides are discussed in detail. The final section (§3.5) summarizes the main points of the chapter.

3.1 The production and classification of vowels

When we produce a vowel, the air flows through the vocal tract with ease; in contrast, when we produce a consonant, the airflow is obstructed to various degrees depending on the types of consonants. Compare the vowel [i], such as the vowel of *bǐ* 'pen' in SC, with the consonant [s], such as the first consonant of *sān* 'three' in SC. When you prolong your production of [s] for as long as your breath allows, you hear a continued hissing sound and may feel that the airflow is more obstructed, but when you do the same for [i], the sound is clear without hissing friction and impediment.

Vowels are typically produced as voiced sounds. Only under very special circumstances do some vowels become voiceless and we will see some examples in §7.3.3. Since vowels are all voiced, the major differences among vowels in terms of vowel quality involve the positions of the tongue and the lips: the tongue can move higher or lower, more toward the front or toward the back, and the lips can be rounded or not rounded.

3.1.1 Aperture: high, mid, and low vowels

Vowels can be differentiated in terms of the degree of openness (i.e. aperture). When the jaw and the tongue are lowered, a more open vowel is produced. Consider the three vowels in (1). Note that in American English the vowel [a] occurs as the first part of the diphthongs (two-vowel sequences) in [aɪ] (as in *buy*) and [aʊ] (as in *how*), and [e] is usually diphthongized as [eɪ]. (See §3.3 for more on diphthongs.) A vowel followed by [ː] means that the vowel is longer than a single vowel, e.g. [iː] is a long vowel, which extends the pronunciation of [i].[1]

(1)　　　　IPA　SC EXAMPLE　　　　　　ENGLISH EXAMPLE
　　HIGH　[i]　　*bǐ*　　[pi]$_{214}$　'pen'　　*beat*　[biːt]
　　MID　　[e]　　*bēi*　[pei]$_{55}$　'cup'　　*bait*　[beɪt]
　　LOW　　[a]　　*hàn*　[xan]$_{51}$　'and'　　*how*　[haʊ]

Compare first the vowel [a] with the vowel [i]. Say [i] and [a] several times in front of a mirror and you should see that your jaw and tongue are lowered and your mouth more open when you produce [a]. Now try to feel where your tongue is: the tongue is closer to the roof of the mouth in [i] but farther away in [a]. Since the tongue position is relatively high in [i] and relatively low in [a], we label [i] as a high vowel and [a] as a low vowel.

The mid vowel [e] has a tongue position lower than [i] but higher than [a] and it is more open than [i] but less open than [a]. Now say [i], [e], [a] slowly for a couple of times and you should feel that the tongue (together with the jaw for most people) is one step lower from [i] to [e] and another step lower from [e] to [a]. The three vowels in (2) also present a set of high, mid, and low vowels. Say [u], [o], [ɑ] slowly to see if you can feel that your tongue is lowered from [u] to [o] and then from [o] to [ɑ].

(2)　　　　IPA　SC EXAMPLE　　　　　　ENGLISH EXAMPLE
　　HIGH　[u]　　*dú*　　[tu]$_{35}$　'to read'　*do*　　[duː]
　　MID　　[o]　　*tóu*　[tʰou]$_{35}$　'head'　　*tow*　[toʊ]
　　LOW　　[ɑ]　　*bāng*　[paŋ]$_{55}$　'to help'　*aunt*　[ɑːnt]

In terms of the degree of openness, a low vowel is more open than a mid vowel, which in turn is more open than a high vowel.[2] The degree of openness generally corresponds to the degree of SONORITY. Of two sounds with the same length, stress, and pitch, a more sonorous sound is perceived as being

---

[1] The English vowel transcriptions mostly follow Ladefoged (2001) and Carr (1999).
[2] In the IPA system, high vowels are labeled as close vowels, mid vowels such as [e] and [o] are close-mid vowels, and low vowels are open vowels (see Appendix A). Here I follow the system of using high, mid, and low for aperture features.

louder. Vowels are more sonorous than consonants, and among vowels, low vowels are more sonorous than mid vowels, which in turn are more sonorous than high vowels. We will come back to the sonority of sounds when we discuss syllable structure in §5.2.2.

We have now seen in (1) and (2) two high, two mid, and two low vowels. To further distinguish these three pairs of vowels, we need to consider another vowel feature.

3.1.2 Place of articulation: front, central, and back vowels

Vowels can also vary by where within the vocal tract the active part of the tongue is located. Produce [i] and [u] for a few times and see if you can feel that the front part of the tongue is pushed relatively forward for [i] and the back part of the tongue is moved relatively backward for [u]. For [i], the front part of the tongue is raised in the front of the oral cavity. In comparison, for [u], the back part of the tongue is bunched up in the back region of the oral cavity and the front part of the tongue lies low behind the lower teeth. While both [i] and [u] are high vowels, [i] is a front vowel and [u] a back vowel. If you produce [e] and [o], you should also find that for [e] the tongue is in a relatively forward position and for [o] the tongue is in a relatively backward position. Therefore, [e] is a front vowel and [o] a back vowel.

If the tongue is in the neutral position without being moved forward or backward, a central vowel is formed. A common central vowel is called *schwa*, transcribed in IPA as [ə]. In English, schwa occurs only in unstressed syllables, such as the first syllable *a* in *about*. English has another mid central vowel, [ʌ], which is used in a STRESSED SYLLABLE, e.g. the vowel in *bus*. In the standard IPA system, the symbol [ʌ] indicates a mid back vowel (Appendix A) but English [ʌ] tends to be lower than [ə] and typically a central vowel (cf. Carr 1999:25; Ladefoged 2001:74).

(3)		IPA	SC EXAMPLE			ENGLISH EXAMPLE	
	MID CENTRAL	[ə]	*hěn*	[xən]$_{214}$	'very'	*about*	[əbaʊt]
	MID CENTRAL	[ʌ]				*bus*	[bʌs]

We have seen three mid vowels, [e], [ə]/[ʌ], and [o], which are differentiated by front, central, and back. As for the low vowels, there are also three types, as shown in (4a).

(4)		IPA	ENGLISH EXAMPLE	
a.	LOW FRONT	[æ]	*bad*	[bæd]
	LOW CENTRAL	[a]	*how*	[haʊ]
	LOW BACK	[ɑ]	*aunt*	[ɑːnt]

		IPA	SC EXAMPLE		
b.	LOW FRONT	[a]	*hàn*	[xan]$_{51}$	'and'
	LOW BACK	[ɑ]	*bāng*	[pɑŋ]$_{55}$	'to help'

The symbol [a] can cause some confusion because: (i) in the IPA vowel system [a] is listed as a front vowel lower than [æ]; (ii) in languages that have only one low vowel, [a] can be used for a central and/or back low vowel; and (iii) in languages that have [a] and [ɑ], [a] may be treated as a front vowel. For English, I use [a] as the central vowel, but for SC [a] is treated as a front low vowel as shown in (4b) (cf. §§5.3, 7.1.1, 7.2.3, and 8.1.5). See Appendix A for more information.

The IPA symbols of the vowels we have discussed so far and their phonetic features are summarized in (5). Neither SC nor English has the high central vowel [ɨ] as a PHONEME but some dialect-accented varieties of SC use it (§12.3.2) and some English speakers also produce [ɨ] in some contexts, e.g. in the plural suffix in a word like *kisses* [kɪsɨz].

(5) Vowel height and backness

	Front	Central	Back
High	i	ɨ	u
Mid	e	ə/ʌ	o
Low	æ/a	a	ɑ

Given this classification, we may assume that the tongue positions of the three front and three back vowels are of the same height in actual articulation. In reality, the high points of the back vowels are lower than the high points of the corresponding front vowels; for example [i] can be raised higher than [u] in the oral tract (Catford 2001:128; Ladefoged 2001:13). In addition, the mid and low vowels are less front or back than the high vowels. The height and backness features therefore are used in relative rather than absolute terms.

3.1.3 Lip position: rounded and unrounded vowels

In addition to the front–back difference, there is an additional difference between [i] and [u] and between [e] and [o]. Say [i] and then [u] in front of a mirror and see how the shape of your lips changes from [i] to [u]. Do the same for [e] and [o]. For [i] and [e], the lips are either in neutral position or spread to the sides. On the other hand, for [u] and [o], the lips are slightly protruded and rounded. Therefore, we call the back vowels [u] and [o] rounded vowels and the front vowels [i] and [e] unrounded vowels.

The low and central vowels listed in (5) above are all unrounded. In general, front, central, and low vowels are typically unrounded, and back non-low vowels are typically rounded. Front rounded vowels, low rounded vowels, or back unrounded vowels are less common but do occur in some languages. For example, French has a series of front rounded vowels, such as high front rounded [y] in *tu* 'you' and mid front rounded [ø] in *peu* 'small',[3] and the Japanese high back vowel is more like the unrounded back vowel [ɯ] although it is often conveniently transcribed as [u].

One of the major differences between British English and American English vowels is that British English has a low back rounded vowel [ɒ] for words such as *hot* and *pot*. For these two words, the vowel is the unrounded [ɑ] in American English.

SC has two additional vowels that English does not have: a high front rounded vowel [y] (as in [ɥy]$_{35}$ *yú* 'fish'), and a mid back unrounded vowel [ɣ] (as in [kɣ]$_{55}$ *gē* 'song').

We have seen three parameters for vowel classification: vowel height, vowel backness, and vowel rounding. The table in (6) summarizes the IPA symbols of the vowels we have mentioned and their vowel features.[4]

(6) Vowel height, backness, and rounding

	Front		Central	Back	
	Unrounded	Rounded	Unrounded	Unrounded	Rounded
High	i	y	ɨ	ɯ	u
Mid	e	ø	ə/ʌ	ɣ	o
Low	æ/a		a	ɑ	ɒ

3.1.4 Tense and lax vowels

English distinguishes four pairs of vowels in terms of tense and lax, as shown in (7a). A lax vowel is slightly lower and more centralized, i.e. closer to the central vowel, than its tense counterpart. For example, the tense vowel [i] is

---

[3] In the American transcription system, [ü] is used for IPA [y] and [ö] is used for IPA [ø] (see Appendix A). In this book, I follow the IPA usage.

[4] I have left out the low front rounded vowel in this table because such a vowel is relatively rare cross-linguistically.

more front and higher than the lax vowel [ɪ], and the tense vowel [u] is more back and higher than the lax vowel [ʊ].[5] Instead of using the terms tense and lax, we can also use mid high for the high lax vowels and mid low for the mid lax vowel (e.g. Ladefoged 2001:36) to reflect the differences in height between tense and lax vowels, as we can see in (7b).

(7) Tense and lax vowels
 a. Tense and lax vowels in English

		Front Unrounded	Example	Back Rounded	Example
High	Tense	i	*beat*	u	*boot*
	Lax	ɪ	*bit*	ʊ	*book*
Mid	Tense	e	*bait*	o	*coat*
	Lax	ɛ	*bet*	ɔ	*core*

 b. Mid-high and mid-low for the lax vowels

	Front Unrounded	Example	Back Rounded	Example
High	i	*beat*	u	*boot*
Mid-High	ɪ	*bit*	ʊ	*book*
Mid	e	*bait*	o	*coat*
Mid-Low	ɛ	*bet*	ɔ	*core*

In English, the tense vowels are longer in length than their lax counterparts.[6] That is why a tense vowel in English is often transcribed with [ː], such as [iː] and [uː], to reflect the length. Since in English tense vowels are long and lax vowels are short, some linguists believe the contrast is long versus short rather than tense versus lax.

The tense–lax difference is PHONEMIC (or DISTINCTIVE/CONTRAS-TIVE) in English. That is, replacing a tense vowel with its corresponding lax

---

[5] In IPA, the high tense vowels are called close vowels, the mid tense vowels are close-mid vowels, and the mid lax vowels are open-mid vowels. No specific term is designated for the high lax vowels (see Appendix A). Here I follow the system commonly used in the English phonetics/phonology literature.

[6] Some feature systems in the literature do not use the features tense and lax. For example, long versus short or peripheral versus non-peripheral (i.e. centralized) have been used.

vowel in a word would change the meaning of the word. For example, the pronunciations of *beat* and *bit* differ only in the tense vowel in the former and the lax vowel in the latter and the two words have different meanings. As mentioned before (§§1.5.2, 2.1.5, 2.2.1), such a pair of words is called a MINIMAL PAIR, which helps us to diagnose distinctive sounds (i.e. phonemes) in a language.

Unlike English, SC does not have a phonemic contrast between tense and lax vowels. In actual pronunciation by some SC speakers, the mid front and back vowels, which are [e] and [o] in the middle of a syllable, are phonetically closer to [ɛ] and [ɔ] when they appear at the end of a syllable, as the examples in (8) illustrate.

(8) SC mid front and back vowel

TENSE	(non-syllable final)	[e]	*bēi*	[pei]	'cup'
		[o]	*gǒu*	[kou]	'dog'
LAX	(syllable final)	[ɛ]	*yě*	[jɛ]	'also'
		[ɔ]	*guǒ*	[kwɔ]	'fruit'

It is important to note that the SC tense and lax vowels in each pair do not differentiate meaning in words. Because of the non-contrastiveness and the phonetic similarities between [e] and [ɛ] and between [o] and [ɔ], in most transcriptions only [e] and [o] are used. There is also much variation from one speaker to another. To avoid complication, we follow the standard practice of using [e] for any front unrounded mid vowel and [o] for any back rounded mid vowel in SC.

3.1.5 Modification of vowels

Vowels can be modified by adding an additional feature. For example, vowels are usually oral but if the VELUM is lowered to allow airflow through the nasal cavity when a vowel is produced, then we have a NASALIZED VOWEL or a nasal vowel. A DIACRITIC tilde mark is placed above a vowel symbol to indicate a nasalized vowel, e.g. [ã]. In English, when a vowel is followed by a nasal consonant, the vowel is nasalized, e.g. *pen* [pẽn]. In SC, the vowel before a nasal consonant is usually nasalized but is not transcribed as such in broad transcriptions. That is, in both SC and English, nasalized vowels are ALLOPHONES of their corresponding oral vowels occurring before a nasal consonant. In some languages, oral and nasal vowels are distinctive phonemes. For example, in French, there is a minimal pair contrasting the oral and nasal mid back rounded vowels: *beau* [bo] 'beautiful' versus *bon* [bõ] 'good'.

Another example of vowel modification is the RHOTACIZED vowel or the rhotic (*r*-colored) vowel, which sounds as if an *r*-like sound is articulated simultaneously throughout the vowel, e.g. the vowel in *bird* in American English. RHOTICS consist of a group of consonants that are orthographically spelled as *r* in the roman alphabetic systems, and a rhotacized vowel has an added *r*-like feature. In North American English, many speakers have a mid central unrounded rhotacized vowel, which has been transcribed variously as [ɚ], or a SYLLABIC CONSONANT [ɹ̩], in words such as *bird* [bɚd], *fur* [fɚ], and *sir* [sɚ]. In many varieties of American English, a vowel preceded by the consonant [ɹ] is also rhotacized, e.g. the low vowel in *car*.

English rhotacized vowels are made either with the tongue tip raised up to the post-alveolar region or with the body of the tongue bunched up in the center of the mouth by keeping the tongue tip down and away from the lower front teeth (Ladefoged 2001:212–13). The root of the tongue is usually retracted slightly backward to cause the slight narrowing of the pharynx. Rhotacization indicates an AUDITORY rather than an ARTICULATORY quality of a vowel, since there is more than one way to produce a rhotacized vowel, but the same auditory effects are achieved, i.e. we hear the same vowel no matter which method of articulation is employed. As mentioned in §1.5.1, the phonetics of a sound consists of articulatory, acoustic, and auditory (perceptual) properties. Articulatory phonetics involves how sounds are produced and perceptual phonetics studies the auditory effects when we perceive sounds.

If the tongue tip is curled back and raised up to the post-alveolar region while a vowel is produced, then we have a retroflexed vowel. A superscript retroflex approximant symbol [ɻ] is added to the vowel symbol to indicate a retroflexed vowel, e.g. *far* [faɻ] in some English varieties (Catford 2001:161–2 and 213). The terms rhotacized vowels and retroflexed vowels are sometimes used interchangeably, since some of these vowels sound similar. For example, in SC, the vowel in *èr* 'two' is called either a retroflexed vowel or a rhotacized vowel. Catford (2001:161–2 and 213), however, maintains the distinction in which a retroflexed vowel has the tongue tip raised up but a rhotacized vowel has bunched-up tongue body and retracted tongue root. SC rhotacized vowels will be discussed later in §3.4.5.

3.1.6 Summary

Vowels are classified according to degree of openness (vowel height), location of the active part of the tongue (vowel backness), and lip position (vowel rounding). The tense and lax difference makes a finer distinction within the category of vowel height. Vowels can also be modified to become nasalized, retroflexed, or rhotacized.

The table in (9) illustrates the classification of vowels. The three central vowels in (9) are all unrounded. I have not mentioned all the vowels that are attested in world's languages because they are irrelevant to our discussion of SC vowels. For a full list of vowels given by IPA, see Appendix A.

(9) Vowel classification

		Front		Central	Back	
		Unrounded	Rounded		Unrounded	Rounded
High	Tense	i	y	ɨ	ɯ	u
	Lax	ɪ				ʊ
Mid	Tense	e	ø		ɤ	o
	Lax	ɛ		ə/ʌ		ɔ
Low		æ/a		a	ɑ	ɒ

In Tables 3.1 and 3.2 we see the vowel charts of American English and SC. In English, the central low vowel [a] occurs in diphthongs (§3.3) and is not phonemic. In SC, the vowel [ɛ] or [æ] may occur in specific contexts, e.g. *tiān* [tjɛn]₅₅ or [tjæn]₅₅ 'sky', which will be discussed in §3.4.3. As we will see later in §3.4, some of the SC vowels in Table 3.2 are not phonemes.

Although this introductory book does not cover acoustic and perceptual phonetics, I do want to mention that the vowel features we introduce here are in fact better viewed as labels for the acoustic/auditory qualities of vowels. For example, a high front vowel [i] has the auditory qualities of high and front

Table 3.1 Chart of American English vowels.

		Front	Central	Back	
		Unrounded		Unrounded	Rounded
High	Tense	i			u
	Lax	ɪ			ʊ
Mid	Tense	e			o
	Lax	ɛ	ə/ʌ		ɔ
Low		æ	a	ɑ	

Table 3.2 Chart of SC vowels.

	Front		Central	Back	
	Unrounded	Rounded		Unrounded	Rounded
High	i	y			u
Mid	e		ə	ɤ	o
Mid	ɛ				
Low					
Low	æ/a			ɑ	

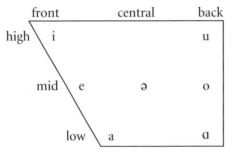

Figure 3.1.   The vowel space.

or is perceived as being high and front. You may find it more difficult for vowels than for consonants to pinpoint exactly the location of your tongue. The tongue positions for the production of vowels are indeed less precise but the different vowels are much more clearly differentiated by their acoustic and auditory phonetic properties (Ladefoged 2001:72 and chapter 8). For those who are interested in reading more about acoustic and perceptual phonetics, see Further Reading.

Now imagine a vowel space that constitutes the available space for the articulation and perception of vowels. We can then plot vowels in the vowel space as illustrated in Figure 3.1. Note that the vowel space diagram has a wider top and a narrower bottom and that the front sloping line is longer than the back vertical line. This is because when the two jaws are wide open there is a wider gap at the front of the mouth than at the back of the mouth. The active part of the tongue in producing a mid and low front vowel is a bit further back toward the central region. A vowel space like this is used to illustrate the relative differences between vowels.

3.2 Glides (semi-vowels)

A syllable contains a NUCLEUS and the MARGINS. For example, for the syllable *bad* in English, the vowel [æ] constitutes the syllable nucleus, and [b] and [d] are the syllable margins: the pre-nucleus margin is the syllable ONSET and the post-nucleus margin is the syllable CODA. The nucleus and the coda form the RIME. The syllable structure is illustrated in (10) below (see also §1.3). We will discuss syllable structure in more detail in chapter 5.

The nucleus is the obligatory unit of the syllable and vowels are in the syllable nucleus. Consonants are generally at the margins of syllables. Occasionally, a consonant may take up the syllable nucleus position. We call such a consonant a SYLLABIC CONSONANT, which is transcribed with a diacritic short line beneath the consonant symbol. For example, the word *rhythm* [ɹɪðm̩] has two syllables, *rhy* [ɹɪ] and *thm* [ðm̩] and the bilabial nasal [m̩] is a syllabic consonant occupying the nucleus of the second syllable. When a vowel-like sound appears in the margin position, it is a GLIDE. For example, the [j] sound for the orthographic *y* as in *yĕ* in SC and *yes* in English is a glide that sounds similar to the vowel [i].

(10)   σ (= syllable)

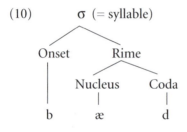

Glides are also called semi-vowels: they are vowel-like sounds but they are not in nuclear position. If we group vowels and glides as a category called VOCOIDS, then vowels are vocoids in nuclear position and glides are vocoids in the syllable margins. In contrast, consonants are generally NON-SYLLABIC (not in nuclear position), but as mentioned earlier some consonants can be SYLLABIC (in nuclear position). In §2.1.4.4 we learned that a glide can be treated as an approximant because it is non-syllabic. To avoid ambiguity we can use the term non-vocoids to refer to true consonants that exclude glides. Consonants, glides, and vowels then are cross-classified as in (11) (cf. Ladefoged 2001:215–16).

(11) Vowels   = syllabic vocoids
      Glides   = non-syllabic vocoids
      Syllabic consonants   = syllabic non-vocoids
      True Consonants   = non-syllabic non-vocoids

SC has three glides and English has two as the examples in (12) show. The glides [j] and [w] are the non-syllabic counterparts of the vowels [i] and [u] respectively. The glide [ɥ] in SC is the non-syllabic counterpart of the high front rounded vowel [y].

(12) SC and English glides

IPA	SC EXAMPLE			ENGLISH EXAMPLE	
[j]	[je]$_{214}$	*yě*	'also'	*yes*	[jɛs]
[w]	[wo]$_{214}$	*wǒ*	'I'	*war*	[wɔɹ]
[ɥ]	[ɥe]$_{51}$	*yuè*	'moon, month'		

In terms of articulation, glides usually differ from vowels by having a slightly narrower channel between the active part of the tongue and the upper part of the oral tract. In terms of the features to use for glides, either vowel features or consonant features have been used. If vowel features are used, [j] is a high front unrounded glide, [w] a high back rounded glide, and [ɥ] a high front rounded glide, all of which appear in the syllabe margins (cf. §2.1.4.4).

3.3 Diphthongs

When a vowel maintains constant vowel quality, i.e. more or less the same tongue and lip positions, throughout its articulation, it is a MONOPHTHONG. However, some vowels change articulatory positions during their production. A vowel that changes its vowel quality within a syllable is called a DIPHTHONG. For example, in [ai], the vowel starts with an [a]-like vowel, glides through the vowel space from the low front or central region toward the high front region and ends in an [i]-like vowel. The vowel space diagram in Figure 3.2 schematizes how SC diphthongs move from one type of vowel quality to another within the vowel space.

Although a diphthong is a vowel that starts with one vowel position and ends in another, for convenience it is often analyzed as a complex vowel with

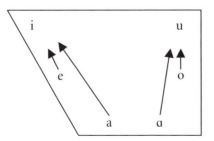

Figure 3.2.   SC diphthongs in the vowel space.

two vowel components. For example, a diphthong like [ai] has [a] and [i] as its components, and we can say that the [a] vowel component is followed by the [i] vowel component in this diphthong. In phonetic transcriptions, a diphthong is then represented with two vowel symbols.

The examples in (13) list the diphthongs from English and those in (14) from SC. In general, English and SC diphthongs are quite similar except that SC does not have [ɔɪ], but you may have noticed two differences in the transcriptions.

(13) English diphthongs

IPA	English Example		IPA	English Example	
[aɪ]	*high*	[haɪ]	[aʊ]	*how*	[haʊ]
[eɪ]	*bay*	[beɪ]	[oʊ]	*bow*	[boʊ]
[ɔɪ]	*boy*	[bɔɪ]			

(14) SC diphthongs

IPA	SC example			IPA	SC example		
[ai]	[kʰai]₅₅	*kāi*	'to open'	[ɑu]	[kɑu]₅₅	*gāo*	'high'
[ei]	[pei]₅₅	*bēi*	'cup'	[ou]	[tou]₅₅	*dōu*	'all'

First, the English diphthongs end in a lax high vowel [ɪ] or [ʊ], whereas the SC diphthongs end in a tense vowel [i] or [u]. Phonetically speaking, SC diphthongs do not reach the height of [i] and [u] in the end and can also be transcribed with [ɪ] or [ʊ]. However, since SC, unlike English, does not have lax vowels as phonemes (§3.1.4), [i] and [u] have been conventionally and conveniently used for the transcription of SC diphthongs. In this book, I follow this practice although you may want to keep in mind that the high vowel ending of a diphthong in SC is similar to that of an English diphthong, i.e. more like a lax vowel.

The second difference is that the English diphthong [aʊ] has a central low vowel but SC diphthong [ɑu] has a back low vowel. In SC, the low vowel before [u] is phonetically similar to English [ɑ] and there is a measurable phonetic difference along the front–back dimension between the low vowel before [i] and that before [u] (Eric Zee and Wai-Sum Lee, personal communication). That is, the low vowel before [u] is further back than the low vowel before [i], and hence [ɑ] is used in [ɑu] and [a] is used before [ai]. In contrast, the two low vowels in English [aɪ] and [aʊ] generally do not differ much as they are more or less in the low central position between front [æ] and back [ɑ] (Ladefoged 2001:74 and 76). Note, however, that the [a]–[ɑ] difference in SC (as also in English) is allophonic rather than phonemic and there is only one low vowel phoneme in SC (see §3.4.3 below). For practical purposes, you may start to pronounce SC diphthongs the way you would English diphthongs, but when you become more proficient in the language and learn more about phonetics and phonology, you might be able to produce and perceive the subtle difference between [a] and [ɑ] in SC diphthongs.

It is important to note that a sequence of two vowels in phonetic transcriptions or orthography does not necessarily indicate a diphthong. What is crucial is that the change of vowel quality occurs within a syllable. When two vowels are sequenced, they may belong to different syllables. For example, in the word *sawing* [sɔːɪŋ], there are two vowels next to each other, but [ɔː] is the nucleus of the first syllable *saw* and [ɪ] is the nucleus of the second syllable *ing*. Therefore, in this particular example, [ɔːɪ] is not a diphthong because the movement from one vowel quality to another does not occur within a single syllable. On the other hand, the vowel [ɔɪ] in *void* [vɔɪd] is a diphthong.

Since it takes some time to move from one vowel position to another, a diphthong is similar to a long vowel monophthong in terms of vowel length. That is, a long vowel [aː] and a diphthong [ai] are similar in length, both of them being longer in vowel duration than a short monophthong vowel [a].

The most common types of diphthongs are those that combine a mid or low vowel with a high vowel, just like those in English and SC. As mentioned in §3.1.1, mid and low vowels are more open than high vowels and hence more sonorous (i.e. louder) than high vowels. This means that diphthongs typically have a more sonorous part and a less sonorous part. For example, in a diphthong like [ai], the more sonorous part is [a].

One potential confusion about the transcription of diphthongs is that there are several competing practices. Some use a sequence of two vowel symbols, e.g. [ai] and [au], as we have done here. To make a distinction between a diphthong and two separate vowels in a sequence, some use a ligature mark over a two-vowel transcription such as [a͡i] and [a͡u] to indicate a diphthong. Alternatively, a diacritic may be placed below the less sonorous part of the diphthongs, e.g. [ai̯] and [au̯]. One may also use the combination of a vowel plus a glide, e.g. [aj] and [aw], to transcribe a diphthong, which highlights the louder and perceptually stronger element of a diphthong as the main nuclear vowel. In terms of pronunciation and perception, the sounds of these different transcriptions are produced and perceived the same way, or at least very similarly. In this book, I continue to use the two-vowel sequence for a diphthong and the glide symbol for a non-syllabic vowel-like sound as defined in the previous section.

In sum, a diphthong is a complex vowel that changes its vowel quality within a syllable. A long vowel such as [aː] is a monophthong that is longer than a short monophthong such as [a]. A long monophthong such as [aː] and a diphthong such as [ai] are of similar length and longer than a short monophthong [a].

The difference between a long monophthong vowel and a diphthong is that throughout the duration of the production, the vowel quality of a long vowel remains more or less the same whereas that of a diphthong changes from one type to another.

3.4 Vowels and glides in SC

This section discusses SC vowels and glides with more examples, determines their phonemic versus allophonic status by showing the context in which a vowel or a group of vowels occurs, and comments on some of the phonetic variations and speaker differences in SC. Practical advice to learners of SC is provided for those vowels that are absent in English.

3.4.1 High vowels/glides and apical vowels

From the discussion in §3.2, we know that SC has three high vowels and three glides, as summarized in (15). The three high vowels in SC are phonemes that can distinguish the meanings of words. For example, *li* [li]$_{51}$ 'power, strength', *lü* [ly]$_{51}$ 'green', and *lu* [lu]$_{51}$ 'road' have different meanings but they differ only in the vowel. That is, replacing one high vowel with another would change the meaning of the word. The examples in (16) all have a monophthong high vowel.

(15) SC high vowels and glides

	Front		Back
	Unrounded	Rounded	Rounded
Vowel	i	y	u
Glide	j	ɥ	w

(16) Examples for high vowels

a. [i] *nǐ* [ni]$_{214}$ 'you'   *mǐ* [mi]$_{214}$ 'rice'
       qī [tɕʰi]$_{55}$ 'seven'   *yī* [ji]$_{55}$ 'one'
b. [y] *lǜ* [ly]$_{51}$ 'green'   *qù* [tɕʰy]$_{51}$ 'to go'
       nǚ [ny]$_{214}$ 'female'   *yú* [ɥy]$_{35}$ 'fish'
c. [u] *shū* [ʂu]$_{55}$ 'book'   *hǔ* [xu]$_{214}$ 'tiger'
       bù [pu]$_{51}$ 'not'   *wǔ* [wu]$_{214}$ 'five'

Many English-speaking learners of SC find it difficult to pronounce [y]. As a high front vowel, [y] has the same tongue position as [i]; the only difference is that [y] has lip rounding. To practice pronouncing [y], say [i] continuously for as long as you can, during which time tightly hold the tongue position but gradually move the lips to the protruded and rounded shape; this is like producing [i] and at the same time trying to say [u] by maintaining the tongue in front position.

Consider now the examples for glides in (17). Notice that all the glides except one are followed by a low or mid vowel. In contrast, in (16) no high vowels are followed by such vowels. Recall that a mid or low vowel is more open and more sonorous than a high vowel (§3.1.1). When a high vowel is followed by a mid or low vowel, a more sonorous vowel is assigned to the nuclear position, and the high vowel before it is then assigned to the onset position. As discussed earlier (§3.2), a high vowel in an onset position is a glide.

(17) Examples for glides

a. [j]	yě	[je]$_{214}$	'also'	yá	[ja]$_{35}$	'tooth'
	jiē	[tɕje]$_{55}$	'street'	xiǎo	[ɕjɑu]$_{214}$	'small'
b. [ɥ]	yuè	[ɥe]$_{51}$	'month'	yún	[ɥyn]$_{35}$	'cloud'
	xué	[ɕɥe]$_{35}$	'to study'	xuǎn	[ɕɥɛn]$_{214}$	'to choose'
c. [w]	wèn	[wən]$_{51}$	'to ask'	wǒ	[wo]$_{214}$	'I'
	duō	[two]$_{55}$	'many'	guì	[kwei]$_{51}$	'expensive'

SC has two more high vowels whose distributions are very limited. Traditionally they are called APICAL vowels. (Recall from §2.1.3.2 that an apical sound is produced with the tongue tip.) The examples in (18) show that the apical vowel [ɿ] appears only after the dental affricates and fricative in syllable final position and the apical vowel [ʅ] appears only after post-alveolar consonants in syllable final position. Both sets of consonants involve the tongue tip in articulation. In *pīnyīn*, the letter *i* is used for both vowels. However, it would be a mistake to produce these vowels as the high front vowel [i].

(18) APICAL VOWEL [ɿ]   APICAL VOWEL [ʅ]

zǐ	[tsɿ]$_{214}$	'son'	zhǐ	[tʂʅ]$_{214}$	'paper'
cí	[tsʰɿ]$_{35}$	'word'	chī	[tʂʰʅ]$_{55}$	'to eat'
sì	[sɿ]$_{51}$	'four'	shí	[ʂʅ]$_{35}$	'ten'
			rì	[ʐʅ]$_{51}$	'day'

As we already know, the term apical means using the tongue tip for articulation. The tip of the tongue is used by some consonants (§§2.1.3.2, 2.2.1, 2.2.3, 2.2.4), but vowels normally involve only the body of the tongue. Apical vowels are therefore unusual vowels that make use of the tongue tip. They appear only after apical consonants. In fact, whether or not apical vowels are real vowels is controversial. Some scholars, such as Chao (1968:24) and Duanmu (2000:36–7), believe that the so-called apical vowels are simply voiced syllabic consonants that are the voiced extension of the preceding consonants into the syllabic nucleus position. Those apical vowels after affricates and fricatives are also called fricative vowels because the syllabic nucleus is the extension of the preceding fricative or the fricative part of an affricate and has the feature of friction (Ladefoged and Maddieson 1996:314). According to Lee and Zee (2003) and Zee (2003a), the apical vowel after dentals is a syllabic apical-laminal or laminal dental (alveolar) approximant, and the apical vowel after post-alveolars a syllabic apical post-alveolar approximant. In this book, I also consider these apical vowels to be syllabic approximants and follow Lee and Zee (2003) in using [ɹ] for both types of syllabic consonants, as shown in (19). In the IPA system, [ɹ] is used for dental, alveolar, and post-alveolar approximants, so the same symbol is used for both dental and post-alveolar approximants in (19). However, it is important to keep in mind that the syllabic consonant [ɹ] after dental consonants should be produced as a dental approximant and that after post-alveolar consonants as a post-alveolar approximant.

(19) Syllabic consonants

	DENTAL APPROXIMANT			POST-ALVEOLAR APPROXIMANT		
a.	zǐ	[tsɹ̩]$_{214}$	'son'	zhǐ	[tʂɻ̩]$_{214}$	'paper'
b.	cí	[tsʰɹ̩]$_{35}$	'word'	chī	[tʂʰɻ̩]$_{55}$	'to eat'
c.	sì	[sɹ̩]$_{51}$	'four'	shí	[ʂɻ̩]$_{35}$	'ten'
d.				rì	[ɻɻ̩]$_{51}$	'day'

In terms of articulation, the tongue tip stays in the same location within the oral cavity throughout the whole syllable. With the exception of the onset consonant [ɻ] in (19d), the syllable onset consonants in (19a–c) are voiceless, but the nuclear part of the syllable, i.e. the syllabic consonant, is voiced. To learn how to pronounce these syllabic consonants, you basically prolong the pronunciation of the consonant. For rì [ɻɻ̩]$_{51}$, you may think of this syllable as having a long consonant [ɻ]. For those six syllables in (19a–c), prolong the pronunciation of the consonant but produce a voiceless consonant in the first phase of the syllable (i.e. the syllable onset) and a voiced one in the second phase of the syllable (i.e. the syllabic nucleus). During the syllabic nuclear phase, there can be a lesser degree of constriction; that is, the tongue tip can be moved slightly away from the teeth or the post-alveolar region at the end of the syllable with little friction.

The front rounded high vowel/glide and the apical vowels are absent in some Chinese dialects, and some dialect-accented speakers of SC may replace them with different vowels. For example, some SC speakers in Taiwan replace an apical vowel with [ɯ] (the high back unrounded vowel) or [u], and replace [y] with [ɨ] (the high central vowel) or [i], as shown in (20) (see §12.3.2 for more details).

(20) PĪNYĪN   SC   TAIWANESE-ACCENTED SC
     sì 'four'   [sɹ]₅₁   [sɯ]₅₁ or [su]₅₁
     lǜ 'green' [ly]₅₁   [lɨ]₅₁ or [li]₅₁

3.4.2 Mid vowels

SC's mid vowels are summarized in (21). Consider first the front unrounded and back rounded vowels, examples for which are given in (22).

(21) SC Mid Vowels

	Front	Central	Back	
	Unrounded	Unrounded	Unrounded	Rounded
Mid	e	ə	ɤ	o

(22) Examples for front unrounded and back rounded mid vowels

a. [e] in diphthong; not in syllable final position
   mèi [mei]₅₁   'sister'   gěi   [kei]₂₁₄ 'to give'
   lèi [lei]₅₁   'tired'   shéi [ʂei]₃₅   'who'

b. [e] in syllable final position
   jiē [tɕje]₅₅ 'street'   xiè   [ɕje]₅₁   'thank'
   tiē [tʰje]₅₅ 'to paste' bié   [bje]₃₅   'don't'

c. [o] in diphthong; not in syllable final position
   tóu [tʰou]₃₅ 'head'   zǒu   [tsou]₂₁₄ 'go, walk'
   gǒu [kou]₂₁₄ 'dog'   shǒu [ʂou]₂₁₄ 'hand'

d. [o] in syllable final position
   duō [two]₅₅   'many'   zuò   [tswo]₅₁ 'do'
   shuō [ʂwo]₅₅   'to speak' guō   [kwo]₅₅   'wok'

Recall from §3.1.4 that for some SC speakers [e] and [o] in syllable final position are phonetically closer to the lax vowels [ɛ] and [ɔ] respectively. Another type of variation is that when [e] and [o] appear in diphthongs, some speakers produce a mid vowel closer to the schwa [ə]. For example, [kei]$_{214}$ sounds like [kəi]$_{214}$, and [kou]$_{214}$ like [kəu]$_{214}$. Therefore, you may see transcriptions that use [e] and [o] in syllable final position and use [ə] when they are in diphthongs, i.e. [əi] and [əu].

For the back vowel, the degree of rounding for [o] in a diphthong is indeed less than that in syllable final position and the rounding may be totally absent in some speakers, but for some SC speakers there is still some degree of rounding for [o] in a diphthong. Variation in the degree of rounding also occurs in English. For example, some English speakers have a lesser degree of or little rounding for [ʊ] in a word like *good*. For the front vowel, there is also variation between [e] and [ə] among SC speakers, although some degree of fronting from the central position is still common. In addition, various Mandarin dialects have much variation between [e] and [ə] and between [o] and [ə] for either syllable medial or final position or for both (Lin 2002). Therefore, when speakers of various Mandarin dialects speak SC (either with or without an accent influenced by the local dialects), variation is typically present.

Despite the phonetic variation, we still use [e] and [o] for syllables like those in (22) because phonetic transcriptions for general purposes need not indicate all the phonetic details and variations among speakers. For the purposes of comparing dialectal differences, narrow transcriptions with phonetic details would then become much more important.

One important generalization we can draw from (22) is that [e] and [o] do not occur in the same environment; that is, they are ALLOPHONES in COMPLEMENTARY DISTRIBUTION but not independent phonemes (see below and the diagram in (27)). If you go through the examples in (22), you should find that [e] is always next to [i] or [j], and [o] is always next to [u] or [w]. This is because, like [i]/[j], [e] is front unrounded, and, like [u]/[w], [o] is back rounded. We can say that the mid vowel is produced with the same backness and rounding as the adjacent high vowel/glide.

When we produce a sequence of sounds, the articulations of adjacent sounds are usually overlapped so as to facilitate the production of the sound sequence, i.e. for ease of articulation. This overlapping of articulations is called COARTICULATION in phonetics. One example from English is the difference between the [k] sound in *cool* and the [k] sound in *key*. Say both words in front of a mirror and pay attention to your lips before and during your production of [k]. You should notice that your lips are slightly rounded when you produce [k] in *cool*. This is because you are anticipating the articulation of a rounded vowel [u] and start the lip rounding articulation for a smoother transition from [k] to the rounded vowel. In a similar fashion, the lips are in an unrounded position for the [k] in *key*, anticipating the articulation of the unrounded vowel [iː]. We can say that the rounding feature of the vowel is extended to the consonant [k] because of coarticulation and for ease of articulation.

In SC, for [ei] and [je] the front unrounded articulation is extended from the high vowel/glide to the mid vowel, making the mid vowel front unrounded, and for [ou] and [wo] the back rounded articulation is adopted by the mid vowel. In phonology, when a sound becomes more like its neighboring sound(s), we have an ASSIMILATION process (see §§7.1.2.1, 7.2, and 7.2.4).

There are some more complications, however. When a mid vowel is preceded by a front rounded glide, we do not have a front rounded mid vowel [ø], as shown in (23). Therefore, we have to say that the mid front unrounded [e] occurs when a mid vowel is next to a high front vowel/glide (either rounded or unrounded) and the mid back rounded [o] occurs when a mid vowel is next to a back rounded vowel/glide.

(23)　[e] after [ɥ]

yuè	[ɥe]$_{51}$	'moon'	*jué*	[tɕɥe]$_{35}$	'to dig'
quē	[tɕʰɥe]$_{55}$	'to lack'	*xuē*	[ɕɥe]$_{55}$	'boots'

What if a mid vowel is adjacent to both a high front and back front vowel/glide? The examples in (24) show that when a diphthong that contains a mid vowel is preceded by a high glide, the mid vowel takes on the following vowel features. More on SC mid vowel assimilation will be discussed in §7.2.4.

(24)　[j] + [ou]　　　　　　　　　　　　[w] + [ei]

yóu	[jou]$_{35}$	'oil'	*wěi*	[wei]$_{214}$	'tail'
jiǔ	[tɕjou]$_{214}$	'wine, liquor'	*guì*	[kwei]$_{51}$	'expensive'

Consider now the examples for the central and back unrounded mid vowels in SC. These two vowels never appear in the same context, i.e. they are allophones in complementary distribution. As we can see in (25), the schwa [ə] occurs only before a consonant such as *n* [n] or *ng* [ŋ], and [ɤ] appears only in a CV syllable (a consonant plus vowel syllable). We can say that there is a rule that changes [ə] to [ɤ] when it is in a CV syllable. In other words, [ə] occurs only when it is before a nasal consonant; in a different position, it changes to a different sound. The mid back unrounded vowel [ɤ] is like the vowel [o] but without lip rounding. You can either produce [o] with slightly spread lips or move the tongue slightly backward when producing the central mid vowel [ə].

🎧 (25) Examples for central and back unrounded vowels

     [ə]   in syllable medial position before a consonant

a. *bèn* [pən]₅₁ 'stupid'   *mén* [mən]₃₅ 'door'

b. *wèn* [wən]₅₁ 'to ask' *děng* [təŋ]₂₁₄ 'to wait'

c. *bīng* [pjəŋ]₅₅ 'ice'   *chūn* [tʂʰwən]₅₅ 'spring'

     [ɤ]   in syllable final position

d. *lè* [lɤ]₅₁ 'happy' *chē* [tʂʰɤ]₅₅ 'car'

  hē [xɤ]₅₅ 'to drink' *rè* [ɹɤ]₅₁ 'hot'

In *pīnyīn*, the letter *e* is used for both [ə] and [ɤ] vowels. In (25c), you may notice that the words 'ice' and 'spring' have the schwa as the main vowel although in *pīnyīn* the letter *e* is absent. This is because SC has a rule that inserts the schwa between the glide [j] and the nasal [ŋ] and between the glide [w] and the nasal [n]. We will discuss these rules in §8.1.5.

In SC, there are three high vowel phonemes that distinguish word meanings. In contrast, SC mid vowels are not phonemes but allophones that occur in different contexts. That is, there is only one mid vowel phoneme and there are four mid vowel allophones, as listed in (26). The diagrams in (27) and (28) illustrate the differences between high and mid vowels in terms of phonological versus allophonic status. Recall that the phoneme is an abstract entity stored in our cognitive phonological system and allophones are actual pronunciations (§1.5.2).

(26) Distributions of SC mid vowels

    [ə] before consonants

    [e] in a diphthong followed by [i]
         in syllable final position preceded by [j] or [ɥ]

    [o] in a diphthong followed by [u]
         in syllable final position preceded by [w]

    [ɤ] in syllable final position in a CV syllable

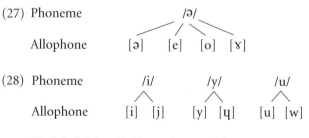

(27) Phoneme   /ə/

     Allophone   [ə]   [e]   [o] [ɤ]

(28) Phoneme   /i/   /y/   /u/

     Allophone   [i] [j]   [y] [ɥ]   [u] [w]

     [i], [y], [u] in syllable nuclear position
     [j], [ɥ], [w] in syllable onset position

In sum, SC has four mid vowels that appear in different environments. We have seen differences in phonetic details and speaker variation for [e] and [o] and how mid vowels are phonologically classified differently from high vowels.

3.4.3 Low vowels

Phonologically speaking, SC has only one low vowel. That is, there is only one low vowel phoneme /a/. However, depending on the context in which the low vowel occurs, the low vowel has different PHONETIC REALIZATIONS. As the examples in (29de) show, when the low vowel is followed by [u] or *ng* [ŋ], the tongue is moved more backward and is more like a back unrounded vowel [ɑ].

(29) SC low vowels

    a. [a] in syllable final position
          yā   [ja]$_{55}$ 'duck'   *bā*   [pa]$_{55}$ 'eight'
    b. [a] in diphthongs ending in [i]
          bái   [pai]$_{35}$ 'white'   *lái*   [lai]$_{35}$ 'to come'
    c. [a] before [n]
          sān   [san]$_{55}$ 'three'   *kàn*   [kʰan]$_{51}$ 'to look'
    d. [ɑ] in diphthongs ending in [u]
          māo   [mɑu]$_{55}$ 'cat'   *lǎo*   [lɑu]$_{214}$ 'old'
    e. [ɑ] before [ŋ]
          táng   [tʰɑŋ]$_{35}$ 'candy'   *bāng*   [pɑŋ]$_{55}$ 'to help'

The examples in (30) show that when the low vowel is between [j]/[ɥ] and [n], the vowel becomes fronted and raised, which is similar to the lower mid vowel [ɛ], the vowel in English *bed*. Recall also that of the two mid vowels, [e] and [ɛ], the lax [ɛ] is lower than the tense [e], so we can also call [ɛ] the lower mid vowel (§3.1.4). However, depending on the speakers, the vowel between [j] and [n] may sound more like [æ], the vowel in English *bad*, and for the vowel between [ɥ] and [n], some speakers keep the low vowel as [a]. The difference between [æ] and [a] is that [æ] is slightly higher and more front than [a].

(30) Low vowel between front glide and [n]

    a. [ɛ] or [æ]   between [j] and [n]
          yǎn   [jɛn]$_{214}$ [jæn]$_{214}$ 'eye'   *liǎn*   [ljɛn]$_{214}$ [ljæn]$_{214}$ 'face'
    b. [ɛ] or [a]   between [ɥ] and [n]
          yuǎn   [ɥɛn]$_{214}$ [ɥan]$_{214}$ 'far'   *xuǎn*   [ɕɥɛn]$_{214}$ [ɕɥan]$_{214}$ 'choose'

For those speakers who have fronted and raised the vowel to [ɛ] or [æ], COARTICULATION is at play again. The glides in (30) are high and front, and, as we have seen in §§2.1.3.2 and 2.2.1, the consonant [n] makes use of the tongue tip/blade for articulation. Amid the flow of articulation, the low vowel, being influenced by the articulations of the two neighboring sounds, is then moved forward and upward to a lower mid vowel [ɛ] or to a higher low front vowel [æ]. For simplicity, we disregard speaker variation and use [ɛ] for the examples like those in (30).

The diagram in (31) illustrates the low vowel phoneme and its allophones, i.e. its different phonetic realizations in different contexts.

(31) Phoneme   /a/

Allophone   [a]   [ɑ]   [ɛ]

[ɑ] before [u] and the velar nasal [ŋ]
[ɛ] between [j]/[ɥ] and the dental nasal [n]
[a] in other contexts

3.4.4 Diphthongs

We have seen in §3.3 that there are four diphthongs in SC. More examples are given in (32).

(32) SC diphthongs

a. [ai]	*ài*	[ai]$_{51}$	'love'	*bái*	[pai]$_{35}$	'white'
	wài	[wai]$_{51}$	'outside'	*mài*	[mai]$_{51}$	'to sell'
b. [ɑu]	*gāo*	[kɑu]$_{55}$	'high, tall'	*bāo*	[pɑu]$_{55}$	'to fold'
	dāo	[tɑu]$_{55}$	'knife'	*hǎo*	[xɑu]$_{35}$	'good'
c. [ei]	*nèi*	[nei]$_{51}$	'inside'	*wěi*	[wei]$_{214}$	'tail'
	měi	[mei]$_{214}$	'beautiful'	*huēi*	[xwei]$_{55}$	'grey'
d. [ou]	*hóu*	[xou]$_{35}$	'monkey'	*gòu*	[kou]$_{51}$	'enough'
	yóu	[jou]$_{35}$	'oil'	*dòu*	[tou]$_{51}$	'bean'

As mentioned in §3.3, in actual articulation, the ending parts of the diphthongs usually fall short of the high vowel position of [i] and [u]. The [i] vowel in a diphthong can become [ɪ] or even [e] in fast speech; [u] in a diphthong can become [ʊ] or [o]. You may have noticed that for [ɑu], the *pīnyīn* system uses *ao* instead of *au*. We can say that there is a rule in which [i] and [u] in diphthongs become lower in height. In our transcriptions, we still use [i] and [u] and disregard the phonetic details and variations that depend on speakers and speech rate.

There are two types of diphthongs: falling diphthongs and rising diphthongs. The diphthongs we have seen so far are falling diphthongs, in which the SONORITY level falls from higher to lower (mid/low vowel quality to high

vowel quality). Recall that mid and low vowels are more open than high vowels and hence more sonorous (i.e. louder) than high vowels (§3.1.1). Some
consider the SC examples such as those in (33) as rising diphthongs; that is,
the sonority level rises from lower to higher (high vowel quality to mid/low
vowel). Moreover, in romanization systems and in most transcriptions of SC
and Chinese dialects, triphthongs with three vowels in a syllable are used, as
the examples in (34) show.

(33) Rising diphthongs?

SC EXAMPLE		RISING DIPHTHONG	GLIDE + VOWEL
xiǎng	'to think'	[ia]	[ja]
xiè	'thank'	[ie]	[je]
xué	'to study'	[ye]	[ɥe]
guān	'to close'	[ua]	[wa]
duō	'many'	[uo]	[wo]

(34) Triphthongs?

SC EXAMPLE		TRIPHTHONG	GLIDE + DIPHTHONG
tiào	'to jump'	[iɑu]	[jɑu]
huài	'bad'	[uai]	[wai]
duì	'correct'	[uei]	[wei]
qiú	'ball'	[iou]	[jou]

However, the first high vowels in these cases can be treated as glides in the
syllable onset, as shown by the second set of transcriptions in (33) and (34).
That is, the high-vowel-like sounds before the nuclear vowel are not analyzed
as vowels in the syllable nucleus. The diagrams in (35) illustrate the relevant
syllabic structures for (33) and (34).

(35) a.

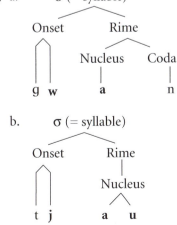

     b.

Note that a falling diphthong occupies the nucleus position as shown in (35b). Under this analysis, SC has only falling diphthongs but no rising diphthongs or triphthongs.

Then why are symbols of vowels often used either in phonetic transcriptions or romanization systems in examples like (33) and (34)? First, it is a tradition in Chinese phonology to treat all VOCOIDS as vowels. Second, in Chinese, as in many languages, glides are the NON-SYLLABIC counterparts of the high vowels: a glide differs from its corresponding vowel by being non-syllabic (§3.2): when a high vowel is assigned to a syllable margin, it becomes a glide (§3.4.1). As we will see in §5.2.2 and §8.1.1, which high vowel becomes a glide is predictable by SYLLABIFICATION rules. Third, the phonetic difference between a vowel and a glide is minimal and whether a vocoid should be part of a diphthong/triphthong or treated as a glide in the syllabic margin is subject to phonological analysis, which varies from one researcher to another.

Under our analysis here, as illustrated in (35), the high vowel before a mid/low vowel is a glide in onset position; a mid or low vowel and its following high vowel form a falling diphthong which appears in the syllable nucleus.

3.4.5 Rhotacized/Retroflexed vowels

The so-called retroflexed vowels occur in the rime *er* in SC and in *ér-huà* rimes (the *r*-suffixed rimes) commonly found in the speech of Beijing speakers. The retroflexed vowels are also referred to as rhotacized (*r*-colored) vowels (e.g. Lee and Zee 2003) or rhotic vowels (Ladefoged and Maddieson 1996:313) because these vowels can be produced in various ways to achieve the same auditory effects, and they usually do not make use of the undersurface of the tongue tip, as one would expect for a retroflex sound (cf. §3.1.5). The *ér-huà* process will be explained and discussed in §8.2, and in this subsection we focus on the articulation and the transcription of the rhotacized/retroflexed vowels.

The rime *er* in SC, as in words like *èr* 'two' and *ér* 'son', is rather unusual. First, the number of morphemes/words using this syllable is very limited in number. Second, no onset consonant can appear before the rime *er*. Third, it is unclear if this rime consists of a single vowel, a syllabic consonant, a diphthong, or a vowel plus a consonant. Similar difficulty also occurs in English for the transcription of the *er*-suffix as in *reader*.

In terms of articulation, the most common way to produce the vowel is to retract the tongue body backward. Some speakers may also raise the tip of the tongue toward the post-alveolar region. Current SC speakers from Beijing seem to use only tongue body retraction (Eric Zee and Wai-Sum Lee, personal communication; Lee and Zee 2003; Zee 2003a). The articulation of this vowel bears some similarities to the rhotacized vowel [ɚ] as in *sir* in some varieties of English (§3.1.5). Because the tongue tip is moved up toward the post-alveolar region during the vowel articulation for some speakers and also because [ɹ] in SC is traditionally considered to be a retroflex approximant (§2.2.4), the vowel in the *er* rime is often labeled as a retroflexed vowel.

There can then be several ways to transcribe *er*, as shown in (36). In the first type of transcription in (36a), the rime consists of a mid central vowel as the syllable nucleus and a post-alveolar approximant in the syllabic coda position, which has been transcribed as either [r] or [ɹ]. In the second and third types of transcriptions in (36bc), the rime has only a single vowel, either rhotacized or retroflexed. Under the two-segment view in the first type, it is also recognized that the mid central vowel before [ɹ] is rhotacized/retroflexed, so for a narrow phonetic transcription, [əɹ] could be either [ɚɹ] or [ə˞ɹ]. A syllabic consonant has also been used sometimes, as shown in (36d).

(36) Transcriptions of the rhotacized/retroflexed vowel

		a.	b.	c.	d.
		[ə] + [ɹ]	rhotacized	retroflexed	syllabic
		[ə] + [r]	vowel	vowel	consonant
ér	'son'	[əɹ]$_{35}$/[ər]$_{35}$	[ɚ]$_{35}$	[ə˞]$_{35}$	[r̩]$_{35}$/[ɹ̩]$_{35}$
ěr	'ear'	[əɹ]$_{214}$/[ər]$_{214}$	[ɚ]$_{214}$	[ə˞]$_{214}$	[r̩]$_{214}$/[ɹ̩]$_{214}$
èr	'two'	[əɹ]$_{51}$/[ər]$_{51}$	[ɚ]$_{51}$	[ə˞]$_{51}$	[r̩]$_{51}$/[ɹ̩]$_{51}$

The suffix used in the *ér-huà* process has been variably transcribed, e.g. [əɹ], [ɹ], [r], or [ɚ] (§8.2.2). When the suffix is added to a word or morpheme, the vowel of the word/morpheme becomes rhotacized (§8.2). The tongue is retracted (with or without the tongue tip being raised) during the production of the vowel and rime. For example, the morpheme in (37a) has a rhotacized/retroflexed rime and vowel when the suffix is added as in (37b), for which three types of transcriptions are shown.

(37) a. Unsuffixed morpheme
     bǎ   [pa]$_{214}$ 'handle'
    b. Suffixed morpheme
     bǎr   [paɹ]$_{214}$ or [paɚ]$_{214}$ or [pa˞ɹ]$_{214}$ 'handle'

For simplicity and convenience, the first type of transcription in (36a) and (37b), i.e. [əɹ] and [aɹ], and the term 'rhotacized' are adopted throughout this book. We will see more examples of rhotacized vowels and rimes in §8.2.

Table 3.3 Vowel phonemes in SC.

	Front		Central	Back	
	Unrounded	Rounded		Unrounded	Rounded
High	i	y			u
Mid			ə		
Low	a				

3.4.6 SC vowel phonemes

Table 3.3 summarizes the vowel phonemes in SC. If you compare this table with Table 3.2 in §3.1.6, you can see that: (i) [ɛ]/[æ] and [ɑ] are absent here because they can be treated as phonetic variants or allophones of the phoneme /a/ in predictable contexts; and (ii) [e], [o], and [ɤ] are also removed because they can be treated as phonetic variants of the phoneme /ə/.

3.5 Summary

In this chapter, we have studied the phonetic features used for describing and classifying SC and English vowels.

- Vowels are classified according to three groups of features indicating basic vowel quality: high-mid-low, front-central-back, and rounded-unrounded (§§3.1.1–3.1.3).
- Vowels can also be pronounced with longer and shorter duration. A long vowel may have consistent vowel quality throughout (a long MONOPHTHONG) or may move from one vowel quality to another (a DIPHTHONG) (§3.3).
- A vowel can be further modified to become NASALIZED (under the influence of an adjacent nasal consonant) or RHOTACIZED or retroflexed (under the influence of an adjacent rhotic or retroflex) (§3.1.5).
- SC and English vowels have been compared for the similarities and differences in phonetic properties (§3.1; Tables 3.1–3.2 in §3.1.6).
- SC has three high vowels and three GLIDES, including the high front rounded vowel and glide that are absent from English. A glide is treated as an ALLOPHONE of its corresponding high vowel PHONEME occurring in ONSET position, i.e. a vowel-like sound that functions like a consonant (§3.2 and §3.4.1).

- The so-called apical vowels in SC are SYLLABIC CONSONANTS occupying the syllable NUCLEUS position and function like vowels (§3.4.1).
- There is only one mid vowel PHONEME in SC but it has four mid vowel ALLOPHONES in mutually exclusive contexts (§3.4.2). There is also only one low vowel phoneme in SC and it has three ALLOPHONES (§3.4.3).
- SC has four DIPHTHONGS: two of which move from a low vowel to a high vowel and the other two from a mid vowel to a high vowel (§3.4.4).
- The RHOTACIZED vowels are vowels with added articulation features similar to the post-alveolar [ɹ], and have retracted tongue body (§3.4.5).
- We have concluded that SC has only five vowel phonemes. The PHONETIC REALIZATIONS or variants of these phonemes, i.e. the actual phonetic pronunciations of these phonemes, are governed by phonological and phonetic rules to be discussed in chapters 7 and 8.

EXERCISES

1 For each of the following phonetic descriptions of a SC vowel or glide, provide the IPA symbol.

PHONETIC DESCRIPTION	IPA SYMBOL
high front unrounded vowel	[i]
a. mid back unrounded vowel	
b. high front rounded vowel	
c. high back rounded glide	
d. low front unrounded vowel	
e. low back unrounded vowel	
f. mid central unrounded vowel	
g. mid front unrounded vowel	
h. mid back rounded vowel	
i. high front rounded glide	
j. high front unrounded glide	
k. high back rounded vowel	

2 For each of the following SC vowels or glides, provide the phonetic description.

IPA	PĪNYĪN/GLOSS		PHONETIC DESCRIPTION
[i]	mǐ	'rice'	high front unrounded vowel
a. [y]	lǜ	'green'	
b. [ɑ]	táng	'suger, candy'	
c. [ə]	děng	'to wait'	

d. [a]   *ài*   'love'
e. [j]   *yŏu*   'oil'
f. [o]   *gŏu*   'dog'
g. [ɤ]   *gē*   'song'
h. [e]   *hēi*   'black, dark'
i. [u]   *shū*   'book'
j. [ɥ]   *xué*   'study'
k. [w]   *suān*   'sour'
l. [ɛ]   *qián*   'money'

3 Each of the following groups of SC vowels/glides have some phonetic properties in common. Choose the most precise and complete description of the shared properties for each group.
Example: [i, y, u] (i) front vowels (ii) high vowels (iii) rounded vowels
The answer is (ii) since all three vowels are high vowels.

a. [y, u, o]
   (i) back rounded vowels (ii) high vowels (iii) rounded vowels
b. [j, ɥ, i, y]
   (i) high vowels (ii) front vowels (iii) high front VOCOIDS (iv) high vocoids
c. [j, e, ɥ, i, y, a]
   (i) front vowels (ii) high vocoids (iii) front vocoids (iv) high vowels
d. [o, e, ə, ɤ, ɛ]
   (i) unrounded vowels (ii) back vowels (iii) mid vowels (iv) low vowels
e. [a, ɑ, o, e, ə, ɤ, ɛ]
   (i) non-high vowels (i.e. mid and low vowels) (ii) mid vowels (iii) low vowels
f. [ɑ, o, u, ɤ]
   (i) non-high back vowels (ii) back vowels (iii) back rounded vowels

4 Give the phonetic transcription for each of the following English words.

Example: *squeeze* [skwiːz]   kids [kʰɪdz]
a. *fight*   b. *strong*   c. *classroom*
d. *tray*   e. *mouse*   f. *throw*
g. *pleasant*   h. *mother*   i. *shoes*
j. *watch*   k. *juice*   l. *spin*

5 Give the phonetic transcription for each of the following SC words. For this exercise, you may use either the tone number, such as tone 1, tone 2, tone 3, tone 4, or the pitch value (see (1) in §1.3).

Example: *bǐ*   'pen' [pi]$_{214}$ or [pi]tone 3
a. *shéi* 'who'   b. *guó* 'nation'   c. *sǐ*   'die'
d. *wài*   'outside'   e. *rén* 'people'   f. *yáng* 'sheep'
g. *xiǎo* 'small'   h. *xiè* 'thank'   i. *kū*   'cry'
j. *hé*   'and'   k. *chī* 'to eat'   l. *èr*   'two'

6   For each of the following pairs of SC vowels, decide if they are separate
    PHONEMES in SC. If yes, find a MINIMAL PAIR to support their phonemic
    status.

    a. [i] and [u]   b. [w] and [u]   c. [i] and [a]
    d. [a] and [ə]   e. [e] and [o]   f. [y] and [i]
    g. [a] and [ɑ]   h. [ə] and [ɤ]   i. [u] and [a]

7   For each of the following SC vowels or glides, identify: (i) the phoneme this
    sound belongs to; (ii) the context(s) it occurs in; and (iii) give an example for
    each context.

    Example: [j]   This is an allophone of /i/ occurring in syllable onset
                   position, e.g. *yè* [je]$_{51}$ 'leaf'

    a. [e]   b. [a]   c. [ə]   d. [ɥ]
    e. [o]   f. [ɛ]   g. [ɑ]   h. [ɤ]

🎧 8   Performance exercise
       Practice the pronunciation of SC vowels/glides and syllabic consonants by
       learning to pronounce the following groups of words. The phonetic
       transcription with a subscripted pitch value for the tone (see (1) in §1.3,
       §4.1.1, §4.1.4) is shown first and the second and third lines provide the *pīnyīn*
       and meaning respectively. Since we have not studied the tones, you may want
       to listen to *The Sounds of Chinese CD* or ask your teacher or a SC speaker to
       help with your practice.

       a. high vowels
          [**li**]$_{35}$ [**lu**]$_{35}$ [**ly**]$_{35}$
          lí   *lú*   *lǘ*
          'fence'   'stove'   'donkey'
       b. high glides: in syllable onset position
          [**je**]$_{51}$ [**ɥe**]$_{51}$ [**wo**]$_{51}$
          yè   *yuè*   *wò*
          'leaf'   'moon'   'to hold'

c. mid front vowel: when preceded by a high front glide or followed by [i]

[ɕje]₂₁₄   [ɕɥe]₂₁₄   [kei]₂₁₄   [kwei]₂₁₄

xiě   *xuě*   *gěi*   *guǐ*

'to write'   'snow'   'to give'   'ghost'

d. mid back rounded vowel: when preceded by [w] or followed by [u]

[xwo]₂₁₄   [tsou]₂₁₄   [tɕjou]₂₁₄

huǒ   *zǒu*   *jiǔ*

'fire'   'to go, to walk'   'alcohol'

e. mid central vowel that occurs before a nasal

[ɹən]₃₅   [ɹəŋ]₃₅

rén   *réng*

'people'   'still'

f. mid back unrounded vowel: when in a CV syllable

[kɤ]₅₅   [tʂʰɤ]₅₅

gē   *chē*

'song'   'car, vehicle'

g. front low vowel: before [n] or [i] or in a vowel-ending syllable

[kan]₅₅   [kai]₅₅   [kwa]₅₅   [tɕja]₅₅

gān   *gāi*   *guā*   *jiā*

'dry'   'should'   'melon'   'home'

h. back low vowel: before [ŋ] and [u]

[mɑŋ]₃₅   [mɑu]₃₅

máng   *máo*

'busy'   'hair'

i. mid-low or mid lax vowel [ɛ]: between high front glide and [n]

[pjɛn]₅₁   [tɕʰjɛn]₅₁   [ɥɛn]₅₁   [tɕʰɥɛn]₅₁

biàn   *qiàn*   *yuàn*   *quàn*

'to change'   'to owe'   'courtyard'   'to urge, to advise'

j. diphthongs

[kai]₂₁₄   [kɑu]₂₁₄   [kei]₂₁₄   [kou]₂₁₄

gǎi   *gǎo*   *gěi*   *gǒu*

'to change'   'to do'   'to give'   'dog'

k. syllabic consonants: in a CV syllable after a dental or post-alveolar affricate or fricative

dental syllabic consonant

[tsɹ̩]₅₁   [tsʰɹ̩]₅₁   [sɹ̩]₅₁

zì   *cì*   *sì*

'self'   'to pierce'   'four'

post-alveolar syllabic consonant

[tʂɻ̩]₅₁	[tʂʰɻ̩]₅₁	[ʂɻ̩]₅₁	[ɻɻ̩]₅₁
zhì	*chì*	*shì*	*rì*
'mole'	'wing'	'thing, matter'	'day, sun'

l. rhotacized vowel

[əɹ]₃₅	[əɹ]₂₁₄	[əɹ]₅₁
ér	*ěr*	*èr*
'son'	'ear'	'two'

4 Tone

In this chapter, we study the phonetic properties of SC tones and how these tones are classified and transcribed. We start with how tone is produced and perceived and what phonetic properties are associated with each type of tone (§4.1). In §4.2, the tones of SC are discussed in detail and practical advice on pronunciation is provided. The final section (§4.3) summarizes the main points of the chapter.

4.1 The phonetic properties and classification of tone

As mentioned in §1.3, other than consonants and vowels, TONE is the third kind of speech element used by languages like SC to distinguish word meanings. That is, a change in the pitch of a word can change the meaning of a word. About 60–70 percent of the world's languages are TONE LANGUAGES (Yip 2002:1), most of which are spoken in Asia, Africa, and central America.

Since tone is manifested by the pitch of the voice, each tone is classified according to: (i) how high or low the pitch is (PITCH LEVEL); and (ii) what the pattern of pitch change is (PITCH CONTOUR). In this section, I first explain informally what tone is (§4.1.1) before we study the phonetic properties of tone (§4.1.2). After clarifying what speech units can manifest tone (§4.1.3), I discuss how tones are classified and transcribed (§4.1.4).

4.1.1 What is tone?

When we speak, the pitch of our voice is changing continuously. The pattern of pitch changes over a phrase or sentence is called INTONATION. Intonation expresses syntactic and contextual meanings but not word meanings. Say the examples in (1) and pay attention to the pitch of your voice. Note the differences between (1a) and (1b) and those between (1c) and (1d).

(1) Intonation

    a. I love my dog.

    b. Do you love your dog?

    c. John! (affirmative answer to 'Who did this?')

    d. John? (uncertainty in an answer to 'Do you know who did this?')

At the end of a statement or an affirmative answer (1ac), the pitch is falling or lowered, but at the end of a question (1bd) the pitch is rising or raised. Intonation adds some additional information for a phrase or sentence; however, whether you raise or lower your pitch, the meaning of each word stays the same (see §10.2.1 for more on intonation).

All languages have intonation. In a non-tone language like English, pitch variations convey only syntactic and contextual information, but in a tone language like SC, pitch variations have the additional function of conveying differences in word meanings. Therefore, tone can be defined as the pattern of pitch changes that affects the meaning of a word.

Using the same examples as in §1.3, we see again in (2) that each of the four examples has a different tone and each word has a different meaning and its own written form as shown by the Chinese characters. Another set of examples is given in (3).

(2) Tonal contrasts in SC

Tone number	Pitch pattern	Pitch value	Example	
1	high level	55	$[ma]_{55}$ *mā* 'mother'	妈
2	high rising	35	$[ma]_{35}$ *má* 'hemp'	麻
3	low falling-rising	214	$[ma]_{214}$ *mǎ* 'horse'	马
4	high falling	51	$[ma]_{51}$ *mà* 'to scold'	骂

(3) Additional examples for the tonal contrasts in SC

Tone number	Pitch pattern	Pitch value	Example	
1	high level	55	$[pa]_{55}$ *bā* 'eight'	八
2	high rising	35	$[pa]_{35}$ *bá* 'pull out'	拔
3	low falling-rising	214	$[pa]_{214}$ *bǎ* 'handle'	把
4	high falling	51	$[pa]_{51}$ *bà* 'father'	爸

The PITCH VALUE is used for the transcription of tone, and in §4.1.4 below, we will see various practices in the transcription of SC tones. As mentioned in §1.3, each number given in the pitch value represents relative PITCH LEVEL (pitch height), with 1 indicating the lowest pitch and 5 the highest pitch on a scale of 1 to 5. By combining two or more pitch value numbers, we can also represent the PITCH CONTOUR (the pattern of pitch change). For example, tone 4 is transcribed as 51, which means this tone is produced by starting with the highest pitch level and quickly moving downward to the lowest pitch level. You can think of the relative high versus low pitch level as the high versus low musical key or note, and a pitch change from a higher to a lower pitch in a falling tone is like the movement from a higher to a lower key on a musical instrument or in singing.

In SC, tone 1 is a high level tone since the pitch is highest at level 5 and the pitch stays the same without going upward or downward, whereas tone 4 is a high falling tone since the pitch starts high and falls down to the low pitch. Tone 2 is a high rising tone because the pitch starts at the mid level of 3 and rises upward to the high level of 5, and tone 3 is a complex low falling-rising as the pitch starts low at level 2, then goes even lower to level 1 before rising up to level 4. Note that tone 3 is low falling-rising only in phrase final position. If tone 3 is followed by another tone, it is simply a low tone: 22 or 21 (see also §4.2.1).

It is important to keep in mind that the pitch scale shows relative rather than absolute pitch values; that is, it only indicates that within a particular pitch range, which could be different from person to person or in different emotional states, if a high tone is assigned a 4 or 5 value then a low tone is at 2 or 1 in order to be identified as a low tone. In addition, a level tone like 55 or 22 can be phonetically slightly falling or rising (e.g. 54, 21) but is still perceived as a level tone.

4.1.2 The phonetic properties of tone

I have described tone and intonation informally in terms of pitch. The question is: what is pitch? Consider first the phonetic term FUNDAMENTAL FREQUENCY (F0). F0 refers to the vibration rate of the vocal folds, i.e. how fast the vocal folds vibrate. The faster the vocal folds vibrate, the higher the F0, and the higher the F0, the higher the pitch.

In a single cycle of vibration, the vocal folds are first brought fairly close together, the air from the lungs then pushes through the narrow glottal opening, which induces a sucking effect to make the vocal folds completely closed to block the air escaping from the lungs, but the pressure built up from the lungs eventually breaks apart the vocal folds, releasing a puff of air (Yip 2002:6–7). F0 is then the number of such cycles occurring in a second. F0 is measured in Hertz (Hz) and one Hertz is one cycle per second. If the vocal folds complete each cycle of vibration 100 times in a second when a sound/tone is produced, then the F0 of that sound/tone is 100 Hertz (Hz). A sound/tone with an F0 of 200 Hz has the vibration rate of the vocal folds at 200 cycles in a second and is perceived as higher in pitch than one with an F0 of 100 Hz.

Unlike F0, which is an acoustic term that refers to the frequency of the vocal folds' vibration of the speech signal itself, pitch is a perceptual term referring to a listener's perception of the F0 of the speech signal. A high tone has higher pitch and higher F0 and a low tone has lower pitch and lower F0. In terms of articulation, the most important factor that determines the pitch of voice is the tension of the vocal folds (Ladefoged 2001:233). When the vocal folds are stretched or stiff, the pitch goes higher; when the vocal folds are slack, the pitch is lowered. Some other phonetic properties also affect the production and perception of tone, such as the length and degree of thickness of the vocal folds, but we do not have to get into these technical details here. For our purposes, we simply say that the primary acoustic correlate of tone is F0, the main articulatory correlate of tone is the tension of the vocal folds, and the perception of tone depends on the perceived pitch level of F0.

4.1.3 The tone bearing unit

SUPRASEGMENTAL PROPERTIES include length, tone, stress, and intonation that are not inherent properties of single consonants or vowels but can be associated with a span of more than one segment. A SEGMENT is a sound unit such as a consonant or a vowel.

In English, STRESS is not a feature of a vowel but of a syllable. In a word like *computer*, there are three syllables: *com*, *pu*, and *ter*, of which the second syllable *pu* is the STRESSED SYLLABLE. Phonetically, a stressed syllable is longer in length, higher in pitch, and/or louder. All these phonetic correlates of stress can be most easily observed on the nuclear vowel of the syllable but that does not mean that stress is a vowel feature. The phonological unit with which stress is associated (the stress bearing unit) in English is either the syllable or the MORA, depending on analyses. A mora is a phonological prosodic weight unit: a HEAVY SYLLABLE has two moras and a LIGHT SYLLABLE has one. A heavy syllable is one that has a long vowel, a diphthong, or a vowel followed by coda in the rime, e.g. syllables that have rimes like [iː], [ai], [ɪn], and [ænd] are heavy syllables and have two moras. A light syllable has only a single short vowel in the rime, e.g. a syllable that has a rime consisting of [ə] is a light syllable and has one mora. In a stress language like English, a heavy syllable tends to be stressed. For example, in a two-syllable verb, if the second syllable is heavy then it is stressed: the word *reply* has a light syllable [ɹɪ] followed by a heavy syllable [plaɪ] and the stress is on the second syllable; in comparison, in the word *carry*, the second syllable [ɹɪ] is light and the stress falls on the first syllable [kʰæ] instead. (See §10.1.1 for more on stress.)

By the same token, tone is not really an inherent vowel feature. A TONE BEARING UNIT is the phonological entity that a tone is associated with. Depending on languages and also depending on different phonological analyses, the tone bearing unit can be the syllable, the rime, the mora, or any SONORANT and vowel segments. The pitch level and/or pitch changes of a tone are indeed most easily observed in the nuclear vowel of a syllable or the sonorant segments within the rime, but tonal features are not the same as vowel features such as high, low, front, and back that indicate vowel quality.

The tone bearing unit in SC has been variously proposed to be the syllable, the rime, or the mora. Phonetically, tone in SC is mostly manifested on the syllable rime, but phonologically any of the above proposals can serve our purposes.

4.1.4 The classification and transcription of tone

In terms of PITCH LEVEL, tones can be classified into high, mid, and low, and in terms of PITCH CONTOUR (the shape of the pitch changes), we distinguish LEVEL TONES versus CONTOUR TONES. A level tone is one that has a relatively consistent pitch level whereas a contour tone is one that changes pitch level within a syllable. For example, a simple high tone is a level tone with a consistent high pitch and a rising tone is a contour tone that starts with a lower pitch level and ends with a higher pitch level within a syllable. A level tone can be high, mid, or low and a contour tone can be rising, falling, rising-falling, or falling-rising. The more complex contour tones such as rising-falling and falling-rising are much less common cross-linguistically. African tone languages mostly have level tones with some contour tones in limited contexts, whereas Asian tone languages have more contour tones with fewer restrictions.

(4) Simple classification of tone

    a. Level tone: high, mid, low
    b. Contour tone: rising, falling, rising-falling, falling-rising

In more complex tone languages, it is also necessary to divide the pitch range into high REGISTER (the higher half of the pitch range) and low register (the lower half of the pitch range), and within each register, level versus contour and high versus low are further differentiated, as illustrated in (5). Note that with this classification, a mid level tone has an ambiguous status: either a high register low or a low register high. Which classification a mid tone belongs to depends on the language. For our purposes, just be aware that a mid tone can pattern with either a high or low register tone.

(5) Classification of tone with register

    a. High register: high   (high level)   low   (mid level)
                           rising   (high rising)   falling   (high falling)
    b. Low register: high   (mid level)   low   (low level)
                           rising   (low rising)   falling   (low falling)

As we have seen in (2) and (3), SC has one high level tone and three contour tones: high rising, low falling-rising, and high falling. There have been various ways to transcribe SC tones, five of which are given in (6). The system in (6a) uses the tone number for convenience with no indication of the pitch values of the tones. This type of transcription is used on the assumption that the reader knows the actual tone value associated with each tone number. The system in (6b) puts diacritic tonal marks on the top of vowels, a system that *pīnyīn* adopts. The diacritic marks mimic the pitch contour to some degree but there is no indication of the pitch level.

(6) TONE 1

	TONE 1	TONE 2	TONE 3	TONE 4
	HIGH LEVEL	HIGH RISING	LOW FALLING-RISING	HIGH FALLING
a.	ma1	ma2	ma3	ma4
b.	mā	má	mǎ	mà
c.	ma˥	ma˦	ma˅˦	ma ˥˩
d.	ma55	ma35	ma214	ma51
e.	ma HH	ma MH	ma LH (LL)	ma HL
f.	ma HH	ma LH	ma LL	ma HL

The systems of (6c) and (6d) are similar in what they can indicate and were introduced by Chao (1930, 1933, 1968). The graphic system in (6c) is known as Chao's tone letters and has been adopted by the IPA to transcribe tones. The system in (6d) is the numerical translation of the graphic system of (6c). The tone letters in (6c) have the vertical bar serving as the reference for the pitch range and the contour line to the left of the vertical bar is used to indicate the pitch contour relative to the pitch range. For tone 1, there is a flat horizontal line on the top end of the vertical line, indicating a high level tone with no pitch movement. The other three tones show pitch movement lines within the appropriate pitch range: tone 2 has the line going from mid to high, tone 3 has a dipping contour in the lower pitch range and tone 4 has a line going from high pitch to low pitch. In (6d), the numbers are used to represent pitch values, with 5 for the highest pitch and 1 for the lowest, indicating both pitch level and contour, as explained earlier in §4.1.1. The numbers can also be superscripted or subscripted (as we have seen in the transcriptions of SC examples in chapters 2 and 3). For tone 1, the number 5 indicates it is a high tone and two 5s means there is no pitch change in the syllable and therefore it is a level tone. Tone 2 is a rising tone in the higher part of the pitch range (high register) with the pitch changes from mid to high. Tone 3 starts with a low tone with very slight dip, then rises to the higher pitch, and tone 4 starts high and falls to the low pitch level. Note that these numbers and their corresponding tone letters are just for relative reference and cannot be taken as absolute pitch values of the tones because in a tonal system the high versus low and level versus contour are relative rather than absolute. For example, we can also transcribe tone 1 as 44 and tone 2 as 24 since the difference between 55 and 44 and that between 35 and 24 are not significant in SC and we still have tone 1 as a high level tone and tone 2 as a relatively higher rising tone. Both systems in (6c) and (6d) are commonly used by fieldworkers transcribing the tones of different Chinese dialects.

The system in (6e) is commonly use by phonologists for the representation of tones, with H for high pitch, M for mid, and L for low. A level tone has just one feature such as HH or LL, and a contour tone has two different features such as HL or LH, indicating the starting and ending points of the contour tone. For tone 1, it is HH for a high level tone. For the rising tone 2, it starts with M and ends with H, and for the falling tone 4, it starts with H and ends with L. Note that for tone 3, it can be represented as LH, starting with L and ending with H to form a low rising tone. As mentioned before, when tone 3 is followed by another tone, it is simply a low tone without the rising part and can be represented as LL. A system without M uses LH for the rising tone and HL for the falling tone, as in (6f).

For our purposes, I will continue to use the numerical system in (6d) for the phonetic transcriptions of examples, but the system of (6e) will be used in the discussion of tonal processes in chapter 9.

4.2 Tones in SC

This section covers the phonetic realizations and phonological status of SC tones. We start with the four PHONEMIC TONES (i.e. tones that differentiate word meanings) and their various PHONETIC REALIZATIONS (§4.2.1), and then introduce the NEUTRAL TONE that occurs only in some contexts (§4.2.2). These tones can vary in some contexts and such tonal variations are discussed in §4.2.3. Practical advice to learners of SC will also be provided.

4.2.1 The four phonemic tones

SC has four basic tones, which are also called citation tones, and they are phonemic, i.e. the change of tone can lead to a change of word meaning. The examples given in (2) and (3) earlier show that these four different tones are four different tonal phonemes. The diagram in (7) illustrates the pitch level and contour of the four tones.

(7)   TONE 1   TONE 2   TONE 3   TONE 4
            HIGH LEVEL   HIGH RISING   LOW FALLING   HIGH FALLING
                                        -RISING
            55/HH   35/MH   214/LH   51/HL

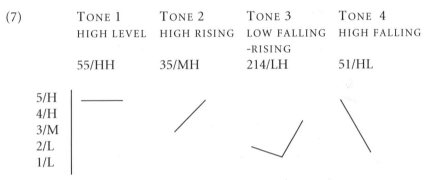

```
5/H
4/H
3/M
2/L
1/L
```

To learn how to produce tones, start by finding out your pitch range. Go to the highest and lowest pitch of your normal speaking range, then find the mid pitch range. You may want to use humming first to feel the differences in pitch level and contour before pronouncing the [ma] syllable with four different tones. For the high level tone (tone 1), start with your higher pitch range and remain high during your humming period or the pronunciation of [ma]. For the high rising tone (tone 2), start at your mid pitch range and move the pitch higher. You can think of this as if you are asking a question in English. As we mentioned in §4.1.1, question intonation in English has a rising pitch for the final syllable, e.g. *John?* For tone 3, you can either: (i) start with your low pitch range and move the pitch a bit higher toward the mid pitch range at the end; or (ii) start with your mid to low pitch range, go down to the lowest pitch and then move the pitch back to the mid pitch range at the end. You may have noticed that I did not ask you to move to the high pitch range at the end despite the fact that the transcription for tone 3 is typically 214. The reason is that although the rising part of tone 3 can reach up to the high pitch range, it most often ends in the mid pitch level. For tone 4, make sure you go the top of your pitch range and move the pitch down. This is similar to the falling intonation in a stressed affirmative emphatic answer in English such as *Yes!*, but note that in English the starting pitch range may not be high enough. One common error in producing the high falling tone in SC by English-speaking learners of SC is that the starting pitch of the falling tone is lower than it should be.

The pitch level and contour in (7) are used in careful speech in pronouncing a single syllable in phrase final position. In non-final position and also in connected speech, tone 3 is basically a low falling or low tone (21 or 22), and tone 4 is mostly realized as 53. The general pattern for tone 3 is that phrase finally it is a low falling-rising tone but it becomes a low or low falling tone without the final rise in non-final position. In fact, even in the phrase final position, tone 3 can be without the final rise in normal or fast speech (Duanmu 2000:221–2). Therefore, one useful strategy to learn to pronounce tone 3 is to treat it simply as a low tone; that is, produce it in the low pitch range with or without a slight falling but without the final rise. According to Chao (1968:28–9), tone 4 becomes 53 when followed by another tone 4. However, in connected speech, tone 4 is also often phonetically a 52 or 53 tone. For tone 4, it is crucial to make it start high in your pitch range and then you can end it in the mid pitch range; that is, the falling range is within the upper half of your pitch range. The diagram in (8) illustrates tone 3 and tone 4 in non-final position and connected speech.

(8) Phonetic variations in tones 3 and 4 in non-final position and connected speech

	TONE 3	TONE 3	TONE 4
	LOW	LOW FALLING	HIGH FALLING
	22	21	53 (OR 52)
	LL	LL	HM

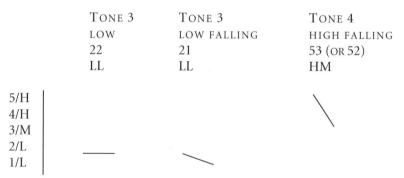

```
5/H
4/H
3/M
2/L
1/L
```

Now use the examples in (9) to practice the pronunciations of the four SC tones. For simplicity, the tone value 51 and 214 are still used for transcriptions of phrase final tones 3 and 4 respectively, but you should be aware of the slight changes in actual pitch values as described above for connected speech. Note also that tone 3 is pronounced like tone 2 before another tone 3 as the highlighted example of (9d) indicates. This tonal change will be discussed in §4.2.3 and §9.4.

🎧 (9) Examples for four SC phonemic tones (T = tone)

a. T1   *tāng* [tʰɑŋ]55   'soup'   *wān* [wan]55   'curve'
   T2   *táng* [tʰɑŋ]35   'candy'   *wán* [wan]35   'to play'
   T3   *tǎng* [tʰɑŋ]214 'lie down'   *wǎn* [wan]214 'late, evening'
   T4   *tàng* [tʰɑŋ]51   'hot'   *wàn* [wan]51   'ten thousand'

b. T1 + T1 = 55 + 55   *fēijī*   [fei]55   [tɕi]55   'airplane'
   T1 + T2 = 55 + 35   *kēxué*   [kʰɤ]55   [ɕɥe]35   'science'
   T1 + T3 = 55 + 214   *gēwǔ*   [kɤ]55   [wu]214   'song and dance'
   T1 + T4 = 55 + 51   *yīnyuè* [jin]55   [ɥe]51   'music'

c. T2 + T1 = 35 + 55   *chábēi* [tʂʰa]35 [pei]55   'tea cup'
   T2 + T2 = 35 + 35   *rénmín* [ɹən]35   [min]35   'people'
   T2 + T3 = 35 + 214   *qímǎ*   [tɕʰi]35 [ma]214   'to ride a horse'
   T2 + T4 = 35 + 51   *tíyì*   [tʰi]35   [ji]51   'suggest, propose'

d. T3 + T1 = 21 + 55   *yǔyīn*   [ɥy]21   [jin]55   'speech sounds'
   T3 + T2 = 21 + 35   *yǔwén*   [ɥy]21   [wən]35   'language'
   T3 + T3 = 35 + 214   *yǔfǎ*   [ɥy]35   [fa]214   'syntax'
   T3 + T4 = 21 + 51   *yǔyì*   [ɥy]21   [ji]51   'semantics'

e. T4 + T1 = 53 + 55   *dàjiā*   [ta]53   [tɕja]55 'all people, everyone'
   T4 + T2 = 53 + 35   *shùlín* [ʂu]53   [lin]35   'woods, forest'
   T4 + T3 = 53 + 214   *fùnǚ*   [fu]53   [ny]214   'women'
   T4 + T4 = 53 + 51   *bìyè*   [pi]53   [je]51   'to graduate'

In connected speech, a tone does not always hold the same pitch level, and the pitch contour can be less obvious or somewhat obscured. For example, the high level tone can be like 44 or 54 or 545 and the high rising tone can be like a 23 tone. In addition, the production of a tone is influenced by adjacent tones. For example, a high level tone after a low tone may become a kind of rising tone. The phonetic details of tonal variations in connected speech are highly complex and we cannot discuss them further. To pronounce tone as native speakers do is not an easy task for adult language learners, especially when a sequence of tones is put together in a phrase or sentence. What can be explained and covered here are the more general patterns of tonal variations, such as those in (8) and others in the following two subsections and in §9.4, to serve as guidelines for learners of SC. To make your tonal pronunciations more native-like requires constant practice and preferably extensive exposure to a SC-speaking environment.

In terms of tonal classification, SC has one level tone and three contour tones. If we divide the pitch range into the higher and lower parts of the pitch range, i.e. high and low registers (as shown in (5)), then we can group the four tones in SC into two types: the high level T1 (55), the high rising T2 (35), and the high falling tones T4 (51 or 53) are tones of high register (within the higher pitch range), and only one tone, the low falling (21) or low falling-rising (214) T3, is within the lower pitch range, a low register tone.

4.2.2 The neutral tone

The NEUTRAL TONE in SC occurs in an unstressed short syllable in non-initial position in a word or phrase and it must be preceded by at least one syllable that has one of the four phonemic tones. The pitch level and contour of the neutral tone varies depending on the preceding tone, as the examples in (10) illustrate (based on Chao 1968:36). For convenience, I use T0 for the neutral tone. In *pīnyīn*, the neutral-toned syllable is treated as toneless with no diacritic tonal mark placed on the vowel. Note that the variants of the neutral tone in (10) is short (represented by one number) and has no pitch contour (no falling or rising). Other studies show that the neutral tone variants have pitch contour. An example of such a system is shown in (11) (based on Cheng 1973:56; cf. Shih 1987 and Yip 2002:181). In (11), the variants of the neutral tone are either falling or rising tones.

(10) The pitch values of the neutral tone I

T1 + T0 = 55 + 2	*māma*	[ma]55	[ma]2	'mother'
	kāi le	[kʰai]55	[lə]2	'have opened, opened'
T2 + T0 = 35 + 3	*yéye*	[je]35	[je]3	'grandfather'
	lái le	[lai]35	[lə]3	'have come, came'
T3 + T0 = 21 + 4	*jiějie*	[tɕje]21	[tɕje]4	'older sister'
	mǎi le	[mai]21	[lə]4	'have bought, bought'
T4 + T0 = 53 + 1	*dìdi*	[ti]53	[ti]1	'younger brother'
	kàn le	[kʰan]53	[lə]1	'have seen, saw'

(11) The pitch values of the neutral tone II

T1 + T0 = 55 + 41	*māma*	[ma]55	[ma]41	'mother'
	kāi le	[kʰai]55	[lə]41	'have opened, opened'
T2 + T0 = 35 + 31	*yéye*	[je]35	[je]31	'grandfather'
	lái le	[lai]35	[lə]31	'have come, came'
T3 + T0 = 21 + 23	*jiějie*	[tɕje]21	[tɕje]23	'older sister'
	mǎi le	[mai]21	[lə]23	'have bought, bought'
T4 + T0 = 53 + 21	*dìdi*	[ti]53	[ti]21	'younger brother'
	kàn le	[kʰan]53	[lə]21	'have seen, saw'

The generalizations from (10) and (11) are that: (i) after the high register tones, i.e. T1, T2, and T4, the neutral tone is low or falling; and (ii) after the low register T3, the neutral tone is high or rising (cf. Cheng 1973:56; Yip 2002:182). Of the three falling neutral tone variants in (11), the one after T1 is higher than the one after T2, and the one after T2 is higher than the one after T4.

The transcriptions in (11) better reflect the actual phonetic pitch movement, and those in (10) better reflect the shortness of the neutral tone. For the practical purposes of learning the pronunciation of the neutral tone, the system in (10) may be easier for most learners. Whichever system you use for your practice, make sure you pronounce the neutral-toned syllable much shorter than the preceding syllable. Think of the neutral-toned syllable as an unstressed syllable in English, e.g. the second syllables *fa* in *sofa*, *ter* in *better*, and *con* in *bacon*. Then I suggest that you first try the simpler pitch value in (10) to serve as the 'target pitch' for the neutral tone. For T1+T0, start with a high level 55 tone and then quickly glide through the pitch range to target the pitch value of 2. For T2+T0, start with a rising 35, then get back to the mid range pitch 3; it is like having a 353 tonal sequence for the span of a long syllable plus a short syllable. For T3+T0, you can think of pronouncing this as a 214 tone but the tone stretches for a span of two syllables, with pitch level 4 or 3 as the target for the neutral-toned syllable. For T4+T0, make sure to start high for the falling 53 tone and then go even lower for the short neutral toned syllable; alternatively, you can also start with 51 and stay low at 1 for the short syllable.

Now that we know the various phonetic realizations of the neutral tone in different contexts, the next question is: does the neutral tone have a basic pitch value of its own? There are different analyses in the literature, but for our purposes, we can think of the syllable with a neutral tone as being toneless (without any tone) and the phonetic pitch value of the toneless syllable results from the extension and influence of the preceding tone. Then the neutral tone is not a phonemic tone like the other four since it has no tone to begin with and it occurs only in highly restricted contexts. An unstressed syllable is typically short in length, weak in prominence (e.g. pitch height, loudness, and intensity), and has a shorter lax vowel or reduced rime (e.g. rime with a more centralized vowel and/or a weakly articulated or deleted coda consonant). In addition, in a tone language, an unstressed syllable tends to lose its original basic tone. The neutral-toned syllable in SC has all the characteristics of an unstressed syllable, so we can treat it as a toneless syllable phonologically. The processes and rules that lead to various pitch values of the neutral tone will be discussed in §9.3.

The neutral tone occurs much more often in the Beijing dialect than in textbook SC and other varieties of SC. In most cases, to have a neutral tone or not does not change word meaning. The second syllables of the examples in

(12ab) may be pronounced with their basic tones or with a neutral tone. The different tonal pronunciations either mark the differences in styles or accents or can be used freely either way, but the meaning of each word remains the same. The examples we saw earlier in (10) and (11) always have a neutral tone regardless of accents or varieties of SC. In a small number of two-syllable words, the one with a neutral tone has a more specialized meaning, as in (12cde) (Cheng 1973:54). In some varieties of SC, however, the examples in (12cde) are pronounced only with the basic tone for both the general and the specialized meanings.

(12)   WITH BASIC TONE   WITH NEUTRAL TONE

     a. *yanjiu*   [jɛn]35 [tɕjou]51   [jɛn]35 [tɕjou]3
             'research'   'research'

     b. *kexue*   [kʰɤ]55 [ɕɥe]35   [kʰɤ]55 [ɕɥe]2
             'science'   'science'

     c. *dongxi*   [tuŋ]55 [ɕi]55   [tuŋ]55 [ɕi]2
             'east and west'   'thing, stuff'

     d. *shenghuo*   [ʂəŋ]55 [xwo]35   [ʂəŋ]55 [xwo]2
             'life'   'livelihood'

     e. *duoshao*   [two]55 [ʂau]214   [two]55 [ʂau]2
             'many and few; more or less'   'how many'

4.2.3 Tonal variations

The pitch level and contour of a tone can change in different contexts. The change of tone due to the influence of adjacent tones is called TONE SANDHI. The most famous tone sandhi rule in SC is tone 3 sandhi: in a sequence of two low tones (two T3s), change the first T3 to the rising T2, as the examples in (13) show. Although the rule seems simple, it becomes much more complex when there is a sequence of more than two low tones in a phase or sentence because which T3 can change also depends on the sentence structure. The more complex examples will be discussed in §9.4.

(13) Examples for T3 sandhi (The arrow → means 'become')

     T3 + T3 → T2 + T3 (i.e. 21 + 214 → 35 + 214)

     xiǎogǒu   [ɕjau]21 [kou]214   →   [ɕjau]35 [kou]214   'puppy'

     hěnhǎo   [hən]21 [xau]214   →   [hən]35 [xau]214   'very good'

     zhǎnlǎn   [tʂan]21 [lan]214   →   [tʂan]35 [lan]214   'exhibition'

     wǔdǎo   [wu]21 [tau]214   →   [wu]35 [tau]214   'dance'

Some tonal changes, unlike T3 sandhi, have rather limited applications, applicable only to a specific syllable or a specific type of expression. In (14), we see the tonal changes specifically for two words, *yī* 'one' and *bù* 'not'.[1] The basic tone is used when these words are pronounced as an isolated single syllable or in phrase final position. When *yī* is followed by T1, T2, and T3, the basic tone (T1) changes to the falling T4, and when it is followed by T4, the tone changes to the rising T2. The tone of *bù* stays as T4 before T1, T2, and T3 (although with the normal change from 51 to 53 in non-final syllable as mentioned §4.2.1) but it changes to the rising T2 when followed by T4. These tonal changes, like tone 3 sandhi, are not optional and must apply.

(14) | basic tone | before T1 | before T2 | before T3 | before T4 |
|---|---|---|---|---|
| **55** | **53** 55 | **53** 35 | **53** 214 | **35** 51 |
| [ji] | [ji] [tjɛn] | [ji] [niɛn] | [ji] [wan] | [ji] [jɑŋ] |
| *yī* | *yì tiān* | *yì nián* | *yì wǎn* | *yíyàng* |
| 'one' | 'one day' | 'one year' | 'one bowl' | 'the same' |
| **51** | 53 55 | 53 35 | 53 214 | 35 51 |
| [pu] | [pu] [xɤ] | [pu] [nan] | [bu] [xɑu] | [bu] [jɑu] |
| *bù* | *bù hē* | *bù nán* | *bù hǎo* | *bú yào* |
| 'not' | 'not drink' | 'not difficult' | 'not good' | 'not want' |

In (15) and (16) we see tonal changes specific to **reduplication**, a morphological or word formation process that repeats a syllable or some segments of a syllable or word. In (15), when a kinship noun is reduplicated to become a disyllabic word, the second repeated syllable becomes a neutral-toned syllable. This tonal change for reduplicated kinship terms is obligatory for SC.

(15) Neutral tone in kinship term reduplication

    a. *dì*　　→　*dìdi*　　　　　　'younger brother'
      [ti]51　→　[ti]53 [ti]　→　[ti]53 [ti]1
    b. *mā*　　→　*māma*　　　　　　'mother'
      [ma]55　→　[ma]55 [ma]　→　[ma]55 [ma]2

The examples in (16) show a tonal pattern specific to some reduplicated adjectives: a monosyllabic adjective is repeated usually with the added *er*-suffix (§3.4.5, §8.2), and the tone of the second repeated syllable becomes a high

---

[1] Chao (1968:45) also mentions two additional words that undergo special tonal changes: *qī* 'seven' and *bā* 'eight'. Both words have T1 and tonal changes are the same as that for *yī* 'one': T1 → T2 before T4 and T1 → T4 before the other three tones. The tonal changes for *qī* 'seven' and *bā* 'eight' are used by a minority of SC speakers and most simply use T1 consistently for these two words.

level tone (T1) regardless of its original tone (based on Cheng 1973: 44–5; cf. Duanmu 2000:228–9). This tonal change is optional and may or may not apply depending on different SC speakers and speech styles.

🎧 (16) Tonal variation in reduplicated adjectives

    a. *màn* [man]51   'slow' → [man]51 [man]**51** + [ɹ]
                           → [man]53 [maɹ]**55**   'slow'
    b. *yuǎn* [ɥɛn]214 'far' → [ɥɛn]214 [ɥɛn]**214** + [ɹ]
                           → [ɥɛn]21 [ɥaɹ]**55**   'far'

    Finally, an optional tonal change applies to T2: it becomes a high level tone (T1) when preceded by T1 and T2 and followed by one of the four basic tones. Two examples from Chao (1968:27–8) are given in (17). This tonal change occurs only in fast speech and may or may not apply depending on different SC speakers. We will come back to this pattern in §9.2.5.

🎧 (17)

    a. *cōng yóu bǐng* 'onion oil cake'
       [tsʰuŋ]55 [jou]**35** [pjəŋ]214   → [tsʰuŋ]55 [jou]**55** [pjəŋ]214
    b. *fēn shuǐ lǐng* 'watershed'
       [fən]55 [ʂwei]**35** [ljəŋ]214   → [fən]55 [ʂwei]**55** [ljəŋ]214

4.3 Summary

This chapter introduces the phonetic properties and classification of tone and discusses the tones in SC and tonal variations.

- Tone is the pattern of pitch variations that can change the meaning of a word. The primary acoustic correlate of tone is F0 (the frequency of the vibration of the vocal folds), the perception of tone depends on the perceived pitch level of F0, and the main articulatory correlate of tone is the tension of the vocal folds (§4.1.2).
- The PITCH LEVEL of a tone can be high, mid, or low and the PITCH CONTOUR of a tone can be level or contour (§4.1.4).
- SC has four PHONEMIC TONES: one LEVEL TONE and three CONTOUR TONES. The high level T1 and two of the contour tones, high rising T2 and high falling T4, are high register tones, and the low falling T3 is a low register tone (§4.2.1).

- The NEUTRAL TONE occurs on a short UNSTRESSED SYLLABLE in phrase final position. The PITCH VALUE of the non-phonemic neutral tone is determined by the preceding tone (§4.2.2).
- Some of the phonemic tones change their tonal pitch values when influenced by neighboring tones (§4.2.3). The most productive TONE SANDHI rule in SC is tone 3 sandhi, which changes T3 to T2 before another T3. Other tonal variations are limited to specific MORPHEMES and/or apply in highly restricted contexts.

Chapter 9 will further explain the processes and rules of tonal variation in SC, and chapter 10 will discuss how tone, stress, and intonation interact in SC.

EXERCISES

1 Give the phonetic transcription for each of the following SC words. Use the numerical pitch value to transcribe the tone.

Example: *bǐ* 'pen' [pi]214

a. *chuáng*	'bed'	b. *jǐn*	'tight'
c. *ruǎn*	'soft'	d. *dāo*	'knife'
e. *shéng*	'rope'	f. *wèi*	'stomach'
g. *kè*	'class'	h. *qiē*	'to cut'
i. *huǒ*	'fire'	j. *zhǐ*	'paper'

2 Give the phonetic transcription for each of the following SC disyllabic words. Use the pitch value to transcribe the tone. Make sure to apply any tonal changes and to give the specific phonetic pitch value for a neutral tone.

Examples:
měiguó 'USA'   [mei]21[kwo]35   (T3 is 21 before another tone)
xiǎogǒu 'puppy' [ɕjau]35[kou]214 (T3 T3 → T2 T3)
dùzi 'abdomen' [tu]53[tsɹ̩]1   (T4 is 53 before another tone, T0 is 1 after T4)

a. *lǎoshǔ*	'mouse'	b. *shīzi*	'lion'
c. *zhèngcháng*	'normal'	d. *dòufu*	'tofu'
e. *wǒmen*	'we'	f. *háizi*	'child'
g. *qiǎnsè*	'light color'	h. *xǐwǎn*	'to do the dishes'
i. *yángnǎi*	'goat milk'	j. *zhūròu*	'pork'

3   Performance exercise I
Each of the following MINIMAL PAIRS differ only in tone. Practice the
pronunciation of each pair.

a. *piāo*   [pʰjɑu]55   'to float'   *piào*   [pʰjɑu]51   'ticket'
b. *qiú*   [tɕʰjou]35   'ball'   *qiū*   [tɕʰjou]55   'autumn'
c. *lǎn*   [lan]214   'lazy'   *làn*   [lan]51   'rotten'
d. *cāi*   [tsʰai]55   'guess'   *cǎi*   [tsʰai]214   'colorful'
e. *miàn*   [mjɛn]51   'face'   *mián*   [mjɛn]35   'cotton'
f. *yú*   [ɥy]35   'fish'   *yǔ*   [ɥy]214   'rain'

4   Performance exercise II
Use the examples in (9) in §4.2.1 to practice the pronunciation of a sequence
of two tones and use the examples in (10) in §4.2.2 to practice the
pronunciation of the neutral tone.

5   Performance exercise III
Listen to *The Sounds of Chinese CD* and identify for each syllable the tone you
hear. Write down first the *pīnyīn* tonal mark on the vowel and then the tone
number T1, T2, T3, or T4 and the pitch value such as 55, 35, 214, and 51.

Example *ba:*		*bá* T2 = 35	*ba:*	*bà* T4 = 51
a. *fan*	fan	fan	fan	
b. *zhu*	zhu	zhu	zhu	
c. *jie*	jie	jie	jie	
d. *xu*	xu	xu	xu	
e. *chuang*	chuang	chuang	chuang	

6   Performance exercise IV
Listen to *The Sounds of Chinese CD* and identify for each syllable the tone you
hear in each disyllabic word/phrase. First, put the *pīnyīn* tonal mark on the
vowel of each syllable. Then write down the tone number T1, T2, T3, T4, or T0
and the pitch value such as 55, 35, 21, 214, 53, or 51 for the basic tones and 2,
3, 4, or 1 for the neutral tone.

Example: *dahan:*   *dàhàn*   T4-T4 = 53–51
            mama: *māma*   T1-T0 = 55–2

Basic tone + basic tone
a. *wuli*   b. *guzhang*   c. *kuhao*
d. *xihuan*   e. *mingli*   f. *canting*

g. *yilang*   h. *gongzuo*   i. *zhengfu*
j. *luyu*   k. *rumen*   l. *niunai*
m. *youqian*   n. *diandeng*   o. *guojia*

Basic tone + neutral tone
p. *lanzi*   q. *shizi*   r. *lao le*
s. *na le*   t. *guozi*   u. *mai le*
v. *pizi*   w. *diu le*

5 Syllable structure

The notion of the syllable is highly difficult to define in phonetic terms (Ladefoged 2001:225–30), but the syllable plays an important role in understanding SUPRASEGMENTAL PROPERTIES such as stress and tone and the organization of PROSODIC STRUCTURE in words, phrases, and sentences. We can think of the syllable as an abstract phonological PROSODIC UNIT at some level of our mental or cognitive system. Sequences of segments are organized into syllables, just like MORPHEMES are organized into words and words are organized into phrases and sentences in the linguistic system.

We have had a basic introduction to syllable structure in earlier chapters (§1.3, §3.2), and in this chapter we study the SC syllable in detail. The chapter starts with the traditional Chinese view of the components within the syllable (§5.1), and then discusses the contemporary view of the representation of the syllable and the basic principles for organizing sequences of segments into syllables (§5.2). There are universal principles for well-formed syllables that apply consistently across all languages, but each language also has its own language-specific constraints on possible syllable types. In §5.3 we examine the permissible syllable types in SC and the absence of some syllable types. The last section (§5.4) summarizes the main points of the chapter. The tables listing all possible syllables in SC can be found in Appendix B.

5.1 The traditional view of Chinese syllable structure

The traditional analysis of the Chinese syllable can be dated back to the sixth century (Cheng 1973:11). On this analysis, tone is considered a property of the whole syllable, and the syllable is divided into two major parts: the INITIAL and the FINAL. The initial is the syllable initial non-glide consonant. The rest of the syllable after the initial consonant is the final, which is further divided into the medial and the RIME. The medial is the glide before the main nuclear vowel, and the rime contains the NUCLEUS and the ending. The nucleus is the main vowel and the ending can be either the post-nuclear vowel (i.e. the second half of a diphthong) or a consonant. The diagram in (1) illustrates the traditional syllable structure in a hierarchical tree structure (cf. Cheng 1973:11; Lin 1989:27; Duanmu 2000:80).[1] A syllable in the form of CGVX (C=consonant, G=glide, V=vowel, X=C or V) is the maximal syllable structure in SC. Every syllable must have the nucleus and in SC the initial, the medial, and the ending are all optional. The possible syllable types in SC are listed in (2). Note that in (2b) the syllable with a SYLLABIC CONSONANT (apical vowel) (§3.4.1) is structurally the same as the normal CV syllable since the syllabic consonant functions like a vowel in that it is the nucleus of the syllable.

(1) The traditional analysis of the Chinese syllable

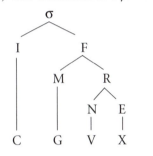

σ = syllable	
I = initial	F = final
M = medial	R = rime
N = nucleus	E = ending
C = consonant	G = glide
V = vowel	X = C or V

(2)   SYLLABLE TYPES   EXAMPLES

a.	V	*è*	[ɤ]51	'hungry'
b.	CV	*mǎ*	[ma]214	'horse'
		sī	[sɹ]55	'silk'
c.	GV	*yā*	[ja]55	'duck'
d.	CGV	*duō*	[two]55	'many'
e.	VC	*ān*	[an]55	'peace, safe'
f.	VV	*ài*	[ai]51	'love'
g.	CVC	*lán*	[lan]35	'blue'
h.	CVV	*lái*	[lai]35	'come'
i.	GVC	*yán*	[jɛn]35	'salt'
j.	GVV	*yào*	[jɑu]51	'medicine'
k.	CGVC	*huàn*	[xwan]51	'to exchange'
l.	CGVV	*huài*	[xwai]51	'bad'

The *pīnyīn* system taught in the classroom also makes use of the notion of the initial and the final and the *pīnyīn* charts/tables are arranged by listing

---

[1] In the literature, sometimes the final is called the rime, and the medial, the nucleus, and the ending are called the head, the body, and the tail respectively.

the initials on the first column and all the finals on the first row (cf. tables in Appendix B).

5.2 Syllable structure and syllabification

In this section, the SC syllable is analyzed in terms of ONSET, RIME, NUCLEUS, and CODA, an approach mostly commonly used for the analysis of syllable structure (§5.2.1). SYLLABIFICATION is a process that assigns a sequence of segments in a word or phrase into appropriate syllable positions, i.e. a process that organizes segments into syllables. In §§5.2.2–5.2.4, the basic linguistic principles of constructing the syllable are introduced and applied to SC. Whenever relevant, English examples are provided for illustration and comparison.

5.2.1 Hierarchical syllable structure

Although the traditional analysis of the syllable has been adopted by researchers in Chinese phonology even until recently (e.g. Cheng 1973; Lin 1989), many newer studies reanalyze the syllable structures of SC and various Chinese dialects with a more contemporary view in the Western linguistics tradition (e.g. Bao 1990, 1996; Duanmu 1990, 2000: chapter 4). On this contemporary view, the pre-nuclear glide in SC is argued to be part of the onset rather than in the rime or in the final. Some also argue that the second vowel component of the diphthong is not part of the coda or the ending; rather the whole diphthong is the nucleus (e.g. Lin 1989; Chung 1989, 1996). In short, the different analyses of the SC syllable structure have been much in debate (see Further Reading). This book adopts an analysis in which the pre-nuclear glide is part of the onset and a diphthong is in the nucleus, as shown in the diagrams in (3ab), illustrated with the examples from (2kl).

(3) SC syllable structure

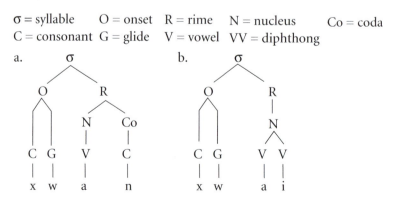

σ = syllable   O = onset   R = rime   N = nucleus   Co = coda
C = consonant G = glide   V = vowel   VV = diphthong

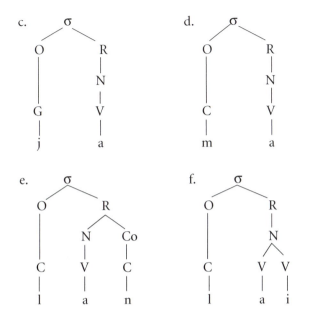

In SC it is possible to have a syllable without an onset, a syllable with only a single consonant or a glide, or a syllable without a coda. The additional examples in (3c-f) show how some of the syllables from (2) are represented. In the diagrams, the labels C, G, and V are used to indicate a timing position within the syllable. A sound SEGMENT (i.e. a consonant, vowel, or glide) that is linked to one position is the normal short segment, whereas a long segment such as a diphthong (3f) or a long vowel (§3.3, §3.1.4) occupies two positions (see (4) below).

A syllable that has no coda is called an OPEN SYLLABLE and a syllable that has a coda is called a CLOSED SYLLABLE. Under the analysis in (3), an open syllable with a monophthong vowel, such as a CV or CGV syllable, is considered to have only one segment in the nucleus. However, phonetically speaking, the single vowel in an open syllable is longer than the vowel in a closed syllable like CVC or CGVC. That is why some linguists represent such an open syllable as illustrated in (4) with a long vowel. A long monophthong vowel is treated as one segment linked to two V positions to indicate the length in the syllable structure. Therefore, syllables like *mǎ* 'horse' and *huā* 'flower' may be transcribed as [ma:]₂₁₄ and [xua:]₅₅ respectively, with a long vowel. For simplicity, I will continue to use a short monophthong vowel in phonetic transcriptions, such as [ma]₂₁₄ and [xua]₅₅, and syllable representations as in (3), but you may want to keep in mind the phonetic fact that a monophthong vowel in an open syllable is longer.

(4)

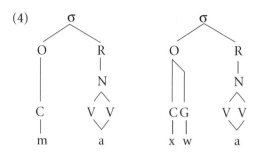

For most analyses of English syllable structure, the pre-nuclear glide is also part of the onset and the diphthong is also under the nucleus node.[2] For example, *swan* [swan] and *sway* [sweɪ] have the same syllable structures as those in (3a) and (3b) respectively. One major difference between the syllable in SC and that in English is that English can have more segments in the onset and coda, e.g. *strange* [streɪndʒ], in which three consonants [str] are in the onset and two consonants [ndʒ] are in the coda. Compared to English, SC has a simpler syllable structure and many fewer syllable types.

5.2.2 Sonority Sequencing Principle

In English, [tɹ] forms a possible onset as in *train*, but cannot be in the coda (e.g. there is no single syllable like *neatr*), whereas the reverse sequence [ɹt] can be in the coda as in *cart* but cannot be in the onset (e.g. there is no single syllable like *rtak*). In SC, a consonant-glide onset like [tw] is good but a glide-consonant onset like [wt] is not possible. This type of restriction occurs not only in English and SC but also consistently in other languages. We can say that there is a universal principle for syllabification, i.e. for the construction of well-formed syllables.

Sound segments differ in the degree of SONORITY, as mentioned in §3.1.1. Of two sounds with the same length, stress, and pitch, a more sonorous sound resonates more and is perceived as being louder. Vowels are more sonorous than consonants. Among vowels, low vowels are more sonorous than mid vowels, which in turn are more sonorous than high vowels. Among consonants, approximants are more sonorous than fricatives, which in turn are more sonorous than stops. All sounds are placed along the SONORITY HIERARCHY as shown in (5).

(5) Sonority hierarchy (more sonorous >> less sonorous)
low vowels >> mid vowels >> high vowels
>> approximants >> nasals >> fricatives >> stops/affricates

---

[2] The status of [j] in [ju] as in *juice* [dʒjus] is less clear as it is sometimes claimed to be in the nucleus rather than in the onset.

Other than the acoustic and auditory characteristics that define the degree of sonority, this sonority hierarchy corresponds to the degree of CONSTRIC-TION in articulation. Vowels have little obstruction of the airstream and hence are more sonorous than consonants. The lower a vowel, the more open the vowel for the air to flow out, and the more sonorous the vowel is. Among the consonants, the more constriction a consonant has, the less air can flow out freely, and the less sonorous the consonant is. This is why low vowels are at the top of the sonority hierarchy and stops, affricates, and fricatives are at the lower end of the sonority hierarchy.

The SONORITY SEQUENCING PRINCIPLE (SSP) as defined in (6) serves as the basic universal principle of organizing segments into syllables (cf. Selkirk 1982). The sonority peak of a syllable is the nuclear segment or the more sonorous segment within the nucleus. In a syllable with a monophthong vowel, the vowel is the sonority peak, and in a syllable with a diphthong, the more sonorous vowel is the peak. The SSP requires that a sequence of onset segments has increasing sonority and a sequence of coda segments has decreasing sonority. That is why [tw] and [tɹ] are good in the onset but not possible in the coda since [t] is less sonorous than [w] and [ɹ].

(6) The Sonority Sequencing Principle (The SSP)
     The syllable has increasing sonority before the nucleus and
     decreasing sonority after the nucleus.

There are some exceptions to the SSP in various languages; for example, in English [st] is a possible onset as in *stand* and yet the first segment [s] as a fricative is more sonorous than the stop [t] in the second segment. Most exceptions to the SSP have been analyzed by linguists in ways to avoid violating the SSP and the details of those analyses do not concern us here. In general SSP has served well as the basic universal principle of organizing segments into syllables and all permissible syllable types in SC observe the SSP.

The SSP also decides which phonemic vowel surfaces as a glide in a sequence of vowels within a syllable. In SC, a phonemic vowel sequence in a syllable like /ia/ and /ua/ is syllabified as [ja] and [wa] respectively because the more sonorous vowel in the sequence (the low vowel) takes the nucleus position and the high vowel becomes a glide. However, if a syllable has only one high vowel, such as /ti/, then the high vowel, being the most sonorous, becomes the syllable nucleus and cannot become a glide.

5.2.3 Maximal Onset Principle

We have so far considered only the syllabification of MONOSYLLABIC words. For a POLYSYLLABIC word, there is the question as to which consonants in the middle of the word should be assigned to the onset of the following syllable and which to the coda of the preceding syllable. For example, in a word like *attract* [ətɹækt], there are two nuclear vowels [ə] and [æ] and hence there are two syllables, i.e. this is a DISYLLABIC word. The question is: where is the syllable boundary that separates the two syllables? That is, how should we syllabify the [tɹ] sequence. We know that [tɹ] cannot be in coda position because it has increasing sonority and violates the SSP. We know that in English [t] may occur in coda position, as in *cat* and *pet*, [ɹ] may occur as a single onset consonant, as in *rain* and *reef*, and [tɹ] may occur in onset position, as in *train* and *tree*. Therefore, we have to decide if the syllabification of *attract* is [ət.ɹækt] or [ə.tɹækt]. (The dot in the phonetic transcription indicates the syllable boundary.) The universal MAXIMAL ONSET PRINCIPLE prefers maximizing the syllabification of consonants to the following onset as long as the resulting onset is a permissible onset of the language in question. That is, [ə.tɹækt] is the correct syllabification for English.

This principle also explains why across languages a single consonant between two vowels is syllabified to the onset of the next syllable rather than the coda of the preceding syllable. For example, *correct* is syllabified as [kʰə.ɹɛkt] with [ɹ] in the onset of the second syllable but not [kʰəɹ.ɛkt]. Why is it that the onset rather than the coda has the priority in syllabification? The most basic syllable type in human language is the CV syllable since all languages have CV syllable structure but not all languages have V or CVC syllable types. In terms of articulation and perception, a CV syllable is easier to produce and easier to perceive, since a rhythm of a sequence of CV syllables consisting of low sonority plus high sonority makes clear the syllable boundaries in a continuous flow of speech. Moreover, in many languages, including SC, only a limited number of consonants are allowed in the coda, and cross-linguistically coda consonants tend to be deleted or weakened by losing some articulatory features. For example, in some varieties of English, the coda [ɹ] is deleted in words like *car* and *park*, or the coda [l] loses consonant constriction and becomes a vowel [ʊ] or glide [w] in words like *feel* and *peel* (Carr 1999:74–5).

Since SC has a rather simple syllable structure and only the nasal consonants [n] and [ŋ] can be in the coda of non-rhotacized rimes, the effects of the Maximal Onset Principle are not as obvious as they are in English. In addition, the one-to-one correspondence between a syllable and a morpheme (and a written character) in most cases (§§1.3–1.4) seems to have made the need for such a principle less necessary for SC. One can say that what the speaker does is to produce each individual morpheme and hence each individual syllable. Consider the two polysyllabic SC words *mŭniú* 'cow', which has two morphemes *mǔ* 'female' and *niú* 'ox, cow', and *mùníhēi* 'Munich', which has one single morpheme because it is a transliterated loanword, but which has three syllables and is written with three characters (§§11.1–11.2). In both cases, the nasal [n] is syllabified as the onset of the second syllable [mu.njou] and [mu.ni.xei], which is in accordance with the Maximal Onset Principle.

However, consider the word *tiānānmén* 'the Tian'an gate at the Tian'anmen Square in Beijing', which has three morphemes: *tiān* 'sky', *ān* 'peace', and *mén* 'door'. Note that *ān* has no onset, and, following the Maximal Onset Principle, one can imagine moving the coda nasal [n] of *tiān* to the second syllable to result in [tiɛ.nan.mən], but this does not happen in SC. The syllabification is typically [tiɛn.an.mən].[3] That is why in *pīnyīn* this word can be written with an apostrophe between the first and second morphemes as *tiān'ānmén* to indicate that [n] remains the coda of the first syllable.

Why is the Maximal Onset Principle not applicable to *ān*? This syllable is one of the so-called 'zero-initial' syllables (see §5.2.4 below) that seem to be without an onset. However, the principle can be kept intact as a universal principle if it can be argued that in SC either reassigning a coda consonant to onset position is prohibited or the zero-initial syllable in fact has onset in its syllable structure representation. We now move on to discuss these analyses.

5.2.4 Resyllabification and the zero-initial syllable

RESYLLABIFICATION is a process in which the affiliation of a segment in a syllable structure can be reassigned through a new round of syllabification when two morphemes or two words are put together. For example, when a vowel-initial morpheme is added after a morpheme or word that ends in a coda consonant, the coda consonant is typically resyllabified as the onset of the vowel-initial morpheme. In English, the word *diplomat* can be syllabified as *di.plo.mat* with [t] in the coda of the third syllable, but when the vowel initial suffix *-ic* is added, the original coda [t] is resyllabified as the onset of the newly added syllable: *di.plo.ma.tic*. Across two words, resyllabification may occur in connected speech, e.g. in a phrase like *catch you* [kʰætʃ] [ju], the coda consonant of the first word [tʃ] sometimes becomes the onset of the second word: [kʰæ.tʃju].

In general, SC does not apply resyllabification across morpheme or word boundaries. That is why a zero-initial syllable does not attract the coda

---

[3] In casual speech, it could become [tiɛn.nan.mən] by lengthening the coda [n] of the first syllable (cf. §8.1.3).

consonant of the preceding syllable to become its own onset. This is a possible language-specific restriction because some languages do prohibit resyllabification across certain grammatical boundaries. However, a better line of explanation is that the zero-initial syllable actually already contains an onset and therefore no resyllabification can occur. One piece of evidence comes from the fact that the zero-initial syllable can often be pronounced with a consonant or glide. As shown in (7), in a zero-onset syllable, if the nucleus is a high vowel, then the onset can be the corresponding glide (which is also reflected in *pīnyīn*), and if the nucleus is a low or mid vowel, then the onset can be [ŋ] or [ʔ] (cf. Duanmu 2000: 82–3; cf. Chao 1948, 1968; Li 1966).[4] Whether or not to insert a consonant and which consonant to use in (7b) varies depending on speakers and different varieties of SC and dialects.

(7) Zero-initial syllables

    a. $[i]_{55}$ → $[ji]_{55}$ *yī*   'one'

        $[y]_{35}$ → $[ɥy]_{35}$ *yú*   'fish'

        $[u]_{214}$ → $[wu]_{214}$ *wǔ*   'five'

    b. $[an]_{55}$ → $[ʔan]_{55}$ or $[ŋan]_{55}$ *ān*   'peace'

The symbol [ʔ] represents a glottal stop, which occurs when the vocal folds are held tightly together, and is used in some contexts in English, e.g. to replace or accompany the word final *p, t,* or *k* consonants: *rat* [ræʔt] (Ladefoged 2001:48–9). Most commonly a glottal stop occurs when an English speaker gives a 'no' reply to a question by saying *uh-uh* [ʔʌ̃ʔʌ]. In classroom teaching, typically no onset sound is explicitly taught for a zero-initial syllable with a mid or low vowel but some speakers and learners naturally produce a glottal stop when such a zero-initial syllable is clearly and intentionally separated from the preceding syllable. For learners of SC, my suggestion is to simply start with the mid or low vowel in such a syllable.

When a zero-initial syllable is a weak toneless syllable, such as the phrase or sentence final injection marker *a*, the coda consonant or the last high vowel of the preceding syllable is geminated (i.e. lengthened) and then the zero-initial *a* has an onset. The onset of the weak syllable usually has [j] (or sometimes [ɦ] for some speakers) when the preceding syllable has a mid or low vowel (cf. Chao 1968; Duanmu 2000:83).

---

[4] Previous studies also include two additional consonants: [ɣ] and [ɦ]. The symbol [ɣ] represents a voiced velar fricative and [ɦ] represents a murmured *h* similar to the *h* sound in *ahead* [əɦɛd] (Ladefoged 2001:124). A murmured sound is produced by holding the vocal folds relatively apart and loosely vibrating as the airstream passes through the glottis. We have learned that a velar fricative such as [x] in SC is produced by leaving a small opening between the back of the tongue and the velum to create friction, and [ɣ] is the voiced counterpart of [x].

(8) Zero-initial function word

    a. *nán a!*   [nan]$_{35}$ [a] → [nan]$_{35}$ [na]$_2$ 'Hard!'

    b. *kuài a!* [kwai]$_{53}$ [a] → [kwai]$_{53}$[ja]$_1$ 'Hurry!'

    c. *wǒ a!*   [wo]$_{21}$ [a] → [wo]$_{21}$ [ja]$_4$ 'Me!'

Since a zero-initial syllable can be pronounced with its own onset segment phonetically, we can claim that the zero-initial syllable is represented as having an onset position, e.g. as in (9a) instead of (9b). The onset position may stay empty, or be filled with a segment identical to a neighboring consonant or high vowel or with some special onset sound variants ((7b) and footnote 4). Under this analysis, SC does not move a coda segment to the onset of the next 'seemingly' vowel-initial syllable as English does because this 'seemingly' vowel-initial syllable actually has an onset in its syllable structure representation. We will discuss the processes that fill the empty onset of a zero-initial syllable in §8.1.3.

(9) a.   b.

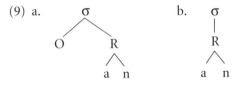

5.3 Phonotactic constraints and gaps in syllable types

Other than the universal principles in organizing segments into syllables, each language also has language-specific constraints on permissible syllable types. PHONOTACTIC CONSTRAINTS (or PHONOTACTICS) are language-specific restrictions on what sequences of segments can be combined. For example, in English, the maximal number of onset segments is limited to three and, more importantly, if there are three consonants in the onset, the first one must be an [s], the second one a stop, and the third one a liquid ([l] or [ɹ]) or glide ([j] or [w]), e.g. *spring, squeeze*.

There are a few general phonotactic constraints in SC, as listed in (10). An asterisk before a linguistic form or representation indicates ungrammaticality or ill-formedness.

(10) General phonotactic constraints in SC

    a. The maximal number of onset segments is limited to two and the second segment must be a glide. For example, [**k**ai], [**w**ai], and [**kw**ai] have permissible onsets but onsets such as *[spl] and *[pl] are illegitimate.

    b. There can be only one coda consonant in SC; it is limited to [n] and [ŋ] in non-rhotacized rimes and can be only [ɹ] in RHOTACIZED

      rimes. For example, *[kam] and *[pat] are not possible syllables in
      SC because of the illicit coda consonants.

  c. The maximal number of segments in the rime is limited to two: either
      a diphthong (counting like two vowel units) or a monophthong (one
      vowel unit) followed by a single consonant. For example, a rime like
      [a], [ɑu], or [an] is allowed but a rime like *[ain] is not.

  d. A rime with a SYLLABIC CONSONANT (or apical vowel) cannot
      have a coda consonant, cannot be preceded by a glide, and must be
      preceded by a consonant with the same PLACE OF
      ARTICULATION. For example, a dental syllabic consonant appears
      only after a dental fricative or affricate, such as [tsɹ̩], [tsʰɹ̩], or [sɹ̩],
      and a post-alveolar syllabic consonant appears only after a
      post-alveolar fricative or affricate, such as [ʂɹ̩] or [tʂɹ̩] (§3.4.1).
      Syllables like *[pɹ̩] and *[wɹ̩n] are not possible.

  e. The high front rounded vowel [y] cannot be the second part of a
      diphthong. For example, the high vowels [i] and [u] can be the
      second half of a diphthong, such as [ai] and [ɑu], but there are no
      diphthongs like *[ay] and *[ey].

  f. A plain schwa [ə] cannot be the only rime segment in a syllable. For
      example, schwa may be in a rime with a coda consonant, such as [ən]
      and [əŋ], but syllables like *[lə] and *[ə] are prohibited.

The first two constraints allow for at most two segments in the onset and at
most one segment in the coda (10ab). In English, the second segment in a two-
segment onset can be a nasal or a liquid, e.g. *snail, train, play*, but in SC the
second segment must be a glide. Like English, SC can have a diphthong in the
nucleus, but, unlike English, the maximal number of segments in the rime is
limited to two (10c). That is, in SC, a rime cannot have both a diphthong and a
coda consonant, e.g. a rime like *[ein] is not allowed. If the nucleus is a syllabic
consonant (apical vowel) as in *sì* [sɹ̩]$_{51}$ 'four' and *shí* [ʂɹ̩]$_{35}$ 'ten' (§3.4.1), there
can be only this nuclear segment in the rime and no glide can intervene between
the initial consonant and the nuclear (10d). The distribution of the high front
rounded vowel [y] is more limited than that of [i] and [u], and the constraint
in (10e) prohibits diphthongs like *[ay] and *[ey] in SC. Finally, the schwa
also has a limited distribution: it must be accompanied by a coda consonant to
form a rime, otherwise it has to be changed to a tense back unrounded vowel,
e.g. [lɤ] and [ɤ] (§8.1.4 and §3.4.2).

   However, some syllable types that fulfill both universal principles and the
general phonotactic constraints in a language can still be absent; e.g. an onset
like *[tsj] or a syllable like *[wɑu] are not possible in SC. In English, although
a stop-lateral onset is good, as in *play* and *glad*, a coronal stop cannot be
followed by a lateral: *[tl] and *[dl] onsets are prohibited. We can say that there

is a gap in the permissible stop-lateral onset sequence. Note that this is not a prohibition against a sequence of [tl] or [dl] since such sequences do occur in words like *Atlantic* and *badly*, in which the stop and the lateral belong to two different syllables: [tl] and [dl] never appear word initially and native speakers consistently place the syllable break between [t] and [l] when asked to isolate the syllables. What is crucial is that a [tl] or [dl] sequence cannot form an onset. There is then an additional specific constraint that prohibits a sequence of a coronal stop and coronal lateral to form an onset.

The gaps in phonological forms (in this case the gaps in syllable types) that have more general patterns and can be explained in terms of general linguistic principles or features are called SYSTEMATIC GAPS. The lack of *[tl] and *[dl] onsets in English may be considered a systematic gap because the stops and the lateral are both coronal and can be explained by a linguistic principle that disfavors segments with the same place of articulation to form an onset. Another example of this type is the lack of [pw] and [bw] onset in English, SC, and many other languages. On the other hand, those gaps that are more idiosyncratic, sporadic, or hard to explain can be considered ACCIDENTAL GAPS. Phonological forms that are considered accidental gaps are potentially possible forms and it just happens by accident that these forms are not present in the language in question. In general, if a native speaker considers a missing form acceptable when it is created (e.g. for the name of a new product), then the missing form is an accidental gap, whereas if a form is not tolerated by a native speaker as a possible form in his/her language, then it is a systematic gap. Sometimes it is not always easy to decide which gaps are systematic and which are accidental, but this distinction at least helps to identify the major constraints in a language.

In SC, other than the general phonotactic constraints, there are a few specific constraints to account for the gaps in syllable types and here we examine the most obvious and systematic ones. These specific constraints usually refer to more specific features such as [coronal], [+high], and [+round]. The square brackets are used for features; the plus and minus indicate the presence or absence of the feature respectively in a segment. We will discuss phonological features in more detail later in §7.1.1, and for the moment consider these features as formal labels for the phonetic/phonological properties of segments.

The constraints listed in (11) concern mainly the CORONAL onset affricates/fricatives and the type of segment that can follow them.

(11) Constraints on onset coronal affricates/fricatives

    a. Alveolo-palatals can occur only before a high front vowel or glide.
      e.g.   [tɕi], [ɕy], [ɕjɑu], and [tɕɥe] are good.
            *[tɕei] and *[ɕa] are bad.

    b. Dental affricates/fricative, post-alveolar affricates/fricative, and velars
       can never occur before a high front vowel or glide.
       e.g. [sai], [ṣei], and [kɑu] are good.
         *[tsja], *[tṣy], and *[ki] are bad.
    c. A dental syllabic consonant occurs only after a dental affricate or
       fricative, and a post-alveolar syllabic consonant occurs only after a
       post-alveolar consonant.

The restrictions given in (11ab) were mentioned earlier in §2.2.5: the alveolo-palatals are in complementary distribution with the dental affricates/fricative, post-alveolar affricates/fricative, and the velar stops. An alveolo-palatal conso-nant, is similar to a high front vowel/glide in that the front part of the tongue is raised high toward the hard palate. We can say that both the alveolo-palatals and high front vowels/glides have the features [−back] (i.e. front or non-back) and [+high] (i.e. high), and the constraints in (11ab) basically state that a con-sonant with [+high, −back] features must be followed by a [+high, −back] vowel/glide. In addition, we also mentioned in §3.4.1 that syllabic consonants (or the so-called apical vowels) occur only after consonants that have the same place of articulation, as stated in (11c).

    The constraint in (12) restricts the segment combination within the rime. A front segment such as a front vowel or a coronal consonant is specified as [−back] (i.e. front) since the articulations of a front vowel and a coronal consonant both occur in the front part of the vocal tract. On the other hand, a back segment with articulations in the back part of the vocal tract, such as a back vowel or a velar consonant, is specified as [+back]. By the same token, a rounded vowel is [+round] and an unrounded vowel is [−round]. In SC, the segments within the rime share the same plus or minus value for the [back] and/or [round] features (cf. Duanmu 2000: 63–4 for a slightly different version).

(12) The segments in the rime must have the same value for [back]/[round].

    a. [in], [yn], [uŋ], [an], and [ɑŋ] are good.
      *[un], *[iŋ], *[yŋ], and *[aŋ] are bad.
    b. [ei], [ou], [ai], and [ɑu] are good.
      *[eu], *[oi], and *[au] are bad.

The same value for [back] must hold between a vowel and a nasal as shown in (12a). Since SC [a] is classified as a front low vowel (§3.1.2, §3.4.3) and specified as [−back], [an] is a good rime. Both [u] and [ŋ] are [+back], so [uŋ] is a good rime, but [un] is not a good rime because [u] is [+back] but [n] is [−back]. Because of this constraint, a schwa must be present between a

VOCOID (a vowel or a glide; §3.2) and a nasal that are opposite in the value for [back]; e.g. [u] is [+back] and [n] is [−back] and they cannot form a rime, but [wən] is a good syllable and we can say that a schwa is inserted between a [+back] /u/ and a [−back] /n/ (see §8.1.5). In (12b), the same restriction applies to a diphthong, which we mentioned earlier in §§3.4.2–3.4.3. We will discuss in §§7.2.3–7.2.4 and §8.1.5 the processes and rules that are applied to fulfill these constraint requirements.[5]

The next constraint, as given in (13), prohibits two high vocoids that have the same [−back] or [+round] feature value within the syllable.

(13) In a syllable that contains GVV, the high glide and the high vowel in the second part of the diphthong cannot be both [−back] or both [+round].

    a. [wai], [wei], [jou], and [jɑu] are good.

    b. *[jai], *[jei], *[ɥai], and *[ɥai] are bad.

    c. *[wɑu], *[wou], *[ɥɑu], and *[ɥou] are bad.

Examples like those in (13a) are allowed because the pre-nuclear high glide and the high vowel at the end of the syllable differ in [back] and [round]. In contrast, the examples in (13b) have a [−back] glide [j] or [ɥ] and a [−back] vowel [i], and the examples in (13c) have a [+round] glide [w] and a [+round] high vowel [u]. Both sets of examples in (13bc) violate the constraint and are illegitimate sequences in SC.

The constraint in (14a) prohibits a labial consonant, [p], [pʰ], [m], or [f], before a rounded (or [+round]) glide, [w] or [ɥ], unless the main vowel is [o]. Note that both labial consonants and rounded glides make use of the lips for articulation, and hence both types of segments are [labial]. In addition, a labial consonant cannot be directly followed by a mid vowel in a CV syllable, as shown in (14b).

(14) Constraints on labial consonants and vocoids

    a. A labial consonant cannot be followed by a rounded glide [w] or [ɥ] when the main vowel is unrounded.

        e.g.   [pwo], [pʰwo], [mwo], and [fwo] are good.

            *[pwa], *[pʰɥe], *[mwei], and *[fwan] are bad.

    b. A labial consonant cannot be followed by a mid vowel in a CV syllable.

        e.g.   [pwo], [pʰwo], [mwo], and [fwo] are good.

            *[pə], *[mɤ], *[fɤ], and *[pʰo] are bad.

---

[5] There is a complication about (12) regarding the schwa. When in a diphthong, a schwa becomes [e] before [i] as in [ei] and becomes [o] before [u] as in [ou] (§3.4.2). But no such changes are required for a schwa before a nasal coda: [ən] and [əŋ] but not *[en] and *[oŋ]. The issue will be taken up in §7.2.4 and §8.1.5.

Finally, the constraint in (15) prohibits a glide + high vowel sequence to differ in backness. We will see in §11.5.4 that English [ju] and [wi] are changed in loanword adaptation.

(15) Constraint on glide + vowel sequences
A glide cannot be followed directly by a high vowel differing in backness: e.g. [ji] and [wu] are good but *[ju] and *[wi] are bad.

It is more difficult to find generalizations and formulate constraints for other missing syllable types in SC. Before a better analysis can be found, let us treat them as accidental gaps, some examples of which are given in (16a). Theoretically speaking, each possible syllable in SC can have any of the four tones, but some good syllables may not have some of the tones and these gaps are also typically treated as accidental gaps, as in (16b). For example, *le* [lɤ] is a permissible syllable in SC but this syllable is either toneless (neutral-toned), such as *le* in *lái le* 'have come/came', or has a falling tone, such as *lè* 'happy', but there is no morpheme or word in current use that has *[lɤ]$_{35}$.

(16) Some examples of accidental gaps

  a. *[ɥa]   *[ɥɑŋ]   *[ɥəŋ]   *[kwəŋ]   *[tia]   *[nia]   *[tin]   *[tiɑŋ]
     *[lwei]   *[nwɑŋ]
  b. *[lɤ]$_{35}$ *[nje]$_{214}$

Based on the specific constraints in (11–15), we can see that on the one hand there is a preference for some similar types of segments to be next to each other, such as the requirement that some coronal consonants must be followed by segments with the same place of articulation as in (11) and the requirement of the same [back] or [round] within the rime in (12); on the other hand, there is also a preference for some similar types of segments not to co-occur, such as the prohibition against two [−back] or [+round] high vowels/glides within the same syllable in (13) and against two labial sounds in (14a). The former type of constraint is ASSIMILATORY (requiring neighboring sounds to be similar) whereas the latter type of constraint is DISSIMILATORY (requiring different sounds in some specific contexts). We will discuss more on assimilatory and dissimilatory processes in §7.2 and §7.1.2.1–7.1.2.2.

5.4 Summary

This chapter shows how sound segments are organized into syllables in SC.

• The universal principle of the SONORITY SEQUENCING PRINCIPLE prohibits an onset in which a glide is followed by a consonant, e.g. *[wt]

(§5.2.2) and a general PHONOTACTIC CONSTRAINT requires that the second segment in a two-segment onset in SC must be a glide (§5.3).

- The general lack of RESYLLABIFICATION in SC is not a counterexample to the MAXIMAL ONSET PRINCIPLE; rather, we can analyze the so-called zero-intial syllables in SC as having an onset in the syllable structure, thereby blocking the resyllabification process (§§5.2.3–5.2.4).

- The language-specific phonotactic constraints and the systematic and accidental gaps in SC syllable types illustrate that how segments are organized into syllables involves both universal and language-specific constraints. That is why languages are similar with respect to the universal principles of syllabification and yet languages can be quite different in which segment sequences are allowed in a syllable.

- The general phonotactic constraints in SC determine which segment is allowed or disallowed in what contexts and how many segments are allowed in certain positions within the syllable structure (as in (10)). The specific syllable structure constraints require or prohibit similar types of segments in certain parts of the syllable structure (as in (11)–(15)), accounting for the systematic gaps (the missing forms) in SC syllables (§5.3).

Appendix B provides five tables listing all the permissible syllables in SC and the empty cells in the tables are non-existent syllables. In the next chapter, we will compare the *pīnyīn* system and the phonetic transcriptions we have set up for SC segments and syllables.

EXERCISES

1 For each of the following SC morphemes/words, give the phonetic transcription and draw a syllable structure tree like those in (3) in §5.2.1.

Example: *mǎi*   'to buy'   [mai]214

a. *huáng*	'yellow'	b. *ài*	'love'
c. *kuài*	'quick, fast'	d. *ruò*	'weak'
e. *jiǎn*	'to pick up'	f. *shǒu*	'hand'
g. *cí*	'porcelain'	h. *péi*	'to compensate'

2　Which of the following syllables are permissible SC syllables and which are not? Identify the applicable universal and/or language-specific constraints that rule out each non-permissible syllable.

Example: [ta] and [wa] are permissible SC syllables. [wta] is not a possible SC syllable because: (i) it violates the SONORITY SEQUENCING PRINCIPLE since [w] has higher sonority value than [t] causing the onset to be in decreasing rather than increasing SONORITY; and (ii) it also violates the general PHONOTACTIC CONSTRAINT in SC that prohibits two segments in the onset unless the second one is a glide ((10a) in §5.3).

[lɤ]	[wsa]	[jin]	[kje]	[pʰwo]
[plai]	[tswn]	[ɑu]	[rtabl]	[xwan]
[ant]	[xetl]	[tʂɥe]	[ʂɹ̩]	[tɹa]
[tjaj]	[swo]	[wəŋ]	[tjɑu]	[ljou]
[tjəŋ]	[twau]	[njɛn]	[tsʰən]	[sə]
[po]	[teu]	[kaɥ]	[xwei]	[pwou]

6 Phonetic transcription and *pīnyīn*

The IPA phonetic transcription system has a unique one-to-one correspondence between a symbol and a sound to provide phonetic information for pronunciation. As a romanization spelling system, *pīnyīn* has specific spelling conventions and the same letter does not always represent the same sound. For example, the letter *u* can be the vowel [u] as in *lù* [lu]$_{51}$ 'road', the glide [w] as in *huài* [xwai]$_{51}$ 'bad, broken', the vowel [y] as in *qù* [tɕʰy]$_{51}$ 'go', and the glide [ɥ] as in *xué* [ɕɥe]$_{35}$ 'learn, study'.

In this chapter, we compare the IPA phonetic transcriptions with the *pīnyīn* romanization system for SC consonants, vowels, and tones. This comparison, together with specific *pīnyīn* spelling rules, provides practice for the correct pronunciation of *pīnyīn* spelled syllables/words and for the correct *pīnyīn* spelling for SC syllables. In §6.1 we compare the corresponding IPA symbols and *pīnyīn* letters for SC consonants, vowels, and tones, and in §6.2 the *pīnyīn* spelling conventions/rules are discussed. The final section (§6.3) summarizes the main points of the chapter.

6.1 IPA transcription and *pīnyīn* spelling

This section starts with the representations of consonants and vowels in IPA and *pīnyīn* (§6.1.1) and then compares the representations of tones in IPA and *pīnyīn* (§6.1.2). Before we start, please keep in mind that the layout and classification of the *pīnyīn* system basically divide the syllable into the INITIAL and the FINAL as in the traditional analysis of the Chinese syllable. From §5.1, we know that the initial includes only the initial non-glide consonant and the final includes the glide, the main vowel, and the final consonant. For example, in *kuài* 'fast, quick', *k* is the initial and *uai* is the final. However, as discussed in §5.2, we have analyzed the Chinese syllable by dividing it into the ONSET and the RIME, with the onset for the initial consonant and the pre-nuclear glide, and the rime for the main vowel/diphthong and the final consonant: for the word *kuài* [kʰwai]₅₁ 'fast, quick', *ku* [kʰw] is in the onset and *ai* [ai] is in the rime. Therefore, the main difference is grouping the pre-nuclear glide with the rime *ai* in *pīnyīn* but with the initial consonant *k* in our current analysis. With this difference in mind, we will better understand some specific *pīnyīn* spelling conventions later in §6.2.

6.1.1 Consonants and vowels

For consonants, the IPA and *pīnyīn* make use of different symbols but the correspondence between the two systems is quite simple. In (1)–(5), we see the corresponding symbols for consonants in IPA and *pīnyīn*.

(1) Symbols for labials

IPA	p	pʰ	m	f
PĪNYĪN	*b*	*p*	*m*	*f*

(2) Symbols for dental stops and the lateral

IPA	t	tʰ	n	l
PĪNYĪN	*d*	*t*	*n*	*l*

(3) Symbols for velars

IPA	k	kʰ	x	ŋ
PĪNYĪN	*g*	*k*	*h*	*ng*

(4) Symbols for dental affricates/fricative and post-alveolars

IPA	ts	tsʰ	s	tʂ	tʂʰ	ʂ	ɻ
PĪNYĪN	*z*	*c*	*s*	*zh*	*ch*	*sh*	*r*

(5) Symbols for alveolo-palatals

IPA	tɕ	tɕʰ	ɕ
PĪNYĪN	*j*	*q*	*x*

As mentioned in §2.2.1, one important difference is that voiceless unaspirated stops [p, t, k] are represented as *b*, *d*, and *g* respectively in *pīnyīn*. Similarly, voiced symbols such as *z*, *zh*, and *j* are also used in *pīnyīn* for the voiceless unaspirated affricates [ts], [tʂ], and [tɕ] respectively, as shown in (4) and (5). For the aspirated stops and affricates, *pīnyīn* basically makes use of voiceless unaspirated symbols, e.g. *p* for [pʰ] and *c* for [tsʰ]. In (3), The use of *ng* in *pīnyīn* for the velar nasal [ŋ] is the same as in English orthography, and *h* is used for the velar fricative [x]. In (4), we can see that in *pīnyīn* the dental and post-alveolar affricates/fricative are differentiated by adding an *h* for the post-alveolar consonants: e.g. dental *s* versus post-alveolar *sh*. The more unusual symbols *j*, *q*, and *x* are used in *pīnyīn* to indicate the alveolo-palatal consonants, as in (5).

For vowels and glides, the correspondence between the IPA and *pīnyīn* becomes more complicated, as shown in (6).

(6) Symbols for vowels

IPA	i	y	u	e/ə/ɤ	o/wo/u	a/ɑ/ɛ
PĪNYĪN	*i*	*ü/u*	*u*	*e*	*o*	*a*

🎧 (7) Examples for vowels

	PĪNYĪN	IPA	
a.	*lǘ*	[ly]$_{35}$	'donkey'
b.	*qù*	[tɕʰy]$_{51}$	'go'
c.	*běi*	[pei]$_{214}$	'north'
d.	*lěng*	[ləŋ]$_{214}$	'cold'
e.	*gē*	[kɤ]$_{55}$	'song'
f.	*gǒu*	[kou]$_{214}$	'dog'
g.	*fó*	[fwo]$_{35}$	'Buddha'
h.	*tiào*	[tʰjɑu]$_{51}$	'jump'
i.	*lán*	[lan]$_{35}$	'blue'
j.	*huáng*	[xwɑŋ]$_{35}$	'yellow'
k.	*qiān*	[tɕʰjɛn]$_{55}$	'thousand'

For the high vowels, the high front rounded vowel [y] is spelled as *ü* when preceded by *l* or *n* but as *u* when preceded by an alveolo-palatal, as the examples in (7ab) show. For the mid unrounded vowels, the letter *e* is used for all the unrounded mid vowels: the mid front [e], the mid central [ə], and the mid back [ɤ], as in (7c–e). For the mid rounded vowels, the letter *o* is used, as in (7fg). Note that the *pīnyīn o* indicates [wo] only when it is preceded by a labial consonant, as in (7g), and it indicates [u] for the second half of the diphthong [ɑu] (7h) or [u] before a velar nasal (see (12b) below). For the low vowel, the letter *a* is used for all the allophones of the low vowels (cf. §3.4.3), as in (7i–k). In *pīnyīn*, the tonal mark is placed above the main vowel or the more sonorous part of a diphthong, which will be discussed below in §6.1.2.

Recall that the glide before the main vowel is traditionally considered to be a high vowel (§3.4.1), but under our current analysis this high vowel is transcribed as a glide since it is treated as a segment in the onset (§5.2.1). In *pīnyīn*, the vowel letters *i*, *u*, and *ü* are used for glides preceded by a consonant, whereas in syllables without an initial consonant, the letters *y*, *w*, and *yu* are used instead for the pre-nuclear glides, as (8) and (9) show.

(8) Symbols for glides

IPA   j   w   ɥ
PĪNYĪN   i/y   u/w   u/yu/y

(9) Examples for glides

    PĪNYĪN   IPA

a. *xiā*   [ɕja]$_{55}$ 'shrimp'
   yā   [ja]$_{55}$ 'duck'
b. *huài*   [xwai]$_{51}$ 'bad, broken'
   wài   [wai]$_{51}$ 'outside'
c. *xuě*   [ɕɥe]$_{214}$ 'snow'
   yuè   [ɥe]$_{51}$ 'moon, month'
   yú   [ɥy]$_{35}$ 'fish'

Since the mid central RHOTACIZED vowel is unrounded, the letter *e* is also used for it in *pīnyīn*, with *r* indicating rhotacization, as in (10). We also see that the letter *i* is used for the so-called apical vowels, which are transcribed as syllabic consonants under current analysis (§3.4.1).

(10) Symbols for rhotacized and apical vowels

IPA   ɚ   ɻ̩
PĪNYĪN   er   i

We have seen that there can be multiple correspondences between a *pīnyīn* letter and the actual vowel/glide IPA symbol. For example, the letter *i* can be the high front unrounded vowel or glide or an apical vowel. The general correspondences between *pīnyīn* letters and IPA symbols for the vowels and glides are summarized in (11)–(13).

(11) *Pīnyīn* letters *i*, *u*, and *ü* and corresponding IPA phonetic transcriptions

    a. *i* in *pīnyīn*
       = [ɹ̩] when *i* is after dental affricates/fricative *z, c, s.*
          e.g.   *zǐ*   [tsɹ̩]$_{214}$ 'purple'
       = [ɻ̩] when *i* is after post-alveolars *zh, ch, sh.*
          e.g.   *shí*   [ʂɻ̩]$_{35}$ 'ten'
       = [i] when *i* is not preceded by *z, c, s, zh, ch, sh* and is the only vowel in a syllable.
          e.g.   *bǐ*   [pi]$_{214}$ 'pen'
             yī   [ji]$_{55}$ 'one'
             xīn   [ɕin]$_{55}$ 'new'

when *i* is after *a* or *e* in a diphthong.

	e.g.	*bǎi*	[pai]$_{214}$	'hundred'
		hēi	[xei]$_{55}$	'black'

= [j] when *i* is followed by a vowel or *ng* and preceded by a consonant.

	e.g.	*tiē*	[tʰje]$_{55}$	'to paste'
		jiā	[tɕja]$_{55}$	'home, family'
		diàn	[tjɛn]$_{51}$	'store'
		qiú	[tɕʰjou]$_{35}$	'ball'
		tīng	[tjəŋ]$_{55}$	'to listen'[1]

b. *u* in *pīnyīn*

= [u] when *u* is the vowel of an OPEN SYLLABLE (a syllable without a coda) or is preceded by *o* in a diphthong.

	e.g.	*kū*	[kʰu]$_{55}$	'cry'
		wǔ	[wu]$_{214}$	'five'
		shǒu	[ʂou]$_{214}$	'hand'

= [w] when *u* is followed by a vowel or *n* and preceded by a consonant.

	e.g.	*huā*	[xwa]$_{55}$	'flower'
		guì	[kwei]$_{51}$	'expensive'
		cūn	[tsʰwən]$_{55}$	'village'[2]

= [y] when *u* is after alveolo-palatals *j*, *q*, *x* and is the only vowel in the syllable.

	e.g.	*jú*	[tɕy]$_{35}$	'orange'
		qù	[tɕʰy]$_{51}$	'go'
		xún	[ɕyn]$_{35}$	'to search'

= [ɥ] when *u* is after alveolo-palatals *j*, *q*, *x* and followed by a vowel.

	e.g.	*juān*	[tɕɥɛn]$_{55}$	'donate'
		xuě	[ɕɥe]$_{214}$	'snow'

c. *ü* in *pīnyīn*

= [y] when *ü* is the vowel in a CV syllable.

	e.g.	*lǜ*	[ly]$_{51}$	'green'

= [ɥ] when *ü* is followed by *e* and preceded by *n* or *l*.

	e.g.	*nüè*	[nɥe]$_{51}$	'to torture'

---

[1] Note that a schwa is inserted in the phonetic representation because as discussed in §5.3 (see constraint (12)), a [−back] (i.e. front) segment [i] cannot be immediately followed by a [+back] segment like a velar nasal [ŋ]. We will discuss the vowel insertion rule in §8.1.5.

[2] A schwa is inserted because a [+back] segment [u] cannot be immediately followed by a [−back] segment like a alveolar nasal [n] (see (12) in §5.3). The vowel insertion rule will be discussed in §8.1.5.

🎧 (12) *Pīnyīn* letters *e*, *o*, and *a* and corresponding phonetic transcriptions

    a. *e* in *pīnyīn*

      = [e] when *e* is next to *i* or after *ju, qu, xu* (cf. 3.4.2).

e.g.	*lèi*	[lei]$_{51}$	'tired'
	xiě	[ɕje]$_{214}$	'to write'
	xué	[ɕɥe]$_{35}$	'to learn'

      = [ə] when *e* is followed by *n, ng,* or *r* (cf. §3.4.2).

e.g.	*bèn*	[pən]$_{51}$	'stupid'
	lěng	[ləŋ]$_{214}$	'cold'
	èr	[əɹ]$_{51}$	'two'

      = [ɤ] when *e* is the vowel of a CV or V syllable (cf. §3.4.2).

e.g.	*gē*	[kɤ]$_{55}$	'song'

    b. *o* in *pīnyīn*

      = [o] when *o* is next to *u* or *w*.

e.g.	*gǒu*	[kou]$_{214}$	'dog'
	huǒ	[xwo]$_{214}$	'fire'
	wǒ	[wo]$_{214}$	'I'

      = [wo] when *o* is preceded by labial consonants *b, p, m, f*.

e.g.	*bō*	[pwo]$_{55}$	'wave'
	fó	[fwo]$_{35}$	'Buddha'

      = [u] when *o* is after *a* in a diphthong.

e.g.	*gāo*	[kɑu]$_{55}$	'high, tall'
	tiào	[tʰjɑu]$_{51}$	'jump'

      when *o* is before *ng*.

e.g.	*dōng*	[tuŋ]$_{55}$	'east'
	qióng	[tɕʰiuŋ]$_{35}$	'poor'

    c. *a* in *pīnyīn*

      = [a] when *a* is at the end of a syllable or before *n, i*.

e.g.	*dà*	[ta]$_{51}$	'big'
	huà	[xwa]$_{51}$	'to draw, to paint'
	gān	[kan]$_{55}$	'dry'
	hǎi	[xai]$_{214}$	'ocean, sea'

      = [ɑ] when *a* is before *ng* or *o* (cf. §3.4.3).

e.g.	*làng*	[lɑŋ]$_{51}$	'wave'
	lǎo	[lɑu]$_{214}$	'old'

      = [ɛ] when *a* is after *i, ju, qu, xu* and before *n* (cf. §3.4.3).

e.g.	*liǎn*	[ljɛn]$_{214}$	'face'
	xuǎn	[ɕɥɛn]$_{214}$	'choose'

🎧 (13) *Pīnyīn* letters *y, w, yu* and corresponding phonetic transcriptions

    a. *y* in *pīnyīn*

      = [j]   when *y* is in syllable initial position not followed by *u*.

          e.g.   *yā*   [ja]$_{55}$ 'duck'

               yóu   [jou]$_{35}$ 'oil'

      = [ɥ]   when *y* is in syllable initial position followed by *u*.

          e.g.   *yú*   [ɥy]$_{35}$ 'fish'

               yún   [ɥyn]$_{35}$ 'cloud'

    b. *w* in *pīnyīn*

      = [w]   when *w* is in syllable initial position.

          e.g.   *wàn*   [wan]$_{51}$ 'ten thousand'

    c. *yu* in *pīnyīn*

      = [ɥ]   when *yu* is in syllable initial position followed by *e* or *an*.

          e.g.   *yuè*   [ɥe]$_{51}$ 'moon'

               yuǎn   [ɥɛn]$_{214}$ 'far'

      = [ɥy] when *yu* is a stand-alone syllable or followed by *n*.

          e.g.   *yú*   [ɥy]$_{35}$ 'fish'

               yún   [ɥyn]$_{35}$ 'cloud'

6.1.2 Tone

As discussed in §4.1.4, PITCH VALUE is used for the transcription of SC tones but the *pīnyīn* system places a diacritic mark above the main vowel of a syllable. Using the syllable *ma* as an example, (14) illustrates the tonal pitch values we use for phonetic transcription and the corresponding diacritic marks in *pīnyīn*. Recall from §4.2.2 that there are various phonetic realizations of the NEUTRAL TONE (T0) depending on the preceding tone, but in *pīnyīn* a neutral-toned syllable is without any tonal diacritic mark.

(14) TONE NUMBER   PITCH VALUE   *PĪNYĪN*

    T1   [ma]55   *mā*

    T2   [ma]35   *má*

    T3   [ma]214   *mǎ*

    T4   [ma]51   *mà*

    T0   [ma]2 or [ma]3   *ma*

                     or [ma]4 or [ma]1

What happens to the tonal diacritic mark when TONE SANDHI (§4.2.3) applies? In *pīnyīn*, the tonal change of tone 3 sandhi is not indicated. When two consecutive syllables have T3 in *pīnyīn*, then usually tone 3 sandhi applies to change the first T3 syllable to T2 (§4.2.3). (I use 'usually' here because it is not always the case that a T3 before another T3 in a sentence must be changed to T2, as we will see in §9.4.) As the example in (15) shows, in both syllables of the word the T3 diacritic mark is used, but in pronunciation the first syllable has T2, as indicated by the phonetic transcription.

(15) Tone 3 Sandhi

PĪNYĪN   PHONETIC TRANSCRIPTION
xiǎojiě   [ɕjɑu]35 [tɕje]214   'miss, lady'

On the other hand, the tonal change for a specific word such as *yī* 'one' and *bù* 'not' discussed in §4.2.3 is indicated in *pīnyīn*. The T1 diacritic mark for *yī* 'one' is changed to T4 when it is before T1, T2, and T3 and to T2 before T4, and the T4 tonal diacritic for *bù* 'not' is changed to T2 before T4. Some examples are given in (16). (Note that T4 is 53 when it is not in word or phrase final position (§4.2.1).)

(16) Tonal changes for *yī* 'one' and *bù* 'not'

PĪNYĪN   PHONETIC TRANSCRIPTION
yī   'one'   [ji]55
yìnián   'one year'   [ji]53 [njɛn]35
yíyàng   'the same'   [ji]35 [jɑŋ]51
bù   'not'   [pu]51
bú kuài   'not fast'   [pu]35 [kʰwai]51

   The next question is: when there is more than one vowel letter in *pīnyīn*, where should the tonal diacritic be placed? This is not a problem at all for our phonetic transcription because the tonal value is indicated for the whole syllable to the right side of the syllable. Now our knowledge of SC syllable structure comes in handy. The rule is simple: place the tonal diacritic on the most sonorous nuclear vowel. That is, when there is a glide followed by a vowel, the vowel receives the tonal diacritic, and when there are two vowel letters for a diphthong, the tonal diacritic is placed on the more sonorous vowel of the diphthong, i.e. the low or mid vowel (§3.3 and §3.4.4). Consider the examples in (17). In (17a), the vowel letters in each example consist of a combination of a glide plus a vowel as shown in the phonetic transcription, so the tonal diacritic goes to the nuclear vowel. In (17b) we have examples containing diphthongs, and the tonal diacritic is placed on the low or mid vowel of the diphthong. In (17c), there is also a diphthong in each example but a *pīnyīn* spelling rule removes the more sonorous mid vowel (see §6.2 below). Of the two high vowel letters left in *pīnyīn*, the first one is a glide in the onset and the second one is the second half of the diphthong under the nuclear node of the syllable (see §5.2.1); the tonal diacritic mark is therefore placed on the second high vowel letter.

(17) Location of tonal mark in *pīnyīn*

    a. *xiā*   [ɕja]55   'shrimp'
        guān   [kwan]55   'close, shut down'
        tiě   [tʰje]214   'steel'
        guō   [kwo]55   'wok'
        yuè   [ɥe]51   'moon, month'
    b. *ài*   [ai]51   'love'
        huài   [xwai]51   'bad'
        hǎo   [xɑu]214   'good'
        niǎo   [njɑu]214   'bird'
        fēi   [fei]55   'to fly'
        shóu   [ʂou]35   'ripe, cooked'
    c. *liù*   [ljou]51   'six'
        duì   [twei]51   'right, correct'

6.2 *Pīnyīn* spelling conventions

In this section, we go over a few special spelling conventions/rules in *pīnyīn*. These conventions can mostly be understood with our knowledge of the syllable structure and phonotactic constraints (§§5.2–5.3), phonological/phonetic rules, and the predictability of a particular sound in certain contexts (chapters 5, 7, and 8).

The first group of general conventions is related to the predictability of particular sounds in some contexts and phonological/phonetic rule application. The first convention concerns the high front rounded vowel [y] or glide [ɥ], which is represented as *ü* in *pīnyīn*. This symbol with two dots above a *u* is used to transcribe the high front rounded vowel in the phonetic transcription tradition in North America (see Appendix A) and in the orthography in languages such as German and French. In *pīnyīn*, the letter *ü* is spelled *u* when preceded by consonants other than *n* and *l*, as the examples in (18) show.

(18) Spelling Convention 1

    a. When *ü* is preceded by alveolo-palatals *j* [tɕ], *q* [tɕʰ], or *x* [ɕ], the two dots are removed and *u* is used.

    b.

use *ü* when preceded by *n, l*			use *u* when preceded by *j, q, x*		
nǚ	[ny]214	'female'	*juǎn*	[tɕɥen]214	'to roll'
lǘ	[ly]35	'donkey'	*qù*	[tɕʰy]51	'to go'
nüè	[nɥe]51	'to torture'	*xué*	[ɕɥe]35	'to study'

Recall that the alveolo-palatals *j* [tɕ], *q* [tɕʰ], and *x* [ɕ] can be followed only by the high front vowels/glides *i* [i]/[j] and *ü* [y]/[ɥ] (§2.2.5 and §5.3). The letter *u* can be used after the alveolo-palatals because it can only be the front rounded vowel/glide [y]/[ɥ] and never the back rounded vowel/glide [u]/[w]. In contrast, both the front rounded vowel/glide *ü* [y]/[ɥ] and the back rounded vowel *u* [u]/[w] can appear after *n* and *l*; for example, compare *lù* [lu]₅₁ 'road' and *nù* [nu]₅₁ 'angry' with the examples in (18b). It is therefore necessary to use the letter *ü* after *n* and *l* to distinguish it from the *u* after *n* and *l*.

The second convention removes the glide *u* [w] in *uo* [wo] after labial consonants, as in (19). We have learned that the vowel sound [o] only occurs next to [u] or [w] (§3.4.2), and it is also predictable that a letter *o* preceded by a labial consonant is pronounced as [wo]; therefore, this simplification of spelling would not cause confusion with other syllables. In addition, for some SC speakers, the pronunciation of [w] after the labial consonants is relatively weak and short, making the syllable sound closer to [o].

(19) Spelling Convention 2

 a. When *uo* [wo] is preceded by *b* [p], *p* [pʰ], *m* [m], or *f* [f], the letter *o* is used.

 b. preceded by labials   preceded by non-labials

bō	[p**wo**]₅₅	'to peel'	*duō*	[t**wo**]₅₅	'many'
pò	[pʰ**wo**]₅₁	'broken'	*guǒ*	[k**wo**]₂₁₄	'fruit'
mó	[m**wo**]₃₅	'to grind'	*zuò*	[ts**wo**]₅₁	'to sit'
fó	[f**wo**]₃₅	'Buddha'	*shuō*	[ʂ**wo**]₅₅	'to say'

The third convention deletes [e] and [o] in some contexts, as the examples in (20) show. Note that *i* and *u* have been changed to *y* and *w* in syllable initial position, which is to be discussed below.

(20) Spelling Convention 3

 a. Delete *e* [e]/[ə] and *o* [o] in the following sequences *uei* [wei], *iou* [jou], and *uen* [wən] when these sequences are preceded by a consonant.

 b. preceded by a consonant   syllable initial position

guǐ	[kwei]₂₁₄	'ghost'	*wěi*	[wei]₂₁₄	'tail'
qiū	[tɕjou]₅₅	'autumn'	*yóu*	[jou]₃₅	'oil'
chūn	[tʂʰwən]₅₅	'spring'	*wèn*	[wən]₅₁	'to ask'

Recall from §3.4.2 that the mid vowel [e] and [o] may have phonetic variation and may be pronounced more like a schwa [ə] by some speakers. A schwa is a vowel that tends to become rather weak in certain contexts, e.g. when it is in a more complex syllable. We can see that these three sequences in (20) all have a pre-nuclear glide, a mid vowel as the main vowel, and the rime is long because it either has a diphthong [ei]/[ou] or a schwa vowel followed by a consonant [ən]. When these sequences are preceded by a consonant, the whole syllable has four positions or segments in the syllable structure: CGVV or CGVC (cf. §5.2.1). When more segments fit into a syllable, the syllable is more crowded and each segment is often somewhat shortened. When a mid vowel is shortened, it is closer to a schwa and may become weak and short in articulation and perception. (We will have more discussion on this in §7.3.2.) This spelling convention not only simplifies the spelling but also reflects the often weaker pronunciation of the mid vowel in these particular contexts. In contrast, a low vowel is phonetically longer and more sonorous than mid and high vowels, so even when it is shortened in a more complex syllable, it is still perceived better than a shortened mid vowel. Unlike *e* and *o*, *a* is not removed from the spelling in a complex syllable, e.g. *kuān* [kʰwan]$_{55}$ 'wide', *biǎo* [pjɑu]$_{214}$ 'watch', and *kuài* [kʰwai]$_{51}$ 'fast'.

The next set of general conventions is related to syllable structure. The convention in (21) is related to zero-initial syllables that begin with a high vowel. In §5.2.4, a zero-initial syllable is analyzed as having an onset position in the syllable structure. If the syllable begins with a high nuclear vowel, then a glide of the same phonetic properties with the high vowel is added in the onset position, e.g. [i] becomes [ji], [u] becomes [wu], and [y] becomes [ɥy]. In *pīnyīn*, a letter indicating an onset glide to a syllable is added when the high vowel is the only vowel letter in the *pīnyīn* syllable and it is in syllable initial position. As you can see from the examples in (21), the glide addition in *pīnyīn* is in the same spirit as our syllable structure analysis of zero-initial syllables by requiring an onset of the syllable. See §8.1.3 for more discussion.

(21) Spelling Convention 4 (The arrow → means 'become' or 'change to')

    a. (i)   Add *y* before a syllable starting with [i], for which [i] is the only vowel in the syllable.

      (ii) Add *w* before a syllable starting with [u], for which [u] is the only vowel in the syllable.

      (iii) Add *y* in a syllable starting with [y], for which [y] is the only vowel in the syllable (and spell the vowel as *u*, cf. (18)).

    b. Examples:

      yī   [ji]$_{55}$ 'one'   [i] zero-initial → [ji]

      yín [jin]$_{35}$ 'silver' [in] zero-initial → [jin]

      yíng [jəŋ]$_{35}$ 'to win' [iŋ] zero-initial → [jiŋ] → [jəŋ] (see §8.1.5)

> *wǔ*   [wu]₂₁₄ 'five'   [u] zero-initial → [wu]
>
> *yú*   [ɥy]₃₅ 'fish'   [y] zero-initial → [ɥy]
>
> *yún*   [ɥyn]₃₅ 'cloud'   [yn] zero-initial → [ɥyn]

A similar and related convention given in (22) changes a high vowel letter to indicate a glide when it is not preceded by an initial consonant. See §8.1.1 for more discussion.

(22) Spelling Convention 5 (The arrow → means 'become' or 'change to')

   a.   When a glide is in syllable initial position

i	[j]	→	*y*
u	[w]	→	*w*
ü/u	[ɥ]	→	*yu*

   b.   preceded by initial consonant   in syllable initial position

   (i)   *xiā*   [ɕja]₅₅ 'shrimp'   *yā*   [ja]₅₅ 'duck'

       qiáo   [tɕʰjɑu]₃₅ 'bridge'   *yāo*   [jɑu]₅₅ 'waist'

       nián   [njɛn]₃₅ 'year'   *yán*   [jɛn]₃₅ 'salt'

       qiáng   [tɕʰjɑŋ]₃₅ 'strong'   *yáng*   [jɑŋ]₃₅ 'sheep'

       jiē   [tɕje]₅₅ 'street'   *yě*   [je]₂₁₄ 'also'

   (ii)   *huā*   [xwa]₅₅ 'flower'   *wà*   [wa]₅₁ 'socks'

       duǒ   [two]₂₁₄ 'hide'   *wǒ*   [wo]₂₁₄ 'I'

       kuài   [kʰwai]₅₁ 'fast'   *wài*   [wai]₅₁ 'outside'

       duǎn   [twan]₂₁₄ 'short'   *wǎn*   [wan]₂₁₄ 'bowl'

       chuáng   [tʂʰwɑŋ]₃₅ 'bed'   *wáng*   [wɑŋ]₃₅ 'king'

   (iii)   *nüè*   [nɥe]₅₁ 'to torture'   *yuè*   [ɥe]₅₁ 'moon'

       juǎn   [tɕɥen]₂₁₄ 'to roll'   *yuán*   [ɥen]₃₅ 'round'

You can see in the phonetic transcriptions that we have treated the pre-nuclear high VOCOID as a glide (§3.4.1 and §5.2.1) in both types of syllables, but in *pīnyīn* the letters representing glides are used only in syllables without an initial consonant.

Spelling rules in an orthographical or romanization system can be arbitrary, but in this section we have seen that the special spelling conventions in *pīnyīn* are easier to understand and memorize when we have knowledge of the phonetics and phonology of SC sounds and syllable structure.

6.3 Summary

This chapter compares the similarities and differences between the *pīnyīn* romanization system and the IPA phonetic transcription system.

- The correspondences between the *pīnyīn* letters and the IPA phonetic symbols for consonants are simple, and it is basically a matter of using different symbols in two different systems for the same sound (§6.1.1).
- However, for the vowels, the correspondences between the phonetic transcriptions and the *pīnyīn* letters are more complicated, mostly because of the different treatment of the pre-nuclear high VOCOID as vowel versus glide (§6.1.1) and the special spelling conventions discussed in §6.2.
- Our phonetic transcriptions of SC tones adopt a different system from the one used in *pīnyīn* (cf. 4.1.4). In general, the correspondence between the two tonal representational systems is quite straightforward although some minor adjustments are needed under TONE SANDHI (§6.1.2).
- The discussion of the spelling conventions of *pīnyīn* (§6.2) not only provides a practical guide to the special spelling rules but also demonstrates that if we utilize what we know about the phonetics and phonology of SC sounds and syllable structure, these spelling conventions become less arbitrary than they at first appear.

A complete list of all SC syllables in *pīnyīn* spelling and corresponding phonetic transcription is given in Appendix B.

EXERCISES

1   For each *pīnyīn*-spelled example below, provide the corresponding phonetic transcription.

	Example:	*báiyù* 'white jade'	[pai]35 [ɥy]51
a.	*huīcè*	'grey color'	
b.	*qiāomén*	'to knock at the door'	
c.	*qúnzi*	'skirt'	
d.	*tōngxùn*	'correspondence, communication'	
e.	*jiànshì*	'knowledge and experience'	
f.	*ruǎnruò*	'weak, feeble'	
g.	*yánzhòng*	'serious'	
h.	*yuánliàng*	'to forgive'	
i.	*chūnqiū*	'spring and autumn'	
j.	*nǚér*	'daughter'	
k.	*wénpíng*	'diploma'	
l.	*jièmò*	'mustard'	

2 For each phonetic transcription below, provide the corresponding *pīnyīn* spelling.

    Example: [pai]35 [ɥy]51 'white jade'   *báiyù*

a. [ɕjuŋ]35 [mɑu]55   'panda'

b. [jən]55 [wu]214   'parrot'

c. [ɕy]55 [tɕʰjou]35   'demand, needs'

d. [ʂwei]21 [pwo]55   'water wave'

e. [njən]35 [ɥɛn]51   'would rather'

f. [ʂɻ]55 [tsʰɻ]35   'poetry'

g. [tʂwən]21 [tɕʰɥe]51   'accurate, precise'

h. [ly]21 [kʰɤ]51   'traveler, passenger'

i. [tʂʰən]35 [ɹən]51   'to admit, to confess'

j. [xuŋ]35 [je]51   'red leaf'

3 Collect five examples for each of the five spelling conventions discussed in §6.2, and for each example provide both *pīnyīn* and phonetic transcriptions.

4 Collect at least twenty SC words you learned in class or you read in Chinese newspapers or magazines (see Appendix C), and provide both *pīnyīn* and phonetic transcriptions for each word.

7 Segmental processes I

A segment or tone may change its phonetic properties in a particular context to achieve ease of articulation or ease of perception to facilitate communication, which we mentioned throughout chapters 2–4 when introducing the articulation of each sound and tone. A SEGMENTAL PROCESS is such a change in context that applies to consonants and vowels, and a TONAL PROCESS is such a change in context that applies to tone. In this chapter and the next, we examine the segmental processes in SC. We will then discuss in more detail how a tone may change in different contexts (chapter 9) or in interaction with other SUPRASEGMENTAL PROPERTIES (§4.1.3) such as STRESS and INTONATION (chapter 10).

An example of a segmental process in English is that any vowel before a nasal coda consonant is nasalized (§3.1.5); for example, the vowel in *pan* /pæn/ is actually nasalized and is pronounced with a nasal vowel as [pʰæ̃n] whereas the vowel in *pad*/pæd/ remains as an oral vowel [pʰæd]. This process of changing an oral vowel phoneme to a phonetically nasalized vowel before a nasal consonant is called VOWEL NASALIZATION.

Since the pronunciation of a sound may change depending on different linguistic contexts, mastering the pronunciation of the sounds of a language without an obvious foreign accent involves not only the correct pronunciation of each individual isolated sound but also the ability to change the pronunciation of a sound in an appropriate context. For example, in English the voiceless stops /p/, /t/, and /k/ are produced with ASPIRATION as [pʰ], [tʰ], and [kʰ] respectively in syllable initial position, e.g. *pat* [pʰæt], *tap* [tʰæp], and *cat* [kʰæt], but they are unaspirated [p], [t], and [k] respectively after [s], e.g. *spot* [spɑt], *stop* [stɑp], and *Scott* [skɑt] (§2.2.1). If you hear the pronunciation of *stop* as [stʰɑp] with an aspirated alveolar stop, you may consider this pronunciation to be with a foreign accent or simply feel that it does not sound quite right. Because each language employs a different set of processes, it is important to learn when and how a sound changes its phonetic properties in a language, in addition to learning the basic pronunciation of each individual sound of the language.

The contextual factors that induce the change of a sound include: (i) adjacent segments or segments within the same syllable or word; (ii) PROSODIC factors such as syllable structure, tone, and stress; and (iii) morphological processes (word formation processes), such as plural noun formation and various types of SUFFIXATION, and sentence structure. A segmental process can be affected by more than one type of these factors.

This chapter introduces basic phonological concepts and discusses the types of segmental processes in SC that are influenced mainly by adjacent segments or tone. In the next chapter, we continue with the discussion of SC segmental processes that are induced mainly by syllable structure and *r*-suffixation (§3.4.5). In §7.1, we study phonological features, NATURAL CLASSES of sounds, PHONOLOGICAL PROCESSES, RULES and CONSTRAINTS, and the distinction between phonological and phonetic processes, and in §7.2 and §7.3, ASSIMILATION, WEAKENING, and REDUCTION processes in SC are discussed. Practical advice for the pronunciation of SC segments in context is provided whenever appropriate. The final section (§7.4) summarizes the main points of the chapter.

7.1 Basic concepts

This section introduces the basic phonological concepts in preparation for the discussion in §7.2. After introducing the notations for phonological features and how sounds can be classified according to these features (§7.1.1), we study what phonological processes and rules are (§7.1.2), how rules and constraints interact (§7.1.3), and how phonological rules differ from phonetic rules (§7.1.4).

7.1.1 Phonological features and natural classes of sounds

In chapters 2 and 3, we learned that each consonant or vowel consists of a set of properties that can be used to classify sounds, such as various places of articulation, various manners of articulation, high, mid, low, etc. Let us call each of these PHONETIC PROPERTIES a PHONETIC FEATURE.

Not all phonetic features are relevant to the phonology of a language. For example, the feature dental versus the feature alveolar is not DISTINCTIVE (or CONTRASTIVE) for SC, which means that replacing a dental articulation with an alveolar one or vice versa does not change the meaning of a word; that is, whether you pronounce SC /n/ with a dental or alveolar place of articulation, the word *nǐ* [ni] 'you' would mean the same. (Recall from §2.2.1 and 2.2.3 that for some speakers, the dental consonants may be articulated at the alveolar ridge.) In contrast, dental/alveolar on the one hand and post-alveolar on the other are distinctive in SC because, for example, replacing a dental unaspirated affricate [ts] with a post-alveolar unaspirated affricate [tʂ] would change the meaning of a word: *zǎo* [tsau]₂₁₄ 'early' and *zhǎo* [tʂau]₂₁₄ 'to look for' are almost the same in pronunciation except that the former has the dental place of articulation and the latter has post-alveolar articulation and the two words have different meanings. In English, the alveolar feature and the post-alveolar feature are also distinctive: *see* [siː] versus *she* [ʃiː].

We already know that a PHONEME is an abstract distinctive or contrastive segment that can differentiate word meaning in a language; e.g. we know that /ts/ and /tʂ/ are separate phonemes in SC, and /s/ and /ʃ/ are separate phonemes in English, based on the fact that there are MINIMAL PAIRS contrasting each pair of sounds (cf. §1.5.2 and §2.2). A DISTINCTIVE FEATURE is a PHONOLOGICAL FEATURE that is relevant to the phonology of a language or can be used in a language contrastively to differentiate one phoneme from another and hence the meaning of one word from another. A universal set of distinctive features consists of a limited number of features that can be used distinctively in human language.

Take English /b/ versus /p/ as an example. The two bilabial stops are identical in all features except one: /b/ is voiced and /p/ is voiceless. Since /b/ and /p/ are separate phonemes in English (§1.5.2 & §2.2.1), the feature [voice], with the square brackets indicating a phonological feature, is distinctive (or phonemic or contrastive) in English and should be included in the universal set of distinctive features. A binary plus and minus notation is used for each phonological feature to indicate the presence or absence of such a feature: [+voice] for /b/ and [−voice] for /p/ (cf. [+back] and [−back] mentioned in §5.3). Consider now the feature [aspirated] and let us take [p] and [pʰ] as an example. As discussed in §2.2.1, [p] and [pʰ] are allophones of the same phoneme /p/ in English because there are no minimal pairs contrasting these two sounds, and [p] appears after [s] and [pʰ] appears in syllable initial position; i.e. replacing one with the other does not change the meaning of a word. In contrast, /p/ and /pʰ/ are separate phonemes in SC, given a minimal pair like *bà* [pa] 'father' and *pà* [pʰa] 'fear'. The only difference between [p] and [pʰ] is a matter of aspiration: [p] is [−aspirated] and [pʰ] is [+aspirated]. Both English and SC have aspirated and unaspirated stops but the feature [aspirated] is non-distinctive in English and distinctive in SC.

The set of phonetic features denotes more detailed phonetic properties whereas the set of phonological features or distinctive features contains only those that are relevant to phonology and can be used distinctively in language. In what follows, I use the terms phonetic features and phonetic properties interchangeably and the term phonological features rather than distinctive features. In (1)–(3), we see the phonological features used by consonants, together with the corresponding phonetic properties discussed in chapters 2 and 3. This is not an exhaustive list of consonant features but it includes those features relevant to our discussion in this and subsequent chapters. The features in (1) denote articulation involving the vocal folds and glottis in the larynx with a simple binary system; e.g. a voiced sound is [+voice] and a voiceless sound is [−voice]. The features in (2) and (3) require some more discussion and explanation.

(1) Laryngeal Features

PHONOLOGICAL FEATURES	PHONETIC PROPERTIES	EXAMPLES
[+voice]/[−voice]	voiced/voiceless	[b]/[p]
[+aspirated]/[−aspirated]	aspirated/unaspirated	[pʰ]/[p]

(2) Place Features

PHONOLOGICAL FEATURES	PHONETIC PROPERTIES	EXAMPLES
Labial	labial	[p] [m] [f]
Coronal: [+anterior]	dental/alveolar	[t] [n] [ts]
Coronal: [−anterior]	post-alveolar	[tʂ] [ʃ]
Coronal: [−anterior] & [−back, +high]	alveolo-palatal	[tɕ] [tɕʰ] [ç]
Dorsal	velar	[k] [x]

For the place features in (2), note first that the three major place features, Labial, Coronal, and Dorsal (§2.1.3), are written with an initial capital letter without square brackets and no plus and minus notations are used for them. Without getting into the theoretical reasons why place features employ a different notation, we just need to keep in mind that each consonant has at least one major place feature. For example, a plain labial sound like [m] has only one place feature, Labial, and has no Coronal or Dorsal feature. Second, in §2.1.3, we learned that there are different types of coronal consonants, and in (2) here we see that the feature [anterior] is used to further divide the coronal consonants. Those coronal sounds articulated on or in front of the alveolar ridge, such as dentals and alveolars, are classified as the anterior part of the coronal articulation and specified as [+anterior]. Those coronal sounds articulated behind the alveolar ridge, such as post-alveolars, have the [−anterior] feature specification. Third, recall from §2.2.5 that the alveolo-palatals in SC are PALATALIZED post-alveolars: these are complex consonants involving both the tongue blade and the front part of the tongue, because in addition to the post-alveolar articulation, the front part of the tongue is also simultaneously raised toward the hard palate, similar to the articulation of [i] or [j]. Since [i] and [j] are high front vowel/glide and hence [−back, +high] (mentioned in §5.3 and discussed below in (5) and §7.2.1), the vowel-like features [−back, +high] are added.

The features [consonantal], [sonorant], and [continuant] in (3), also called the major class features, cross-classify different types of segments in terms of the manner of articulation. The feature [consonantal] divides all segments into VOCOIDS (vowels and glides), which are [−consonantal], and non-vocoids (true consonants), which are [+consonantal].[1] The feature [sonorant] divides all consonants into two groups: [−sonorant] stops, affricates, and fricatives that have complete or stronger obstruction of the airflow and [+sonorant] nasals and approximants that allow air to flow out of the vocal tract with less or little obstruction. The feature [continuant] divides all segments into two groups along a different dimension: [−continuant] oral and nasal stops that have complete obstruction of the airflow within the oral tract and [+continuant] fricatives and approximants that allow air to escape through the oral tract.

(3) Major class and manner features

PHONOLOGICAL FEATURES	PHONETIC PROPERTIES	EXAMPLES
[+consonantal]	consonants	[t] [s] [n] [l]
[−consonantal]	glides and vowels	[j] [w] [i] [u]
[+sonorant]	nasal, approximant	[m] [l]
[−sonorant]	stop, fricative, affricate	[t] [s] [ts]
[+continuant]	fricative and approximant	[ʂ] [f] [l] [ɹ]
[−continuant]	oral stop and nasal stop	[p] [n]
[+nasal]	nasal	[n] [m]
[−nasal]	oral	[d] [b]
[+lateral]	lateral	[l]
[−lateral]	central or non-lateral	[ɹ] [t] [f]

Affricates start like a [−continuant] stop and release like a [+continuant] fricative (see §2.1.4.3). As shown in (4), we can use two features to clearly distinguish stops, nasals, fricatives, affricates, and approximants. We can also group stops, fricatives, and affricates together as OBSTRUENTS (§2.1.6) that

---

[1] In some languages, a glide can be classified as [+consonantal] under certain analyses. In SC, since a glide is simply a high vowel in a non-nuclear position in the syllable (§3.2, §3.4.1), it is analyzed as [−consonantal].

are specified as [−sonorant], and then group nasals and approximants together as SONORANTS (§2.1.6) that are [+sononrant].

(4) Stops   =   [−sonorant]   [−continuant]

    Nasals   =   [+sonorant]   [−continuant]

    Fricatives   =   [−sonorant]   [+continuant]

    Approximants =   [+sonorant]   [+continuant]

    Affricates   =   [−sonorant]   [−continuant] [+continuant]

Aside from being [−consonantal], a vowel/glide has the relevant vowel features as given in (5). Following the binary plus and minus feature system, the three-way high–mid–low and front–central–back vowel properties are classified with three features: [high], [low], and [back]. In SC, since the glides are variants of high vowels in non-nuclear position in the syllables, the glides also bear the vowel features. The central vowels have traditionally be given the feature [+back], but in some analyses a central vowel has no [back] feature specification. For example, a central low vowel can be [+low, +back] or simply [+low], and a schwa can be [−high, −low, +back] or simply [−high, −low]. As we will see below (§7.2.4, §8.1.5), we will treat the central mid vowel as having no [back] specification. In other words, a front vowel is [−back], a back vowel is [+back], and a central vowel is unspecified for backness, i.e. neither [+back] nor [−back]. The features [−high] and [+low] are not the same: [+low] is specified for low vowels only but [−high] is for both mid and low vowels. By the same token, [−low] and [+high] are not the same: [+high] is used for high vowels only but both high and mid vowels are [−low]. A mid vowel is therefore specified as [−high, −low].

(5) Vowel features

PHONOLOGICAL FEATURES	PHONETIC PROPERTIES	EXAMPLES
[+high]	high vowels	[i] [y] [u]
[+low]	low vowels	[a] [æ] [ɑ]
[−high] [−low]	mid vowels	[e] [o] [ə]
[−back] (Coronal)	front vowels	[i] [y] [e]
[+back] (Dorsal)	back	[u] [o] [ɑ]
[+round] (Labial)	rounded vowels	[u] [o] [y]
[−round]	unrounded vowels	[a] [i] [e]

In general, a rounded vowel/glide is also considered to have a Labial feature because rounding involves the lips. Therefore, [u] and [w] are specified as [Labial, +round], and [p] and [b] are simply [Labial]. In addition, since vowel articulation involves the body of the tongue, vowels are also widely considered to be Dorsal segments. In some feature theories (e.g. Clements and Hume 1995), [−back] vowels are given the feature Coronal and [+back] vowels the feature Dorsal. For our purposes, we make use of the basic vowel features in (5) but will use Labial, Coronal, and Dorsal when necessary for explanation.

Some features are used by both consonants and vowels. The feature [+nasal] is also used for a nasal vowel, and all vowels are [+voice] except in some limited contexts in some languages. Consonants that have a SECONDARY ARTICULATION (§2.2.5), a vowel-like articulation superimposed on the primary consonant articulation, are specified with a vowel feature such as [−back] or [+round]. For example, as mentioned above and in §2.2.5, alveolo-palatals in SC are palatalized post-alveoalrs, having [−back, +high] features in addition to the primary post-alveolar articulation. A LABIALIZED stop like [kʷ] in Cantonese, which has a [u]/[w]-like secondary articulation with lip rounding that is superimposed on the primary velar articulation, has a [+round] feature in addition to the primary Dorsal feature. A consonant articulated in the front part of the vocal tract (e.g. alveolars) can sometimes be analyzed as being [−back] and a consonant articulated in the back part of the vocal tract (e.g. velars) can be specified as [+back]. We have seen in §5.3 and will see later in §§7.2.3–7.2.4 that in SC the alveolar [n] is treated as [−back] and the velar [ŋ] as [+back].

With the phonological features in place, the notion of NATURAL CLASSES of sounds can now be introduced. A natural class of sounds is a group of sounds that share a set of phonological features and behave as a group with respect to some PHONOLOGICAL PROCESSES or CONSTRAINTS. For example, all vowels in English, SC, and most languages become nasalized vowels, i.e. become [+nasal], next to a nasal consonant; voiceless stops in English become [+aspirated] in syllable initial position; and alveolo-palatals in SC can appear only before a high front vowel/glide (§2.2.5 and §5.3). We can then state that vowels form a natural class of sound that bears the feature [−consonantal], that the voiceless stops form a natural class of sound that can be defined with the features [+consonantal, −voice, −sonorant, −continuant], that alveolo-palatals form a natural class of sounds defined as [Coronal, −anterior, −back, +high], and that high front vowels/glides form a natural class of sounds bearing the features [−consonantal, +high, −back].[2]

---

[2] Technically the set of features that define a natural class of sounds must include all segments in the class and exclude all other segments. For example, for the natural class of voiced oral stops, a featural definition like [+consonant, +voice, −continuant] does include all three voiced stops but fails to exclude nasal stops, which also have all these three features. To exclude nasals, which are [+sonorant], the natural class of voiced oral stops should be defined as [+consonantal, +voice, −continuant, −sonorant,].

The concept of natural classes is useful in generalizing phonological processes/rules and constraints. For example, instead of stating the English aspiration process with three separate rules: [p] becomes [pʰ] syllable initially, [t] becomes [tʰ] syllable initially, and [k] becomes [kʰ] syllable initially, we can simply consolidate these three rules into one: voiceless stops become aspirated syllable initially. This is not only economical but also provides much better insights into the sound system of a language. As we will see in §7.1.2.4, §7.2, and chapter 8, phonological rules tend to refer to natural classes of sounds.

In the next subsection, we turn to the topic of what phonological processes and phonological rules are.

7.1.2 Phonological processes and rules

A PHONOLOGICAL PROCESS generally refers to a general process that is commonly adopted across languages and a PHONOLOGICAL RULE contains information on language-specific execution of the process. For example, as mentioned above, many languages nasalize a vowel next to a nasal consonant, which is called the process of VOWEL NASALIZATION. However, the rule for vowel nasalization in English, SC, and many languages is that a vowel is nasalized before a nasal consonant, but in some languages the rule for vowel nasalization can be for a vowel to become nasalized after a nasal consonant. Most common phonological processes across languages are either ASSIMILA-TORY or DISSIMILATORY in nature (cf. §5.3) or are sensitive to PROSODIC STRUCTURE like syllable or stress.

7.1.2.1 Assimilation

ASSIMILATION occurs when a sound becomes more similar to a neighboring sound or some sound within the same syllable. For example, VOWEL NASAL-IZATION mentioned above is a kind of assimilation process because an oral vowel becomes a nasal vowel before a nasal consonant, i.e. an oral vowel is changed to be more like the following consonant in terms of nasality. Another example of assimilation is that the English plural SUFFIX for nouns -s is pronounced either as [s] or [z] depending on the final sound of the noun: if a noun ends in a voiced sound, the plural suffix is pronounced as a voiced [z] (e.g. *dogs* [dɔgz], *zoos* [zuz]), and if a noun ends in a voiceless sound, the plural suffix is pronounced as a voiceless [s] (e.g. *cats* [kʰæts]). That is, the plural suffix has the same [voice] feature specification as its preceding segment. This process is called VOICING ASSIMILATION, i.e. assimilation in terms of the [voice] feature. In SC, the requirement that alveolo-palatals must be followed by a high front vowel/glide (§5.3) can also be viewed as being assimilatory in the sense that alveolo-palatals have the [−back, +high] features (i.e. the front part of the tongue is raised), which are shared by a high front vowel/glide. This specific assimilation process is called PALATALIZATION, which will be discussed in more detail in §7.2.1.

The more similar the neighboring sounds are, the more easily the articulators can move efficiently from one sound to the next; therefore, one major reason for assimilation is to achieve ease of articulation. The need for ease of articulation, however, must be balanced against the need for ease of perception for efficient communication. If all neighboring segments sound the same, then it becomes difficult for the listener to detect exactly which sequence of sounds and which word have been uttered.

7.1.2.2 Dissimilation

DISSIMILATION occurs when a sound becomes less similar to a neighboring sound or another sound within the same syllable to achieve ease of perception, i.e. to better distinguish one sound from another. We can think of tone 3 sandhi, which changes the first T3 in a T3 T3 sequence to a T2 (§4.2.3, §9.2.2, §9.4), as a kind of dissimilation process that makes the two originally identical tones less similar. In §5.3, we also learned that in English, a labial consonant cannot be followed by the rounded glide [w] as in *[pwa]. Since a rounded glide and a labial consonant both involve the lips in articulation, they both have the Labial feature and we see that two similar sounds in terms of the Labial feature cannot be in the syllable onset, which is a dissimilatory constraint that demands the two segments in the onset be different in terms of the Labial feature. The English plural suffix is pronounced as [əz] (or [iz] by some speakers) when the preceding noun ends in a SIBILANT (a fricative or affricate with high-frequency friction) like [s], [z], [ʃ], [ʒ], [tʃ], and [dʒ], e.g. *kisses* [kɪsəz], *roses* [ɹozəz], *churches* [tʃɚtʃəz]. A vowel is inserted between a sibilant at the end of the noun and the plural suffix, another sibilant, so that we can hear both sibilants clearly. Therefore, this VOWEL INSERTION process between two sibilants is to break apart two similar sounds and can be considered dissimilatory in nature.

7.1.2.3 Prosodically conditioned processes

A prosodically conditioned segmental process is one sensitive to syllable structure, stress, tone, or intonation. In English, the lateral /l/ is a plain alveolar in syllable onset position but becomes a lateral that has the back of the tongue raised, transcribed as [ɫ], when it is in coda position: e.g. *lift* [lɪft] versus *fill* [fɪɫ]. This process is called VELARIZATION, which raises the back of the tongue toward the velum in addition to the primary alveolar articulation, and it is sensitive to syllable structure. English also has a segmental process sensitive to stress. In English a vowel often becomes a schwa or a short lax high vowel when it is not stressed. For example, the first syllable of the word *grammar, gra* [græ], is stressed and has the vowel [æ], but in the word *grammatical,* the same first syllable is no longer stressed (because the stress is now on the second syllable) and the vowel becomes a schwa: *gra* [grə]. This process is called VOWEL REDUCTION, which makes a vowel shorter and more centralized (closer to the central region of the vowel space). A prosodically conditioned process can be for ease of articulation and/or for ease of perception. For example, having a reduced shorter vowel in unstressed position is articulatorily easier because an unstressed syllable is shorter in duration than a stressed syllable. Perceptually, a full strong vowel in a stressed syllable and a reduced weak vowel in an unstressed syllable make it easier to hear the prosodic rhythm.

7.1.2.4 Phonological rules

With this basic understanding of phonological processes, we now turn to phonological rules. Phonological rules provide formal notations to describe phonological processes in a particular language. For English aspiration and vowel nasalization, we can write rules like those in (6).

(6) Two English phonological rules

    a. English aspiration[3]
      (i) Voiceless stops become aspirated in syllable initial position.
      (ii) <u>Formal rule</u>: [−continuant, −voice] → [+aspirated]/ $_\sigma$[__
      (iii) <u>Informal rule</u>: Voiceless stops → [+aspirated] / syllable initially
    b. English vowel nasalization
      (i) Vowels become nasalized before a nasal coda consonant.
      (ii) <u>Formal rule</u>: [−consonantal] → [+nasal]/__ [+nasal, +consonantal]$_\sigma$
      (iii) <u>Informal rule</u>: Vowels → [+nasal] / __ [+nasal] consonants in coda

The arrow → means 'to become' or 'to change to' and the slash / means 'in the environment of'. The notation '__' indicates the location this change occurs; for

---

[3] The English aspiration rule is more complicated than this. See footnote 10 in §1.5.2.

example, _X means 'before X', X_ means 'after X' and X_Y means between
X and Y. The sequences σ[_ and _]σ indicate that the change occurs at the
beginning and at the end of a syllable respectively. For our purposes, we do
not need to focus on the technical aspects of the formal rules, so an informal
notation is usually sufficient. The main difference between the formal and the
informal ones in (6) is the use of a smaller number of feature specifications
and special notations in an informal rule.

A rule tells us what the actual pronunciation of a phoneme or morpheme
is. A PHONEME or a MORPHEME (minimal meaningful unit composed of
a phoneme or a sequence of phonemes; §1.3) constitutes the UNDERLYING
REPRESENTATION (abbreviated as UR) of a sound or a morpheme. ALLO-
PHONES are different phonetic realizations (or pronunciations) of a phoneme
and ALLOMORPHS are different phonetic realizations of a morpheme. These
phonetic realizations constitute the SURFACE REPRESENTATION (abbreviated as SR). You can think of underlying representation as the abstract representation stored in our mental dictionary and surface representation as the
actual pronunciation. A phonological rule describes how a sound in underlying representation becomes a modified sound in surface representation and in
what contexts, as illustrated in (7).

(7) underlying representation → rule application → surface representation

Consider first the diagrams in (8) (similar to those used in §1.5.3 and §2.2.1)
to explain the notion of phoneme and allophone: in SC the unaspirated [p]
and aspirated [pʰ] are contrastive (i.e. belong to separate phonemes) but in
English they are not (i.e. they are allophones).

(8)

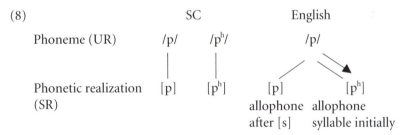

If there is a phonetic realization or allophone that is different from the phoneme,
as in the case of English in (8) between [pʰ] and /p/ indicated by an arrow, then
a phonological rule, formulated as the aspiration rule in (6a), applies to the
underlying representation /p/ and the result of the rule application is the surface
representation [pʰ].

The same idea applies to the underlying representation of a morpheme.
Assuming that the underlying representation of the English plural suffix s is

/z/, there are three allomorphs for this plural morpheme, as illustrated in (9).[4] Note that two allomorphs differ from the underlying representation of the morpheme, so two rules apply in this case, as the examples in (10) show.

(9) The English plural morpheme and its allomorphs

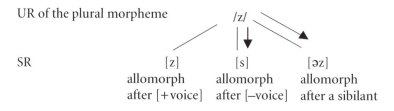

UR of the plural morpheme   /z/

SR   [z]   [s]   [əz]
                       allomorph   allomorph   allomorph
                      after [+voice]   after [−voice]   after a sibilant

(10) Rules for English plural formation

    a. English vowel insertion rule between two sibilants
       A vowel is inserted between sibilants.
       Rule 1: /z/ → [əz] / sibilant __ sibilant
    b. English voicing assimilation rule for the plural morpheme
       The plural morpheme becomes voiceless after a voiceless segment.
       Rule 2: /z/ → [−voice] / [−voice]__

c. Examples	cats	kisses	dogs
UR	/kæt/ /z/	/kɪs/ /z/	/dɔg/ /z/
Rule 1	- - - -	kɪsəz	- - - -
Rule 2	kæts	- - - -	- - - -
SR	[kæts]	[kɪsəz]	[dɔgz]

In the first two examples in (10c) we see how a sound in the UR is changed by rule application. For the example of *cats*, the UR for the plural /z/ becomes [s] by Rule 2, and Rule 1 is irrelevant for this example because Rule 1 applies only when there are two sibilants. For the *kisses* example, Rule 1 first changes the underlying /z/ to [əz] and Rule 2 cannot apply to this example because after the insertion of the vowel, /z/ is now after [ə] and is no longer after a voiceless segment. The *dogs* example does not undergo either rule and the plural is [z] in the SR. An illustration like (10c), in which the UR, the SR, and the effects of rule application are shown, is called a DERIVATION. When there is more

---

[4] The choice of /z/ as the underlying representation of the English plural suffix is not without controversy, although it is the most common analysis. One reason for this choice is to allow for a simple rule system to generate all three allomorphs, as shown in (10) and explained below. Another reason is that a rule like /z/ → [s] after a voiceless sound (assimilation) and a vowel insertion rule to break up two adjacent sibilants (dissimilation) are common natural rules cross-linguistically. Therefore, which underlying representation to set up often depends on how natural the rules and how economical the rule system would be.

than one rule to derive an SR from a UR, the first rule applies to the UR and the subsequent rules apply one by one to the output of the previous rule.

A rule can be obligatory or optional. An OBLIGATORY RULE in a language always applies as long as the specifications stated in the rule are met. The examples we have discussed so far are obligatory rules. An OPTIONAL RULE may or may not apply to a particular representation, depending on speakers and most often depending on speech rate and style. For example, in faster casual speech, the velar nasal in the suffix *ing* can become an alveolar nasal, e.g. *going* /goɪŋ/ → [goɪn], and this change from [ŋ] to [n] is an optional rule.

This section has introduced the basic concepts of phonological processes and rules. A sound often undergoes a process/rule in a language for ease of articulation and/or ease of perception. Before discussing the segmental processes/rules in SC, I would like to briefly explain the differences between rules and constraints and those between phonological rules and phonetic rules.

7.1.3 Rules and constraints

A RULE changes a sound to another in some context and a CONSTRAINT prohibits or requires a certain combination of sounds in some context. In the previous section, we have seen examples of phonological rules and in §5.3 we discussed a number of constraints that determine possible SC syllables. Both rules and constraints reflect which sound can occur in what context, but rules are 'active' in that they make changes from one representation to another, and constraints are 'passive' in that they simply express what is allowed or not allowed.

Sometimes constraints are simply static statements or descriptions of possible and impossible sound combinations and linguistic representations, but constraints can often be viewed as the reasons why rules apply. For example, to help understand the vowel insertion rule between two sibilants in English plural noun formation (§7.1.2.4), we can say that there is a constraint that prohibits two adjacent sibilants within the same syllable and the vowel insertion rule 'repairs' or 'removes' a violation of the constraint. That is, when /z/ is added to a sibilant-ending noun in the process of forming a plural noun, a representation that violates the no-two-sibilants constraint is created:* /kɪsz/. To avoid the violation, the rule of vowel insertion breaks apart the two sibilants and the resulting surface representation contains only legitimate syllables: [kɪ.səz].

A number of SC examples that illustrate this relationship between constraints and rules will be discussed in §§7.2–7.3 and chapter 8. This concept of rule application as a repair for illicit representation (or as avoidance of constraint violation) is called a CONSTRAINT-BASED APPROACH, which will also become useful when we discuss loanword adaptation in chapter 11.

7.1.4 Phonological rules versus phonetic rules

In §7.1.2 above we saw a few examples of phonological processes and rules. There are also phonetic processes and rules and it is not always easy to decide if a process or rule is phonological or phonetic. One general criterion is that phonological processes/rules are CATEGORICAL since they produce a clear category of sound distinguishable from another, whereas phonetic processes/rules can be GRADIENT since they produce either a range of sounds that differ only in smaller phonetic details or a variable group of sounds depending on speech style and speech rate. In other words, phonological rules create distinct classes of sounds in a SR but phonetic rules create a continuum of sounds depending on speech style and speech rate. For example, a vowel is typically shorter and more reduced or can even be deleted in fast speech but stays relatively constant in slow or formal speech. This type of variation is often considered to be phonetic in nature. In contrast, the change of [aɪd] in *divide* [dɪvaɪd] to [ɪʒ] in *division* [dɪvɪʒən] after the addition of the suffix *ion* is considered phonological since both the vowel and the consonant make a consistent change from one category of sound to another: [aɪ] to [ɪ] and [d] to [ʒ].

When a rule changes a phoneme to an allophone, it is called an ALLOPHONIC RULE. Depending on different analyses, some allophonic rules may be considered phonological and some phonetic. This is where the distinction between phonological and phonetic rules becomes more complicated. The aspiration rule in English is an allophonic rule that changes an unaspirated voiceless stop (a phoneme) to an aspirated voiceless stop (an allophone in English), and the property of aspiration or the feature [aspirated] stays relatively constant regardless of speech rate although the degree or the amount of aspiration may vary depending on speech rate. If we follow the categorical versus gradient/variable criterion, we can say that the rule of aspiration is phonological but the degree or amount of aspiration (how much aspiration is present) is gradient and variable and hence phonetic.

Some of the segmental processes/rules in SC to be discussed below and in the next chapter are controversial in terms of their classification as phonological or phonetic processes/rules. For our purposes, we study the major processes/rules, be they phonological or phonetic, to better understand which sounds change their phonetic properties in what contexts and why. Practically speaking, for learners of SC, this knowledge can help fine-tune their pronunciation and/or listening comprehension.

7.2 Assimilation in SC

This section covers the processes/rules of assimilation and related constraints in SC. We know from §7.1.2.1 that, under the assimilation process, a sound becomes similar in certain feature(s) to an adjacent sound. When a sound changes only a portion of its features to be the same as its neighboring sound, it is called PARTIAL ASSIMILATION, since the sound under change does not become totally identical with its neighboring sound. TOTAL ASSIMILATION makes a sound identical to its neighboring sound. In this section, we examine four cases of partial assimilation in SC, one for consonants (§7.2.1) and three for vowels (§§7.2.2–7.2.4).

7.2.1 Palatalization

From §2.2.5 and §5.3, we learned that alveolo-palatals can appear only before high front vowels/glides, [i]/[j] and [y]/[ɥ]. One analysis can be that there is simply a constraint requiring such a restriction. This constraint, however, mimics the common process of PALATALIZATION cross-linguistically, in which a coronal or velar consonant becomes a palato-alveolar or an alveolo-palatal before high front or front vowels (e.g. in English *got you* /gɑtju/ → [gɑtʃju]). Palatalization is an assimilation process because a high front vowel/glide makes use of the front part of the tongue to approach the hard palate, and the consonant before such a vowel/glide also moves away from the alveolar ridge or velum to get closer to the hard palate.

Therefore, an alternative analysis is to posit a rule that changes some underlying phonemes to become alveolo-palatals before high front vowels/glides. If there is a rule, there is an underlying representation (UR) to which the rule applies to yield the surface representation (SR). As mentioned in §2.2.5, the underlying phonemes for SC alveolo-palatals remain controversial: some argue for the velars /k, k^h, x/ and some for the dental /ts, ts^h, s/. If we adopt the latter view (Duanmu 2000), the palatalization rule in SC can be stated and formulated as in (11a–b) and the derivations of three examples are given in (11c).

(11) Consonant palatalization in SC

    a. Dental affricates/fricative become alveolo-palatals before high front vowels/glides.

    b. Rule: Dental affricates/fricative
             → [−back, +high]/__ [−back, +high] vocoids

    c. Examples:

	jīn 'gold'	*qīn* 'to invade'	*xīn* 'new'
UR	/tsin/$_{55}$	/ts^{h}in/$_{55}$	/sin/$_{55}$
rule (11b)	tɕin$_{55}$	tɕ^{h}in$_{55}$	ɕin$_{55}$
SR	[tɕin]$_{55}$	[tɕ^{h}in]$_{55}$	[ɕin]$_{55}$

Since both high front vowels/glides are [−back, +high] and the dentals are not, the dentals take on the [−back, +high] feature to become alveolo-palatals (which are Coronal and [−back, +high]). This palatalization rule is then a case of partial assimilation.

However, in §11.4.1, we will see that both English velar stops and coronal fricatives/affricates are changed to alveolo-palatals before high front vowels/glides, two examples of which are given in (12), where [s] and [k] before a high front vowel in English become [ç] and [tç] respectively in SC loanwords.

(12) Loanword examples:

ENGLISH		SC	
Wisconsin [sɪn]	→	*wēisīkāng**xīn***	[wei.sɹ.kʰɑŋ.**çin**]
Kentucky [kʰi]	→	*kěndéjī*	[kʰən.tɤ.**tçi**]

The generalization for both the native words and borrowed words is that no dentals/alveolars, post-alveolars, or velars can appear before a high front vowel/glide. Therefore, instead of having one fixed UR for the palatalization rule as in (11), we can adopt a constraint-based analysis (§7.1.3): there is a constraint as in (13a) and any constraint violation is corrected by the repair rules in (13b) that change an offending consonant to a corresponding alveolo-palatal. Rule 1 changes a dental/alveolar or a post-alveolar fricative and affricate to an alveolo-palatal fricative and affricate respectively, e.g. [s, z, ʃ] → [ç] and [ts, dʒ] → [tç]. Rule 2 changes a velar stop or fricative to an alveolo-palatal affricate or fricative respectively, e.g. [k] → [tç] and [x] → [ç].

(13) SC palatalization constraint and rules

    a. Palatal Constraint
            Coronal fricatives/affricates and velar obstruents cannot be
            followed by high front vowels/glides.
    b. Palatalization Rule 1:
            Coronal fricatives/affricates
                → [−back, +high] / __[−back, +high] vocoids
    c. Palatalization Rule 2:
            Velar obstruents
                → [−back, +high] / __[−back, +high] vocoids

Palatalization is an obligatory rule in SC, which means the Palatal Constraint (13a) can never be violated and the palatalization rules (13bc) must apply if there is a violation of the constraint. We will see in §11.4.1 how the constraint and repair rules in (13) apply to modify a foreign word adopted into SC. For various analyses of SC palatalization, see Further Reading for references for Chinese segmental processes.

7.2.2 Vowel nasalization

As in English, an oral vowel before a nasal consonant in SC becomes nasalized. The vowel nasalization rule is the same as in (6b) in §7.1.3. It has been claimed that vowel nasalization is an optional phonological rule (Duanmu 2000:73). The degree of nasalization may vary among speakers, but, phonetically speaking, there is almost always at least some degree of nasalization for the vowel before a nasal coda consonant. However, a vowel with a smaller degree of nasalization may not be recognized as a nasal vowel phonologically because it is difficult to detect.

The degree of vowel nasalization in SC also differs depending on the type of nasal consonant: a vowel before a velar nasal is more strongly nasalized than the one before an alveolar nasal (Zhang 2000). As we will see in §8.2.4, this phonetic gradient difference in the degree of nasalization plays a role in the changes of the nasal-ending rimes under *r*-suffixation.

7.2.3 Low vowel assimilation

From §3.4.3, we learned that SC has only one low vowel phoneme /a/, which has three allophones: [a], [ɑ], and [ɛ]. This means that there exist two rules: one changes the low vowel to a low back vowel [ɑ] and the other changes the low vowel to the mid lax or low mid vowel [ɛ], as shown in (14) and (15). These rules apply only within the domain of a syllable, as the examples in (14b) show.[5]

(14) Low Vowel Backing

    a. Rule: [+low] vowels → [+back] / __ [+back]
                (The low vowel becomes [+back] before [u] and [ŋ])

    b. Example: *gāo*   'high'   *gāng*   'steel'

UR	/kau/$_{55}$		/kaŋ/$_{55}$
rule (14a)	kɑu$_{55}$		kɑŋ$_{55}$
SR	[kɑu]$_{55}$		[kɑŋ]$_{55}$

    c. Constraint: The segments in the rime must have the same values for [back] and [round] (cf. (12) in §5.3).

    d. Constraint: A low rounded vowel is prohibited.

The backing rule in (14a) is an assimilation rule because both [u] and [ŋ] make use of the back part of the tongue to approach the velum and the low

---

[5] In a disyllabic word in which the low vowel is in the first syllable followed by a [+back] segment in the second syllable, the rule does not apply, e.g. *wa wa* [wa]$_{35}$[wa]$_3$ 'baby, doll'.

vowel also moves toward the back. If we specify both [u] and [ŋ] with [+back], then the low vowel takes on the same feature and becomes a [+back] low vowel. The derivation in (14b) shows that the rule applies to produce a [+back] low vowel. Recall also from §5.3 that in SC the segments in the rime share the same [back] and [round] feature, as in (14c). Making sure that a low underlying vowel is [+back] before another [+back] segment in the rime satisfies this requirement. That is, in a constraint-based approach, one can consider the assimilation rule in (14a) a response to the specific PHONOTACTIC CON-STRAINT in (14c) that requires a certain combination of adjacent segments in a syllable. We will see that the same constraint is responsible for mid vowel assimilation (§7.2.4) and mid vowel insertion (§8.1.5). The reason that the low vowel does not become [+round] before a rounded [u], i.e. [ɑu] but not *[ɒu], can be attributed to the fact that SC does not allow a rounded low vowel, as the constraint in (14d) indicates. This is not an unusual constraint since rounded low vowels are much less common than high and mid rounded vowels cross-linguistically.

The fronting/raising rule in (15ab) is also an assimilation rule. The glides are [+high, −back] because they raise the front part of the tongue toward the hard palate and the alveolar nasal can be considered [−back] because it makes use of the tongue blade to touch the alveolar ridge located in the front part of the oral tract. The low vowel, being influenced by both segments, becomes a front vowel ([−back]) and is raised up one step from a low vowel to a mid vowel ([−low]). The low vowel does not go all the way to become a high vowel since such a drastic change of vowel height would make it confusing with other syllables, e.g. [jin]$_{55}$ 'music', and also make it difficult to recognize the original [+low] vowel. The examples in (15c) show that, as the first step, the underlying high vowel is syllabified as a glide in the onset (mentioned in §3.4.1 and §5.2.1 and to be discussed again in §8.1.1), and then the fronting/raising rule applies to produce the surface representation.

(15) Low Vowel Fronting/Raising

    a. The low vowel becomes [−back] and [−low] between front glides [j]/[ɥ] and the alveolar nasal coda [n].

    b. Rule: [+low] vowels → [−back, −low] / [−back, +high] __ [n]

    c. Example: *tiān*   'sky'   *yuán*   'round'

UR	/tʰian/$_{55}$	/yan/$_{35}$	
glide formation	tʰjan$_{55}$	ɥan$_{35}$	
rule (15ab)	tʰjɛn$_{55}$	ɥɛn$_{35}$	
SR	[tʰjɛn]$_{55}$	[ɥɛn]$_{35}$	

The backing rule in (14) is quite consistent for most SC speakers but the fronting/raising rule in (15) could be an optional rule for some speakers. As mentioned in §3.4.3, some speakers may produce a low front vowel [æ], i.e. only fronting but no raising, or have a low vowel [a], i.e. no fronting or raising.

7.2.4 Mid vowel assimilation

SC has only one mid vowel phoneme /ə/, which has four allophones: [ə], [e], [o], and [ɤ] (§3.4.2). This means that there are three changes: the first one changes the schwa to [e], the second one to [o], and the third one to [ɤ]. In this subsection we discuss the first two changes and leave the third one for §8.1.4.

Instead of positing one assimilation rule from /ə/ to [e] and another one from /ə/ to [o], we can actually formulate only one rule, as shown in (16a), since the mid vowel simply copies whatever [back] and [round] features an adjacent high vowel or glide has.

(16) Mid Vowel Assimilation I

    a. Rule: mid vowels

        → [αback, βround]/ next to [αback, βround, −consonantal]
        A mid vowel has the same [back] and [round] feature values as an adjacent high vowel/glide.

    🎧 b. Examples:

	bēi 'cup'	*xiě* 'write'	*gǒu* 'dog'	*guō* 'wok'
UR	/pəi/$_{55}$	/ɕiə/$_{214}$	/kəu/$_{214}$	/kuə/$_{55}$
glide	- - - -	ɕjə$_{214}$	- - - -	kwə$_{55}$
rule (16a)	pei$_{55}$	ɕje$_{214}$	kou$_{214}$	kwo$_{55}$
SR	[pei]$_{55}$	[ɕje]$_{214}$	[kou]$_{214}$	[kwo]$_{55}$

This rule states that a mid vowel assimilates to an adjacent high vowel/glide, i.e. [−consonantal] segments, in terms of the [back] and [round] features. The symbols α and β in (16a) mean they can be either a plus or a minus. If both α and β are plus, then the adjacent high vowel/glide is [+back, +round], i.e. [u]/[w], and the mid vowel becomes [+back, +round], i.e. [o]. If both α and β are minus, then the adjacent high vowel/glide is [−back, −round], i.e. [i]/[j], and the mid vowel becomes [−back, −round], i.e. [e]. If α is minus and β is plus, then the adjacent high glide is [−back, +round], i.e. [ɥ]. In this case, only the glide is relevant because the high front rounded vowel cannot be the second part of a diphthong, i.e. *[ay] or *[ey] (§5.3). Of course, a fourth logical possibility is a [+back, −round] vowel, but SC has no high back unrounded vowel/glide. The examples and derivations in (16b) show that both glide formation (§8.1.1) and assimilation apply in the second and fourth examples. Glide formation is not applicable to the first and third examples since the high vowel part of a diphthong is part of the syllable nucleus (§5.2.1).

However, the examples in (17a), in which the glide is high front rounded, seem to be exceptions to the rule: only the [−back] feature of the high front rounded glide is adopted by the mid vowel and the [+round] feature is left out. That is, we do not get a front rounded mid vowel *[ø] as rule (16a) predicted. The reason is that cross-linguistically it is a relatively less common vowel and SC is among those languages that prohibit a mid front rounded vowel. In general a front rounded vowel is less common, more difficult in articulation, and in terms of perception, it is somewhere between [e] and [o] and is more easily confused with these two more common vowels

(17) Mid vowel preceded by high front rounded glide

a. *xué*   'study'   /ɕyə/$_{35}$ →   [ɕɥe]$_{35}$*[ɕɥø]$_{35}$
    yuè   'month'   /yə/$_{51}$ →   [ɥe]$_{51}$*[ɥø]$_{51}$

b. Constraint: No mid front rounded vowel [ø].

c. Rule: Remove [+round] from [ø] to produce [e].

d. Examples:

	xué 'study'	*yuè* 'month'
UR	/ɕyə/$_{35}$	/yə/$_{51}$
glide	ɕɥə$_{35}$	ɥə$_{51}$
rule (16a)	ɕɥø$_{35}$	ɥø$_{51}$
constraint (17b)	*ɕɥø$_{35}$	*ɥø$_{51}$
rule (17c)	ɕɥe$_{35}$	ɥe$_{51}$
SR	[ɕɥe]$_{35}$	[ɥe]$_{51}$

We can then say that there is a constraint that prohibits [ø] in SC and this constraint prompts a repair rule to change this non-permissible vowel to a permissible one. The constraint and the repair rule are given in (17bc). In (17d), we see that assimilation rule (16a) produces illicit representations bared by constraint (17b), but with the rule in (17c) we can make an adjustment to the representation to yield a well-formed SR. The result is still an assimilation process because the mid vowel becomes more similar to the glide in terms of [−back].

The next complication arises when the mid vowel is flanked by both front and back high vowels/glides. Should the mid vowel assimilate to [−back, −round] or [+back, +round]? The examples in (18) show that the high vowel in the diphthong rather than the glide in the onset determines the assimilation outcome. That is, the mid vowel assimilates to the following high vowel but not to the preceding high glide.

(18) Mid vowel flanked by high vowel and glide

liŭ	'willow'	/liəu/$_{214}$	→	[ljou]$_{214}$ *[ljeu]$_{214}$
shuĭ	'water'	/ʂuəi/$_{214}$	→	[ʂwei]$_{214}$ *[ʂwoi]$_{214}$

The solution lies in the syllable structure. Recall from §5.2.1 that a diphthong, in this case the mid vowel and its following high vowel, belongs to the nucleus and rime, whereas the high glide belongs to the onset, as illustrated in (19).

(19)

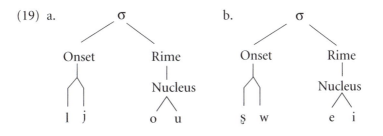

The mid vowel then has a closer relationship to the high vowel in the nucleus/rime because they have the same syllabic affiliation. When the mid vowel has to choose between two high vocoids for assimilation, the one in the rime wins over the one in the onset. There is a general constraint that requires application of a rule in a smaller domain before such application in a larger domain (cf. §9.4 for tone 3 sandhi application in phrases/sentences). In this particular case, after the application of mid vowel assimilation within the rime, further assimilation to the glide in the onset does not apply. Think of the possible outcome: if we apply the rule again between [o] and [j] in (19a) and between [e] and [w] in (19b), we either produce a prohibited sound [ø] (violating constraint (17b)) or there is simply no way to have a vowel that is simultaneously [−back] and [+back], required by the preceding and the following high vowel/glide.

For SC, let us set up two domains for the application of mid vowel assimilation: the rime and the syllable. The rule applies first within the rime and then within the syllable. The constraint that regulates how mid vowel assimilation rule (16a) should apply is given in (20a), and we can derive the correct outputs as shown in (20b).

(20) Mid vowel assimilation II

    a. Constraint:　Apply mid vowel assimilation within the rime first; if the rule has applied within the rime, it does not reapply in the same syllable.

b. Examples with two high vocoids

	liŭ 'willow'	*shuĭ* 'water'
UR	/liəu/$_{214}$	/ʂui/$_{214}$
glide	ljəu$_{214}$	ʂwəi$_{214}$
rule (16a) constrained		
by (20a)	ljou$_{214}$	ʂwei$_{214}$
SR	[ljou]$_{214}$	[ʂwei]$_{214}$

c. Constraint: The segments in the rime must have the same values for [back] and [round].

Note that mid vowel assimilation within the rime, like the low vowel assimilation in (14a) in §7.2.3, can be considered a rule to fulfill the requirement that the rime segments cannot be different in terms of [back] and [round] features, repeated in (20c) (same as (14c) in §7.2.3 and (12) in §5.3). This constraint on the rime also explains why mid vowel assimilation fails to apply when the mid vowel is preceded by a glide and followed by a coda consonant, e.g. [wən] but not *[won], and [jəŋ] but not *[jeŋ], since the two segments in a rime like *[on] or *[eŋ] differ in the [back] and/or [round] features and violate this rime constraint. See also §8.1.5 for more details.

As mentioned in 3.4.2, the degree of fronting, backing, or rounding of the mid vowel can vary depending on different speakers and different Mandarin dialects (cf. Lin 2002). Under some analyses, the assimilation within the rime (i.e. within a diphthong) is an optional rule (cf. Duanmu 2000:73): /əi/ and /əu/ can optionally stay as [əi] and [əu] respectively, although assimilation still applies when the mid vowel is preceded by a glide: [je], [wo], and [ɥe]. Note that when these diphthongs are preceded by a glide, the mid vowel is not assimilated to the glide either: /iəu/ → [jəu] and /uəi/ → [wəi]. In this type of speech and analysis, the rule/constraint system has to be changed in a way to prohibit assimilation of the mid vowel to the glide when the mid vowel is part of a diphthong. See references for Chinese segmental processes in Further Reading for different analyses of mid vowel assimilation. Later, in §7.3.2, we will see examples of VOWEL REDUCTION that makes [e] or [o] become a schwa in fast speech.

7.3 Weakening and reduction in SC

7.3.1 Consonant weakening

A CONSONANT WEAKENING process is one in which a voiceless stop becomes voiced or a consonant with greater CONSTRICTION becomes one with less constriction: stop → fricative and fricative → approximant. The explanation for and analyses of consonant weakening are relatively complex, so let us simply adopt the view that there is a strength hierarchy for consonants as in (21), in which voiceless stops have the highest strength and approximants the weakest.

(21) Consonant Strength Hierarchy

Strongest < ———————————————— > Weakest
voiceless stops – voiced stops – fricatives – approximants

Note that this strength hierarchy seems to be the SONORITY HIERARCHY (§5.2.2) in reverse: of these consonants, approximants are most sonorous and voiceless stops are least sonorous. For our purposes, we can say that a less sonorous consonant is more 'consonant-like' and less 'vowel-like' and it is given the label as being stronger.

If one type of consonant becomes another type that is to the right side on the strength hierarchy in (21) when next to a vowel or SONORANT, then it is a weakening process. Weakening facilitates faster and smoother transition of sounds for ease of articulation. If a voiceless stop becomes voiced, or a voiced stop becomes fricative, or a fricative becomes an approximant next to a vowel or sonorant, the consonant is becoming a little bit more like a vowel or sonorant in terms of voicing and/or the degree of constriction, since vowels and sonorants are voiced and have freer airflow through the oral or nasal cavities. For example, a voiced stop has complete obstruction of the airflow, but by opening up a little to become a fricative when it is next to a vowel, the articulatory transition from or to its surrounding vowels becomes more efficient.

With this basic idea of what a consonant weakening process is, we can now examine the examples in (22). The neutral tone is not marked in *pīnyīn*, and in the transcriptions the phonetic tone value used in Chao (1968:36) is adopted (§4.2.2).

(22) Consonant weakening in SC

   a. Under neutral tone:
      voiceless stop/affricate → voiced stop/affricate
      stop → fricative
      fricative → approximant

li$_{35}$ **pa**$_3$	→ li$_{35}$ **ba**$_3$	*líba*	'fence'
ti$_{53}$ **ti**$_1$	→ ti$_{53}$ **di**$_1$	*dìdi*	'younger brother'
xai$_{35}$ **tsʅ**$_3$	→ xai$_{35}$ **dzʅ**$_3$	*hái zi*	'child'
tswo$_{53}$ **tʂə**$_1$	→ tswo$_{53}$ **dʐə**$_1$	*zuò zhe*	'sitting'
pʰi$_{53}$ **ku**$_1$	→ pʰi$_{53}$ **ɣu**$_1$	*pìgu*	'buttocks'

$$kɤ_{55}\ kɤ_2 \quad \rightarrow\ kɤ_{55}\ ɣə_2 \qquad \textit{gēge} \qquad \text{'older brother'}$$
$$wan_{21}\ ʂaŋ_4 \quad \rightarrow\ wan_{21}\ ɻəŋ_4 \qquad \textit{wǎnshang} \qquad \text{'evening'}$$
$$pau_{53}\ ʂaŋ_1 \quad \rightarrow\ pau_{53}\ ɻɔ̃_1 \qquad \textit{bào shang} \qquad \text{'in the newspaper'}$$

b. In the second syllable of a trisyllabic expression:

stop/affricate → fricative or approximant

$$kaŋ\ kaŋ\ tɕʰy \rightarrow kaŋ\ ɣaŋ\ tɕʰy \quad \textit{gānggāng qù} \quad \text{'just went'}$$
$$pu\ tʂɻ\ tau \quad \rightarrow pu\ ɻɻ\ tau \quad \textit{bù zhīdào} \quad \text{'don't know'}$$

In SC, the consonant undergoing the weakening process is usually in a neutral-toned syllable (Cheng 1973:82) as in (22a), or in a second position of a trisyllabic (three-syllable) expression (Duanmu 2000:256) as in (22b). (I omit the tone in the examples in (22b) for ease of presentation; the tones are marked on the *pīnyīn* for each example.) The last three examples in (22a) also show vowel/rime reduction, [ɤ] → [ə] and [aŋ] → [əŋ] or [ɔ̃], which will be discussed in the next subsection. Consonant weakening in SC is an optional rule and applies most commonly to frequently used words and expressions in casual speech.

7.3.2 Vowel reduction and rime reduction

In the discussion of English VOWEL REDUCTION in an unstressed syllable (§7.1.2.3), we learned that a vowel in a prosodically weak syllable (a syllable without stress or tone) tends to be reduced: the vowel becomes shorter, centralized, or lax; i.e. it is moved closer to the mid central region of the vowel space. In the extreme case of vowel reduction, the vowel is deleted. Vowel reduction can also be viewed as a kind of WEAKENING process.

Recall from §4.2.2 that the neutral-toned syllable in SC is unstressed and shorter. Because a neutral-toned syllable is prosodically weak, the vowel and rime in a neutral-toned syllable tend to be reduced. A reduced vowel is shorter and centralized or lax or even deleted, and a reduced rime also becomes shorter in duration through reducing the main vowel, deleting a vowel or coda, and/or merging two segments in the rime into one segment.

In SC, both vowel reduction and RIME REDUCTION rules are optional; they may or may not apply depending on speakers, speech rate, and style, and they are more likely to apply in casual or fast speech. It is also important to note that the use of neutral tone varies greatly among different SC speakers. For example, the SC spoken in Beijing has many words with neutral tone but textbook SC has fewer such words and some SC varieties spoken in areas outside of Beijing have only a handful. Since the reduction process is conditioned by the presence of the neutral tone, a speaker applies a vowel or rime reduction rule when he/she has a neutral tone for the word. Therefore, not all examples given below are used by all SC speakers.

Consider first the examples in (23). These examples have a simple rime that contains only one nuclear segment and has no coda.

(23) Vowel reduction under neutral tone

    a. low vowel   → schwa

        t^{h}ou$_{35}$ fa$_3$ → t^{h}ou$_{35}$ fə$_3$ *tóufa*   'hair'

        xən$_{53}$ ta$_1$ → xən$_{53}$ tə$_1$ *hèn ta*   'hate him'

    b. mid back vowel → schwa

        kɤ$_{55}$ kɤ$_2$ → kɤ$_{55}$ kə$_2$ *gēge*   'older brother'

    c. low vowel   → schwa or [e]

        tʂaŋ$_{55}$ tɕja$_2$ → tʂaŋ$_{55}$ tɕjə$_2$ *zhāngjia*   'Zhang family'

                      tʂaŋ$_{55}$ tɕje$_2$

        tɕ^{h}jaŋ$_{55}$ ɕja$_2$ → tɕ^{h}jaŋ$_{55}$ ɕjə$_2$ *xiāngxia*   'countryside'

                      tɕ^{h}jaŋ$_{55}$ ɕje$_2$

    d. low vowel   → schwa or [o]

        ɕjau$_{53}$ xwa$_1$ → ɕjau$_{53}$ xwə$_1$ *xiàohua*   'joke'

                      ɕjau$_{53}$ xwo$_1$

        xwaŋ$_{35}$ kwa$_3$ → xwaŋ$_{35}$ kwə$_3$ *huánggua*   'cucumber'

                      xwaŋ$_{35}$ kwo$_3$

The low and mid back vowels in a simple rime (a rime with a single vowel) as in (23ab) may become schwa – a short, lax, mid central vowel. In (23cd) we see that when the low vowel is preceded by a glide in a simple-rime syllable, the low vowel can either be reduced to a schwa or [e] after [j] and [o] after [w]. This means that the mid vowel assimilation rule optionally applies after the low vowel is reduced to a schwa.

The examples in (24) have a complex rime that contains either a diphthong or a vowel plus a nasal.

(24) Vowel reduction and rime reduction[6]

    a. [ai] → [əi] or [ei] or [ɛ]

        [au] → [əu] or [ou] or [ɔ]

      (i) nai$_{21}$ nai$_4$ → nai$_{21}$ nəi$_4$ *nǎinai*   'grandma'

                     nai$_{21}$ nei$_4$

                     nai$_{21}$ nɛ$_4$

---

[6] There is no recording for these examples in the CD because these more complex reduction processes are difficult to produce individually without a speech context.

(ii) mai_{21} **mai_4** $\rightarrow$ mai_{21} **mǝi_4**   *mǎimai*   'trade'

mai_{21} **mei_4**

mai_{21} **mɛ_4**

b. [low vowel + nasal] $\rightarrow$ [schwa + nasal] or nasalized schwa

(i) nǝŋ_{35} **kan_3** $\rightarrow$ nǝŋ_{35} **kǝn_3**   *nénggan*   'capable'

nǝŋ_{35} **kə̃_3**

ɕi_{21} **xwan_4** $\rightarrow$ ɕi_{21} **xwǝn_4**   *xǐhuan*   'to like'

ɕi_{21} **xwə̃_4**

(ii) wan_{21} **ʂaŋ_4** $\rightarrow$ wan_{21} **ɹǝŋ_4**   *wǎnshang*   'evening'

wan_{21} **ɹə̃_4**

ɕi_{55} **waŋ_2** $\rightarrow$ ɕi_{55} **wǝŋ_2**   *xīwang*   'to hope'

ɕi_{55} **wə̃_2**

c. front glide + low vowel + nasal $\rightarrow$ front glide + schwa + nasal

or high vowel + nasal

(i) /ɕin/$_{55}$ /ɕ**ian**/

ɕin_{55} **ɕjɛn_2** $\rightarrow$ ɕin **ɕjǝn_2**   *xīnxian*   'fresh'

ɕin **ɕin_2**

(ii) /ku/$_{55}$ /n**ian**/

ku_{55} **njɑŋ_2** $\rightarrow$ ku_{55} **njǝŋ_2**   *gūniang*   'girl'

ku_{55} **niŋ_2**

In (24a), the low vowel is reduced to either a schwa or [e]/[o], but the whole rime can also be reduced to one segment. The diphthong [ai] contains the [+low] feature for the first half and [+high, −back, −round] for the second half. Merging these two parts into one MONOPHTHONG vowel produces a mid front lax vowel [ɛ] that is [−back, −round, −high, −low], i.e. a vowel that retains the [−back, −round] feature and compromises on the height features since no vowel can be both high and low. The same can be said about the change of [ɑu] ([+low] plus [+high, +back, +round]) to a back rounded mid lax vowel [ɔ] ([+back, +round, −high, −low]). The examples in (24b) are similar in that either the low vowel is reduced to a schwa or the schwa and the nasal in the rime are further reduced by merging the two segments into one nasalized schwa that retains the mid central vowel and the [+nasal] feature of the nasal coda. In (24c), the underlying low vowel is reduced to a schwa or is even deleted, making the pre-nuclear high glide fill in as the main nuclear vowel.

Another type of optional vowel reduction is conditioned by syllable types. The mid vowel [e] or [o] may also be reduced to schwa or even deleted when they are part of a diphthong and appear in a syllable that has an initial consonant and a pre-nuclear glide. Again this vowel reduction process applies more commonly in casual or fast speech. Compare the examples in (25a) and (25b).

🎧 (25) Mid vowels in GVV and CGVV syllables

    a. GVV syllable

         /iəu/$_{35}$ →   [you]$_{35}$ *yóu*   'oil'

         /uəi/$_{214}$ →   [wei]$_{214}$ *wěi*   'tail'

    b. CGVV syllable

    (i)   /liəu/$_{35}$ →   [ljou]$_{35}$ *liú*   'to flow'

                               [ljəu]$_{35}$

                               [lju]$_{35}$

    (ii)   /tsuəi/$_{51}$ →   [tswei]$_{51}$ *zuì*   'sin'

                                 [tswəi]$_{51}$

                               [tswi]$_{51}$

We can see that for a zero-initial syllable in (25a) the mid vowel is generally not reduced (although a schwa may appear for some speakers; cf. §7.2.4), whereas for a CGVV syllable, in (25b), the mid vowel is more likely to be reduced to a schwa or even deleted.

You may have noticed that some reduced syllables contain rimes that are prohibited by some of the syllable structure constraints discussed in §5.3. For example, there is a constraint requiring the rime segments to have the same [back] and [round] features ((12) in §5.3), so a rime like [iŋ] in (24c) should not have occurred, and [ju] and [wi] in (25b) are supposed to be banned also ((15) in §5.3). There is actually no contradiction: syllable structure constraints regulate phonological representations and optional vowel/rime reduction that depends on speech rate and style is generally considered to be a phonetic process. Phonetic processes may produce a sound, a sequence of sounds, or a syllable that is at odds with well-formed phonological representation but is quite natural with respect to phonetic mechanisms and principles.

7.3.3 Vowel devoicing

When a vowel, which is originally voiced, becomes voiceless when next to a voiceless consonant, we have a VOWEL DEVOICING process. This is a kind of assimilation process. SC vowel devoicing is an optional rule that may or may not apply, but when it applies, it occurs most commonly in an unstressed neutral-toned syllable in fast speech. Therefore, this can also be viewed as a kind of reduction/weakening process. In very fast speech, a devoiced vowel may sound like it has been deleted.

Not all vowels can be devoiced: in general a high vowel after a voiceless fricative/affricate or a voiceless aspirated stop in a neutral-toned syllable is most likely to be devoiced, and the syllabic consonants, which are originally voiced and occur only after voiceless affricates and fricatives, also tend to be devoiced in a neutral-toned syllable (Duanmu 2000:257–8; Zee 2003b, personal communication). Some examples are given in (26), in which a devoiced vowel/syllabic consonant is marked by a circle diacritic underneath.

(26) Vowel devoicing under neutral tone

a. high vowel → [−voice]/ [−voice] fricative/affricate___

li$_{53}$ tɕʰi$_1$	→	li$_{53}$ tɕʰi̥$_1$	*lìqi*	'physical strength'
tuŋ$_{55}$ ɕi$_2$	→	tuŋ$_{55}$ ɕi̥$_2$	*dōngxi*	'thing, object'
tai$_{53}$ fu$_1$	→	tai$_{53}$ fu̥$_1$	*dàifu*	'doctor'
swan$_{53}$ ʂu$_1$	→	swan$_{53}$ ʂu̥$_1$	*suànshu*	'arithmetic'
tʂʰu$_{55}$ tɕʰy$_1$	→	tʂʰu$_{55}$ tɕʰɣ̥$_1$	*chūqu*	'go out'

b. high vowel → [−voice]/ [−voice, +aspirated] stop ___

| wən$_{53}$ tʰi$_1$ | → | wən$_{53}$ tʰi̥$_1$ | *wènti* | 'question' |
| ɕin$_{55}$ kʰu$_2$ | → | ɕin$_{55}$ kʰu̥$_2$ | *xīnku* | 'laborious' |

c. syllabic consonant → [−voice]/ [−voice] fricative/affricate ___

ʂɻ$_{53}$ tsɻ$_1$	→	ʂɻ$_{53}$ tsɻ̥$_1$	*shìzi*	'persimmon'
san$_{55}$ tsʰɻ$_2$	→	san$_{55}$ tsʰɻ̥$_2$	*sānci*	'three times'
jou$_{21}$ ji$_{53}$ sɻ$_1$	→	jou$_{21}$ ji$_{53}$ sɻ̥$_1$	*yǒu yìsi*	'interesting'
li$_{53}$ tʂɻ	→	li$_{53}$ tʂɻ̥$_1$	*lìzhi*	'lichee fruit'
tan$_{53}$ ʂɻ̍	→	tan$_{53}$ ʂɻ̥$_1$	*dànshi*	'but'

Among the affected segments, syllabic consonants and [i] seem more likely to be devoiced than [u], which in turn is more likely to be devoiced than [y]. Among the consonants that trigger vowel devoicing, voiceless fricatives and aspirated affricates and stops seem more likely to make the next nucleus devoiced. In addition, when the phonetic realization of the neutral tone is low with a pitch level of 1 after high falling T4 or 2 after high level T1, vowel devoicing is also more likely to occur.

Devoicing in (26) all occurs in the final syllable since that is where neutral tone usually occurs. In a non-final position, a high vowel or syllabic consonant may also undergo devoicing, but only if it is after an aspirated consonant in a syllable with a low tone, i.e. T3 in non-final position (see also Duanmu 2000:257–8). Two examples are given in (27). Similar cases of vowel devoicing also occur in English, such as *potato* and *tomato*, in which the first vowel can be devoiced.

(27) Vowel devoicing after aspirated C in a non-final low-toned syllable

$$t\varphi^h i_{21}\ s_{J55} \quad \rightarrow \quad t\varphi^h \underset{\circ}{i}_{21}\ s_{J55} \qquad q\breve{\imath}s\bar{\imath} \quad \text{'cheese'}$$
$$t^h u_{21}\ tou_{51} \quad \rightarrow \quad t^h \underset{\circ}{u}_{21}\ tou_{51} \qquad t\breve{u}d\grave{o}u \quad \text{'potato'}$$

For learners of SC, it is relatively difficult to master the phonetic details of consonant weakening, vowel/rime reduction, and vowel devoicing without close and frequent interactions with native speakers in a natural SC-speaking environment. However, being aware of these facts should help improve comprehension when listening to SC speakers' casual conversation.

7.4 Summary

This chapter introduces the basic concepts of phonology, the interaction of phonology with phonetics, and discusses major assimilation, weakening, and reduction processes in SC.

- SEGMENTAL PROCESSES, which apply commonly across languages, change the phonetic/phonological properties of consonants or vowels in various contexts. A PHONOLOGICAL RULE describes the specific details of a process in a particular language and converts an UNDERLYING REPRESENTATION to a SURFACE REPRESENTATION (§7.1.2.4).
- Distinctive PHONOLOGICAL FEATURES are those that are referred to in phonological organization and processes. A NATURAL CLASS of sounds exhibit similar phonological behavior, pattern together in PHONOLOGICAL PROCESSES and RULES regularly, and can be technically defined in terms of phonological features (§7.1.1).
- Both RULES and CONSTRAINTS are used to describe and explain changes of sounds in various contexts. In the CONSTRAINT-BASED APPROACH, a rule applies if a relevant constraint is violated and needs a fix-up to derive a permissible SURFACE REPRESENTATION (§7.1.3).
- Phonological rules produce categorical changes of sounds whereas PHONETIC RULES yield gradient and variable changes involving phonetic details that are less detectable, and dependent on speech rate (§7.1.4).
- SC ASSIMILATION processes/rules produce: (i) alveolo-palatals before high front vowels/glides; (ii) nasalized vowels before a coda nasal; (iii) back low vowels before [+back] segment, [u] and [ŋ]; (iv) a mid lax vowel [ɛ] between a front glide and [n] when the vowel is an underlying low vowel; and (v) mid vowels [e] and [o] next to high front vowels/glides and high back rounded vowel/glide respectively (§7.2).

- SC CONSONANT WEAKENING changes a voiceless stop to voiced, a stop to a fricative, or a fricative to an approximant when the consonant is between vowels/sonorants (§7.3.1).
- SC VOWEL REDUCTION, RIME REDUCTION, and VOWEL DEVOICING (§§7.3.2–7.3.3) generally occur in a neutral-toned syllable in casual conversation. A vowel is reduced to a mid vowel (most commonly schwa), segments in the rime may be merged into one segment, and a vowel is devoiced when preceded by a voiceless and/or aspirated OBSTRUENT. Vowel deletion may occur in some cases of vowel/rime reduction and vowel devoicing in fast speech.

In the next chapter, additional segmental processes are covered: syllable-based processes and changes of rimes under *r*-suffixation.

EXERCISES

1   For each of the following examples, give the *pīnyīn* and identify all the constraint(s) and/or rule(s) that have applied.

Example: /pəi/214 → [pei]214 'north'
            běi
            Constraint: the rime segments share the same [back] and [round]
                        features.
            Rule: mid vowel assimilation

a.	/kau/$_{55}$	→ [kau]$_{55}$	'high, tall'
b.	/suə/$_{55}$	→ [swo]$_{55}$	'shrink'
c.	/iaŋ/$_{214}$	→ [jãŋ]$_{214}$	'itchy'
d.	/mian/$_{51}$	→ [mjẽn]$_{51}$	'noodle'
e.	/piə/$_{35}$	→ [pje]$_{35}$	'don't'
f.	*Keats* [kʰits] (English)	→ [tɕi]$_{53}$ [tsʰɻ]$_{35}$ (SC)	'Keats'
g.	*show* [ʃou] (English)	→ [ɕjou]$_{51}$ (SC)	'show'
h.	[kãn]$_{53}$ [fa]$_1$	→ [kãn]$_{53}$ [fə]$_1$	'viewpoint'
i.	[mãn]$_{35}$ [ɥẽn]$_3$	→ [mãn]$_{35}$ [ɥən]$_3$	'to complain'
		or [mãn]$_{35}$ [ɥə̃]$_3$	
j.	[kãŋ]$_{55}$ [kãn]$_2$	→ [kãŋ]$_{55}$[ɣə̃]$_2$	'just now'
k.	[ɕjau]$_{21}$ [tʂʰɻ]$_4$	→ [ɕjau]$_{21}$ [tʂʰɻ]$_4$	'snack'
l.	[tɕʰin]$_{55}$ [tɕʰi]$_2$	→ [tɕʰin]$_{55}$ [tɕʰi]$_2$	'relatives'

2   For each of the following examples, give the surface representation by applying the rule(s) provided.

Example:

yuán   /yan/$_{35}$ 'round'
Rules: glide formation, vowel nasalization, and low vowel fronting/raising
→   [ɥɛ̃n]$_{35}$

a. *wéibō*   /uəi/$_{35}$ /puə/$_{55}$ 'microwave'
   Rules: glide formation, mid vowel assimilation
b. *diànnǎo*   /tian/ /nau/   'computer'
   Rules: glide formation, low vowel fronting/raising, vowel nasalization,
               and low vowel backing
c. *Jim* (English) [dʒɪm]   'Jim'
   Rule: Consonant palatalization
   →   [__i]$_{35}$ [mu]$_{214}$ (SC)
d. *sān ge*   [sān]$_{55}$ [kɤ]$_2$ 'three items'
   Rules: consonant weakening and vowel reduction
e. *liánjie*   [ljɛ̃n]$_{35}$ [tɕje]$_3$ 'connect together'
   Rule: vowel reduction
f. *nǎodai*   [nɑu]$_{21}$ [tai]$_4$ 'head'
   Rule: vowel reduction
g. *xiūxi*   [ɕjou]$_{55}$ [ɕi]$_2$ 'take a rest'
   Rule: vowel devoicing
h. *guānsi*   [kwan]$_{55}$ [sɹ̩]$_2$ 'lawsuit'
   Rule: vowel devoicing

3 Collect five examples for each assimilation rule discussed in §7.2. For each
       example, give the *pīnyīn* spelling, the underlying representation, and the
       surface representation.

4 Whenever you have a chance, listen carefully to SC speakers' casual
       conversation, and collect examples for each weakening/reduction rule
       discussed in §7.3. For each example: (i) transcribe what you hear; (ii) identify
       the word in *pīnyīn* and phonetic transcription before rule application;
       and (iii) describe the changes made to the word by rule application.

8 Segmental processes II

This chapter continues the discussion of SC processes by studying: (i) segmental processes that are motivated by syllable structure constraints; and (ii) segmental processes that are induced by *r*-suffixation.

In chapter 5 we studied syllable structure and the permissible and non-permissible syllable types in SC. As we will see in §8.1, some segmental processes are induced by universal syllable structure principles or language specific PHONOTATIC CONSTRAINTS. As mentioned in §3.4.5, in some SC words, the suffix *r* is added to the last syllable; for example, *huà* becomes *huàr* 'painting, picture'. Various segmental processes apply to the rime of an *r*-suffixed syllable. In §8.2 I introduce the use and function of the *r*-suffix (§8.2.1), set up the phonological and phonetic representations of the suffix (§8.2.2), and discuss how the rime of a syllable changes when *r*-suffixation applies (§§8.2.3–8.2.4). The last section (§8.3) summarizes the main points of the chapter.

8.1 Syllable-based processes

8.1.1 Glide formation

The discussion in §3.2, §3.4.1, and §5.2.1 suggests that SC glides are essentially underlying high vowels that surface in non-nuclear position. When an underlying high vowel is syllabified as part of the onset, it is transcribed as a glide under our analysis. SYLLABIFICATION is a process in which a sequence of segments are associated with a syllable, and when a high vowel is followed by a mid or low vowel, which is more sonorous than a high vowel, the mid or low vowel is syllabified as the nucleus and the high vowel is associated with the onset position (§5.2). In (1) we see that a glide is derived by linking an underlying high vowel to the onset position. The syllable representation in which a high vowel is linked to the onset is interpreted and transcribed as a glide, and the dotted lines in (1b) indicate the syllabification process of associating segments to a syllable.

(1) Glide formation

   a. Rule: high vowel → glide / in onset position

🎧 b. Examples: *xiā* 'shrimp'   *guì* 'expensive' *yuǎn* 'far'
      UR   /çia/$_{55}$ /kuəi/$_{51}$ /yan/$_{214}$

	Onset Rime	Onset Rime	Onset Rime
Glide formation & assimilation	ç i a	k u e i	y ɛ n
SR	ç i a	k u e i	y ɛ n
Transcription	[çja]	[kwei]	[ɥɛn]

8.1.2 Syllabic consonants (apical vowels)

Recall from §3.4.1 that the SYLLABIC CONSONANTS (or the so-called apical vowels) in SC appear only after dental and post-alveolar affricates and fricatives and that they are voiced sonorants that share the same place of articulation as the preceding consonants. Consider how a syllabic consonant is derived, as illustrated in (2).

(2) Syllabic consonant formation

   a. Constraint 1: A syllable must have a nucleus segment.
   b. Rule 1:   A dental and post-alveolar affricate/fricative extends to an empty nucleus.
   c. Constraint 2: A SC nucleus must be [+voice, +sonorant].
   d. Rule 2:   Dental/post-alveolar affricate/fricative
                        ⟶ [+ voice, +sonorant] in nucleus

🎧 e. Examples: *sī* 'silk'   *zhǐ* 'paper'   cf. *shū* 'book'
      UR   /s/$_{55}$ /tʂ/$_{214}$ /ʂu/$_{55}$

   f. Syllabifi-   Onset Nucleus   Onset Nucleus   Onset Nucleus
      cation   s   tʂ   ʂ   u

   g. Rule 1   Onset Nucleus   Onset Nucleus
                        s   tʂ   ---

   h. Rule 2   Onset Nucleus   Onset Nucleus
                        s [+voice   tʂ [+voice   ---
                           +sonorant]   +sonorant]

i. SR   Onset Nucleus   Onset Nucleus   Onset Nucleus

s [+voice   tʂ [+voice   ʂ   u

+sonorant]   +sonorant]

Transcription   [sɹ̩]₅₅   [tʂɹ̩]₂₁₄   [ʂu]₅₅

We can think of the process of deriving a syllabic consonant as involving two steps, formulated as two rules in (2bd). Based on the CONSTRAINT-BASED APPROACH (§7.1.3), rules 1 and 2 in (2bd) are responses to violations of constraints 1 and 2 in (2ac) respectively. Dental and post-alveolar fricatives and affricates, referred to by these rules, form a NATURAL CLASS of sound (§7.1.1) because both of them share the features Coronal, [−sonorant] and [+continuant]. Let us now go through the examples and derivations in (2e–i). First, the UR for a syllable that has a syllabic consonant contains a single consonant and this consonant is syllabified to the onset, as the first two examples in (2ef) show. The third example, which has the same kind of consonant but has a vowel in the UR, is provided for comparison. Second, because constraint 1 requires that a syllable nucleus must contain a segment, rule 1 applies to extend the onset consonant to fill the empty nucleus, i.e. to double the consonant in duration to expand into the two-segment length. The process of making a segment longer is called lengthening or GEMINA-TION. (Note that cross-linguistically a lengthened or geminated affricate can only have the fricative portion lengthened, e.g. [tss] rather than *[tsts].) A segment that is doubly linked to two syllable positions, as in the outcome of the application of rule 1 in (2g), is considered a geminate or long segment. When a consonant is linked to the syllable nucleus, we have a syllabic consonant (§3.2). Third, a syllable nucleus prefers a more sonorous segment (§5.2.2) and yet the onset consonant, which is [−sonornant, −voice], is low in sonority, which is in violation of constraint 2. Therefore, the extended portion of the consonant receives the features [+voice, +sonorant] to become a voiced sonorant more suitable for a nucleus, as shown in (2h). We can see that the third example does not undergo rule 1 and rule 2 since it does not have an empty nucleus to begin with. Finally, the SR and IPA transcription are shown in (2i).

This process of creating a syllabic consonant is natural and simple to understand in terms of this constraint-based view: (i) an empty nucleus is prohibited since a syllable without a nucleus is not a legitimate syllable; hence, the preceding consonant is lengthened to fill the nucleus position to create a syllabic consonant; (ii) however, a voiceless obstruent is not sonorous enough to be a legitimate SC nucleus, so the nucleus portion of the lengthened consonant becomes a voiced sonorant without changing the place of articulation.

8.1.3 Zero-initial syllables

In §5.2.4, we adopted the view that a 'zero-initial' syllable actually has a syllable onset position, which may be filled by a consonant or glide. Recall also the fact that the onset of a zero-initial syllable beginning with a mid or low vowel may be a glottal stop [ʔ] or a velar nasal [ŋ] depending on speakers and different varieties of SC and dialects. The example in (3) illustrates how a consonant is inserted to fill the empty onset. The rule is prompted by the need to provide a segment to the onset position of a zero-initial syllable. When a consonant that is not originally present in the UR is added to a SR, it is a process of CONSONANT INSERTION. For speakers without consonant insertion, the onset remains empty.

(3) Consonant insertion for 'zero-initial' syllables

    a. Constraint: A syllable must have an onset segment.
         Rule: Insert a velar nasal or a glottal stop in an empty onset
                         followed by a low or mid vowel.
    b. Rule application

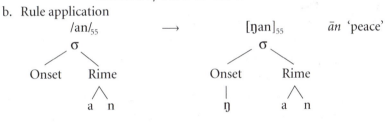

$/an/_{55}$ ⟶ $[ŋan]_{55}$ *ān* 'peace'

In some cases, the onset position of a zero-initial syllable completely copies an adjacent sound, again a lengthening/gemination process (cf. §8.1.2). Consider the examples in (4a) first (cf. examples (7) in §5.2.4), which are all 'zero-initial' syllables that start with a high vowel in the UR. We see that a glide identical in all features to the following vowel fills the onset position in SR. The constraint and rule are given in (4b). This process is also motivated by the need for an onset segment; that is, to avoid having an empty onset, the onset copies the following high vowel. The complete copying of the vowel for the onset segment may also be treated as a case of TOTAL ASSIMILATION (cf. §7.2).

(4) Gemination I

    🎧 a. *yīn* 'sound'   *yú* 'fish'   *wǔ* 'five'
            UR   SR   UR   SR   UR   SR
            $/in/_{55} → [jin]_{55}$ $/y/_{35} → [ɥy]_{35}$ $/u/_{214} → [wu]_{214}$
      b. Constraint: A syllable must have an onset segment.
          Rule: An empty onset before a high vowel is filled with a
                           corresponding glide.
      c. UR $/in/_{55}$ $/y/_{35}$ $/u/_{214}$

d. Syllabification

Onset Rime	Onset Rime	Onset Rime
i n	y	u

e. Rule application

Onset Rime	Onset Rime	Onset Rime
i n	y	u
= [jin]	= [ɥy]	= [wu]

f. SR and transcription

Onset Rime	Onset Rime	Onset Rime
i n	y	u
= [jin]$_{55}$	= [ɥy]$_{35}$	= [wu]$_{214}$

The UR segments in (4c) are associated to the syllable rime as the diagrams in (4d) show. The diagrams in (4e) illustrate rule application with the dotted lines indicating that all the vowel features are copied to the onset. The SRs are given in (4f). Remember that when both the onset and the rime have the same set of features, as indicated by a single vowel [i], [y], or [u] associated with both the onset and the rime, that means we have two identical segments in the syllable. As we just learned from §8.1.1, in SC high vowels in non-nuclear position becomes glides, but a high vowel and its corresponding glide still share the same set of phonological features and the only difference between them is that they occupy different syllable positions. In addition, similar to what we saw in the previous subsection, when a segment is doubled as two segments in a phonological rule, this is called a process of gemination.

The process of gemination also applies across two syllables when the second syllable is a FUNCTION WORD consisting of a zero-initial weak syllable that is shorter and neutral-toned. A function word serves a grammatical function and has less concrete meaning than a CONTENT WORD such as a noun, verb, adjective, and adverb. For example, articles, such as *a, an, the, those,* and prepositions, such as *to, for, up, down,* are function words. SC particles, such as the question marker *ma* and *ne,* are also function words. The interjection marker in SC is a zero-initial neutral-toned syllable *a.* As the examples in (5ab) show, the onset of this weak syllable copies the last segment of the preceding syllable if that segment is a nasal consonant, a high vowel, or a syllabic consonant; otherwise, the onset is filled with [j] as shown in (5b).[1] As shown in (6a), the same syllable constraint is in operation but the rules are different from those in (4) because the contexts are different.

---

[1] In addition to [j], other consonants, such as the glottal stop [ʔ] and glottal fricative [ɦ], are possible depending on speakers and dialects. See also §5.2.4 and footnote 4 in §5.2.4.

(5) Examples for the zero-initial weak syllable *a*

a. *kàn a*   'Look!'   /k^{h}an/$_{51}$ /a/   →   [k^{h}an]$_{53}$ [na]$_1$

    máng a   'Busy!'   /maŋ/$_{35}$ /a/   →   [maŋ]$_{35}$ [ŋa]$_3$

    lái a   'Come!'   /lai/$_{35}$ /a/   →   [lai]$_{35}$ [ja]$_3$

    zǒu a   'Go!'   /tsəu/$_{214}$ /a/   →   [tsou]$_{21}$ [wa]$_4$

    chī a   'Eat!'   /tʂ^h/$_{55}$ /a/   →   [tʂ^{h}ɻ]$_{55}$ [ɹa]$_2$

    sì a   'Four!'   /s/$_{51}$ /a/   →   [sɹ]$_{53}$ [ɹa]$_1$

b. *wǒ a*   'Me!'   /uə/$_{214}$ /a/   →   [wo]$_{21}$ [ja]$_4$

    tā a   'Him!'   /ta/$_{55}$ /a/   →   [ta]$_{55}$ [ja]$_2$

    hē a   'Drink!'   /xə/$_{55}$ /a/   →   [xɤ]$_{55}$ [ja]$_2$

    qiē a   'Cut!'   /tɕ^{h}iə/$_{55}$ /a/   →   [tɕ^{h}je]$_{55}$ [ja]$_2$

(6) Gemination II and consonant insertion

a. Constraint: A syllable must have an onset segment.

    Rule 1:   An empty onset after a consonant or a high vowel in a function word copies the consonant/high vowel.

    Rule 2:   [j] fills an empty onset after a mid/low vowel in a function word.

b. Examples: [k^{h}an]$_{51}$ [a]   [lai]$_{35}$ [a]   [uo]$_{214}$ [a]

c. Syllabification (O = onset R = rime)

```
O   R   O R       O   R   O R       O   R   O R
|   /\  |         |   /\  |         |   |   |
kʰ  a n   a       l   a i   a       u   o     a
```

d. Rule 1

```
O   R   O R       O   R   O R
|   /\⋱ |         |   /\⋱ |         ----
kʰ  a n   a       l   a i   a
```

e. Rule 2

```
                                    O   R   O R
----              ----              |   |   ⋮ |
                                    u   o   j a
```

f. SR and transcription

```
O   R   O R       O   R   O R       O   R   O R
|   /\/ |         |   /\/ |         |   |   | |
kʰ  a n   a       l   a i   a       u   o   j a
[kʰan]₅₃ [na]₁    [lai]₃₅ [ja]₃     [wo]₂₁ [ja]₄
```

The syllabification of the examples in (6b) is shown in (6c), in which the onset of the interjection marker is empty. In (6d) we see that rule 1 applies to the first two examples by extending the nasal and the final vowel to the empty onset. The third example is unaffected by rule 1 since the first syllable does not end in a consonant or a high vowel, but it does undergo rule 2 that inserts [j] to fill the empty onset, as illustrated in (6e). The SRs and transcriptions are provided in (6f).

The gemination and consonant insertion processes in (3), (4), and (6) are motivated by the same constraint: the need to provide a segment for the onset of a zero-initial syllable. In a content word, as seen in (3) and (4), the onset is filled by a glide identical to the following high vowel or by an inserted consonant if the following vowel is not high. In a function word that does not have a high vowel, as shown in (5) and (6), the onset is filled by the preceding high vowel or consonant or by an inserted consonant when the preceding segment is a mid/low vowel.

8.1.4 Mid vowel tensing

In §7.2.4, we saw that an underlying mid vowel /ə/ is assimilated to an adjacent high vowel/glide to become [e] or [o]. The same underlying mid vowel has another allophone in a simple CV or V syllable: [ɤ], as we can see in the examples in (7) (cf. §3.4.2). An onset consonant may optionally be inserted in zero-initial syllables in (7b) to become [ʔɤ] through the consonant insertion rule discussed in the previous subsection.

(7) Examples for the allophone [ɤ] of the phoneme /ə/

$$
\begin{array}{llllll}
\text{a.} & /lə/_{51} & \rightarrow & [lɤ]_{51} & & lè & \text{‘happy’} \\
 & /kə/_{55} & \rightarrow & [kɤ]_{55} & & k\bar{e} & \text{‘song’} \\
 & /xə/_{35} & \rightarrow & [xɤ]_{35} & & h\acute{e} & \text{‘river’} \\
 & /sə/_{51} & \rightarrow & [sɤ]_{51} & & sè & \text{‘color’} \\
 & /tʂʰə/_{55} & \rightarrow & [tʂʰɤ]_{55} & & ch\bar{e} & \text{‘car, vehicle’} \\
 & /ɹə/_{51} & \rightarrow & [ɹɤ]_{51} & & rè & \text{‘warm, hot’} \\
\text{b.} & /ə/_{51} & \rightarrow & [ɤ]_{51} & \rightarrow\ [ʔɤ] & è & \text{‘hungry’} \\
 & /ə/_{35} & \rightarrow & [ɤ]_{35} & \rightarrow\ [ʔɤ] & \acute{e} & \text{‘goose’} \\
\end{array}
$$

In SC, a schwa cannot form a rime by itself ((10f) in §5.3). Schwa is a mid central lax vowel and is shorter than all other vowels. That is why, when a vowel is reduced in a short unstressed and/or neutral-toned syllable, it tends to become a schwa (§7.1.2.3 for English and §7.3.2 for SC). A rime requires at least some length to manifest stress or phonemic tone and schwa is too short to form a rime by itself in SC. If a schwa is followed by a consonant, the rime is longer with two segments, but if it is not, it is changed to a longer tense back vowel that is also mid and unrounded. Let us call this a mid vowel tensing rule, which is to lengthen the duration of a mid vowel in a simple rime since a tense vowel is longer than a lax vowel (§3.1.4). The constraint and the rule are given in (8a) and sample derivations in (8b).

(8)   Mid vowel tensing
   a. Constraint: A schwa cannot appear in a simple V rime
       Rule: A schwa in a simple V rime becomes tense and ba ck
   b. UR   /lə/   /ə/
       Syllabification   Onset Rime   Onset Rime
                              | | |
                              l   ə   ə

       Tensing   Onset Rime   Onset Rime
                              | | |
                              l   ɤ   ɤ

       C Insertion   Onset Rime   Onset Rime
                              | | ⋮ |
                              l   ɤ   ʔ   ɤ

       SR   Onset Rime   Onset Rime
                              | | | |
                              l   ɤ   ʔ   ɤ

Note, however, that the rime [ɤ] is reduced back to [ə] under neutral tone (§7.3.2) because a neutral-toned syllable is short enough to tolerate schwa as its nucleus. For example, the second syllable of the word *gēge* 'older brother' has a neutral tone and is pronounced as $[kɤ]_{55}$ $[kə]_2$.

8.1.5 Mid vowel insertion and high vowel split

SC has a rime constraint that requires the segments in the rime to share the same [back] and [round] features (§5.3, §7.2.3, §7.2.4). The SRs of the examples in (9a) do not violate the constraint since the mid and low vowels undergo the low and mid vowel assimilation rules discussed in §§7.2.3–7.2.4. The examples in (9b), however, seem to be counterexamples to the rime constraint since we do not have SRs like *[en] or *[ɤŋ] as one would expect the schwa to become [−back] [e] before a [−back] nasal [n] and [+back] [ɤ] before a [+back] nasal [ŋ]. Phonetically speaking, the schwa often moves a little frontward before [n] but is not fronted enough to sound like [e], and it also moves a little backward before [ŋ] but is not backed enough to sound like [ɤ]. These small phonetic details are not obviously detectable and traditionally have not been transcribed.

(9) Rime constraint: rime segments share the same [back] and [round] features

   a.   mid and low vowels

	táng 'candy'	*táu* 'peach'	*běi* 'north'	*gǒu* 'dog'
UR	/tʰaŋ/$_{35}$	/tʰau/$_{35}$	/pəi/$_{214}$	/kəu/$_{214}$
Assimilation	tʰɑŋ	tʰɑu	pei	kou
SR	[tʰɑŋ]$_{35}$	[tʰɑu]$_{35}$	[pei]$_{214}$	[kou]$_{214}$

b. Mid vowel followed by a coda nasal

	hěn 'very'	lěng 'cold'
UR	/xən/$_{214}$	/ləŋ/$_{214}$
SR	[xən]$_{214}$	[ləŋ]$_{214}$
	*[xen]$_{214}$	*[lɤŋ]$_{214}$

In modern phonological analysis, schwa is treated as a neutral vowel that has the tongue in its neutral position – not back, not front, not high, not low – and hence is not specified with any phonological vowel features. A neutral vowel, like an 'invisible' segment, does not technically enter into the computation of the sameness of feature values. Alternatively, one can change the wording of the constraint to: 'the two segments in the rime cannot have the opposite values for [back] and [round]' as in Duanmu (2000:63), and then a rime like [ən] and [əŋ] does not violate the constraint since the schwa has no [−back] nor [+back] specification and hence no opposite values in [back] in such rimes. Another alternative solution is to say that unlike a low vowel that stays as [−back] before [n] (/an/ → [an]) or becomes [+back] before [ŋ] (/aŋ/ → [ɑŋ]), a schwa undergoes assimilation only when next to a vowel/glide but not next to a nasal for some phonetic and phonological reasons. For example, the change of schwa to [e] before [n] seems too drastic a change for a short neutral vowel under the influence of a nasal consonant, and the change of schwa to [ɤ], as discussed in §8.1.4, is a lengthening process that occurs only in a simple rime and may be prohibited in a complex rime with a coda. For different analyses, see references for Chinese segmental processes in Further Reading.

For our purposes, let us simply assume that this rime constraint is in effect: (i) for diphthongs, e.g. [ei], [ou], [ɑu]; and (ii) for a complex rime with a high or low vowel followed by a coda nasal, e.g. [an], [ɑŋ], [in], [yn], [uŋ]. Given this understanding of the rime constraint, consider now the URs and the SRs of the examples in (10). The examples in (10a) show that [i]/[y] can be followed by [n] in a rime whereas [u] and [n] cannot form a [un] rime because they differ in backness: [u] is [+back] and [n] is [−back]. The same problem appears in the first and third examples of (10b): [i]/[y] and [ŋ] cannot form a rime because [i] and [y] are [−back] and [ŋ] is [+back].

🎧 (10) High vowels followed by a coda nasal

a.

	xīn 'new'	lún 'wheel'	qún 'skirt'
UR	/çin/$_{55}$	/lun/$_{35}$	/tɕʰyn/$_{35}$
SR	[çin]$_{55}$	[lwən]$_{35}$	[tɕʰyn]$_{35}$
		*[lun]$_{35}$	

b. | *bīng* 'ice' | *dōng* 'east' | *qióng* 'poor'
UR | /piŋ/$_{55}$ | /tuŋ/$_{55}$ | /tɕʰyŋ/$_{35}$
SR | [pjəŋ]$_{55}$ | [tuŋ]$_{55}$ | [tɕʰjuŋ]$_{35}$
    | *[piŋ]$_{55}$ | | *[tɕʰyŋ]$_{35}$

The solution to avoid illicit forms such as *[un] and *[iŋ] is to syllabify the high vowel to the onset position and a schwa is inserted to fill the nucleus left behind by the moved high vowel, as illustrated in (11). The solution to avoid the illicit form *[yŋ] is to split the [y] into [iu] with the [u] in the nucleus position, as illustrated in (12).[2]

(11) Mid vowel insertion I

a. Constraint 1: The high vowel and the coda nasal must have the same value of [back].
b. Rule 1: Syllabify [i] before [ŋ] and [u] before [n] to the onset.
c. Constraint 2: A syllable must have a nuclear segment.
d. Rule 2: Insert [ə] to the empty nucleus.
e. Examples: *bīng* 'ice'   *lún* 'wheel'
    UR /piŋ/$_{55}$ /lun/$_{35}$
    Rule 1 Onset Nucleus Coda   Onset Nucleus Coda
            ╱╲ | ╱╲ |
            p i   ŋ   l u   n
f. Rule 2 Onset Nucleus Coda   Onset Nucleus Coda
            ╱╲   ⋮ | ╱╲   ⋮ |
            p i ə   ŋ   l u ə   n
g. SR and transcription
            Onset Nucleus Coda   Onset Nucleus Coda
            ╱╲ | | ╱╲ | |
            p i ə   ŋ   l u ə   n
            [pjəŋ]$_{55}$ [lwən]$_{35}$

Rule 1 in (11b) applies to avoid violation of the rime constraint in (11a), and we can see in (11e) that by syllabifying the high vowel to the onset, the nucleus and the coda in the rime would not have contradictory values for [back] since the nucleus is empty. Rule 2 in (11d) applies to avoid violation of the constraint in (11c) that prohibits an empty nucleus. As we can see in (11f), by inserting a schwa to the empty nucleus, we no longer have an empty nucleus. The SRs and transcriptions are given in (11g).

---

[2] The final *iong* in *pīnyīn* can sometimes be transcribed as [ɥəŋ] or [ɥuŋ] depending on different researchers (e.g. Cheng 1973:22–3).

In (12), we can see how and why /yŋ/ is transformed to [iuŋ].

(12) High vowel split

a. Constraint 1: The high vowel and the coda nasal must have the same value of [back].
b. Rule 1: Syllabify [y] before [ŋ] to the onset.
c. Constraint 2: A syllable must have a nuclear segment.
d. Rule 2: [y] is split into two segments [i] and [u] to fill the empty nucleus with [u].
e. Example: *qióng* 'poor'
UR /tɕʰyŋ/$_{35}$
Rule 1 Onset Nucleus Coda
tɕʰ y ŋ
f. Rule 2 Onset Nucleus Coda
tɕʰ i u ŋ
g. SR and transcription
Onset Nucleus Coda
tɕʰ i u ŋ
[tɕʰjuŋ]$_{35}$

With the same process and motivation as in (11ab), [y] before [ŋ] is syllabified to the onset so that the [−back] [y] does not form a rime with the [+back] [ŋ], as we can see in (12abe). The empty nucleus also needs to be filled by a vowel, as demanded by the constraint (12c), the same one as in (11c). The difference is that the solution to avoid having an empty nucleus here is to apply the high vowel split rule in (12d) instead of the schwa insertion rule in (11d). The vowel [y] is complex in that it is both [−back] and [+round], and it can be split into two segments: a [−back] [i] and a [+round] [u]. As shown in (12f), the [u] segment fills the nucleus, and in (12g) we see the SR and transcription.

For some speakers, the rime [uŋ] is pronounced more like [ɔŋ] and [juŋ] more like [jɔŋ], and in fact, in *pīnyīn*, [uŋ] is spelled as *ong* and [juŋ] as *iong*, reflecting the [ɔŋ]/[jɔŋ] type of pronunciation. This change of [uŋ] to [ɔŋ] is optional and variable depending on speakers and different varieties of SC. For example, speakers in Taiwan commonly use the [ɔŋ] pronunciation (§12.3.2).

From §8.1.3, we learned that for a zero-initial syllable that begins with a high vowel, the onset segment is the glide identical to the high vowel by a gemination process, as the examples in (13) show. In (13a), the rime is simple, and in (13b), there is a coda nasal after the high vowel. Consider now other zero-initial syllables consisting of an underlying high vowel followed by a coda nasal in (14).

🎧 (13) Zero-initial syllables

        a. /i/$_{55}$ → [ji]$_{55}$ *yī*   'one'

           /y/$_{35}$ → [ɥy]$_{35}$ *yú*   'fish'

           /u/$_{214}$ → [wu]$_{214}$ *wǔ*   'five'

        b. /in/$_{35}$ → [jin]$_{35}$ *yín*   'silver'

           /yn/$_{35}$ → [ɥyn]$_{35}$ *yún*   'cloud'

🎧 (14) Zero-initial syllables

        a. /iŋ/$_{214}$ → [jəŋ]$_{214}$ *yǐng* 'shadow'

           /un/$_{51}$ → [wən]$_{51}$ *wèn*   'to ask'

        b. /yŋ/$_{51}$ → [juŋ]$_{51}$ *yòng*   'to use'

        c. /uŋ/$_{55}$ → [wəŋ]$_{55}$ *wēng* 'old man'

The examples in (14a) follow the constraints and rules in (11) to syllabify the underlying high vowel as a glide to the onset and insert a schwa for the nucleus. The example in (14b) also follows the constraints and rules in (12) to split the underlying [y] into [i] and [u] and syllabify [i] as the glide and [u] as the nuclear vowel. The example in (14c) may seem unexpected, since we saw earlier in (10b) that an underlying /uŋ/ stays as [uŋ] since both segments are [+back]. An underlying /uŋ/ stays as [uŋ] only when it is preceded by an initial consonant, e.g. /luŋ/$_{35}$ → [luŋ]$_{35}$ *long* 'dragon'. In a zero-initial syllable, /uŋ/ would have an empty onset that needs to be filled. The solution in this case is to fill the onset with the vowel, and the empty nucleus left behind is filled by an inserted schwa. The constraints, rules, and derivations are illustrated in (15).

(15) Mid vowel insertion II

        a. Constraint 1: A syllable must have an onset segment.

        b. Rule 1:   Syllabify /u/ in a zero-initial syllable to the onset.

        c. Constraint 2: A syllable must have a nuclear segment.

        d. Rule 2:   Insert [ə] to the empty nucleus.

        e. Example: *wēng* 'old man'

           UR   /uŋ/$_{55}$

           Rule 1   Onset Nucleus Coda
                               ╲   │
                              u   ŋ

        f. Rule 2   Onset Nucleus Coda
                            │   ┊   │
                            u   ə   ŋ

        g. SR and transcription
                       Onset Nucleus Coda
                            │   │   │
                          u   ə   ŋ   [wəŋ]$_{55}$

Rule 1 in (15b) is the same as rule 1 in (11b) but they are motivated by different constraints: (15b) applies in response to the lack of an onset (15a), which is the same as the constraint in (4b) in §8.1.3, whereas rule (11b) applies to avoid two segments in the rime that differ in backness. Constraint 2 and rule 2 in (15cd) are the same as those in (11cd). Rules 1 and 2 of (15) apply as shown in (15ef) and the SR and transcription are shown in (15g). Later, in §§8.2.3–8.2.4, we will see again that an empty nucleus is filled by a schwa through the same mid vowel insertion process.

In this subsection and the previous four subsections, we have seen various processes/rules in response to constraints maintaining well-formed syllable structure. In addition, different processes and rules may be adopted in different contexts to satisfy the same syllable structure constraint, and sometimes the same process/rule can be motivated by different constraint requirements. In the next subsection, we discuss an optional process that sometimes produces abnormal syllables.

8.1.6 Syllable contraction

Syllable contraction occurs when two syllables in a sequence are merged into one syllable that has some segments or features from both syllables. Occasionally more than two syllables can be contracted into one in fast speech. In this subsection we focus only on the contraction of two syllables. Syllable contraction occurs mostly in high frequency words or phrases in casual conversation. A small number of contracted syllables are used so often that they may become regular words, some of which have written forms. The example in (16a) has a written form but those in (16bc) do not. Most contracted syllables do not become regular words, nor do they have written forms.

(16) Syllable contraction I

    a.   *bú* 'not'   *yào* 'want'   →   *bié*   别   'don't'
        $[\text{pu}]_{35}$ $[\text{j}\alpha\text{u}]_{51}$ → $[\text{pje}]_{35}$

    b.   *zhè* 'this'   *yī* 'one'
        $[\text{tʂɤ}]_{51}$ $[\text{ji}]_{51}$ → $[\text{tʂei}]_{53}$ 'this one'

    c.   *nà* 'that'   *yī* 'one'
        $[\text{na}]_{51}$ $[\text{ji}]_{55}$ → $[\text{nei}]_{53}$ 'that one'

In (16a), the contracted syllable takes the onset segments of both syllables, [pj], and the mid vowel [e] (which may result from vowel reduction of [ɑu] to a mid vowel that is assimilated to the glide) becomes the nucleus. Each example in (16bc) takes the onset of the first syllable and combines the vowels of the first and the second into a diphthong. The change of [nai] to [nei] in (16c) is either caused by vowel reduction or by the desire to be parallel to (16b). Note that the tone in the contracted syllable in (16a) takes the tone of the first syllable, but the contracted tones in (16bc) start the same with the first syllable but fall short of the low at the end for a falling tone.

A contracted syllable almost always takes the initial onset consonant and sometimes the glide of the first syllable of the word or phrase on which it is based. As for the rime, some part of the rime in the second syllable most often appears in the contracted syllable, but the rime of the first syllable and the onset of the second syllable may also contribute to the final contracted form. The resulting tone usually combines the tones of the two in some compromised way. As a matter of principle, the contracted syllable tends to take segments from the left edge of the first syllable and from the right edge of the second syllable and to accommodate as many elements as can be tolerated by the speakers and the speech rate. These general rules and principles are necessarily somewhat vague since variations and exceptions do occur. The examples in (17) illustrate these general rules/principles for SC syllable contraction. (For additional examples of syllable contraction, see Duanmu (2000:258–9) and Tseng (2005).)

🎧 (17) Syllable contraction II

    a. *zhèyàng*   'so, this way, like this'
       [tʂɤ]$_{53}$ [jɑŋ]$_{51}$ →   [tɕjɑŋ]$_{51}$

    b. *suóyǐ*   'therefore'
       [swo]$_{35}$ [ji]$_{214}$ →   [swei]$_{53}$ or [swɛ]$_{53}$

    c. *shíhòu*   'time'
       [ʂʅ]$_{35}$ [xou]$_{51}$ →   [ʂou]$_{53}$

    d. *bǐjiǎo*   'comparatively'
       [pi]$_{35}$ [tɕjɑu]$_{214}$ →   [pjɑu]$_{352}$

    e. *kéyǐ*   'may, can'
       [kʰɤ]$_{35}$ [ji]$_{21}$ →   [kʰəi]$_{52}$

    f. *tāmen*   'they'
       [ta]$_{55}$ [mən]$_{2}$ →   [tam]$_{53}$

    g. *shéme*   'what'
       [ʂɤ]$_{35}$ [mə]$_{3}$ →   [ʂəm]$_{353}$

Some contracted syllables are not the normal well-formed syllables in SC. For example, (17fg) have a labial nasal in the coda and (17e) does not have [e] before [i] as one would expect. The tones also may not be one of those typical SC tones we expect, as the examples in (17dg) show. Since a contracted syllable tends to combine the sound/tone elements from two syllables so as to convey the meaning of the original syllables, compromises may have to be made by violating some phonotactic constraints. In fact, if contracted syllables are always identical to some well-formed non-contracted syllables, confusion and miscommunication could happen. In addition, this is a phonetic and optional process in fast speech and is not regulated by phonological constraints (§7.3.2). These are some of the reasons why odd syllable types and tones are tolerated.

The diagrams in (18) demonstrate how the segments and tone in two syllables are rearranged into one syllable for the example in (17d).

(18) Syllable contraction derivation

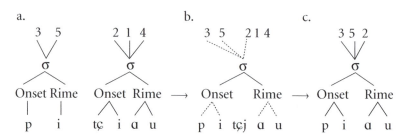

In (18a), there are two syllables, but syllable contraction provides only one syllable for the segments and tones in the original two syllables to fit in. The dotted lines in (18b) show which tones and segments are chosen to be associated with this single syllable. The unassociated segments and tones are removed and the final contracted syllable is obtained as in (18c).

8.2 *r*-suffixation

In §7.1.2 the discussion of the segmental changes in English plural noun formation showed that segmental changes can also be induced by word formation processes. In this section, we study the segmental changes when *r*-suffixation applies. In §8.2.1 the use and function of *r*-suffixation are introduced, in §8.2.2 the UR and SR of the suffix are set up, and in §§8.2.3–8.2.4 the phonological processes/rules involved under *r*-suffixation are examined.

8.2.1 The use and function of the *r*-suffix

The *r*-suffix is often identified as a diminutive suffix that denotes 'smallness' or 'a little bit', but in some cases a suffixed noun simply implies that the object is a familiar object. For example, the *r*-suffixed noun *huār* [xwaɹ]₅₅ can simply mean 'flower' rather than 'small flower'.

SC has only a small number of suffixes (see Li and Thompson 1981: 36 and Packard 1990, 2000), and SC suffixes are usually in the form of one single syllable with a neutral tone. For example, when *zi* [tsɹ̩] 'noun suffix' is added to the noun *yǐ* [ji]₂₁₄ 'chair', a disyllabic word *yǐzi* [ji]₂₁ [tsɹ̩]₄ 'chair' is created with a neutral tone in the second syllable. Unlike a suffix like *zi*, the *r*-suffix does not form a stand-alone syllable; rather, it is attached to the preceding syllable to be part of its rime. For example, when the noun *huā* [xwa]₅₅ 'flower' is suffixed with /ɹ/, the suffixed word *huār* [xwaɹ]₅₅ 'flower' is pronounced as one syllable with the suffix occupying the coda position.

The suffix /ɹ/ originates in the word /əɹ/₃₅ *ér* 'son, child'. The relationship is also evident in the orthography: the written character 儿 for *ér* 'son, child' is also used to represent the suffix. For example, the suffixed noun *huār* [xwaɹ]₅₅ 'flower' is monosyllabic but is written with two characters: 花 儿. Normally one character represents one syllable (§§1.3–1.4) but this is a special case where two characters represent one syllable. In some Mandarin dialects and in the history of Mandarin, this suffix is actually a separate syllable with a neutral tone: e.g. [xwa]₅₅ [əɹ]₂ 'flower'. In the Beijing dialect on which SC is based, we can say that there is an obligatory process of syllable contraction that merges the suffix with the preceding syllable (see §§8.2.3–8.2.4 below).

In textbook SC and most varieties of SC, *r*-suffixation, which is called *ér-huà* 儿 化 in Chinese, is limited to a small number of words, but speakers of the Beijing dialect and SC speakers from Beijing apply *r*-suffixation extensively to many nouns and some verbs/adjectives. Some SC speakers, especially those in the southern part of China, such as Hong Kong and Shanghai, and in Taiwan and Singapore, either pronounce the suffix as a separate syllable or do not even exhibit the *r*-suffixation process at all.

Not only does the application of *r*-suffixation vary greatly among SC speakers, the segmental changes applied under *r*-suffixation also have variations depending on the age of the speakers and the speakers' local dialects. For ease of presentation and discussion, we will not discuss all the variations. In addition, since *r*-suffixation is limited in use in textbook SC and many SC speakers' speech, the discussion will be based on more commonly used words.

For learners of SC, it is not necessary to learn all these *r*-suffixed words, and sticking to only those words used in the textbooks and national broadcasts would be good enough. Remember that although the pronunciation of SC is based on the Beijing dialect, SC is not identical to the Beijing dialect in all linguistic aspects and usage (§1.2), and also note that extensive *r*-suffixation is a special dialectal feature of some Mandarin dialects including the Beijing dialect. For those who are interested in learning to pronounce *r*-suffixed words, the best strategy is to learn form SC speakers from Beijing. The need for us to spend some time understanding the segmental changes induced by *r*-suffixation is for the practical purpose of being able to better comprehend the speech of those SC speakers who do use *r*-suffixed words more extensively.

8.2.2 Phonological and phonetic representations of the suffix

Before we study the processes/rules and relevant constraints that apply to a syllable upon *r*-suffixation, we should decide first the phonological and phonetic representations of the suffix. As mentioned above, there have been many different analyses of the segmental changes under Beijing *r*-suffixation. The underlying phonological representation for the suffix ranges from /əɹ/, /ɚ/, and /ɹ/ to a non-segment single feature [rhotic] or [retroflex], and the phonetic realization of the suffix ranges from [r], [ɹ], a rhotacized vowel [ɚ], and/or a rhotic/retroflex feature on the vowel/rime of the preceding syllable.

In §3.4.5, various transcriptions and descriptions of the *er* syllable were discussed, and [əɹ] has been used for the mid central RHOTACIZED vowel for convenience and ease of presentation. For the suffix *r*, let us set up the UR as /ɹ/ (cf. Lin 1989) and the resulting SR of the rhotacized rime/vowel through *r*-suffixation is marked with an [ɹ] at the end of the rime, e.g. [aɹ], or on the vowel with a superscript, e.g. [oʲ]. A form like [aɹ] is a rhotacized complex rime consisting of two segments in the rime, whereas a form like [oʲ] is a simple rime containing a single rhotacized vowel. Although the post-alveolar symbol [ɹ] is used here, many speakers simply retract the tongue body backward and do not raise the tongue tip to the post-alveolar region (§3.4.5; Lee and Zee 2003).

8.2.3 Suffixation to syllables with a simple rime

In the examples in (19), the syllable preceding the *r*-suffix has a simple rime consisting of only one segment, either a vowel or a syllabic consonant.

(19) Simple rime suffixed with /ɹ/

    I. Low vowel + /ɹ/

    a. $[xwa]_{53} + /ɹ/$ → $[xwaɹ]_{53}$

                                 huàr   'painting, picture'

        $[na]_{53} + /ɹ/$ → $[naɹ]_{53}$

                                   nàr   'there'

    II. Mid vowel + /ɹ/

    b. $[tʂɤ]_{53} + /ɹ/$ → $[tʂɤʲ]_{53}$

                                   zhèr   'here'

        $[kɤ]_{55} + /ɹ/$ → $[kɤʲ]_{55}$

                                   gēr   'song'

c. $[\text{kwo}]_{55} + /\text{ɹ}/$ → $[\text{kwo}^{\text{ɹ}}]_{55}$

guōr   'wok'

d. $[\text{ɕjɑu}]_{21}[\text{ɕje}]_{35} + /\text{ɹ}/$ → $[\text{ɕjɑu}]_{21}[\text{ɕje}^{\text{ɹ}}]_{35}/[\text{ɕjɔɹ}]_{35}$

xiǎoxiér 'small shoes'

III. High vowel + /ɹ/

e. $[\text{tɕi}]_{55} + /\text{ɹ}/$ → $[\text{tɕjɔɹ}]_{55}$

jīr   'chicken'

f. $[\text{ɥy}]_{35} + /\text{ɹ}/$ → $[\text{ɥɔɹ}]_{35}$

yúr   'fish'

g. $[\text{ku}]_{21} + /\text{ɹ}/$ → $[\text{ku}^{\text{ɹ}}]_{35}$

gǔr   'drum'

IV. Syllabic consonant + /ɹ/

h. $[\text{tsɻ̩}]_{53} + /\text{ɹ}/$ → $[\text{tsɔɹ}]_{53}$

zìr   'written character'

$[\text{tʂɻ̩}]_{55} + /\text{ɹ}/$ → $[\text{tʂɔɹ}]_{53}$

zhīr   'twig'

In (19a), for a simple rime with a low vowel, the suffix is added to create a complex rhotacized rime, but in (19bcd), a mid vowel is rhotacized and maintains a simple rime in the *r*-suffixed syllable. A back mid vowel differs from a front mid vowel in that a rhotacized mid front vowel [e^{ɹ}] can also lose its [−back] feature and have a variant in the form of a rhotacized rime [ɔɹ] (19d). For the high front vowels in (19ef), the high vowel is syllabified to the onset to become a glide and the rime becomes [ɔɹ], whereas the high back vowel in (19g) is simply rhotacized and stays in the rime. In (19h), the syllabic consonant is deleted and the *r*-suffixed rime is [ɔɹ].

The major generalization is that a rhotacized rime is possible for a low and mid vowel but a high front vowel or a syllabic consonant cannot be rhotacized or stay in a rhotacized rime. Rhotacization and high front vowels/syllabic coronal consonants are incompatible because of contradictory articulatory gestures: rhotacization involves the retraction of the tongue body and yet a high front vowel and a syllabic coronal consonant involves the raising and/or advancing of the front of the tongue. To resolve the incompatibility, a schwa is inserted to create a central mid rhotacized vowel [ɔɹ] for the rime, as in (19efh). The fact that a mid front vowel may lose its [−back] feature (19d) but a back vowel does not lose its [+back] feature (19bc) also indicates that a central or back mid vowel is more compatible with rhotacization.

The movement of the incompatible high vowel to the onset position indicates that the *r*-suffixed syllable retains as many segments/features as can be tolerated from the original syllable, which is the same as the syllable contraction process we saw in §8.1.6. A syllabic consonant, however, cannot be in the onset nor can it be part of a complex rime (§5.3). Moreover, as discussed in §8.1.2, a syllabic consonant is simply an extension of an onset coronal consonant. To accommodate the suffix, the syllabic consonant cannot appear.

Using the examples in (19abeh), the diagrams in (20) illustrate how the suffix and the segments of its preceding syllable manage to fit into one single syllable.

(20) Derivation of *r*-suffixation I

    a. Onset Rime   ⟶   Onset Rime

        tʂ   ɤ ɹ   tʂ   ɤˀ

    b. Onset Rime   ⟶   Onset Rime

        x u a ɹ   x u a ɹ

    c. Onset Rime   ⟶   Onset Rime   ⟶   Onset Rime

        tɕ i   ɹ   tɕ i   ə ɹ   tɕ i   ə ɹ [tɕjəɹ]

    d. Onset Rime   ⟶   Onset Rime   ⟶   Onset Rime

        ts   ɹ   ts   ə ɹ   ts   ə ɹ

This process is similar to syllable contraction as shown in (18) in §8.1.6. In (20a), all segments can be accommodated and the mid vowel and the suffix is merged to create a single rhotacized mid vowel, but for a low vowel, the suffix and the vowel does not merge, as shown in (20b). In (20c) the high vowel is associated to the onset, leaving behind an empty nucleus, and a schwa is inserted to fill the nucleus position. In (20d), the coronal consonant is linked only to the onset and does not extend to the nucleus (cf. (2fg) in §8.1.2), and an empty nucleus is also filled with a schwa to create a mid central rhotacized vowel.

8.2.4 Suffixation to syllables with a complex rime

In the examples in (21), the syllable preceding the *r*-suffix has a complex rime consisting of either a diphthong or a vowel followed by a coda nasal.

(21) Complex rime suffixed with /ɹ/

    I. Diphthongs + /ɹ/
    a. [kʰou]₂₁[tai]₅₃   + /ɹ/   →   [kʰou]₂₁[taɹ]₅₃
                             kǒudàir   'pocket'
    b. [ji]₅₃[xwei]₂₁   + /ɹ/   →   [ji]₅₃[xwəɹ]₂₁
                              yìhuěir   'in a moment'

c. [waɹ]₃₅ [pʰjɑu]₅₁ + /ɹ/   →   [waɹ]₃₅[pʰjɑuˀ]₅₁
                                              wánrpiàor   'amateur'

       [tʰou]₃₅   + /ɹ/   →   [tʰouˀ]₃₅
                                                tóur   'head'

II. Vowel-[n] + /ɹ/
d. [kwan]₅₅   + /ɹ/   →   [kwaɹ]₅₅
                                                guānr   'government official'

e. [jɛn]₂₁   + /ɹ/   →   [jaɹ]₂₁
                                                yǎnr   'eye'

f. [wan]₃₅   + /ɹ/   →   [waɹ]₃₅
                                                wánr   'play, fun'

g. [kən]₅₅   + /ɹ/   →   [kəɹ]₅₅
                                                gēnr   'root'

h. [kwən]₂₁   + /ɹ/   →   [kwəɹ]₂₁
                                                gǔnr   'to roll'

i. [tɕin]₅₅   + /ɹ/   →   [tɕjəɹ]₅₅
                                                jīnr   'today'

j. [ji]₅₃[tɕʰyn]₃₅ + /ɹ/   →   [ji]₅₃[tɕʰyəɹ]₃₅
                                                jì qúnr   'a flock of'

III. Vowel-[ŋ] + /ɹ/
k. [jɑŋ]₅₁   + /ɹ/   →   [jɑ̃ɹ̃]₅₁
                                                yàngr   'appearance, shape'

l. [mjəŋ]₃₅   + /ɹ/   →   [mjə̃ɹ̃]₃₅
                                                míngr   'tomorrow'

m. [kʰuŋ]₅₃   + /ɹ/   →   [kʰũɹ̃]₅₃
                                                kòngr   'free time'

The examples in (21abij) again show the incompatibility of a high front vowel with [ɹ]. The high front vowel part of the diphthongs [ai] and [ei] is deleted (21ab) and its position is filled by the suffix; on the other hand, the high back part of the diphthongs [ɑu] and [ou] in (21c) is retained and the whole rime is rhotacized. In (21ij), a high front vowel moves away from the suffix to become a glide and a schwa is inserted to fill the vacated nucleus position. Note also that a coda nasal is replaced by the suffix (20d–j). Since a low vowel becomes [ɛ] only between a high front glide and [n] (§7.2.3), when [n] is removed, the context for the low vowel fronting/raising rule disappears. That is why in (21e) the vowel in the *r*-suffixed rime returns to a low vowel.

One important generalization for the examples with nasal deletion is that the deletion of [n] does not lead to vowel nasalization of the rime as shown in (21d–j), whereas the [+nasal] feature of [ŋ] is retained on the vowel as shown in (21k–m). The coda nasal is removed because SC does not allow both a nasal and a [ɹ] in the coda. The fact that vowel nasalization is stronger before [ŋ] than before [n] was mentioned in §7.2.2. Although this difference in the degree of nasalization is phonetic in nature, its effects show up in the phonological processes under *r*-suffixation (Zhang 2000). This is one good case demonstrating that phonology and phonetics are closely interconnected despite their differences (§1.5.3). Note also that [n] was given a [−back] feature and [ŋ] a [+back] feature in our analyses of low vowel assimilation (§7.2.3), mid vowel insertion (§8.1.5), and some phonotactic constraints (§5.3). A [−back] [n], like a high front vowel, is less compatible with rhotacization, and a [+back] [ŋ], like a back vowel, survives in some way leaving behind a [+nasal] feature. We can analyze the difference by saying that [n] is deleted but [ŋ], like a back vowel, is retained and merged with the vowel when [ɹ] is added.

The diagrams in (22) provide sample derivations for the examples (21aeik). The derivation in (22a) shows that, given the single syllable, [i] is not associated due to its incompatibility with [ɹ], yielding an output with [i] deleted.

(22) Derivation of *r*-suffixation II

In (22b), the syllable before the suffix results from a low vowel assimilation rule that changes the underlying /a/ to [ɛ] between a high front glide and [n]: /ian/ → [jɛn] (§7.2.3). However, when [n], like a high front vowel, cannot be syllabified due to its incompatibility with [ɹ], the low vowel reappears because the context necessary for [ɛ] to appear is no longer present since the low vowel is now between a high front glide and [ɹ]. Like the example in (20b) in §8.2.3, the high vowel in (22c) is linked to the onset since neither [i] and [n] can directly precede [ɹ]. The high front vowel can be syllabified as an onset but the coda nasal cannot be accommodated. The lack of a nuclear vowel is then resolved by an inserted schwa. In comparison, a velar nasal is compatible with [ɹ] and stays, but since there cannot be more than three segments in a SC rime (§5.3), the vowel and the nasal are merged into a nasalized vowel. (Recall that in §7.3.2, a vowel and a coda nasal can also be merged under the process of rime reduction.)

In 8.1.6, the syllables resulting from syllable contraction may be violating SC phonotactic constraints. Similarly, the only possible unsuffixed rime that can have [ɹ] is [ɚɹ], and yet the *r*-suffixed rimes allow for other rhotacized vowels. Syllable contraction and *r*-suffixation, then, demonstrate that although some parts of the phonotactic constraints are never violated, some may be marginally violated under morphological or phonetic processes.

The segmental changes under *r*-suffixation and their variations among speakers can be rather complex. I have limited the discussion to one general type that exhibits the major and common generalizations among different varieties. Those who are interested in additional data and different analyses, see Further Reading for references.

8.3 Summary

This chapter discusses the role syllable structure and phonotactic constraints play in SC segmental changes. These segmental processes can be purely phonological/phonetic or can be effected by morphology or lexical information.

- High vowels in SC are syllabified to the onset to become glides when they are followed by a mid or low vowel (§8.1.1). This conforms to the SONORITY SEQUENCING PRINCIPLE in syllabifying the most sonorous segment, a low or mid vowel, to the nucleus (§5.2.2).
- SYLLABIC CONSONANTS are created by lengthening an initial dental or post-alveolar fricative/affricate to fill an empty nucleus position (§8.1.2).
- The segment that fills an empty onset position in a zero-initial syllable is either a copy of the high vowel in the same syllable through GEMINATION or is realized with a glottal or velar consonant when the vowel is mid or low. When the zero-initial syllable is a FUNCTION WORD, the onset is filled either with a copy of the high vowel or nasal in the preceding syllable through geminiation or with [j] when the preceding syllable ends in a mid or low vowel (§8.1.3).
- Mid vowel tensing occurs in a simple V rime when such a rime calls for a longer vowel than schwa (§8.1.4).

- Mid vowel insertion (§8.1.5) between a high glide and a coda nasal occurs either to satisfy the constraint that requires the rime segments to share the same value in [back] or to fill in an empty nucleus. The high vowel split rule which changes [y] to [iu] applies to avoid the illicit rime [yŋ] in which the two segments also differ in backness.
- SYLLABLE CONTRACTION produces a single syllable that combines the segments and tones of two syllables (§8.1.6). This process applies most commonly to disyllabic words or phrases used in high frequency and in casual speech.
- Similar to the syllable contraction process, the *r*-suffix is combined with its preceding syllable to produce a single *r*-suffixed syllable. The incompatibility of a [−back] segment, such as high front vowels and [n], with the suffix [ɹ], and the prohibition of having more than two rime segments, lead to various segmental processes such as glide formation, mid vowel insertion, segment deletion, and segmental merger that produces a nasalized vowel (§8.2).

Chapters 7 and 8 have discussed an array of segmental changes in different phonological/phonetic and morphological contexts. In the next chapter, we study what tonal processes occur to change an underlying tone to a different tone and in what contexts.

EXERCISES

1   For each of the following examples, give the *pīnyīn* and identify all the constraint(s) and/or rule(s) that have applied.

Example: /s/55 → [sɹ̩]55   'silk'
          sī

Syllabic consonant formation (§8.1.2)

a. /ɕin/214   →   [ɕjən]214   'awake'
b. /ən/55   →   [ʔən]55   'favor'
c. /tun/51   →   [twən]51   'ton'
d. /tʂə/55   →   [tʂɤ]55   'to cover'
e. /tʂʰ/214   →   [tʂʰɹ̩]214   'tooth'
f. /tʰian/55 /a/   →   [tjɛn]55 [na]2   'my goodness!'
g. /ɹə/53 /a/   →   [ɹɤ]53 [ja]1   'hot!'
h. /ɕyŋ/35   →   [ɕjuŋ]35   'bear'
i. /yn/55   →   [ɥyn]55   'dizzy'

j.   [twei]$_{53}$ [la]$_1$ →   [tʁa]$_{531}$ 'that's right'

k.   [ɹu]$_{35}$ [kwo]$_{214}$ →   [ɹwo]$_{352}$ 'if'

l.   [ɥe]$_{53}$ + ɹ   →   [ɥeʴ]$_{51}$ or [ɥəɹ]$_{51}$ 'moon'

m.   [jaŋ]$_{35}$ + ɹ   →   [jãɹ]$_{35}$ 'sheep'

2   For each of the following examples, give the surface representation by applying the rule(s) provided.

Example:

tūn	/tʰun/$_{55}$	'to swallow'

Rules: glide formation (§8.1.1) and mid vowel insertion (§8.1.5)

→   [tʰwən]$_{55}$

a.   *yíng*   /iŋ/$_{35}$ 'to win'

Rules: glide formation in empty onset and mid vowel insertion

b.   *zí*   /ts/$_{35}$ 'china, porcelain'

Rule: syllabic consonant formation

c.   *hǎo a*   /xau/$_{21}$ /a/

Rules: low vowel backing and gemination to fill empty onset

d.   *dǎ a*   /ta/$_{21}$ /a/   'Hit!'

Rule: consonant insertion to fill empty onset

e.   *dé*   /tə/$_{35}$ 'virtue'

Rule: mid vowel tensing

f.   *yòng*   /yŋ/$_{51}$ 'to use'

Rules: glide formation in empty onset, and high vowel split

g.   *pánr*   [pʰan]$_{35}$ + /ɹ/   'plate, dish'

Rules: *r*-suffixation and [n] deletion

h.   *gāngr*   [kɑŋ]$_{55}$ + ɹ   'urn, jar'

Rules: *r*-suffixation, and merger of low vowel and velar nasal

i.   *dāor*   [tɑu]$_{55}$ + ɹ   'knife'

Rule: *r*-suffixation

j.   *bēir*   [pei]$_{55}$ + ɹ   'cup'

Rules: *r*-suffixation and [i] deletion

k.   *jiēr*   [tɕje]$_{55}$ + ɹ   'street'

Rule: *r*-suffixation

l.   *chēr*   [tʂʰɤ]$_{55}$ + ɹ   'car'

Rule: *r*-suffixation

3   Collect five examples for each syllable-based rule discussed in §§8.1.1–8.1.5. For each example, give the *pīnyīn* spelling, the underlying representation, and the surface representation.

4   Whenever you have a chance, listen carefully to SC speakers' casual
    conversation and collect examples for syllable contraction. For each example:
    (i) transcribe the contracted syllable you hear; (ii) identify the original word
    with uncontracted syllables; and (iii) describe the segmental and tonal
    changes made to the word by syllable contraction.

5   Whenever you have a chance, listen carefully to Beijing SC speakers' speech
    and collect examples for r-suffixation. For each example: (i) transcribe the
    r-suffixed word; (ii) identify the original unsuffixed word; and (iii) describe the
    changes made to the unsuffixed word by r-suffixation.

9 Tonal processes

In §4.2.3, TONE SANDHI was defined as a process in which a tone is changed due to the influence of adjacent tones and a few examples of SC tonal variations were presented. In addition to adjacent tones, tonal changes can be influenced by a particular word, a morphological or phonological process, or prosodic, word, and sentence structures. This chapter examines how and why a tone is changed, and in what context, in SC. We start with an introduction of tone features and tonal processes relevant to SC in §9.1 before studying the tonal changes applying to the four PHONEMIC TONES in §9.2. The phonetic variations of the neutral tone are analyzed in §9.3, and in §9.4 we examine how the application of tone 3 sandhi is determined by PROSODIC and MORPHO-SYNTACTIC factors. The final section (§9.5) summarizes the main points of the chapter.

9.1 Tone features and tonal processes

In the transcription of tone, we have adopted a PITCH VALUE system that indicates both the PITCH LEVEL and pitch movement (PITCH CONTOUR): on a scale of 1 to 5, 5 has the highest pitch and 1 has the lowest, and 55 indicates no movement (a LEVEL TONE), whereas 35 and 51 show rising and falling pitch movements respectively (CONTOUR TONES). For phonology, the small phonetic difference in pitch level, e.g. that between 1 and 2 or between 4 and 5, is usually not important. What is more important is low versus high pitch, and the differences between level tones and rising/falling contours. The basic phonological features used for a tonal system can simply be L (low tone), and H (high tone), and M (mid tone) for some languages. A level tone is then LL (low level) or HH (high level), a rising tone is LH, and a falling tone is HL (cf. §4.1.4).

Most analyses of SC tone make use of only H and L, but, for our specific purposes, let us use H, L, and M to better match the numerical phonetic transcription system. The correspondences between the phonological tone features and the pitch values used for transcription are shown in (1a), and (1b) shows how SC tones are represented with tone features.

(1) Tonal feature and pitch value

a. TONAL FEATURE   PITCH VALUE
   H (high)   4 or 5
   M (mid)   3
   L (low)   1 or 2

b. SC TONE   TONAL FEATURE   PITCH VALUE
   Tone 1   HH   55
   Tone 2   MH   35
   Tone 3   LL (before another tone)   21
                    LH (in phrase final syllable)   214
   Tone 4   HL (in phrase final syllable)   51
                    HM (before another tone)   53

A TONE BEARING UNIT (TBU) is the phonological entity with which a tone is associated, and in SC the TBU can be the syllable, the rime, or the MORA (see § 4.1.3) depending on different analyses. A common analysis of SC tone is to assign two moras (i.e. two TBUs) for each 'full syllable' (i.e. each non-neutral-toned syllable), with each tone feature associated with one mora; for a 'weak syllable' (i.e. a neutral-toned syllable), there is only one mora and one tone feature (cf. Duanmu 2000: chapter 10). The reason that there are usually two tone features for each SC syllable is because most syllables have two moras. For ease of presentation without getting into the technical aspects of phonological representation and theory, let us use the syllable as the TBU to which tone features are linked. When two tone features belong to the same syllable, the syllable has two lines linking the two tone features as illustrated in (2a). When a tone feature, e.g. L, is linked to two syllables, as in (2b), the representation indicates that both syllables have a low tone and in this particular case the first syllable has a falling HL tone and the second one has a single low tone.

(2) a. high level tone   falling tone   b. falling low

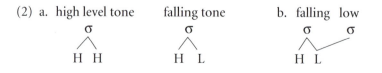

ATONAL PROCESS can be assimilatory or dissimilatory. If a tone becomes more similar to a neighboring tone, it is an ASSIMILATION process. If a tone becomes less similar to an adjacent tone, it is a DISSIMILATION process. When two identical tones are next to each other, dissimilation may apply, resulting in the change of one of the tones to another tone (as in tone 3 sandhi) or in the deletion of one of the tones. Tonal assimilation can be analyzed as TONE SPREAD that extends a tone to an adjacent TBU. For example, the diagrams in (3) show that the high tone in the first syllable is spread to the next syllable. A doubly linked H tone means that the high tone extends to span two syllables resulting in two high tones. This is similar to the analyses for syllabic consonants in §8.1.2 and zero-initial syllables in §8.1.3, in which a single segment is linked to two syllable positions and becomes a long segment.

(3) Tone spread

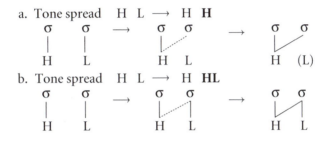

The H tone spread may result in different phonetic outputs depending on languages. In (3a) high tone spread displaces the low tone originally linked to the second syllable, and a tone that is not linked to a TBU is either deleted or becomes a floating tone waiting for an opportunity to surface again, e.g. when some suitable TBU comes along through a morphological process such as suffixation. In (3b), the second syllable is associated with both the spread H and the original L, resulting in a HL falling tone for the second syllable.

Like vowel or consonant insertion and deletion, there are also processes like TONE INSERTION and TONE DELETION. For example, when a syllable has no tone, a tone can be inserted to give the syllable a tone (similar to the insertion of a schwa to fill an empty nucleus discussed in §8.1.5 and §8.2), and when a syllable becomes unstressed, its original tone may be deleted. Similar to vowel or rime reduction (§7.3.2), TONE REDUCTION is a process in which a tone is shortened or simplified when its host syllable is shorter and weaker. There are other tonal processes used in various tone languages (see Yip 2002), but this basic understanding of tonal processes should be sufficient for our purposes.

There are also less noticeable phonetic tonal changes called TONAL COAR-TICUALTION, which may change the pitch level/contour and the exact time when the pitch level/contour of a tone is manifested. For example, when a high level tone is preceded and followed by a low tone in a sequence of three syllables, we do not have a discrete division such as low pitch for the whole first syllable, high pitch for the whole middle syllable, and low pitch for the whole third syllable, although phonologically this is how we represent each tone and its associated syllable. Phonetically it is necessary to produce smooth pitch transition from one tone to another due to physiological constraints and for ease of articulation. In this particular example, because it takes some time to move from a L pitch target to a H pitch target, the high pitch is realized in the later part of the middle syllable and may linger shortly at the beginning of the third syllable (Xu 1999; Yip 2002:8–9). Moreover, there is a natural smooth gliding pitch movement from L to H and then H to L that is more like a sequence of low-rising-high-falling, even though phonologically there are no rising and falling tones. It is not always an easy task to separate tonal coarticulation from tone sandhi or other tonal processes, and tonal coarticulation can be rather complex. In what follows, only the major tonal processes most commonly identified in the Chinese phonology literature are covered, but possible tonal coarticualtion effects will be mentioned whenever appropriate. For more examples and discussion of tonal coarticulation, see Yip (2002:8–10), Chen (2000:23–38), and references for tone in Further Reading.

9.2 Tonal processes for the four phonemic tones

In this section, we examine in more detail the tonal changes that apply to the four phonemic tones introduced in chapter 4. A PHONEMIC TONE is the underlying tone associated with each syllable and it may change to a tone with a different phonetic pitch value in the SURFACE REPRESENTATION through tonal processes/rules.

9.2.1 T3 and T4 reduction

In the first case, T3 and T4 are simplified or shortened when they are followed by another tone, as shown in (4) and (5).

(4) T3 reduction

    a. LH⟶ LL/ ___ another tone
    b. Example: *lǎoyīng* 'eagle' [lɑu]**214** [jəŋ]55 ⟶ [lɑu]**21** [jəŋ]55

      σ   σ   σ   σ

     /\ /\ ⟶ /\ /\

    L H H H   L L H H

(5) T4 reduction

    a. HL⟶HM/___ another tone

    b. Example: *dòngwù* 'animal' [tuŋ]**51** [wu]51 ⟶ [tuŋ]**53** [wu]51

$$\begin{array}{ccc} \sigma \quad \sigma & & \sigma \quad \sigma \\ \wedge \quad \wedge & \rightarrow & \wedge \quad \wedge \\ \text{H L H L} & & \textbf{H M} \text{ H L} \end{array}$$

A syllable in phrase final position is longer in duration and can afford to preserve fully the pitch level and contour of its tone, whereas a syllable in non-final position is somewhat shorter, so a complex tone may be reduced. In (4), a complex tone like T3 is simplified by dropping the final rise (the H tone feature), and in (5), the falling tone T4 is cut short in the sense that the fall can only reach the middle of the pitch range (HM) rather than going all the way down to reach the low pitch level (HL). Tonal reduction can often be considered a tonal coarticulation effect: for example, T4 is cut short of its falling part so as to fulfill the need to smoothly and quickly move to the next tone.

9.2.2 Tone 3 sandhi

The second case is TONE 3 SANDHI, which changes a T3 to T2 before another T3. In terms of production, the changed T3 (the T2 derived from T3) before another T3 is not completely identical to T2 in that the changed T3 has slightly lower overall FUNDAMENTAL FREQUENCY (F0) (§4.1.2) than that of regular T2 in the same context (Zee 1980; Peng 2000). However, native speakers do not seem to reliably detect the minor differences between a changed T3 and the real T2 in perceptual tests (Wang and Li 1967; Peng 2000). Let us simply assume that the changed T3 is the same as T2.

    Given the T3 reduction rule in (4), a T3 before another tone is a LL tone. This LL tone then changes to MH (T2) before another T3, which can be either a phrase final T3 (LH) or a non-phrase final T3 (LL), as shown in (6a). The examples in (6bc) illustrate the change of the first T3 from LH to LL and finally to MH.

🎧 (6) Tone 3 sandhi: T3 T3 → T2 T3

    a. Rule: LL⟶MH/ __ LH or LL (i.e. T3⟶T2/__ T3)

    b. Example 1:   *lǎoshǔ* 'mouse'

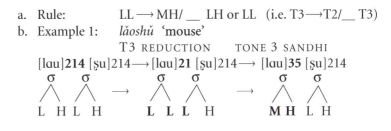

                    T3 REDUCTION   TONE 3 SANDHI

       [lɑu]**214** [ʂu]214⟶[lɑu]**21** [ʂu]214⟶ [lɑu]**35** [ʂu]214

$$\begin{array}{ccccc} \sigma \quad \sigma & & \sigma \quad \sigma & & \sigma \quad \sigma \\ \wedge \quad \wedge & \rightarrow & \wedge \quad \wedge & \rightarrow & \wedge \quad \wedge \\ \text{L H L H} & & \textbf{L} \text{ L} \textbf{L} \text{ H} & & \textbf{M H} \text{ L H} \end{array}$$

c. Example 2:   *lǎoshǔyào* 'mouse drug (poison used to kill mice)'
   [lɑu]**214** [ʂu]**214** [jɑu]51   ⟶   [lɑu]**21** [ʂu]**21** [jɑu]51   (T3 reduction)
                                       ⟶   [lɑu]**35** [ʂu]**21** [jɑu]51   (Tone 3 sandhi)

$$\text{T3 REDUCTION} \qquad \text{TONE 3 SANDHI}$$

σ   σ   σ   σ   σ   σ   σ   σ   σ
∧   ∧   ∧   →   ∧   ∧   ∧   →   ∧   ∧   ∧
L HL HH L   **L   LL LH** L   **M HL** LH L

Given the representation with the tone features, tone 3 sandhi basically changes
from a LL tone to a high rising tone (MH) before a L tone feature. As mentioned
in §7.1.2.2 and §9.1, this can be treated as a dissimilation rule since the LL tone
is changed to differ from the following L. The purpose of this change may be
attributed to ease of perception. High pitch is more salient and easier to perceive,
and when there is a sequence of three or four Ls it becomes more difficult to
perceive the pitch change from one tone to another and from one syllable to
another. By changing the first T3 to a higher pitch, the tonal transition between
the two syllables becomes more detectable. When there are more than two T3
syllables in a row, how tone 3 sandhi is applied becomes more complicated.
Compare the two examples in (7), in which T3, T2, and *pīnyīn* are used for
simplicity.

🎧 (7)   Tone 3 sandhi in phrases/sentences

a. *mǐ lǎoshǔ hǎo*   Mic key Mouse is good'
   T3 T3 T3 T3   →   T3 **T2 T2** T3
b. *gǒu yǎo lǎoshǔ*   'The dog bit the mouse'
   T3 T3 T3 T3   →   **T2** T3 **T2** T3

As you can see, the same sequence of four T3s produces two different surface
tone sandhi patterns. This suggests that the change of T3 to T2 is not determined
simply by being followed by another T3. How prosodic and syntactic factors
determine which T3 undergoes tone sandhi and which T3 does not will be
discussed in §9.4.

9.2.3 Tonal change for *yī* and *bù*

The third case is the change of tone in two specific words: *yī* 'one' and *bù* 'not'
(see (14) in §4.2.3 for a full set of examples). The tone for *yī* 'one' is HH (T1)
in phrase final position, but it changes to HL (T4) in non-phrase final position
by rule (8a). This HL tone then becomes HM by the T4 reduction rule in (4)
before T1, T2, and T3, as the derivation in (8b) illustrates. Before another T4,
however, the HL tone derived by rule (8a) further changes to MH (T2) before
another T4 by rule (8c), as illustrated by the derivation in (8d).

(8) Tone sandhi for *yī* 'one' and *bù* 'not'

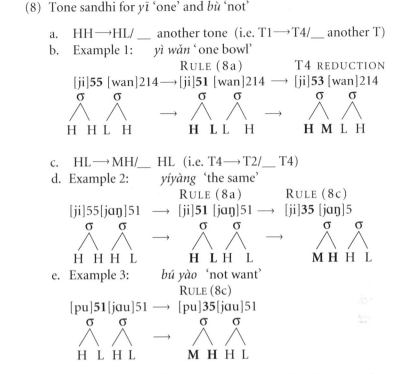

    a.   HH⟶HL/ __ another tone (i.e. T1⟶T4/__ another T)

    b.   Example 1:   *yì wǎn* 'one bowl'

RULE (8a)   T4 REDUCTION

[ji]55 [wan]214⟶[ji]51 [wan]214 ⟶ [ji]53 [wan]214

σ σ   ⟶   σ σ   ⟶   σ σ

H HL H   H LL H   H M L H

    c.   HL⟶MH/__ HL (i.e. T4⟶T2/__ T4)

    d. Example 2:   *yíyàng* 'the same'

RULE (8a)   RULE (8c)

[ji]55[jaŋ]51 ⟶ [ji]51 [jaŋ]51 ⟶ [ji]35 [jaŋ]5

σ σ   ⟶   σ σ   ⟶   σ σ

H H H L   H L H L   M H H L

    e.   Example 3:   *bú yào* 'not want'

RULE (8c)

[pu]51[jau]51 ⟶ [pu]35[jau]51

σ σ   ⟶   σ σ

H L H L   M H H L

The rule in (8a) seems to be an arbitrary change for this particular word, but the rule in (8c) can be treated as another case of dissimilation: change the first T4 in a sequence of two T4s. This T4 dissimilation rule, however, is very limited in its application since it applies only when the first T4 is for the word *yī* 'one' or *bù* 'not'. The derivation in (8e) shows that the T4 of *bù* 'not' also becomes T2 when followed by another T4 by applying rule (8c).

9.2.4 Tonal changes in reduplication

The fourth case is the loss of tone in reduplicated kinship nouns (a kinship noun formed by repeating the same syllable). As shown in (9), the copy or repeat of the monosyllabic morpheme becomes unstressed and can only bear a neutral tone (see §9.3 below for how the neutral tone is realized).

(9) Tonal changes for reduplicated kinship nouns

    a.   A monosyllabic kinship noun is reduplicated.

    b.   The reduplicated syllable is unstressed and loses the tone.

    c.   Example: *mā*⟶*māma* 'mother'

    d. REDUPLICATION   TONE LOSS   NEUTRAL TONE REALIZATION

σ σ   ⟶   σ σ   ⟶   σ σ

H H H H   H H   H H L

The examples we have seen so far involve OBLIGATORY RULES. The next two cases of tonal changes involve OPTIONAL RULES; that is, the rules may or may not apply depending on speakers and/or speech rate (§4.2.3). In (10), we see in some reduplicated adjectives (adjectives formed by repeating the same adjective syllable), the second repeated syllable, regardless of its original tone, is changed to T1 (HH). This rule is specific to this morphological process and used only by some SC speakers, especially those who use *r*-suffixation (§8.2.1).

(10) Tonal changes for reduplicated adjectives

      a. The tone on the repeated syllable bears a HH tone.
      b. Example: *màn* [man]51 'slow'

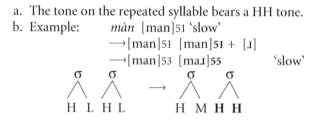

                  →[man]51 [man]51 + [ɹ]
                  →[man]53 [maɹ]55   'slow'

9.2.5 Tone 2 sandhi

TONE 2 SANDHI in (11) occurs only in fast speech and the rule may or may not apply, depending on the speakers. This rule for T2 can be analyzed as an assimilation rule that spreads the H tone feature of the first syllable to replace the M feature of T2 in the second syllable, as illustrated in (11a), in which T in the third syllable represents any one of the four phonemic tones.

(11) Tone 2 sandhi

      a. MH→HH after HH or MH and before one of the four tones
          (i.e. T2→T1 after T1 or T2 and before T1, T2, T3, or T4)

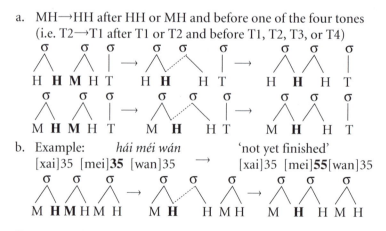

      b. Example: *hái méi wán*   'not yet finished'
             [xai]35 [mei]35 [wan]35   →   [xai]35 [mei]55[wan]35

The diagrams in (11ab) show that the H spread rule results in a HH second syllable with the original M feature removed. In fast speech, each non-phrase final syllable is much shorter and ease of articulation is an important factor to facilitate fast movement of articulation; under these circumstances, deletion and/or assimilation is more likely to occur. Another important factor is that in such a three-syllable expression, the middle syllable is least stressed and hence its original complex tone is simplified. We will discuss the effect of stress on tone 2 sandhi in §10.1.2. Since the application of this rule depends on speech rate and has variation, it may be treated as a phonetic tonal coarticulation rule.

9.3 The phonetic realizations of the neutral tone

The neutral-toned syllable is an unstressed syllable shorter than a normal syllable and must be in non-initial position in an expression (§4.2.2). Neutral-toned syllables are limited to: (i) FUNCTION WORDS such as the question marker *ma* as in *nǐ lái ma?* 'you-come-question marker; are you coming?' and suffixes (e.g. *zi* as in *yǐzi* 'chair'); (ii) the reduplicated syllable of a disyllabic kinship term, as mentioned in §4.2.3 and §9.2.4 above (e.g. *mèimei* 'younger sister'); and (iii) the final syllable in some disyllabic words (e.g. *dōngxi* 'things, stuffs'). While the neutral-toned function words, suffixes, and reduplicated kinship terms are present in most SC speakers' speech, speakers vary with regard to which disyllabic words contain a neutral-toned syllable. For example, SC speakers in northern China, such as in Beijing, have more words with a neutral tone. In addition, when a syllable becomes unstressed and much shortened, such a syllable cannot bear its original phonemic tone and hence becomes a neutral-toned syllable accompanied with vowel/rime reduction (§7.3.2). For example, *xiàtiān* may be pronounced without a neutral tone as [ɕja]53 [tʰjɛn]55 or with a neutral tone as [ɕja]53 [tʰjə]1.

The generalizations for the phonetic realizations of the NEUTRAL TONE are that: (i) if a neutral tone is immediately preceded by a phonemic tone (i.e. one of the four basic underlying tones in SC), it is low after T1 and T4, mid or low after T2, and mid or high after T3 (cf. §4.2.2); and (ii) if it is immediately preceded by another neutral tone, it has a low tone. We can see that in most cases, the neutral tone is phonetically in the lower part of the pitch range. How to represent the neutral-toned syllable phonologically is a debated issue. It can simply be toneless as in (12a) or actually have a single L tone feature as in (12b). In what follows, the toneless representation as in (12a) will be adopted to better match the fact that it is not a phonemic tone, and the low tone in the surface representation can be attributed to the default phonetic pitch level for an unstressed syllable (see also Duanmu 2000:224).

(12) Phonological representation of the neutral tone

    a. σ   b. σ
                     |
                     L

Now that we have decided on the phonological representation of the neutral tone, we can turn to the derivations of various phonetic pitch values of this toneless syllable. As discussed in §4.2.2, there are at least two sets of descriptions for the pitch values of the neutral tone, as shown in (13). This book has adopted the first system in (13a) for phonetic transcription. If we use the tone features, we obtain the patterns in these two systems as shown in (14).

🎧 (13) Pitch values of the neutral tone

    a. System I

T1 + T0 = 55 + 2	*māma*	[ma]55	[ma]2	'mother'
T2 + T0 = 35 + 3	*lái le*	[lai]35	[lə]3	'came'
T3 + T0 = 21 + 4	*jiějie*	[tɕje]21	[tɕje]4	'older sister'
T4 + T0 = 53 + 1	*kàn le*	[kʰan]53	[lə]1	'saw'

    b. System II

T1 + T0 = 55 + 41	*māma*	[ma]55	[ma]41	'mother'
T2 + T0 = 35 + 31	*lái le*	[lai]35	[lə]31	'came'
T3 + T0 = 21 + 23	*jiějie*	[tɕje]21	[tɕje]23	'older sister'
T4 + T0 = 53 + 21	*kàn le*	[kʰan]53	[lə]21	'saw'

(14) Tone features of the neutral tone

    a. System I

        T1 + T0 = HH + L   T2 + T0 = MH + M

        T3 + T0 = LL + H   T4 + T0 = HM + L

    b. System II

        T1 + T0 = HH + HL   T2 + T0 = MH + ML

        T3 + T0 = LL + LM   T4 + T0 = HM + LL

The main difference is that the first system makes use of a short single tone, which reflects the shortness of the syllable and tone. On the other hand, the second system describes the neutral tone as a contour tone, encoding more phonetic details about the transition and movement from the end of the preceding tone to the end of the neutral tone. However, the two systems in (14) actually do not differ much. After HH (T1), the pitch is going down to target L and the two systems differ in encoding or not encoding this falling movement in the neutral tone. After MH (T2), the pitch falls and the two systems differ in detailing how much it falls: to M or to L via M. After LL (T3) the pitch rises and the two systems differ in detailing how much it rises: to H or to M. After HM (T4), the pitch falls further to L and the two systems do not differ. This is one reason why in §4.2.2 I suggested that either system may be adopted to practice the pronunciation of the neutral tone, although I personally find the first system easier in teaching and learning.

For a phonological analysis that does not need to encode all phonetic details even in the surface representation, we can basically use system I for illustration. Consider first the neutral tone after T3 and T4. As discussed in §9.2.1, these two tones undergo tonal reduction when followed by another tone because a non-final syllable is shorter. However, if the following tone is a toneless syllable, then the part of the original tone that cannot be accommodated in the non-final syllable can fill in the toneless syllable, as shown in (15).

(15) The neutral tone after T3 and T4

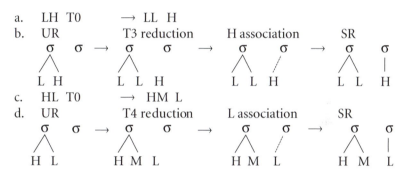

When T3 is reduced in non-final position, the H feature of T3 is removed before another tone since no available tone bearing unit is available for it. However, when T3 is followed by a toneless syllable as in (15ab), there is a perfect match: the toneless syllable needs a tone in phonetic pronunciation and the H feature needs a tone bearing unit. Therefore, the H feature is associated to the toneless syllable. Similarly, when T4 reduction applies, the falling range of the HL tone is cut short to HM and the L feature is also removed when the following syllable has a tone. In (15cd), we see that when the following syllable is toneless, the L feature fills in to give the neutral tone a pitch value.

When preceded by T1 and T2, the toneless syllable is provided with a default L tone, which is similar to the insertion of a schwa to fill an empty nucleus, as discussed in §8.1.5 and §8.2. The process is illustrated in (16).

(16) The neutral tone after T1 and T2

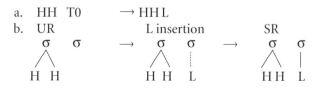

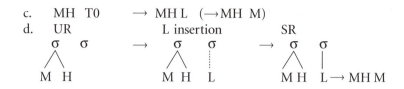

c.   MH T0   → MH L (→MH M)
d.   UR   L insertion   SR

You may have noticed that although the SR of the neutral tone after T2 in (16cd) is associated with a L feature, the transcription in system I is M and in system II is ML. The SR is the phonological output that needs not encode all phonetic details, so the adjustment of L to M can be treated as being regulated by phonetics. Phonetically, going from a high pitch to a low pitch necessarily involves going through the mid part of the pitch range. However, there is a difference between the H–L transition in (16ab) and that in (16cd): the neutral tone after T1 in (16a) has a sharp fall that quickly reaches the low pitch range, whereas the neutral tone after T2 in (16b) has a slower fall that reaches the mid or mid-low area of the pitch range. The difference can be attributed to the fact that T1 is a level tone and T2 a contour tone. T2 is a rising tone that takes more time and effort to manifest than a level tone like T1. It is then relatively easy to have a quick transition from the plain level HH to fall directly to L. On the other hand, the movement from M to H and then to the opposite direction toward L has a more difficult maneuver and transition, and given the short duration of the neutral-toned syllable, the phonological target of L is phonetically achieved at M.

This section has tried to explain why a neutral tone has different phonetic realizations when preceded by different tones. Phonologically the toneless syllable either receives an unassociated tone feature left behind by tonal reduction of the preceding tone (T3 and T4) or is filled with a default inserted L feature. The phonetic interpretations and adjustments of the SRs then match the phonetic transcriptions of the neutral tone in different contexts.

9.4 Tone 3 sandhi in complex words and phrases

Tone 3 sandhi is deceptively simple in terms of the rule description, and yet its application becomes rather complicated when there are more than two T3s in a word or phrase. This section examines when and how tone 3 sandhi is applied in a complex word or in a phrase/sentence. The data and the explanation for tone 3 sandhi application are complex, and only the basic general principles will be discussed due to space limitations and the introductory nature of this book. References for more data and different analyses are provided in Further Reading. The analytic approach adopted in this section mainly follows Chen (2000: chapter 9) and Shih (1986, 1997).

Before we examine more examples of tone 3 sandhi, we need to have a basic understanding of the prosodic and morpho-syntactic factors that determine the domains within which tone 3 sandhi applies. In §9.4.1 the relevant prosodic units and morpho-syntactic domains are introduced, and then tone 3 sandhi examples are presented and analyzed in §9.4.2.

9.4.1 Prosodic and morpho-syntactic domains

Moras, syllables, and feet belong to a set of PROSODIC UNITS that organize and regulate the rhythm of utterances. Prosodic units are not sound segments but provide the domains and/or anchors for SUPRASEGMENTALS (§4.1.3) such as length, tone, stress, and intonation. Each prosodic unit is organized into a higher level of prosodic unit according to the prosodic hierarchy in (17a). Rime segments are organized into moras: a light syllable has a simple rime with only one short vowel and has one mora; a heavy syllable has a complex rime with a long vowel, a diphthong, or a vowel plus coda, and has two moras (cf. §5.2.1). Onset segments and moras are then organized into syllables and syllables are organized into feet. In (17b) we see an example of the prosodic representation for the word *magazine* [mægəziːn], in which σ = syllable and μ = mora and a long vowel occupies two moras.

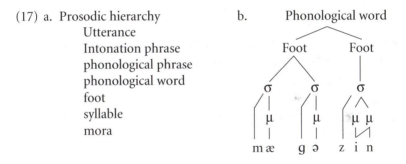

(17) a. Prosodic hierarchy   b.   Phonological word
             Utterance
             Intonation phrase
             phonological phrase
             phonological word
             foot
             syllable
             mora

A universally preferred foot structure is 'binary' in the sense that a FOOT contains either two syllables or a heavy syllable with two moras. In (17b), the first foot contains two light syllables and also two moras, and the second foot contains one heavy syllable with two moras. For stress languages, the assignment of stress depends on foot structure. In English the primary stress is assigned to the rightmost foot, so the stress in (17b) is on the last syllable. Under special circumstances, a single light syllable foot and/or a superfoot with more than two syllables are possible in some languages.

The prosodic units relevant to our discussion of tone 3 sandhi are the syllable and the foot. For SC, the preferred foot structure is a DISYLLABIC foot and such a foot constitutes the basic domain within which tone 3 sandhi must apply. However, the foot discussed here for SC differs from the foot for stress assignment in that the foot does not carry stress and it may contain more than two syllables. It is sometimes called a stressless foot (Duanmu 2000:242) or a 'minimal rhythmic unit' (Chen 2000:366) to differentiate it from the prosodic units normally assumed in (17a). For simplicity, let us still treat this SC prosodic unit as a foot. (For a different analysis of tone 3 sanhdi with a stress foot, see Duanmu 2000: chapter 11.)

The examples in (18) illustrate how to group syllables into feet.

(18) Parsing syllables into feet

$$
\begin{array}{lll}
\text{a.} & \sigma \sigma \sigma \sigma & \to (\sigma \sigma)(\sigma \sigma) \\
\text{b.} & \sigma \sigma \sigma & \to \sigma (\sigma \sigma) & \to (\sigma \sigma \sigma) \\
\text{c.} & \sigma \sigma \sigma & \to (\sigma \sigma) \sigma & \to (\sigma \sigma \sigma) \\
\text{d.} & (\sigma \sigma)(\sigma \sigma) & \to (\sigma \sigma \sigma \sigma)
\end{array}
$$

In (18a), a four-syllable word or phrase is grouped into two disyllabic feet. However, when there is an unfooted single syllable, as in (18bc), this free syllable may join an adjacent foot to form a larger prosodic domain (or a superfoot). In fast speech, some foot boundaries may be removed to create an even larger domain, as in (18d).

The question now is how to parse a sequence of syllables into feet. In (18bc), you may have noticed that there are two ways to build the basic binary foot for a three-syllable sequence, either starting from the right edge as in (18b) or starting from the left edge as in (18c). Consider the numerical expression or phone digits of a sequence of *jiǔ* 'nine' in (19).

(19) Sequences of T3s

a. *jiu jiu jiu jiu*   (*jiu   jiu*) (*jiu jiu*)
   T3   T3   T3   T3   → (**T2** T3) (**T2** T3)

b. *jiu jiu jiu jiu jiu*   (*jiu   jiu*) (*jiu   jiu*) *jiu*
   T3   T3   T3   T3   T3 → (**T2** T3) (**T2** T3) T3
                        (*jiu   jiu*) (*jiu   jiu   jiu*)
          → (**T2** T3) (**T2** **T2** T3)

The example in (19b) shows that the disyllabic feet are built from left to right so that the last syllable is left alone. If we were to pair up the syllables going from right to left, the first syllable would have been the initially unfooted syllable. This free last syllable in (19b) then joins the preceding foot to form a three-syllable domain. In both examples in (19), tone 3 sandhi then applies once each prosodic domain is built. The rules we have established so far are as follows:

(20) Foot building for tone 3 sandhi (preliminary version)

    a. Build a disyllabic foot proceeding from left to right.

    b. Incorporate an unfooted free syllable to an adjacent foot.

Given these rules, for a four-syllable expression one expects that the foot structure and tone sandhi pattern in (19a) is the only possibility. However, the example in (21), which we mentioned in §9.2.2, contradicts this assumption. The derivation in (21b) shows that we must build the disyllabic foot for the second and third syllable first in order to get the correct result.

(21) Foot building in a four-syllable expression

    a. *mǐ lǎoshǔ hǎo*   'Mickey Mouse is good'

        T3 T3 T3 T3   →   T3 **T2 T2** T3

    b. *mǐ lǎoshǔ hǎo*   'Mickey Mouse is good'

        T3 T3 T3 T3   →   T3 (**T2** T3) T3

                      →   (T3 **T2** T3) T3

                      →   (T3 **T2 T2** T3)

Once the disyllabic foot in the middle is set up, we are left with two unfooted syllables: one at the left edge and the other at the right edge. After incorporating the left-edge free syllable, tone 3 sandhi does not apply since there are no two adjacent T3s within the three-syllable domain. After incorporating the right-edge free syllable, tone 3 sandhi applies to the third syllable since it is followed by a T3 within the final four-syllable domain. Now we derive the correct tone pattern for this phrase.

The reason why we build the first disyllabic foot in the middle in this example is because FOOT BUILDING must start from the smallest morpho-syntatic domain, in this case *lǎoshǔ* 'mouse'. Morphological domains are set up for words and COMPOUNDS (complex words that combine two or more simple words, e.g. *classroom, courtyard*), and syntactic domains are set up for phrases and sentences. The distinction between the word level structure and the phrase level structure is important for setting up the domains for tone 3 application as we will see below. Note that a noun with a MODIFIER that describes or specifies the noun, such as *xiǎo lǎoshǔ* 'small mouse', is also treated as a word (see Chen 2000:§9.3 for details), although syntactically such a complex noun is often classified as a noun phrase. That is, a simple noun, a compound noun, and a complex noun [modifier + noun] are all treated as words rather than phrases.

The foot building rules in (20) are basically correct but they must apply within a word proceeding from the smaller domain to the larger domain before applying to a phrase, as illustrated in (22a). The different domains are represented with square brackets, as in (22b).

(22) Food building based on morpho-syntactic domains

a. Word:

	lǎoshǔ	'mouse'
	mǐ lǎoshǔ	'Mickey Mouse'

Phrase:

	mǐ lǎoshǔ hǎo	'Mickey Mouse is good'
b. [[*mǐ* [*lǎoshǔ*]] *hǎo*]		[[Mickey [mouse]] is good]

With the complex noun *mǐ lǎoshǔ*, *lǎoshǔ* is the base noun and *mǐ* is used to specify what kind of *lǎoshǔ* it is, so *lǎoshǔ* is the first domain to set up. In (22b), there are three pairs of brackets, the innermost pair are for *lǎoshǔ*, the next pair for the larger noun *mǐ lǎoshǔ* and the outermost pair for the whole phrase. Space limitation prevents a full discussion of SC morpho-syntactic structures, but necessary explanation will be provided when we discuss each example.

With the information of the morpho-syntactic domains, the foot building rules can be modified as in (23).

(23) Foot building for tone 3 sandhi (final version)

a. Build disyllabic feet proceeding from left to right.
b. Incorporate an unfooted free syllable to an adjacent foot.
c. This foot building process applies first within a word starting from the smallest domain to the subsequent larger domains step by step.
d. The foot building process applies to the smallest domain of the phrase and then to the whole phrase proceeding from left to right.

The rule in (23c) states that, for a complex word, the foot building process and tone sandhi application must start from the smallest domain, to the next larger domains, and finally to the largest domain. Once this is done, the foot building process/tone sandhi application then scan the phrase to see if (23ab) may still apply to the smallest domain of the phrase, and if not, the foot building process goes from left to right for the entire phrase.

It is also important to note that the numerical expressions in (19) above do not have any syntactic structure, so only rules (23ab) apply. The example of *mǐ lǎoshǔ hǎo* is now analyzed as in (24).

(24) [[*mǐ* [*lǎoshǔ*]] *hǎo*]   '[[Mickey [Mouse]] is good]'

T3 T3 T3 T3	
(**T2** T3)	Word: disyllabic foot; tone sandhi
(T3 **T2** T3)	Word: incorporation; no tone sandhi
(T3 T2 **T2** T3)	Phrase: incorporation; tone sandhi

Let us start with an analysis of the word and phrase to determine the morpho-syntactic brackets or domains of this example. The next step is to build a disyllabic foot within the smallest domain of the word and tone sandhi applies. At the next larger domain for the complex noun, the unfooted syllable at the left edge joins the existing foot, but no tone sandhi applies since there are no two T3s in a sequence. At the phrase level, the unfooted syllable at the right edge is incorporated into the three-syllable foot by rule (23b), then tone sandhi can and must apply to the third syllable.

The next subsection analyzes additional examples with minor refinement of the basic rules that we have set up for tone 3 sandhi application.

9.4.2 Examples

Consider the four-syllable examples in (25), each of which has different morpho-syntactic structures or brackets but all of which have the same tone 3 sandhi pattern.

🎧 (25) Four-syllable sentences with different morpho-syntactic brackets

a. old-watch-very-good   '[[the old watch] [is very good]]'
   [[*lǎo biǎo*] [*hěn hǎo*]]
   T3 T3 T3 T3   → **T2** T3 **T2** T3

b. I-hit-mouse   '[I [hit [the mouse]]]'
   [*wǒ* [*dǎ* [*lǎoshǔ*]]]
   T3 T3 T3 T3   → **T2** T3 **T2** T3

c. which-kind-dog-good   '[[[which kind] of dog] is better]?'
   [[[*něi zhǒng*] *gǒu*] *hǎo*]
   T3 T3 T3 T3   → **T2** T3 **T2** T3

A sentence is divided into two major parts: the SUBJECT and the PREDICATE. The subject in (25a) is the 'old watch', and the predicate is 'very good'; in (25b) the subject is 'I' and the predicate 'hit the mouse'; and in (25c) the subject is 'which kind of dog' and the predicate is 'better'. Note that, in the SC examples (25ac), the adjective alone constitutes the predicate and does not need a *be* verb like *is* in English. In these examples, the subject is the entity before the verb/adjective and the predicate is the rest of the sentence that contains a verb/adjective. A predicate may contain simply a verb/adjective as in (25ac) or a verb plus an OBJECT as in (25b), in which the object, 'the mouse', is the receiver of the action of 'hitting'. There is always a bracket division between the subject and the predicate.

With the basic understanding of the morpho-syntactic brackets of these examples, foot building and tone 3 sandhi apply as shown in (26).

(26) Analyses of examples in (25)

    a. [[*lǎo biǎo*] [*hěn hǎo*]]   '[[the old watch] [is very good]]'
        T3 T3 T3 T3

        (**T2** T3) T3 T3   Word: disyllabic foot; tone sandhi
        (**T2** T3) (**T2** T3)   Phrase: disyllabic foot; tone sandhi

    b. [*wǒ* [*dǎ* [*lǎoshǔ*]]]   '[I [hit [the mouse]]]'
        T3 T3 T3 T3

        T3 T3 (**T2** T3)   Word: disyllabic foot; tone sandhi
        (**T2** T3) (**T2** T3)   Phrase: disyllabic foot: tone sandhi

    c. [[[*něi zhǒng*] *gǒu*] *hǎo*] '[[[which kind] of dog] is better]?'
        T3 T3 T3 T3

        (**T2** T3) T3 T3   Phrase: disyllabic foot; tone sandhi
        (T2 T3) (**T2** T3)   Phrase: disyllabic foot; tone sanhdi

In (26ab), after a disyllabic foot is built for the words *lǎo biǎo* and *lǎoshǔ*, the remaining two syllables are grouped into a disyllabic foot at the phrasal stage. In (26c), the smallest domain of the phrase is given a foot first and the remaining syllables in the phrase form another disyllabic foot.

    Consider now the four-syllable examples in (27ab), which have different tone sandhi patterns from those in (26). The brackets between (27a) and (27b) are different but they share the same tone sandhi pattern.

🎧 (27) Different morpho-syntactic brackets with the same tone sandhi pattern

    a. Mickey-mouse-good
        [[*mǐ* [*lǎoshǔ*]] *hǎo*]   '[[Mickey [Mouse]] is good]'
        T3 T3 T3 T3

        T3 (**T2** T3) T3   Word: disyllabic foot; tone sandhi
        (T3 T2 T3) T3   Word: incorporation; no tone sandhi
        (T3 **T2 T2** T3)   Phrase: incorporation; tone sandhi

    b. search-president-palace
        [*zhǎo* [[*zǒngtǒng*] *fǔ*]]   '[looking for [the [presidential] palace]]'
        T3 T3 T3 T3

        T3 (**T2** T3) T3   Word: disyllabic foot; tone sandhi
        T3 (T2 **T2** T3)   Word: incorporation; tone sandhi
        (T3 **T2 T2** T3)   Phrase: incorporation; no tone sandhi

Example (27a) was analyzed in the previous subsection, and the explanation for (27b) is similar. The complex word *zǒngtǒng fǔ* 'presidential palace' is the object of the verb *zhǎo*, so there is a division between them. Within the complex noun, the smaller bracket or domain is 'president' *zǒngtǒng*, so the disyllabic foot starts there and tone sandhi applies. The syllable for 'palace' *fǔ* of the complex word is then incorporated to form a three-syllable domain within which tone sandhi applies again. Finally, at the phrase level, the left edge syllable, the verb, is incorporated and no tone sandhi applies.

We have seen that examples with different morpho-syntactic structures may or may not have the same tone sandhi patterns because tone sandhi application crucially relies on the PROSODIC DOMAINS built through the foot building process. Although the foot building process requires some information about morpho-syntactic structures, the domains within which tone sandhi must apply is not identical to the morpho-synatic domains delimited by the brackets.

Some expressions may have more than one tone sandhi pattern because of optional tone sandhi or a faster speech rate. We have seen that within each prosodic domain, tone 3 sandhi obligatorily applies. When two adjacent T3s belong to different prosodic domains, as in (28a), the application of tone 3 sandhi can be optional, as shown in (28b).

(28) Optional tone 3 sandhi application

    a. Old-Li-search-shoes

       [[*lǎo lǐ*] [*zhǎo xié*]]   '[[Old Li] [looks for shoes]]'

       T3 T3 T3 T2

       (**T2** T3) T3 T2   Word: disyllabic foot; tone sandhi

       (T2 T3) (T3 T2)   Phrase: disyllabic foot; no tone sandhi

    b. (T2 T3) (T3 T2)

       (T2 **T2**) (T3 T2)   optional rule

In addition, a T3 can optionally change to T2 before a T2 that was derived from a T3 (cf. Shen, J. (1994) cited by Duanmu (2000:241)), usually in casual or fast speech. In normal or slow speech, the tone pattern for example (29a) is T2 T3 T2 T3 as predicted. In fast casual speech, however, the two prosodic domains can be merged into one as shown in (29b), and then tone sandhi applies from left to right: targeting the leftmost T3 before targeting the one to the right.

(29) Multiple tone sandhi patterns

    a. Old-Li-search-pen

       [[*lǎo lǐ*] [*zhǎo bǐ*]]   '[[Old Li] [looks for pens]]'

       T3 T3 T3 T3

       (**T2** T3) T3 T3   Word: disyllabic foot; tone sandhi

       (T2 T3) (**T2** T3)   Phrase: disyllabic foot; tone sandhi

b. (T3 T3 T3 T3)   One prosodic domain in fast speech
    (**T2** T3 T3 T3)   Tone sandhi proceeding from left to right
    (T2 **T2** T3 T3)
    (T2 T2 **T2** T3)

Another interesting fact about variation in tone 3 sandhi patterns is that an expression with the smaller brackets or domains crowded toward the left side, as examples (30ac) show, usually has one tone sandhi pattern, whereas an expression with the smaller brackets or domains toward the right side, as in examples (30bd), may have more than one pattern. The example in (30c) is taken from Chen (2000:383).

(30) Left-oriented and right-oriented bracketing

a. mouse-run   b. buy-rice-wine
    'the mouse is running'   'to buy rice wine'
    [[*lǎoshǔ*] *pǎo*]   [*mǎi* [*mǐ jiǔ*]]
        T3 T3 T3   T3 T3 T3
    →   **T2 T2** T3   →   T3 **T2** T3
                                   or   **T2 T2** T3

c. exhibition-hall-director   d. small-female-tiger
    'exhibition hall director'   'small female tiger'
    [[[*zhǎnlǎn*] *guǎn*] *zhǎng*]   [*xiǎo* [*mǔ* [*lǎohǔ*]]]
        T3 T3 T3 T3   T3 T3 T3 T3
    →   **T2 T2 T2** T3   →   **T2** T3 **T2** T3
                                   or   T3 **T2 T2** T3
                                   or   **T2 T2 T2** T3

The alternative additional tone sandhi patterns in (30bd) occur in fast casual speech, as demonstrated by the analyses in (31).

(31) Analyses of examples in (30)

a. [[*lǎoshǔ*] *pǎo*]   '[[the mouse] is running]'
    (**T2** T3) T3   Word: disyllabic foot; tone sandhi
    (**T2 T2** T3)   Phrase: incorporation; tone sandhi
    Optional in fast speech
    (T3 T3 T3)   one prosodic domain in fast speech
    (**T2 T2** T3)   tone sandhi from left to right
b. [*mǎi* [*mǐ jiǔ*]]   '[to buy [rice wine]]'
    T3 (**T2** T3)   Word: disyllabic foot; tone sandhi
    (T3 T2 T3)   Phrase: incorporation; no tone sandhi

Optional in fast speech

    (T3 T3 T3)   one prosodic domain in fast speech

    (**T2 T2** T3)   tone sandhi from left to right

c. [[[*zhǎnlǎn*] *guǎn*] *zhǎng*]   '[[[exhibition] hall] director]'

    (**T2** T3) T3 T3   Word: disyllabic foot; tone sandhi

    (T2 **T2** T3) T3   Word: incorporation; tone sandhi

    (T2 T2 **T2** T3)   Word: incorporation; tone sandhi

Optional in fast speech

    (T3 T3 T3 T3)   one prosodic domain for all syllables

    (**T2 T2 T2** T3)   tone sandhi from left to right

d. [*xiǎo* [*mǔ* [*lǎohǔ*]]]   '[small [female [tiger]]]'

    T3 T3 (**T2** T3)   Word: disyllabic foot; tone sandhi

    T3 (T3 T2 T3)   Word: incorporation; no tone sandhi

    (**T2** T3 T2 T3)   Word: incorporation; tone sandhi

Optional in fast speech I

    T3 (T3 T3 T3)   one prosodic domain for [*mǔ* [*lǎohǔ*]]

    T3 (**T2 T2** T3)   tone sandhi from left to right

    (T3 T2 T2 T3)   incorporation; no tone sandhi

Optional in fast speech II

    (T3 T3 T3 T3)   one prosodic domain for all syllables

    (**T2 T2 T2** T3)   tone sandhi from left to right

The example in (31b) has the pattern T3 T2 T3 when we apply the normal foot building process and tone sandhi application, but there is also an optional fast speech process in which a single prosodic domain is formed and tone sandhi applies from left to right (cf. (29b) above) to produce a different sandhi pattern. On the other hand, for (31a), even when we create a single prosodic domain for fast speech, the tone sandhi pattern would be identical: T2 T2 T3. Therefore, we have only one pattern for (31a) but two patterns for (31b). The example in (31c) is a compound noun. Because the whole expression is a complex word, the foot building process and tone sandhi application must apply step by step from the innermost domain, *zhǎnlǎn* 'exhibition', to the next domain, *zhǎnlǎn guǎn* 'exhibition hall', before getting to the outermost domain *zhǎnlǎn guǎn zhǎng* 'exhibition hall director', according to the rules in (23abc) in §9.4.1. Again, if the optional fast speech rule applies, the tone sandhi pattern would be the same. Finally, in (31d), the normal pattern is T2 T3 T2 T3, but in fast speech, either the word 'female tiger' [*mǔ* [*lǎohǔ*]] forms a single prosodic domain or the whole expression forms a single prosodic domain, resulting in two additional sandhi patterns.

We have seen so far that expressions with different morpho-syntactic structures may or may not have the same tone sandhi patterns. One may then expect
that if two examples have identical bracketing structure, they must have the
same tone sandhi pattern. Each pair of examples, i.e. (32ab) and (32cd), have
the same bracketing structure but they do not have the same tone sandhi pattern. The pattern with an asterisk indicates an impossible pattern, or at least a
bad pattern, for most SC speakers.

(32) Same brackets but different tone sandhi patterns

a. I-want-buy-pen
   'I want to buy pens'
   [*wǒ* [*xiǎng* [*mǎi bǐ*]]]
      T3 T3 T3 T3
   → **T2** T3 **T2** T3
   or **T2 T2 T2** T3
   *T3 **T2 T2** T3

b. small-female-tiger
   'small female tiger'
   [*xiǎo* [*mǔ* [*lǎohǔ*]]]
      T3 T3 T3 T3
   → **T2** T3 **T2** T3
   or T3 **T2 T2** T3
   or **T2 T2 T2** T3

c. I-want-buy-flower
   'I want to buy flowers'
   [*wǒ* [*xiǎng* [*mǎi huā*]]]
      T3 T3 T3 T1
   → **T2** T3 T3 T1
   or **T2 T2** T3 T1

d. small-female-boar
   'small female boar'
   [*xiǎo* [*mǔ* [*jězhū*]]]
      T3 T3 T3 T1
   → T3 **T2** T3 T1
   or **T2 T2** T3 T1
   *T2** T3 T3 T1

The example in (32b) can have the T3 T2 T2 T3 pattern but (32a) cannot,
and (32c) can have the T2 T3 T3 T1 pattern but (32d) cannot. What is crucial
in explaining the differences in these examples is to distinguish words from
phrases. For words, foot building must apply to the smaller domain prior to
the larger domains, but for phrases, once a disyllabic foot is built for the smallest
domain, the foot building process goes from left to right for the entire phrase
(see (23cd)). The examples on the right, i.e. (32bd), are classified as words but
those on the left, i.e. (32ab), are phrases.

Example (32b) has already been analyzed in (31d). The derivations of the
remaining three examples in (32) are shown in (33). For the phrases that contain
no words longer than one syllable, as in (33ab), there is no foot building process
at the word level. At the phrasal level, after a disyllabic foot for the smallest
domain is set, additional disyllabic feet are built from left to right (cf. rule
(23d) in §9.4.1). The optional rules then provide the alternative patterns. The

example in (33c), however, is a complex word, just like the example (30d)/(32b) analyzed in (31d). The foot building process at the word level applies to the smallest domain, then to the next two larger domains. The optional fast speech rule yields the alternative pattern. Given the rules we have set up, there is no way to derive the asterisked patterns shown in (32ad).

(33) Analyses of examples in (32)

a. [*wǒ* [*xiǎng* [*mǎi bǐ*]]]   '[I [want to [buy pens]]]'
    T3 T3 T3 T3   Word: not applicable
    T3 T3 (**T2** T3)   Phrase: disyllabic foot for the smallest
                                    domain; tone sandhi
    (**T2** T3) (**T2** T3)   Phrase: disyllabic foot for the rest; tone
                                    sandhi
    Optional in fast speech
    (T3 T3 T3 T3)   one prosodic domain in fast speech
    (**T2 T2 T2** T3)   tone sandhi from left to right
b. [*wǒ* [*xiǎng* [*mǎi huā*]]]   '[I [want to [buy flowers]]]'
    T3 T3 T3 T1   Word: not applicable
    T3 T3 (T3 T1)   Phrase: disyllabic foot for the smallest
                                    domain; no tone sandhi
    (**T2** T3) (T3 T1)   Phrase: disyllabic feet for the rest; tone sandhi
    Optional rule between two T3s in different prosodic domains (28b)
    (T2 **T2**) (T3 T1)
c. [*xiǎo* [*mǔ* [*jiězhū*]]]   '[small [female [boar]]]'
    T3 T3 (T3 T1)   Word: disyllabic foot; no tone sandhi
    T3 (**T2** T3 T1)   Word: incorporation; tone sandhi
    (T3 T2 T3 T1)   Word: incorporation; no tone sandhi
    Optional in fast speech
    (T3 T3 T3 T1)   one prosodic domain in fast speech
    (**T2 T2** T3 T1)   tone sandhi from left to right

    In some phrases, the normal tone 3 sandhi reading cannot be derived by the rules we have set up. This class of exception involves certain function words (Chen 2000:§9.4; Zhang 1997). The examples in (34a) and (34b) have the same bracketing structure. However, (34a) has a function word, the preposition 'than', and allows for one additional tone sandhi pattern, T2 T3 T2 T3, which is prohibited for (34b).

(34) Expressions with and without a function word

    a. dog-than-horse-good   b. horse-very-good-raise
       'dogs are better than horse'   'horses are easy to raise'
       [*gǒu* [[*bǐ mǎ*] *hǎo*]]   [*mǎ* [[*hěn hǎo*] *yǎng*]]
          T3 T3 T3 T3   T3 T3 T3 T3
      → **T2** T3 **T2** T3   → T3 **T2 T2** T3
      or T3 **T2 T2** T3   or **T2 T2 T2** T3
      or **T2 T2 T2** T3   *****T2** T3 **T2** T3

The subject is *gǒu* 'dogs' in (34a) and *mǎ* 'horses' in (34b), and the predicate contains an adjective/verb and covers the next three syllables in both cases. There is therefore a major division between the subject and the predicate. Within the predicate, in (34a), the preposition and the noun *bǐ mǎ* 'than horse' form a syntactic unit to specify in what way dogs are good, and in (34b), *hěn hǎo* forms a syntactic unit to specify the degree of difficulty in raising horses. Given these syntactic brackets, the tone sandhi patterns of (34b) are shown in (35). Those same two patterns in (34a) can be derived the same way.

(35) Analysis of example (34b)

    [*mǎ* [[*hěn hǎo*] *yǎng*]]
       T3 T3 T3 T3   Word: not applicable
       T3 (**T2** T3) T3   Phrase: disyllabic; tone sandhi
      (T3 T2 **T2** T3)   Phrase: incorporation; tone sandhi
   Optional in fast speech
      (T3 T3 T3 T3)   one prosodic domain in fast speech
      (**T2 T2 T2** T3)   tone sandhi from left to right

What needs to be explained is why (34a) has an additional pattern T2 T3 T2 T3. A function word can be prosodically grouped with its preceding syllable, which is called a process of cliticization (Chen 2000:401–403). With the application of cliticization, the special pattern for (34a) can be derived as in (36). Since the example in (34b)/(35) does not contain a function word, cliticization cannot apply and a pattern like (36) therefore is not possible.

(36) Analysis of example (34a)

    [*gǒu* [[*bǐ mǎ*] *hǎo*]]   'dogs are better than horses'
    (**T2** T3) T3 T3   cliticization; tone sandhi
    (**T2** T3) (**T2** T3)   Phrase: disyllabic foot; tone sandhi

Finally, when a T3 syllable before another T3 is emphasized, it must be changed to T2. The example in (37a) has a non-emphatic pattern. If the verb 'buy' is emphasized, such as in the context of 'only BUY good books, not sell good books', the emphatic reading has a different pattern.

🎧 (37) Normal and emphatic patterns

<table>
<tr><td>a.</td><td>only-buy-good-book</td><td>b.</td><td>only-BUY-good-book</td></tr>
<tr><td></td><td>only buy good books</td><td></td><td>only BUY good books</td></tr>
<tr><td></td><td>[zhǐ [mǎi [hǎo shū]]]</td><td></td><td>[zhǐ [MǍI [hǎo shū]]]</td></tr>
<tr><td></td><td>T3 T3 T3 T1</td><td></td><td>T3 T3 T3 T1</td></tr>
<tr><td></td><td>→ T2 T3 T3 T1</td><td></td><td>→ T3 T2 T3 T1</td></tr>
<tr><td></td><td>or T2 T2 T3 T1</td><td></td><td></td></tr>
</table>

The normal reading in (37a) can be derived as in (38a). For an emphatic reading, a prosodic boundary must be placed to the left of the emphatic syllable, resulting in the different reading, as shown in (38b).

(38) Analyses of examples in (37)

a. [zhǐ [mǎi [hǎo shū]]]

T3 T3 (T3 T1)	Word: disyllabic foot
(**T2** T3) (T3 T1)	Phrase: disyllabic foot; tone sandhi
Optional rule between two T3s in different feet	
(T2 **T2**) (T3 T1)	

b. [zhǐ [**MǍI** [hǎo shū]]]

T3 T3 (T3 T1)	Word: disyllabic foot
T3 (**T2** T3 T1)	Emphatic prosodic boundary to the left of the emphatic syllable; incorporation; tone sandhi
(T3 T2 T3 T1)	phrase: incorporation; no tone sandhi

This subsection has provided a number of examples with complex words and phrases/sentences and demonstrated how tone 3 sandhi ought to apply. Since the number of complex words and phrases/sentences that can be created is unlimited, which is one of the most important defining properties of human language, one can come up with many additional examples of various tone 3 sandhi patterns. The building of prosodic domains in interaction with morpho-syntactic structures, together with additional rules, constitutes the basic set of rules and principles for all potential examples involving tone 3 sandhi application.

9.5 Summary

This chapter introduces tone features, presents tonal processes in SC, and explains how and why these processes occur.

- T ONE FEATURES, H, M, and L are adopted. TONAL PROCESSES include ASSIMILATION (or TONE SPREAD), DISSIMILATION, TONE REDUCTION, TONE DELETION, and TONE INSERTION (§9.1).
- T3 and T4 undergo tone reduction to shorten 214 to 21 (i.e. LH → LL) and 51 to 53 (i.e. HL → HM) respectively before another tone (§9.2).
- T ONE 3 SANDHI changes a T3 to T2 before another T3, which is analyzed as a dissimilation process (§9.2.2).
- Some tonal changes are limited in application, such as those applying to *yī* 'one', *bù* 'not', and reduplicative kinship terms and adjectives (§9.2.3).
- T ONE 2 SANDHI occurs only in fast speech to change T2 to T1 after T1 or T2 and before another tone (§9.2.5). This phenomenon is accounted for as a kind of assimilation by the H tone spread rule. The involvement of stress in this case will be discussed in §10.1.2.
- The neutral-toned syllable is toneless and receives its tone feature either from the last tone feature of reduced T3 and T4, i.e. H and L respectively, or through a default L feature insertion (§9.3).
- In complex words and phrases/sentences, how and when tone 3 sandhi applies is determined by the PROSODIC DOMAINS built through the interaction with MORPHO-SYNTACTIC domains (§9.4). Speech rate and emphasis also affect tone 3 sandhi patterns.

EXERCISES

🎧 **1**   For each of the following examples, provide the tonal derivation using the tone features H, M, and L and identify the tonal process(es)/sandhi rule(s) involved.

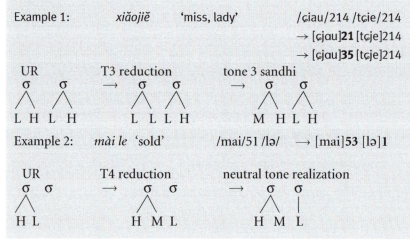

a. *shùlín*   'forest'   /ʂu/51 /lin/35   → [ʂu]**53** [lin]35

b. *mǎlù*   'road'   /ma/214 /lu/51   → [ma]**21** [lu]51

c. *yídìng*   'definitely'   /i/55 /tiŋ/51   → [ji]**35** [tiən]51

d. *búqù*   'not go'   /pu/51 /tɕʰy/51   → [pu]**35** [tɕʰy]51

e. *yìnián*   'one year'   /i/55 /nian/35   → [ji]**51** [njɛn]35

    → [ji]**53** [njɛn]35

f. *xīyáng sēn*   'American ginseng'   /ɕi/55 /jaŋ/35 /sən/55

    → [ɕi]55 [jaŋ]**55** [sən]55

g. *hǎohǎor*   'good, well'   /xau/214

    →   [xɑu]214 [xɑu]214 + [ɹ]

    →   [xɑu]**21** [xɑu]214 + [ɹ]

    →   [xɑu]**21** [xɑuɹ]**55**

h. *nǎinai*   'grandmother'   /nai/214 /nai/   → [nai]**21** [nai]**4**

i. *huán le*   'returned'   /xuan/35 /lə/   → [xwan]35 [lə]**3**

j. *dìfang*   'place, location'   /ti/51 /faŋ/   → [ti]**53** [fəŋ]**1**

k. *dōngbian*   'east side'   /tuŋ/55 /pian/   → [tuŋ]55 [pjən]**2**

l. *yěmǎ*   'wild horse'   /iə/214 /ma/214

    → [je]**21** [ma]214 → [je]**35** [ma]214

m. *hǎo jǐ zhǒng*   'quite a few kinds'   /xau/214 /tɕi/214 /tʂuŋ/214

    →   [xɑu]**21** [tɕi]**21** [tʂuŋ]214

    →   [xɑu]**35** [tɕi]**35** [tʂuŋ]214

    →   [xɑu]**35** [tɕi]**55** [tʂuŋ]214

2 Collect examples for the tone sandhi rules/processes discussed in §§9.2–9.3.
For each example: (i) give the underlying tones (both numerical pitch values
and tone features); (ii) identify the processes/rules involved; and (iii) give the
tonal derivation leading to the surface representation. You may follow the two
examples given in Exercise 1.

🎧 **3** Review the analysis of tone 3 sandhi discussed in §9.4. For each of
the following examples, present the derivation with foot building
and tone 3 sandhi application that leads to the surface sandhi
patterns.

Example:

xiǎo lǎoshǔ pǎo le   small-mouse-run-*le*   'the small mouse ran away'

   T3 T3 T3 T3 T0   → T3 **T2** T3 T3 T0 or T3 **T2 T2** T3 T0

[[*xiăo* [*lăoshŭ*]] [*păo le*]]   morpho-syntactic brackets
   T3 T3 T3 T3 T0   underlying tone
   T3 (**T2** T3) T3 T0   word: disyllabic foot; tone sandhi
   (T3 T2 T3) T3 T0   word: incorporation; no tone sandhi
   (T3 T2 T3) (T3 T0)   phrase: disyllabic foot
Optional rule between two T3s in different prosodic domains
   (T3 T2 **T2**) (T3 T0)

a. *zhăo zhănlăn guăn*   'looking for the exhibition hall'
   T3 T3 T3 T3   →   T3 **T2 T2** T3
  [*zhăo* [[*zhănlăn*] *guăn*]]   morpho-syntactic brackets
  look for – exhibition – hall

b. *xiăo mŭmă hăo*   'the small female horse is good'
   T3 T3 T3 T3   →   T3 **T2 T2** T3
  [[*xiăo* [*mŭmă*]] *hăo*]   morpho-syntactic brackets
  little – female horse – good

c. *xiăng măi gŭshū*   'want to buy antique books'
   T3 T3 T3 T3   →   **T2** T3 T3 T1 or **T2 T2** T3 T1
  [*xiăng* [*măi* [*gŭshū*]]]   morpho-syntactic brackets
  want – buy – old book

d. *xiăng MĂI gŭshū*   'want to BUY antique books (not to sell . . .)'
   T3 T3 T3 T3   →   T3 **T2** T3 T1
  [*xiăng* [*MĂI* [*gŭshū*]]]   morpho-syntactic brackets
  want – BUY – old book

e. *gŏu bĭ mă xiăo*   'dogs are smaller than horses'
   T3 T3 T3 T3   →   **T2** T3 **T2** T3 or T3 **T2 T2** T3
                or **T2 T2 T2** T3 (fast speech)
  [*gŏu* [[*bĭ mă*] *xiăo*]]   morpho-syntactic brackets
  dog – than – horse – small

f. *gŏu hĕn hăo yăng*   'dogs are easy to raise'
   T3 T3 T3 T3   →   T3 **T2 T2** T3
                or **T2 T2 T2** T3 (fast speech)
  [*gŏu* [[*hĕn hăo*] *yăng*]]   morpho-syntactic brackets
  dog – very good – raise

g. *xiăo mă păo*   'the small horse is running'
   T3 T3 T3   →   **T2 T2** T3
  [[*xiăo mă*] *păo*]   morpho-syntactic brackets
  little horse – run

h. *mǎi hǎo jiǔ*   'buying good wine'

   T3 T3 T3   →   T3 **T2** T3 or **T2 T2** T3 (fast speech)

   [*mǎi* [*hǎo jiǔ*]]   morpho-syntactic brackets

   buy – good wine

i. *xiǎo mǔ lǎoshǔ*   'small female mouse'

   T3 T3 T3 T3   →   **T2** T3 **T2** T3

                or T3 **T2 T2** T3 or **T2 T2 T2** T3 (fast speech)

   [*xiǎo* [*mǔ* [*lǎoshǔ*]]]   morpho-syntactic brackets

   small – female mouse

j. *wǒ xiǎng mǎi jiǔ*   'I want to buy wine'

   T3 T3 T3 T3   →   **T2** T3 **T2** T3 or **T2 T2 T2** T3 (fast speech)

   [*wǒ* [*xiǎng* [*mǎi jiǔ*]]]   morpho-syntactic brackets

   I – want – buy – wine

k. *xiǎo mǔ jěmāo*   'small female wild cat'

   T3 T3 T3 T1   →   T3 **T2** T3 T1 or **T2 T2** T3 T1 (fast speech)

   [*xiǎo* [*mǔ* [*jěmāo*]]]   morpho-syntactic brackets

   small – female – wild cat

l. *wǒ xiǎng xiě shū*   'I want to write a book'

   T3 T3 T3 T1   →   **T2** T3 T3 T1 or **T2 T2** T3 T1 (fast speech)

   [*wǒ* [*xiǎng* [*xiě shū*]]]   morpho-syntactic brackets

   I – want – write book

m. *mǐ lǎoshǔ xiǎng zhǎo hǎo mǐjiǔ*   'Mickey Mouse wants to look for good rice wine'

   T3 T3 T3 T3 T3 T3 T3 T3   →   T3 **T2** T3 **T2** T3 T3 **T2** T3

                or T3 **T2** T3 **T2 T2** T3 **T2** T3 (fast speech)

   [[[*mǐ* [*lǎoshǔ*]] [*xiǎng* [*zhǎo* [*hǎo* [*mǐjiǔ*]]]]]]

   Mickey – Mouse – want – look for – good – rice wine

n. *wǒ xiǎng mǎi xiǎo mǔmǎ*   'I want to buy the small female horse'

   T3 T3 T3 T3 T3 T3   →   **T2 T2** T3 T3 **T2** T3

                or **T2 T2 T2** T3 **T2** T3

   [*wǒ* [*xiǎng* [*mǎi* [*xiǎo* [*mǔmǎ*]]]]]   morpho-syntactic brackets

   I – want – buy – small – female horse

4 Create or collect complex words and sentences with three or more T3s in a sequence. For each example: (i) present the tone sandhi pattern(s) based on your judgment; (ii) check with native speakers of SC to see what the possible tone 3 sandhi pattern(s) are; and (iii) provide an analysis to derive the attested patterns.

10 Stress and intonation

I have mentioned several times that the NEUTRAL TONE occurs in an UNSTRESSED SYLLABLE (§4.2.2 and §9.3). The question that naturally arises is: as a tone language, does SC really have STRESS? Recall also from §4.1.1 that TONE makes use of pitch variation to distinguish word meaning, whereas INTONATION is the pitch variation pattern to convey the syntactic and contextual meaning of a phrase or sentence. The next question that arises is: since both tone and intonation are expressed by pitch variation, how can SC separate tone from intonation?

This chapter discusses: (i) the extent to which stress is manifested in SC and how tone and stress interact in SC (§10.1); and (ii) the basic patterns of intonation in SC and how tone and intonation can be separated and interact in SC (§10.2). The final section (§10.3) summarizes the main points of the chapter.

10.1 Stress and tone

This section gives a brief introduction to what stress is (§10.1.1) before discussing whether SC exhibits stress and how tone and stress may interact (§10.1.2).

10.1.1 What is stress?

SC is a tone language and English is a stress language. In §4.1.1, we learned that TONE is the pattern of pitch changes that can differentiate word meanings. Then what is stress? STRESS is also a SUPRASEGMENTAL PROPERTY of the syllable. A STRESSED SYLLABLE is made more prominent or salient than an UNSTRESSED SYLLABLE in a word, a phrase, or in the flow of speech by being higher in pitch, longer in duration, and/or louder. For example, in the three-syllable word *horizon*, the second syllable *ri* has stress but the first syllable *ho* and the third syllable *zon* are without stress. In terms of articulation, a stressed syllable is produced with more respiratory energy and laryngeal activity (Ladefoged 2001:93), and in terms of perception, a stressed syllable stands out as more prominent or salient than its surrounding unstressed syllables.

The pattern of stress creates a pattern of rhythm in a stress language. In the above example, we have an unstressed-stressed-unstressed or weak-strong-weak rhythm. Stress patterns tend to alternate between stressed and unstressed syllables in an utterance. For example, in a four-syllable word like *intonation*, the first and third syllables are stressed but the second and the fourth syllables are not. Between the first and third stressed syllables, the third one has more promi-nence than the first one, so this English word has a PRIMARY STRESS on the third syllable and a SECONDARY STRESS (i.e. a lesser degree of stress) on the first syllable. The tendency of stress alternation to create rhythm is phono-logically expressed by the foot structure discussed earlier in §9.4.1. Recall that a FOOT is a PROSODIC UNIT that contains two syllables (or two MORAS depending on languages). Of the two elements within a foot, one must be more prominent than the other, hence the resulting rhythm. As illustrated in (1), when we group the sequence of four syllables in *intonation* into two feet, the first syllable is more prominent than the second one in the first foot and the third one is more prominent than the fourth one in the second foot.

(1) Stress alternation expressed by stress feet

$$
\begin{array}{llll}
in & to & na & tion \\
(\sigma & \sigma) & (\sigma & \sigma) \\
x & & x & \\
& & x & \\
\end{array}
$$

σ = syllable; ( ) = foot domain
x indicates prominence/stress

The two prominent stressed syllables, the first one and the third one, can be further differentiated in terms of degree of stress/prominence. In English, the stressed syllable on the rightmost foot is given an additional prominence mark 'x': the syllable with two 'x' marks has the highest degree of stress among the four syllables, the syllable with one 'x' mark has a lesser degree of stress and the syllables without the 'x' mark have no stress.

Some stress languages have a left-prominent foot: the left element of a foot has more prominence/stress, as in (2a). English is one such language as we have seen in (1). Some stress languages have a right-prominent foot: the right element of a foot has more prominence/stress, as in (2b). In both systems, there is an alternation of stress but the rhythmic patterns are different: one is stressed-unstressed (2a) and the other is unstressed-stressed (2b).

(2) a. left-prominent foot   b. right-prominent foot
      (σ σ)   (σ σ)
       x   x

Stress can also be used to emphasize a particular word or syllable contrasting with another one in a phrase/sentence. For example, if someone misheard when you are leaving, you can correct him/her or emphasize the time by saying *I'm leaving NOW not this evening,* with an emphatic or contrastive stress on *now* as opposed to *this evening.* SC, like all other languages, also has this kind of sentence level emphatic stress. The question is whether SC has the kind of word stress a stress language has.

10.1.2 Stress in SC and its interaction with tone

Stress in SC is phonetically manifested mainly by the expansion of pitch range and time duration, and sometimes by an increase of loudness (Chao 1968:35; Shih 1988:93; Shen 1989b:59–60). Expansion of pitch range means that a high-pitched tone become even higher and a low-pitched tone becomes even lower in a stressed syllable; that is, the range of pitch space is enlarged when producing a stressed syllable.

The most obvious and uncontroversial exhibition of word stress in SC is demonstrated by those disyllabic words with a NEUTRAL TONE. As shown in the example in (3), when the first syllable has a full tone (non-neutral tone) and the second one has the neutral tone (i.e. is toneless), the foot structure is left-prominent with the first syllable stressed and the second one unstressed. The vowel and/or rime in a neutral-toned syllable is often reduced (§7.3.2), which is in accordance with cross-linguistic tendency of vowel/rime reduction in unstressed syllables.

(3)   *dōngxi*   [tuŋ]55 [ɕi]2   'things, stuffs'
      tone: T1   T0
      foot: (σ σ)
      stress: x

However, when each syllable in a word has a full tone, as in most words in SC, it is not clear which syllable is stressed (cf. Chao 1968:38; Chen 2000:288). This is a situation very different from English, because English speakers are readily able to identify which syllable is stressed in a word and yet SC speakers' judgments of SC words without a neutral tone vary and are often inconsistent. Duanmu (2000:144) suggests that it is difficult to detect stress in SC because the most important phonetic cue for stress is F0 (FUNDAMENTAL FREQUENCY;

§4.1.2), but F0 is already used by SC for tone to contrast word meanings and hence cannot be used freely for stress.

Because of the difficulty in identifying phonetic stress in SC, in the literature some claim that SC has no stress in words without a neutral tone, and those who maintain that SC does have stress for all words disagree in whether the SC stress foot is left-dominant or right-dominant or can be both depending on different words. Nonetheless, there seems to be a common belief among some researchers that phonologically SC has a foot structure of some sort, although phonetically stress is difficult to detect. For example, the PROSODIC DOMAIN within which TONE 3 SANDHI applies can be treated as a kind of foot (cf. §9.4.1), or can be analyzed as a left-dominant stress foot (Duanmu 2000: chapter 11). Another example is the strong tendency for a SC word to be minimally two syllables long (Duanmu 2000:140 and chapter 7), which means a SC word tends to be at least a foot. To make a monosyllabic morpheme into a disyllabic word, either the monosyllabic morpheme is reduplicated, e.g. *dì* 'younger brother' → *dìdi* 'younger brother', or another morpheme, either with the same meaning or with empty meaning, is added, e.g. *shǔ* 'mouse' → *lǎoshǔ* 'mouse', *yǐ* 'chair' → *yǐzi* 'chair', *xué* 'study' plus *xí* 'study' → *xuéxí* 'study'. For the name of a country, there is no need to add *guó* 'country' to a country name that is more than one syllable long: e.g. *Rìběn* 'Japan' not *Rìběnguó, *Xībānyá* 'Spain' not *Xībānyáguó, but *guó* must be added to a monosyllabic country name: e.g. *Měiguó* 'America, USA' not *Měi, *Déguó* 'Germany' not *Dé. Although SC does have monosyllabic words, many of them have disyllabic counterparts: e.g. *huà* and *túhuà* 'painting, picture', *diàn* and *shāngdiàn* 'store, shop'. For a review of the controversy of SC stress and the evidence for phonological stress (foot structure with stress) in SC in particular and in Chinese in general, see Chen (2000: chapter 7) and Duanmu (2000: chapter 6).

For the practical purposes, learners of SC may not have to be concerned much about SC stress, given its elusive nature, but it is still necessary to produce and comprehend the pronunciation of the stressed (full-toned) versus unstressed (neutral-toned) syllables of those disyllabic words with a neutral tone. For example, the example in (3) would have a different meaning if it is pronounced with a full tone in the second syllable: *dōngxī* [tuŋ]55 [çi]55 'east and west'. For those SC speakers who do not have a neutral tone for disyllabic words, the full-toned version can mean either 'things, stuffs' or 'east and west'.

The most common interaction between tone and stress in SC is the occurrence of the neutral tone. When a syllable becomes unstressed either in a particular word for a particular meaning (e.g. as in (3)) or in fast casual speech, its original tone is lost and it becomes a neutral-toned or toneless syllable (cf. §9.3). The reason for the tone loss is that an unstressed syllable is short and weak, making it difficult to manifest fully the pitch change of a tone: there is not enough time and hence it is more difficult for a speaker to manipulate the pitch change, and also the syllable is not prominent enough to help listeners to perceive the pitch change even if the tone is implemented in articulation. When a neutral-toned syllable becomes stressed either in slow careful speech or because of emphatic stress, the original tone appears. For example, *péngyou* [pəŋ]35[jou]3 'friend', with a neutral tone in the second syllable, becomes *péngyŏu* [pəŋ]35[jou]214 with tone 3 in the second syllable when the word is emphasized. For speakers who do not generally have a neutral tone for this word, the second syllable may lose its tone and sound like a neutral tone in fast speech.

A case of stress-sensitive tone sandhi in SC is TONE 2 SANDHI (§4.2.3 and §9.2.5), which changes a MH tone (T2) to a HH tone (T1) when it is preceded by a HH tone (T1) or a MH tone (T2) and followed by another PHONEMIC TONE. In §9.2.5, tone 2 sandhi is analyzed as a kind of tonal ASSIMILATION or TONE SPREAD that changes a M feature to a H feature after another H feature, as in (4) (see §9.2.5 for the full analysis).

(4) Tone 2 sandhi

> HH MH   T   →   HH HH   T
> MH MH   T   →   MH HH   T

What is puzzling about this tonal assimilation process is that it occurs only in a three-syllable expression and only if the third tone is a phonemic tone. If we have a disyllabic word with T1 or T2 in the first syllable and T2 in the second syllable, no sandhi applies, as shown in (5ab). If we have a three-syllable expression but the third syllable has a neutral tone (i.e. not a phonemic tone), then no tone sandhi applies either, as the example in (5c) shows.

(5) a. *fēidié* [fei]55 [die]35   'flying saucer'
         HH MH (*HH HH)
     b. *méi lái* [mei]35 [lai]35   'did not come'
         MH MH (*MH HH)
     c. *hái méi ne*   [xai]35 [mei]35 [nə]3   'not yet'
         MH MH T0 → MH MH L (*MH HH L)

The explanation for the puzzle lies in the fact that in a three-syllable expression with a phonemic full tone in the third syllable, the third syllable has most prominence, and the middle syllable has least prominence. A syllable in a weak position tends to lose its tone and/or is subject to assimilation, especially in fast speech, so tone 2 sandhi, which applies only in fast speech, occurs only when tone 2 is in a prosodically weak position (Chen 2000:299–302; Yip 1980:291; Shih and Sproat 1992; Zhang 1988). When the third syllable has a neutral tone, as in (5c), tone 2 sandhi of the middle syllable does not apply because in this case it is the third syllable, not the middle syllable, that is in a prosodically weak position.

10.2 Intonation and tone

This section starts with a brief introduction to intonation in §10.2.1. Examples of some basic intonation patterns of SC and how tone and intonation are expressed and interact in SC are discussed in §10.2.2.

10.2.1 What is intonation?

We have learned that the pattern of pitch variation that can differentiate word meaning is called tone. INTONATION is also expressed by various patterns of pitch changes (e.g. high versus low and rising versus falling), but intonation does not distinguish word meaning. It instead expresses syntactic and contextual meanings such as statement, question, affirmation, command, surprise, emphasis, etc. The two SC examples in (6a) show that the tonal differences yield two different meanings. In (6bc), we see that if the same word has two different intonation patterns, the word meaning does not change but one intonation pattern expresses affirmation (6b) and the other a question (6c). The lowered/falling pitch to express affirmation and the raised/rising pitch to express a question are similar to the intonation patterns in English, as in (6d), in which the meaning of the word does not change although each example has a different pitch pattern.

(6)

  a. *mǎi*   [mai]214   'to buy'   tone: LH
       mài   [mai]51   'to sell'   tone: HL
  b. *mǎi*   'buy!'   tone: LH
                            intonation: lowered/falling pitch
  c. *mǎi*   'buy?'   tone: LH
                            intonation: raised/rising pitch
  d. Buy!   intonation: lowered/falling pitch
     Buy?   intonation: raised/rising pitch

In a non-tone language like English, pitch variation is used only for intonation. Analyses of English intonation typically make use of tone features (i.e. H and L) to show the ups and downs of pitch in a phrase/sentence (e.g. Liberman

1975; Pierrehumbert 1980). For example, in a plain statement as in (7a), the final syllable has a falling pitch pattern to end in a lower pitch, whereas in a simple yes-no question as in (7b), the final syllable has a rising pitch pattern to end in a higher pitch. The arrows indicate the direction of the pitch change, and the tone features indicate the pitch contour.

(7) a.   ↘   b.   ↗
    He is going to come.   Is he going to come?
                H L   L H

On the other hand, in a tone language, pitch variation is used for both tone and intonation. Because of the need for tone to distinguish word meaning, the pitch contour for the intonation cannot be as freely exploited as that in a non-tone language. Otherwise, a drastic change of pitch contour for intonation purposes could alter the meaning of a word. For example, if in a question, a falling tone (T4: HL) in the final syllable is changed to a rising pitch pattern (LH) by a question intonation, then the word may be misheard as a different word with a T3. In §10.2.2, we will see how SC expresses intonation without disturbing the tonal pitch pattern needed to distinguish word meaning.

In general, there is a gradual downtrend of pitch over the entire course of an intonational phrase (an utterance with a specific intonation pattern), which is called DECLINATION. Because of this, a high tone at the beginning of an utterance is higher in pitch than a high tone in the middle of an utterance, and a high tone at the end of an utterance is further lowered phonetically. Therefore, the H versus L tone features, either for tone or intonation, only indicate relative pitch level (cf. §4.1.1).

10.2.2 Intonation in SC and its interaction with tone

To avoid the potential conflict between tone and intonation, SC, like many other tone languages (especially Asian tone languages), makes use of sentence-final PARTICLES to indicate certain groups of syntactic and contextual meanings expressed by intonation in a non-tone language. These sentence-final particles are FUNCTION WORDS, and in SC they are monosyllabic and have a neutral tone. Some examples are given in (8). For more examples and explanation of the use of particles, see Chao (1968: §8.5) and Li and Thompson (1981: chapter 7).

🎧 (8) SC particles

    a. *ma*   'question marker'
                 tā shì xuéshēng ma?   'Is he a student?'
                 he-is-student-*ma*

b. *ba*   'supposition, solicit agreement'

nǐ huì lái ba   'You will come, I suppose'

you-will-come-*ba*

wǒmen zǒu ba   'Let's go, shall we?'

we-go-*ba*

SC still has intonation, but with the use of particles the change of pitch contour for intonation purposes is minimized to some extent. According to Shen (1989b:26–7), SC has three basic types of intonation pitch movements, as in (9) (with minor modifications and simplifications). The main difference between a statement and a question is that the starting pitch of a question is higher than that of a statement and the overall pitch level of a question is also higher than that of a statement.

(9) Basic types of intonation pitch movements

a. Type I for statements (e.g. *tā míngtiān lái.* 'he will come tomorrow')
Starting mid, moving higher to mid-high, and falling to low at the end.

b. Type II for questions with high utterance-final pitch (e.g. *tā míngtiān lái?* 'he will come tomorrow?')
Starting mid-high, moving to high, dropping very slightly before ending in high or mid high.

c. Type III for questions with low utterance-final pitch (e.g. *shéi míngtiān lái?* 'who will come tomorrow?')
Starting mid-high, moving to high, sloping down to low at the end.

d.

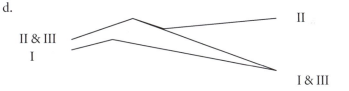

Although there is some degree of pitch movement for intonation purposes, Shen (1989a,b) maintains that in SC the basic contour of a tone (i.e. level, falling, rising) remains recognizable and easily perceived even though intonation inevitably causes some minor modifications or distortion of the tone. For example, the high level tone (T1) tends to be slightly falling in a statement and slightly rising in a question, but the tone is not altered beyond recognition since it is still perceived by the speakers in her experiments as T1. In addition, when more than one tone appear in a sequence, TONAL COARTICULATION changes each tone somewhat for a smooth transition from one tone to another (§9.1). Such changes are expected by native speakers of SC and hence do not affect the recognition of a tone.

If the pitch contour of each tone remains pretty much intact (after taking into consideration tonal coarticulation effects), how can intonation be expressed and recognized? As we have seen in (9), there is a difference in the degree of overall pitch level between a statement intonation and a question intonation. Therefore, the first strategy is to manipulate the pitch level: (i) the pitch level of the whole utterance may be raised higher or be depressed lower; and/or (ii) the high pitch of a tone gets higher and the low pitch of a tone gets even lower (cf. Chao 1933:131–2; Shen 1989a,b). The second strategy is to add a H or L pitch after the tone features of the sentence final syllable (Chao 1933:132–3).

The examples in (10) illustrate the second strategy of tone feature addition. For example, affirmative intonation on a rising tone produces a rising-falling contour as in (10a), question intonation on the same rising tone produces a rising tone that stretches longer and higher at the end, as illustrated in (10b), and question intonation on a falling tone results in a falling-rising pitch contour as in (10c).

(10) Phrase final tone addition

    a. *máng!*   '(really) busy!'
       tone MH (35) + affirmative intonation $L \rightarrow MHL = 351$
    b. *máng?*   '(did you say) busy?'
       tone MH (35) + question intonation $H \rightarrow MH^+ = 36$
    c. *màn?*   '(did you say) slow?'
       tone HL (51) + question intonation $H \rightarrow HLM = 513$

However, based on phonetic experiments, Shen (1989b) argues that the expression of SC intonation mainly involves the change of the overall pitch level of an utterance and does not add an additional tone feature at the end of an utterance. For example, the overall pitch level of a question is higher than that in a statement for the same sequence of words, as illustrated in (11), with the solid and dotted lines indicating the relative lower and higher pitch level respectively for the whole utterance. At either the higher or lower pitch level, the basic tonal contour is retained, as indicated by the tone features. Under this view, the pitch movement of intonation as a whole is superimposed onto the pitch movements of tones; that is, pitch movements of tone and intonation act simultaneously.

(11) Higher pitch level for questions: HH MH HH MH *tā míngtiān lái?*
     Lower pitch level for statements: _____ *tā míngtiān lái.*
                       HH MH HH MH

Shen's argument for the lack of tone feature addition at the end of an utterance is based on the experimental results showing that, for the same intonation, the utterance-final pitch basically has the pitch contour of any of the four SC tones. In (12), I give four examples that have the same statement intonation but terminate in different tones. These examples do not all have a final falling pitch contour as one would find in English statements; rather, the final syllable has a falling pitch only when it has a falling tone (12d).

🎧 (12)

	EXAMPLE		UTTERANCE FINAL PITCH CONTOUR
a.	*wǒ xǐhuān māo*		Level or slightly falling
	I-like-cat	'I like cats'	
b.	*wǒ xǐhuān qián*		High rising
	I-like-money	'I like money'	
c.	*wǒ xǐhuān gǒu*		Low or low rising
	I-like-dog	'I like dogs'	
d.	*wǒ xǐhuān shù*		Falling
	I-like-tree	'I like trees'	

In a colorless normal utterance without expressive emotion and special emphasis, which is the main data from Shen (1989b), intonation is indeed manifested by a higher or lower pitch level for the whole utterance without much distortion of the tones and there is no addition of a H or L intonation tone feature to the utterance-final tone. However, in an emotive and expressive utterance, especially with the emphasis of an utterance-final word, tone feature addition as described in Chao (1933), and like those examples in (10), does occur.

Unlike the full tones, the neutral tone is more strongly affected by intonation. Since a neutral-toned syllable is toneless, its pitch value is shaped by the preceding phonemic tone, as discussed and analyzed in §9.3. However, the pitch value of a neutral tone is also affected by intonation. The phonetic facts are rather complex and here I mention only a few based on Shen (1989b:38–48). In general, the neutral tone combines the pitch value at the end of the preceding full tone and the pitch value imposed by intonation (Shen 1989b:48). For example, if the pitch value of the neutral tone is high after T3, it becomes higher if the intonation at that point is raised, such as toward the end of a question with a rising intonation. However, there are some special situations. First, the question particle *ma*, unlike other neutral-toned particles and syllables, always ends with a high pitch, regardless of the tone of its preceding syllable (Shen 1989b:41). Second, in an utterance with DECLINATION (§10.2.1), such as in a statement, the pitch level of the neutral tone is higher at the beginning and lower at the end because of the gradual downtrend of the intonation (Shen 1989b:41). Third, when two or more neutral tones occur in succession, the first neutral tone is conditioned both by the preceding tone and the intonation, but the second and the subsequent neutral tones are controlled solely by sentence intonation (Shen 1989b:40–41). In the example in (13), which is a question ending with a lower final pitch (type III in (9)), the first neutral-toned syllable *le* has a mid pitch level since it is after a T2 (§9.3). In the middle of the sentence, the intonation has begun to fall after the higher point at *lái*, and the next two neutral-toned syllables *mei* and *you* have low pitch values since the intonation has low pitch toward the end of the sentence.

(13) Two or more neutral tones in succession

44   35   3   2   1   pitch value
tā   lái   le   mei   you?
he-come-perfective aspect-not-have
'Has he come yet?'

In this subsection, the basics of SC intonation and its interaction with tone are discussed. For more details, different views, and advanced topics in this area, see relevant references in Further Reading.

10.3 Summary

This chapter introduces what stress and intonation are and discusses how tone interacts with stress and intonation in SC.

- A stressed syllable is commonly higher in pitch, longer in duration, and/or louder, and hence is perceived as more prominent or salient than an unstressed syllable. The pattern of stress tends to create a pattern of rhythm that alternates between stressed and unstressed syllables (§10.1.1).
- It is uncontroversial that in a disyllabic SC word with the neutral tone, the first syllable with a full tone is stressed and the second syllable with the neutral tone is unstressed, but in a disyllabic word with two full tones, it is not clear which one has the stress (§10.1.2).
- Although it is difficult to detect stress phonetically in SC, there have been proposals that SC has abstract stress/foot structure phonologically (§10.1.2).
- In SC, tone interacts with stress in at least three cases: (i) the neutral tone occurs when a syllable becomes unstressed; (ii) tone 2 sandhi occurs only when tone 2 is in a weakly stressed (or unstressed) position in a

three-syllable expression; and (iii) the domain of tone 3 sandhi application may be considered a foot (§10.1.2).

- Like tone, intonation also makes crucial use of pitch, but, unlike tone, it expresses syntactic and contextual meanings rather than differences in word meaning (10.2.1).
- Three basic intonation patterns in SC have been introduced. A question intonation has an overall higher pitch level than a statement intonation (§10.2.2).
- Except for the neutral tone, the tonal contour remains recognizable with the superimposition of intonation (§10.2.2).
- In an expressive and/or emphatic utterance, an intonation pitch value is added to the tone of the final syllable (§10.2.2).
- Since the neutral tone is toneless, it is subject to the influence of intonation more easily than the four phonemic tones (§10.2.2).
- In general, the pitch value of the neutral tone is conditioned by both the preceding phonemic tone and intonation. However, in a sequence of neutral tones, the neutral tones after the first one are controlled solely by intonation (§10.2.2).

EXERCISES

1   Decide if each of the following statements is true or false. For each false statement, provide the correction.

a. As in English, it is easy to detect word stress in SC.
b. For a word with a neutral tone, such as shēnghuo [ʂən]55[xwo]2 'livelihood', the neutral-toned syllable is unstressed, but for a word with full tones such as shēnghuó [ʂən]55[xwo]35 'life', it is unclear or debatable which syllable is stressed.
c. Unlike English, SC cannot use stress for emphasis or focus in a phrase or sentence.
d. Tone 2 sandhi applies in a three-syllable sequence when the T2 is preceded by T1 or T2 and followed by either a phonemic tone or a neutral tone.
e. Tone 2 sandhi applies because in the three-syllable sequence the second syllable that T2 is associated with has least prominence.
f. The prosodic domain within which tone 3 sandhi applies (§9.4) is analyzed by some as a foot.
g. SC speakers can expand the pitch range (e.g. a high tone becomes higher and a low tone becomes lower) and/or syllable length to indicate stress.

h. Both tone and intonation make use of pitch variation to indicate meaning differences. Intonation conveys syntactic and contextual meanings in phrases/sentences but does not distinguish word meaning, whereas tone distinguishes word meaning.

i. Tone languages often use sentence-final particles or other function words to convey certain syntactic or contextual meanings that are typically expressed by intonation in a non-tone language.

j. Both English and SC have a falling intonation pattern at the end of a statement and an affirmative expression.

k. In SC, the pitch level and pitch contour of a tone become unrecognizable in a sentence when superimposed by intonation.

l. In SC, the intonation pattern for a question has an overall lower pitch level than that for a statement.

m. In an expressive, emotive and/or emphatic utterance, an intonation pitch value is added to the tone of the final syllable. For example, in a question intonation, *mài* HL (51) 'sell' → *mài*? HLM (513) '(did you say) sell?' and for an affirmative intonation, *lái* MH (35) 'come' → *lái*! MHL (351) '(definitely) will come'.

n. Both types of questions, such as *nǐ xǐhuān gǒu*? 'you like dogs?' and *shéi xǐhuān gǒu* 'who likes dogs?', have a rising intonation at the end of the sentence.

o. The neutral tone is conditioned by the preceding tone but is not affected by intonation.

p. A neutral tone preceded by another neutral tone is affected solely by intonation.

2 Record conversations by native speakers of SC and listen carefully to the recording several times. First, identify: (i) examples with a neutral tone, tone 2 sandhi, and tone 3 sandhi; and (ii) examples of questions, statements/ affirmative expressions, and emotive/expressive or emphatic phrases/sentences. Second, for each example, describe and explain: (i) the tone sandhi pattern(s); (ii) the interaction of tone and stress; (iii) the intonation pattern; and/or (iv) the interaction of tone and intonation.

11 Loanword adaptation

One common way for a language to borrow a word from a foreign language is to make any necessary changes to the sounds of the foreign word to fit the native language's phonetic and phonological systems. For example, the state name *Texas* [tʰɛk.səs], a DISYLLABIC word, is borrowed into SC with the pronunciation of *dékèsàsī* [tə]₃₅ [kʰə]₅₃ [sa]₅₃ [sɹ]₅₅, a four-syllable word. The expansion of the number of syllables is due to the fact that SC does not allow [k] and [s] in syllable coda position (§5.3), and adding a vowel after [k] and a syllabic consonant after [s] makes the word conform to the permissible syllable structure in SC. Consonants and vowels may also change during the sound adaptation process.

This chapter illustrates and explains how phonetic/phonological principles in general and SC's phonetic and phonological systems in particular shape the pronunciations of the loanwords borrowed from English. Since not all loanwords are borrowed through adaptation of sounds, §11.1 introduces how SC loanwords are created through different adaptation processes. After a general introduction to the process of sound adaptation (§11.2), we examine how SC makes adjustments for syllable structure (§11.3), consonants (§11.4), and vowels (§11.5) in loanword adaptation. The final section (§11.6) summarizes the main points of the chapter.

11.1 Loanwords in SC

In the history of Chinese, extensive borrowing of foreign words occurred when Buddhism was spread to China and large numbers of Buddhist texts were translated. This spanned roughly the period from the second century AD to the thirteenth century. The new wave of extensive borrowing of foreign words began in the sixteenth century when Western missionaries came to China, and since then most new loanwords have come from European languages and some from Japanese. English has been the major source of new loanwords since the early twentieth century. Older loanwords were mostly created by Western missionaries and translators of foreign books. Modern loanwords are mostly created by intellectuals, translators, and media people who know English or relevant foreign languages.

A foreign word can be borrowed into SC directly from the source language, with modifications of the original sounds as necessary. The adapted word is represented by Chinese characters that simulate the adapted pronunciation, with each character for one syllable, as shown in (1). Although each Chinese character commonly represents a MORPHEME and hence has some meaning associated with it (§1.4), the characters in a sound-based loanword are used mainly for the purpose of representing the sounds and syllables and may not convey any meaning, as in this case.

🎧 (1) ENGLISH   CHARACTER   *PĪNYĪN*   IPA TRANSCRIPTION
       Texas   德克萨斯   *dékèsàsī* $[tə]_{35}[k^hə]_{53}[sa]_{53}[s\textipa{\textturnr}]_{55}$

This sound-based borrowing method is commonly used for proper names, such as the name of a place, a person, or the brand name of a product. We will have more examples and discussion in the next few sections.

The sound-based method is commonly used by languages in borrowing foreign words. For example, the Chinese city *Shanghai* is pronounced as $[ʂɑŋ]_{53}[xai]_{214}$ in SC, but English speakers typically pronounce it as $[ʃæŋhai]$, although in English the orthographic spelling is directly adopted from Chinese *pīnyīn*. In Japanese, the English word *hotel* is pronounced as *hoteru* and is represented with Japanese orthographic scripts in the written form.

A meaning-based method is often used by SC when borrowing foreign words. There are two types of meaning-based adaptations. The first type literally translates the meaning of each MORPHEME in the source word, as the examples in (2a) show. The second type creates a brand new Chinese word in an attempt to capture the major characteristic or essence of the foreign concept or object without a morpheme-by-morpheme translation, as in (2b). Combinations of both types are possible, as in (2c), where one morpheme is a direct translation while the other one is not. In general, the meaning-based method is mostly adopted for new objects and concepts, whereas the sound-based method is used mostly for foreign proper names.

🎧 (2)   ENGLISH   CHARACTER &   *PĪNYĪN* &
                       MEANING   IPA TRANSCRIPTION
          a. *football*   足球   *zúqiú*
                          'foot-ball' $[tsu]_{35}[tɕ^hjou]_{35}$
             honeymoon 蜜月   *mìyuè*
                          'honey-moon' $[mi]_{53}[ɥe]_{51}$

	bull market	牛市		*niúshì*
		'bull-market'		[njou]$_{35}$[ʂ̩ɹ]$_{51}$
	microwave oven	微波炉		*wēibōlú*
		'micro-wave-oven'		[wei]$_{35}$[pwo]$_{55}$[lu]$_{35}$
	Microsoft	微软		*wēiruǎn*
		'micro-soft'		[wei]$_{35}$[ɹwan]$_{214}$
	Newsweek	新闻周刊		*xīnwén zhōukān*
		'news-weekly'		[ɕin]$_{55}$[wən]$_{35}$
				[tʂou]$_{55}$[kʰan]$_{55}$
b.	*computer*	电脑		*diànnǎo*
		'electric/electronic-brain'		[tjɛn]$_{53}$[nɑu]$_{214}$
	train	火车		*huǒchē*
		'fire-vehicle'		[xwo]$_{21}$[tʂʰɤ]$_{55}$
	movie	电影		*diànyǐng*
		'electric/electronic-image'		[tjɛn]$_{53}$[jəŋ]$_{214}$
	typewriter	打字机		*dǎzìjī*
		'hit-character-machine'		[ta]$_{21}$[tsɹ]$_{53}$[tɕi]$_{55}$
c.	*computer*	计算机		*jìsuànjī*
		'compute-machine'		[tɕi]$_{53}$[swan]$_{53}$[tɕi]$_{55}$
	television	电视		*diànshì*
		'electric/electronic-vision'		[tjɛn]$_{53}$[ʂ̩ɹ]$_{51}$

The same foreign word may have more than one corresponding Chinese word. Such a situation usually arises when different groups of SC speakers come up with different loanwords. The SC translated word for *computer* in (2c) was used by SC speakers from mainland China and the one in (2b) by SC speakers from Taiwan, but (2b) has recently gained popularity among many speakers from China. Additional meaning-based variants include the word *software*, which is *ruǎnjiàn* 'soft-piece' in China but *ruǎntǐ* 'soft-body/entity' in Taiwan, and the word *hardware*, which is *yìngjiàn* 'hard-piece' in China and *yìngtǐ* 'hard-body/entity' in Taiwan. Examples for different sound-based loanwords include the state of *Michigan*, which is *mìzhí'ān* in China and *mìxìgān* in Taiwan, and the name *Bush* (from President Bush), which is *bùshí* in China and *bùxī* in Taiwan. Sometimes, one group uses the sound-based method while the other uses the meaning-based method. For example, for the word *laser*, the sound-based loanword, *léishè*, is used in Taiwan and the meaning-based loanword, *jīguāng* 'excited-light', is used in China.

Among the same group of speakers, multiple Chinese versions for the same foreign word can co-exist and one of them may eventually become the norm. This situation occurs most often to the sound-based loanwords because there can be more than one way to adapt the sounds of a foreign word into SC (see §11.2 below). If both a meaning-based loanword and a sound-based loanword are available for the same foreign word, the meaning-based one is often preferred or tends to become the final accepted norm. For example, the English word *engine* can be either *yǐnqíng* (sound-based) or *fādòngjī* 'launch-machine' (meaning-based), but the latter is preferred by many SC speakers and may be considered the standard norm (see also Chen 1999:104–105).

Some SC loanwords combine the sound-based and the meaning-based methods. Each example in (3a) shows that the first part of the loanword is sound-based and the second part is meaning-based. Sometimes, it is possible for a sound-based loanword to use characters that reflect the meaning or essence of the foreign word to some extent or in a humorous way, as the examples in (3b) show.

(3) | ENGLISH | CHARACTER & MEANING | PĪNYĪN & IPA TRANSCRIPTION |
|---|---|---|
| a. *Cambridge* | 剑桥 '*cam*-bridge' | *jiànqiáo* [tɕjɛn]₅₃[tɕʰjɑu]₃₅ |
| *beer* | 啤酒 '*beer*-alcohol' | *píjiǔ* [pʰi]₃₅[tɕjou]₂₁₄ |
| *motorcycle* | 摩托车 '*motor*-vehicle' | *mótuōchē* [mwo]₃₅[tʰwo]₅₅[tʂʰɤ]₅₅ |
| b. *mini* | 迷你 'enchant-you' | *mǐnǐ* [mi]₃₅[ni]₂₁₄ |
| *laser* | 雷射 'thunder-shoot' | *léishè* [lei]₃₅[ʂɤ]₅₁ |
| *radar* | 雷达 'thunder-reach' | *léidá* [lei]₃₅[ta]₃₅ |

Because Japanese *kanji* (Chinese characters used by Japanese) is almost identical to Chinese characters, SC has also borrowed *kanji* written words coined by Japanese (Chen 1999:102). Although the same written characters are pronounced differently in Japanese and in SC, it is easy to take the written forms and pronounce them in SC. For example, the word for 'bank' is written as 银行 ('silver-company') in both languages. This term was coined by Japanese through the meaning-based method and is pronounced as *ginko*. Chinese later borrowed it directly through the written form but pronounce it in Chinese, which is *yínháng* in SC.

We have had a brief review of how SC borrows words from other languages. In what follows, we will focus on loanwords created through the sound-based method since this type of loanword showcases how the sounds of a foreign word can be adjusted to conform to the native language's phonetic/phonological rules and constraints.

11.2 Sound adaptation in SC loanwords

When creating a loanword through the sound-based method, different aspects of the phonetic and phonological systems need to be examined: syllable structure, consonants, vowels, and SUPRASEGMENTALS. We will not discuss how English stress is changed to tone in SC in the loanword adaptation process because it is not clear if the stressed syllable in English is consistently turned into a particular tone in SC (e.g. tone 1 or tone 4) and this area awaits further research. For simplicity, in the loanword examples discussed below, tones will be marked on the *pīnyīn* but will not be included in the IPA phonetic transcriptions.

The next three sections (§§11.3–11.5) discuss how an English syllable is adjusted to conform to the permissible syllable types in SC (§11.3), what English consonants are changed to what SC consonants (§11.4), and what English vowels are changed to what SC vowels (§11.5). In general, changes are made in order to conform to permissible SC phonetic and phonological forms so that the adapted word can be easily pronounced by SC speakers. Before we study each of these areas in detail, we need to be aware of a few important characteristics of sound-based loanwords in SC.

First, there can be more than one way to make changes to the sounds and syllables during the loanword adaptation process. As mentioned earlier, *Michigan* and *Bush* have two adapted versions in SC. Another example is *Disney* (for the Disney theme park), which has been adapted as either *dísīnài* (an older version used in Taiwan) or *díshìní* (a newer one used in China and Hong Kong and by some speakers in Taiwan more recently). In general, as long as the adapted loanword imitates the sounds of the foreign word and follows the SC phonetic and phonological systems, it is considered acceptable. If more than one version co-exist initially, one of them often becomes the conventionalized norm after a while.

Second, some Chinese characters have routinely been used for the sound-based adaptation of foreign proper names, which to some extent makes it easier to process loanwords and separate them from native words in reading. For example, the four characters used to represent the loanword adapted from the word *Texas* in (1) are typical ones used in sound-based loanwords. Since each such character represents the pronunciation of a particular syllable in SC, its main function is to simulate some syllable(s) in English. For example, the characters in (4) are typically used to simulate syllables such as [li] and [ɹi] in English. As mentioned in §11.1, the original meaning of a character used in a sound-based loanword is usually irrelevant and ignored. However, as with most Chinese personal names, there is a tendency to use certain characters for male names and others for female names. The characters in (4a) are most likely to be used for male names (both in native Chinese names and adapted foreign names), whereas those in (4b), with meanings associated with flower or beauty, are typically used for female names.

(4)   CHARACTER/PĪNYĪN/MEANING   EXAMPLE

　　　a. 利 *lì* 'interest, profit'   *Henry*   亨利 *hēnglì*
　　　　 理 *lǐ* 'reason'   *Charlie* 查理 *chálǐ*
　　　b. 莉 *lì* 'jasmine'   ***Lilly***   莉莉 ***lìlì***
　　　　　　　　　　　　　　　　　　　　 Mary   玛莉 *mǎlì*
　　　　 丽 *lì* 'beautiful'   *Mary*   玛丽 *mǎlì*

Third, the sound-based adaptation process generally matches the pronunciation of an adapted word as closely as possible to that of the original foreign word. However, the choice of characters to represent an adapted loanword can be influenced by several factors that may not result in the closest match. The most common reason for deviation from the pronunciation of the foreign word is the need or the desire to use characters with good or attractive meanings, for example, in promoting or marketing a product or avoiding the use of characters or syllables similar to taboo words. In addition, China and Taiwan may avoid using identical loanwords for the same foreign name. I already mentioned earlier that *Bush* is adapted as *bùshí* in China but *bùxī* in Taiwan. Another example is *Regan*, which is *lǐgēn* in China and *léigēn* in Taiwan. In terms of phonetic closeness, the Taiwan versions better match the English pronunciations, but the deviation exhibited in China's versions is still within the acceptable range in the sound adaptation process. Furthermore, some loanwords may have been borrowed through a local dialect and may contain sounds and syllables peculiar to the local dialect and how it adapts a foreign word.

Since there can be variation and potential deviation in the sound-based adaptation process, we cannot cover every possible case in this introductory book and the generalizations or rules discussed in the following sections do not intend to be comprehensive. Instead, we examine sample examples to gain a basic understanding of how the SC phonetic and phonological features, rules and constraints are relevant to the adaptation of sound-based loanwords.

11.3 Syllable structure adjustment

English has a more complex syllable structure than SC does in the sense that English allows more consonants in the onset and coda (§5.2.1). The example

Texas mentioned earlier has illustrated why a disyllabic English word becomes four syllables long in SC. Recall that in the syllable onset, SC allows only one segment (a consonant or a glide) or two segments (a consonant plus a glide) and in the coda only [n] and [ŋ] are allowed. Although in some varieties of SC, a [ɹ] coda is possible after many different vowels when *r*-suffixation applies (§8.2), the SC loanword adaptation process follows the syllable structure of unsuffixed forms. That is, the only syllable that may contain a [ɹ] coda is *er* [əɹ]. However, since *er* can be phonetically treated as a rhotacized vowel [ɚ] (§3.4.5, §8.2.2), we may also claim that there is no [ɹ] coda in SC.

When an English syllable contains an onset or a coda not permitted by SC, two strategies are commonly employed: (i) insertion of a syllable nucleus; or (ii) consonant deletion.

11.3.1 Nucleus insertion

Consider first the examples of nucleus insertion in (5), in which a dot in the phonetic transcription indicates a syllable boundary, and remember that some English words have more than one loanword in SC. In each example in (5), we see that the number of syllables is increased in SC by adding additional syllable nuclei, a vowel, or a syllabic consonant.

(5)   ENGLISH   SC

   a. *Strauss*   [stɹaʊs]   ***shǐ.tè.láo.sī***   [ʂɹ.tʰɤ.lɑu.sɹ]
                           sī.tè.láo.sī   [sɹ.tʰɤ.lɑu.sɹ]

   b. *Franklin*   [fɹæŋ.klɪn]   ***fù.lán.kè.lín***   [fu.lan.kʰɤ.lin]
                            fó.lán.kè.lín   [fwo.lan.kʰɤ.lin]

   c. *Vermont*   [vɚ.mɑnt]   ***fó.méng.tè***   [fwo.məŋ.tʰɤ]
   d. *Roberts*   [ɹɑ.bɚts]   ***luó.bó.zī***   [lwo.pwo.tsɹ]
                           luó.bó.cì   [lwo.pwo.tsʰɹ]

   e. *Richards*   [ɹɪ.tʃɚdz]   ***lǐ.chá.zī***   [li.tʂʰa.tsɹ]
   f. *Richmond*   [ɹɪtʃ.mənd]   ***lì.qì.méng***   [li.tɕʰi.məŋ]
   g. *Mark*   [mɑɹk]   ***mǎ.kè***   [ma.kʰɤ]
                           mài.kè   [mai.kʰɤ]

   h. *Brook*   [bɹʊk]   ***bù.lǔ.kè***   [pu.lu.kʰɤ]
   i. *Jim*   [dʒɪm]   ***jí.mǔ***   [tɕi.mu]
   j. *Frances*   [fɹɑn.səs]   ***fǎ.lán.xī.sī***   [fa.lan.ɕi.sɹ]
   k. *Frederick*   [fɹɛ.də.ɹɪk]   ***fěi.dé.liè.kè***   [fei.tɤ.lje.kʰɤ]
   l. *Truman*   [tɹu.mən]   ***dù.lǔ.mén***   [tu.lu.mən]

Nucleus insertion creates a simple CV syllable. In (5a), the three-consonant onset and the [s] coda are not possible in SC, so a vowel or a syllabic consonant is inserted after the first two consonants and the last consonant. We also see nucleus insertion after English [f] and [k] in (5b) and after [b] in (5h), since [fr], [kl], and [bɹ] are not a possible onsets in SC, after [t] in (5c), since a [nt] coda is not allowed in SC, after [ts] and [dz] in (5de), after [tʃ] in (5f), and after [k] in (5g), because again these are not possible SC codas.

You may have noticed that different types of vowels and syllabic consonants have been inserted. The choice of which segment to insert depends on the preceding consonant. We can envision that what is inserted is not a specific vowel or syllabic consonant but an empty syllable nucleus. In §8.1 we have seen that SC fills an empty onset or empty nucleus position either by extending an adjacent sound or by adding some default choice of consonant or vowel. The nucleus insertion process in loanword adaptation follows a similar pattern. In general, /ə/ is the basic vowel to fill the inserted empty nucleus and it becomes [ɤ] in a simple CV syllable, as in (5abcghk), through the mid vowel tensing process discussed in §8.1.4. However, we also see other vowels and syllabic consonants. Which type of nucleus to use depends on the consonant to be modified and follows the rule/constraint system in SC.

First, in (5adej), a syllabic consonant is used after a dental or post-alveolar fricative or affricate. In §8.1.2 we learned that a syllabic consonant fills an empty nucleus after a dental/post-alveolar fricative/affricate. For example, the syllable *si* is /s/ in UNDERLYING REPRESENTATION and surfaces as [sɹ̩] after insertion of an empty nucleus and extension of the [s] to fill the empty nucleus. In the loanword adaptation process, SC tries to convert English consonants such as [s], or [ts] to a well-formed SC syllable and naturally makes use of the same process. Although in SC [ɤ] can also appear as a nuclear vowel after a dental/post-alveolar fricative/affricate in a CV syllable (e.g. *se* [sɤ]₅₁ 'color'), the use of a syllabic consonant makes the resulting syllable sound closer to the original English consonant. For example, *si* [sɹ̩] is a better match to English [s] than *se* [sɤ] in terms of perception and pronunciation.

Second, in (5f), a high vowel is inserted. The palato-alveolar affricate [tʃ] in English is converted into an alveolo-palatal affricate [tɕʰ] in SC since SC does not have [tʃ], and [tɕʰ] is the best match in pronunciation and perception. The mid vowel [ɤ] is not used because an alveolo-palatal in SC can only be followed by a high vowel/glide (§7.2.1, §2.2.5, §5.3). The inserted empty nucleus in this example is therefore filled with a high front vowel, resulting in [tɕʰi].

Third, in (5bhi), [u] or [wo] appears after a labial consonant. In SC, a labial consonant cannot be followed by [ɤ] (§5.3). When the consonant is a labial, the inserted empty nucleus takes on the labial feature of the consonant, resulting in a rounded vowel. Since both labial consonants and rounded vowels make use of lips in articulation, this is a case of ASSIMILATION (§7.1.2.1). If a high rounded vowel is chosen, then [u] appears, but if a mid rounded vowel [o] is chosen, it has to be adjusted to [wo] since [o] in SC occurs only next to a [w] or in a diphthong [ou]. Both [u] and [wo] are more commonly used than [ou] after a labial consonant because: (i) SC has a limited number of characters representing a labial plus [ou] syllable and there is no character for [pou]; and (ii) the insertion of [u] or [wo] after a labial makes the resulting syllable sound closer to the original labial consonant in English.

Finally, we see in (5jk) that the vowel inserted after [f] is not a rounded one and in (5l) that the vowel inserted after [t] is not [ɤ]. This is not what we expected but note that the inserted vowel in each case is similar to the first vowel in the original English word, as though the inserted nucleus simply copies the first vowel. This 'vowel copying' process sometimes happens when the relevant consonant appears in an onset consonant cluster, especially when the second consonant is [ɹ].

In summary, the inserted nucleus is by default a schwa that appears as [ɤ] in general, but it must be a syllabic consonant after a dental/post-alveolar fricative/affricate, a high front vowel after an alveolo-palatal, and a rounded vowel after a labial consonant. Occasionally, the inserted nucleus may copy the neighboring vowel when the insertion occurs inside an onset consonant cluster.

11.3.2 Consonant deletion

Consider now examples of consonant deletion in (6). One obvious observation based on these examples is that all the consonants that do not show up in the SC loanwords are coda consonants. Consonant deletion applies more commonly to coda consonants, to consonants that are less easily perceived, and to consonants in a longer sequence of consonants or in longer words.

(6)   ENGLISH   SC
   a. *Richmond*   [ɹɪtʃ.mənd]   *lì.qí.méng*   [li.tɕʰi.məŋ]
   b. *Netherlands* [nɛ.ðə.ləndz]   *ní.dé.lán*   [ni.tɤ.lan]
   c. *Mark*   [mɑɹk]   *mǎ.kè*   [ma.kʰɤ]
                                     mài.kè   [mai.kʰɤ]
   d. *Denmark*   [dɛn.mɑɹk]   *dān.mài*   [tan.mai]
   e. *Richard*   [ɹɪ.tʃɚd]   *lǐ.chá*   [li.tʂʰa]
   f. *Richards*   [ɹɪ.tʃɚdz]   *lǐ.chá.zī*   [li.tʂʰa.tsɹ]

In (6cd) we see that [ɹ] is omitted in the SC loanwords since it is not a possible coda consonant except in *r*-suffixed words, but as mentioned earlier, syllable structure adjustment for loanword adaptation in SC is based on the syllable structure of unsuffixed words. In different varieties of English, the phonetic realization of the phoneme /ɹ/ after a vowel in the same syllable has much variation: it may be deleted or it may behave more like a glide and make the vowel rhotacized. This fact may contribute to the tendency to drop a post-nuclear [ɹ] in the adaptation process. In terms of perception, it is not easy to hear clearly the boundary between a back vowel and the following coda [ɹ]. Therefore, deletion of [ɹ] in SC loanword adaptation occurs more often after back vowels, as in these examples (see §11.4.3 below for more details).

A stop consonant within a sequence of coda consonants and/or in word final position is more likely to delete, as in (6abde). If an alveolar stop is followed by [s] or [z], then they may be converted to an affricate in SC, as in (6f). However, in (6b), the same word-final [dz] simply deletes. Although a four-syllable loanword for *Netherlands* such as *ní.dé.lán.zī* (by converting [dz] to [ts] and inserting a syllabic consonant) is a possibility, the shorter three-syllable version has become the accepted norm. Consonant deletion is more likely to occur when there is more than one segment in the coda and/or if the sequence of consonants have the same place of articulation. In (6b), there are three coda consonants in the last syllable [ndz] and they are all alveolars. By the same token, in (6a), the final stop [d] shares the same place of articulation with the preceding [n] in a complex coda and it is deleted in the corresponding SC loanword. In terms of perception, a stop, especially when next to a HOMORGANIC sonorant (such as a nasal or an approximant) or a fricative, is harder to perceive and this relative difficulty in perceptibility explains its vulnerability to deletion in the adaptation process.

Another factor that favors the deletion of [dz] in (6b) is the tendency to avoid creating loanwords with too many syllables. Initial adaptation of an unfamiliar foreign word tends to preserve as many segments as possible to avoid potential confusion with other loanwords, but when a loanword becomes frequently used with no potential confusion with other loanwords, a version with a smaller number of syllables is often preferred.

The concern for avoiding confusion also keeps similarly sounding foreign names distinct in the loanwords. In English the difference between (6e) and (6f) is the additional final [z] in (6f). In the corresponding SC loanwords, the distinction is maintained by converting the final stop and fricative [d] and [z] in (6f) to an affricate followed by an inserted syllabic consonant. In contrast, the coda consonant [d] in (6e) is simply deleted.

Finally, the preference for shorter loanwords does not mean a preference for MONOSYLLABIC loanwords. On the contrary, a minimum of two syllables, i.e. a foot (§10.1.1), is much preferred. For example, the final [k] in (6c) is retained with vowel insertion so that the loanword can be at least two syllables long. In comparison, the final [k] in (6d) can be deleted since the loanword is already two syllables long.

To summarize, consonants or consonant clusters that are not allowed in SC coda position can be deleted during the adaptation process. Deletion is more likely to occur if such a consonant: (i) is less perceptible in a particular context (e.g. [ɹ] after a back vowel, or a stop in a complex coda, in word final position, or next to a homorganic sonorant or fricative); or (ii) appears in a complex coda and/or in a longer word. Consonants that potentially can be subject to deletion may be retained instead to maintain a distinction between similarly-sounding names or the two syllables minimum preference for SC loanwords.

11.4 Adaptation of consonants

An English consonant is changed or slightly modified: (i) when it is not part of the SC consonant system; (ii) when its combination with adjacent segments is not allowed by SC PHONOTACTICS; or (iii) when a minor change can lead to the use of a character preferred by the translator or user (cf. §11.2).

The general principle in consonant adaptation is that either an identical consonant or a phonetically similar consonant is used by SC to replace the English counterpart. When a consonant appears in both English and SC, the same consonant is used most of the time. For example, SC [f] is used for an English [f], onset nasals [n] and [m] are used respectively for English onset [n] and [m], and English onset glide [j] and [w] mostly correspond to [j] and [w] respectively in SC. However, for some consonants shared by both languages, a small range of variation is often allowed. For example, either [p] or [pʰ] can be used for the English [p] (see §11.4.3 below) and either [n] or [ŋ] can be used for a coda [n] in English (see §11.4.4 below).

When an English consonant is not part of the SC consonant system, a replacement that bears some phonetic similarities with the English consonant is adopted. For example, [x] is used to replace English [h] when the following vowel is not a high front vowel: for example, *Harris* is adapted to *hālìsī* [**xa**.li.sɹ̩]. However, there can be more than one choice for the replacement of certain English consonants. For example, SC does not have [v], and the consonant that is used to replace English [v] can be [w] or [f]: for example, *Victoria* is adapted as *wéiduōlìyà* [**wei**.two.li.ja] and *Steve* as *shǐdìfū* [ʂɹ̩.ti.**fu**]. All these sounds make use of the lips and share the feature Labial. The decision of which labial to use to replace [v] sometimes depends on which character is preferred in the adaptation of a particular English word, but since both [v] and [w] are voiced, the use of [w] seems relatively more common. Another example is English [θ], which can be adapted as [s], [ʂ], or [ç]: *Arthur* as *yǎsè* [ja.**sɤ**], *Samantha* as *shāmànshā* [**ʂa**.man.ʂa], and *Timothy* as *tímóxī* [tʰi.mwo.**çi**]. Replacing [θ] with [s] is most common since SC [s] is also a dental fricative, but [ç] must be used if it is followed by a high front vowel/glide since SC does not allow a syllable like *[si] (§5.3, §7.2.1, §11.4.1).

In addition, some consonant–vowel combinations in English are not possible in SC and hence are replaced by permissible consonant–vowel combinations in SC. For example, SC has [ɹ] but it cannot be followed by a high front vowel/glide (§5.3; §7.2.1), so an English syllable like [ɹi] is adapted as [li] in SC (cf. (4) in §11.2).

In what follows, the consonant adaptation processes involving CORONAL fricatives/affricates, velars, oral stops, liquids, and nasals are discussed.

11.4.1 Coronal fricatives/affricates and velars

Consider first the examples in (7), illustrating the corresponding SC sounds used for English [s] and [z].

(7)   ENGLISH   SC

  a. *Simon*   [saɪ.mən]   *sài.méng*   [sai.məŋ]

    Scott   [skɑt]   *shǐ.kǎo.tè*   [ʂɹ.kʰɑu.tʰɤ]

  b. *James*   [dʒeɪmz]   *zhān.mǔ.sī*   [tʂan.mu.sɹ]

    Jazz   [dʒæz]   *jué.shì*   [tɕɥe.ʂɹ]

    Zola   [zoʊ.lə]   *zwǒ.lā*   [tswo.la]

  c. *Lansing*   [læn.sɪŋ]   *lán.xīn*   [lan.ɕin]

    New Zealand   [nju.zi.lənd]   *niǔ.xī.lán*   [njou.ɕi.lan]

  d. *Roberts*   [ɹɑ.bɚts]   *luó.bó.zī*   [lwo.pwo.tsɹ]

        luó.bó.cì   [lwo.pwo.tsʰɹ]

    Richards   [ɹɪ.tʃɚdz]   *lǐ.chá.zī*   [li.tsʰa.tsɹ]

    Hertz   [hɚts]   *hè.zī*   [xɤ.tsɹ]

    Keats   [kʰits]   *jì.cí*   [tɕi.tsʰɹ]

English alveolar fricative [s] appears mostly as dental [s] and post-alveolar [ʂ] in SC loanwords, and the voiced [z], which SC does not have, appears mostly as [s] or [ʂ] but sometimes as [ts] or [tʂ], as the examples in (7ab) show. However, in (7c), we see that if [s] and [z] appear before a high front vowel, an alveolo-palatal is used in SC because a dental fricative cannot be followed by a high front vowel (§5.3, §7.2.1). In addition, if [s] and [z] appear after [t] and [d] respectively, an affricate appears in SC, as shown in (7d). Note that either the aspirated affricate [tsʰ] or the unaspirated [ts] can be used for the [t] + [s] sequence in English, but a sequence of [d] + [z] in English is converted to an unaspirated [ts]. We will see the same pattern for stops below in §11.4.2.

English palato-alveolar fricatives/affricates, which SC lacks, are generally replaced by alveolo-palatal fricatives/affricates in SC, as shown in (8a), but they can sometimes be converted to post-alveolar fricatives/affricates when not followed by a high vowel, as the examples in (8b) show. Alveolo-palatals in SC are closest matches to palato-alveolars in English in terms of articulatory and auditory properties (§2.2.5), but since English palato-alveolars are produced in the post-alveolar region, they can also be replaced by post-alveolars in SC.

(8)   ENGLISH   SC
   a. *Sheraton*   [ʃɛ.ɹə.tən]   *xǐ.lái.dēng*   [ɕi.lai.təŋ]
      Shoemaker   [ʃju.meɪ.kʰə]   *xiū.mài.kè*   [ɕjou.mai.kʰɤ]
      Churchill   [tʃɚ.tʃɪl]   *qiū.jí.ěr*   [tɕʰjou.tɕi.ɑɹ]
      Jim   [dʒɪm]   *jí.mǔ*   [tɕi.mu]
   b. *Shakespeare* [ʃeɪk.spɹɹ]   *shā.shì.bǐ.yà*   [ʂa.ʂɹ.pi.ja]
      Charlie   [tʃɑɹ.li]   *chá.lǐ*   [tʂʰa.li]
      Johnson   [dʒɑn.sən]   *zhān.shēng*   [tʂan.ʂəŋ]
                                         zhān.sēn   [tʂan.sən]

A velar stop [k] or [g] in English normally corresponds to a velar stop in SC and we have mentioned earlier that [h] in English is normally replaced by the velar fricative [x] in SC. However, in SC the three velars [k, g, x], as well as dental and post-alveolar fricatives/affricates, must not be followed by a high front vowel or glide due to the palatal constraint discussed in §7.2.1. Therefore, an English [k], [g], or [h] followed by a high front vowel/glide becomes an alveolo-palatal in SC, as shown in (9a). The same conversion to alveolo-palatals applies to English alveolars and palato-alveolars followed by a high front vowel/glide, as shown in (9b). Sometimes, the relevant consonant may not be followed by a high front vowel in English, but if the English vowel is converted to a high front vowel or a high front glide plus vowel combination in SC (see §11.5 for vowel adaptation), the consonant changes accordingly, as the examples in (9c) show.

(9)   ENGLISH   SC
   a. *Kingston*   [kʰɪŋ.stən]   *jīn.sī.dùn*   [tɕin.sɹ.tun]
      Gilbert   [gɪl.bɚt]   *jí.ěr.bó.tè*   [tɕi.ɑɹ.pwo.tʰɤ]
      Hillary   [hɪ.lə.ɹi]   *xī.lā.ruǐ*   [ɕi.la.ɹwei]
   b. *Lansing*   [læn.sɪŋ]   *lán.xīn*   [lan.ɕin]
      New Zealand [nju.zi.lənd]   *niǔ.xī.lán*   [njou.ɕi.lan]
      Schiller   [ʃɪ.lə]   *xí.lè*   [ɕi.lɤ]
      Shoemaker   [ʃju.meɪ.kʰə]   *xiū.mài.kè*   [ɕjou.mai.kʰɤ]
      Churchill   [tʃɚ.tʃɪl]   *qiū.jí.ěr*   [tɕʰjou.tɕi.ɑɹ]
      Jim   [dʒɪm]   *jí.mǔ*   [tɕi.mu]
   c. *California*   [kʰæ.lə.for.njə]   *jiā.lì.fú.ní.yà* [tɕja.li.fu.ni.ja]
      Churchill   [tʃɚ.tʃɪl]   *qiū.jí.ěr*   [tɕʰjou.tɕi.ɑɹ]

To summarize, when English coronal fricatives/affricates are not followed by a high front vowel or glide, the alveolar fricatives, [s] and [z], are converted to dental or post-alveolar fricatives/affricates in SC, and the palato-alveolar fricatives/affricates, [ʃ], [ʒ], [tʃ], and [dʒ], mostly correspond to SC alveolo-palatals and sometimes post-alveolars. When English coronal fricatives/affricates, velar stops, and [h] or their SC counterparts are followed by a high front vowel/glide, alveolo-palatals are used in the SC loanwords.

11.4.2 Oral stops

English has voiced and voiceless stop PHONEMES but a voiceless stop has two ALLOPHONES: voiceless aspirated in syllable initial position and voiceless unaspirated after /s/; on the other hand, SC has no voiced stops but has voiceless unaspirated and voiceless aspirated phonemes (§2.1.4, §1.5.2, §2.2.1). In the loanword adaptation process, an English voiceless stop, either phonetically aspirated or unaspirated, can be converted to either voiceless unaspirated or aspirated relatively freely in SC, as the examples in (10a–c) show, but in (10d) we see that an English voiced stop corresponds to a voiceless unaspirated stop in SC (cf. Shih 2004).

🎧 (10)   ENGLISH   SC

   a. *Peggy*   [pʰɛ.gi]   *pèi.jī*   [pʰei.tɕi]
      Peter   [pʰi.tɚ]   *bǐ.dé*   [pi.tɤ]
      Spencer [spɛn.sɚ]   *shǐ.bīn.sài* [ʂɹ.pin.sai]
   b. *Tom*   [tʰɑm]   *tāng.mǔ*   [tʰaŋ.mu]
      Texas   [tʰɛk.səs]   *dékèsàsī*   [tə.kʰə.sa.sɹ]
      Steve   [stiv]   *shǐ.tí.fū*   [ʂɹ.tʰi.fu]
                                 shǐ.dì.fū   [ʂɹ.ti.fu]
      Stone   [stoʊn]   *shǐ.dōng*   [ʂɹ.tuŋ]
   c. *Carter* [kʰɑɹ.tɚ]   *kǎ.tè*   [kʰa.tʰɤ]
      Kennedy [kʰɛ.nə.di]   *gān.nǎi.dí*   [kan.nai.ti]
      Scotland [skɑt.lənd]   *sū.gé.lán*   [su.kɤ.lan]
      Scott   [skɑt]   *shǐ.kǎo.tè*   [ʂɹ.kʰɑu.tʰɤ]
   d. *Bush*   [bʊʃ]   *bù.xī*   [pu.ɕi]
                                 bù.shí   [pu.ʂɹ]
      Bill   [bɪl]   *bǐ.ěr*   [pi.ɔɹ]
      David   [dei.vɪd]   *dà.wèi*   [ta.wei]
      Disney   [dɪs.ni]   *dí.sī.nài*   [ti.sɹ.nai]
                                 dí.shì.ní   [ti.ʂɹ.ni]
      Gallup   [gæ.ləp]   *gài.luò.pǔ*   [kai.lwo.pʰu]
      Green   [gɹin]   *gé.lín*   [kɤ.lin]

As mentioned before, phonetic similarity plays the major role in sound-based adaptation but it is common to tolerate a small range of variation. It seems that for voiceless stops, the matching of the feature [−voice] is good enough, and the presence or absence of aspiration does not seem to matter. On the other hand, voiced OBSTRUENTS such as stops and coronal fricative/affricates are most likely to be adapted as voiceless unaspirated obstruents in SC because of closer phonetic similarity: aspiration is associated only with voiceless obstruents in both English and SC. There are, however, a limited number of exceptions to this strong tendency. For example, the word *beer* is adapted with a combination of both sound-based and meaning-based processes (see (3a)) as *píjiŭ* [pʰi.tɕjou], in which the first syllable imitates the sound and the second syllable means 'alcohol'. Note that in this case, the English [b] is adapted as an aspirated [pʰ]. The character used for the syllable [pʰi] is used only for sound-based loanwords and not for native SC words. Another example is the name *George* [dʒɔːɹdʒ], which is usually adapted as *qiáozhì* [tɕʰjɑu.tʂɻ̩] with the first voiced affricate corresponding to an aspirated affricate in SC. An exception to the general patterns in SC loanword adaptation can be attributed to the preference for a particular written character or just an idiosyncratic use of the original translator.

11.4.3 Liquids

Both English and SC have the liquids [l] and [ɹ], but they behave slightly differently during SC loanword adaptation. Consider first the liquids in onset position. As shown in (11), while English [l] appears also as [l] in SC loanwords, English [ɹ] can become either [ɹ] or [l]. The variation may be due to the fact that in SC [l] can combine with more types of rimes than [ɹ] can, and there are also more characters available for [l] initial syllables than those for [ɹ] initial syllables.

(11) ENGLISH			SC	
Lamb	[læm]		*lán.mŭ*	[lan.mu]
Lewis	[luis]		*lù.yì.sī*	[lu.ji.sɻ]
			liú.yì.shì	[ljou.ji.ʂɻ]
Lisa	[li.sə]		*lì.shā*	[li.ʂa]
Laura	[lɔ.ɹə]		*luó.lā*	[lwo.la]
Hillary	[hɪ.lə.ɹi]		*xī.lā.ruĭ*	[ɕi.la.ɹwei]
			xǐ.lái.lì	[ɕi.lai.li]
Rita	[ɹi.tə]		*lì.tǎ*	[li.tʰa]
			ruì.tǎ	[ɹwei.tʰa]
Redford	[ɹɛd.fɚd]		*ruì.dé.fú*	[ɹwei.tɤ.fu]
Rice	[ɹaɪs]		*lài.sī*	[lai.sɻ]
Rose	[ɹoʊz]		*luó.sī*	[lwo.sɻ]

Note that in the examples *Rita* and *Redford*, the English [ɹ] is followed by a front vowel, and since no SC [ɹ] can be followed directly by a high or mid front vowel, the corresponding [ɹ]-onset syllable in SC is one that has a [w] glide. The addition of [w] may also be accounted for by the fact that the onset [ɹ] in English has some degree of lip-rounding and can be narrowly transcribed as [ɹ^w] (Shih 2004).

Shih (2004) observes that, when the English liquids appear in the rime (either in nucleus or coda position), they tend to become [əɹ] in SC if they are preceded by a high or mid front vowel, as in (12a), and to be deleted if they are preceded by a mid or low back vowel, as in (12b). Occasionally, an English [l], especially when it is a syllabic consonant, may also be turned into a vowel or diphthong, two examples of which from Shih (2004) are given in (12c).

(12)   ENGLISH   SC
   a. *Bill*   [bɪl]   *bǐ.ěr*   [pi.əɹ]
      Hilton   [hɪl.tən]   *xī.ěr.dùn*   [ɕi.əɹ.tun]
      Hegel   [heɪ.gl̩]   *hēi.gé.ěr*   [xei.kɤ.əɹ]
      Sears   [sɪɹz]   *xī.ěr.sī*   [ɕi.əɹ.sɹ̩]
      Blair   [blɛɹ]   *bù.lái.ěr*   [pu.lai.əɹ]
                                 bù.léi.ěr   [pu.lei.əɹ]
   b. *Harold*   [hæ.ɹəld]   *hā.luò.dé*   [xa.lwo.tɤ]
      Barbara   [baɹ.bə.ɹə]   *bā.bā.lā*   [pa.pa.la]
      Mark   [maɹk]   *mǎ.kè*   [ma.kʰɤ]
                                 mài.kè   [mai.kʰɤ]
      Harvard   [haɹ.vəd]   *hā.fó*   [xa.fwo]
   c. *Rachel*   [ɹeɪ.tʃl̩]   *ruì.qiū*   [ɹwei.tɕʰjou]
      bagel   [beɪ.gl̩]   *bèi.guǒ*   [pei.kwo]

In English, there can be an ultra-short vowel-like transition from a high/mid front vowel to the liquid, so the liquid can be better perceived and hence seems to be retained in SC. On the other hand, a syllabic liquid or a liquid after a back vowel is perceptually more difficult to distinguish from a back vowel and therefore it is often deleted or sometimes converted to [wo] or [ou] in SC. However, there are some exceptions to these general rules, as shown in (13).

(13)   ENGLISH   SC
   a. *Gilbert*   [gɪl.bɚt]   *jí.bó.tè*   [tɕi.pwo.tʰɤ]
      Darwin   [daɹ.wən]   *dá.ěr.wén*   [ta.əɹ.wən]
   b. *Paul*   [pʰɔl]   *bǎo.luó*   [pau.lwo]
      Dole   [doʊl]   *dù.ěr*   [tu.əɹ]
      Gore   [gɔɹ]   *gāo.ěr*   [kau.əɹ]

For the exceptions in (13a), where an [l] after a high front vowel is unexpectedly deleted and an [ɹ] after a back vowel is unexpectedly retained in SC, there does not seem to be a good explanation, but note that *Gilbert* can also be adapted as *jí.ěr.bó.tè* (see (9a)) by retaining the liquid after the high front vowel. Since SC loanword adaptation involves many different factors, as mentioned in §11.2, we can only talk about generalizations that have a strong tendency rather than absolute rules. The exceptions in (13b), on the other hand, can be attributed to the preference for a SC loanword to be at least two syllables long (§11.3.2). The English names in (13b) are all monosyllabic syllables with one liquid coda after a back vowel. To change them into two syllables in SC, either a vowel is inserted after the liquid or the liquid becomes a separate *er* syllable.

In sum, in the onset position, English [ɹ] can be adapted as [l], [ɹ], or sometimes [ɹw]. Within the rime, English liquids after a high/mid front vowel usually become *er* in SC and those after a mid/low back vowel are usually deleted in SC. A liquid after a back vowel in a monosyllabic name is retained so that a DISYLLABIC loanword can be created.

11.4.4 Nasals

The English nasals [n] and [m] in syllable onset position mostly correspond to [n] and [m] respectively in SC loanwords. Since SC does not allow [m] in coda position, an English coda [m] is replaced by either [n] or [ŋ], as shown in (14a). If the coda [m] appears in a monosyllabic word, then [m] appears as the onset of an inserted vowel, as in (14b), so that a disyllabic loanword can be created. The inserted vowel is [u] since an inserted nucleus is typically a rounded vowel after a labial consonant (§11.3.1). Note that the first syllable in such a disyllabic loanword may or may not retain a nasal coda: compare the first two examples and the third example in (14b).

(14) ENGLISH   SC
  a. *William* [wɪ.ljəm]   *wēi.lián* [wei.ljɛn]
    Adam   [æ.dəm]   *yà.dāng*   [ja.taŋ]
  b. *Lamb*   [læm]   *lán.mǔ*   [lan.mu]
    Tom   [tʰɑm]   *tāng.mǔ*   [tʰɑŋ.mu]
    Tim   [tʰɪm]   *tí,mǔ*   [tʰi.mu]
  c. *Green*   [gɹin]   *gé.lín*   [kɤ.lin]
    Stone   [stoʊn]   *shǐ.dōng* [ʂɹ.tuŋ]
    Harding [hɑɹ.dɪŋ]   *hā.dìng*   [xa.tjəŋ]
    Lansing [læn.sɪŋ]   *lán.xīn*   [lan.ɕin]

d. *Wayne*	[weɪn]	*wéi.ēn*	[wei.ən]
Maine	[meɪn]	*miǎn.īn*	[mjɛn.in]
		miǎn.ēn	[mjɛn.ən]
King	[kɪŋ]	*jīn.ēn*	[tɕin.ən]

In (14c), we see that [n] and [ŋ] are used freely for either [n] or [ŋ] in English. The variation can be attributed to the fact that the place of articulation of a coda nasal is less perceptible than that of an onset nasal, and hence the variation. In (14d), the two-syllable minimum preference also leads to the insertion of a vowel to create a disyllabic loanword. However, there is a small number of exceptions: for example, *Ann* can be adapted as the monosyllabic loanword *ān* [an] in SC. In addition, vowel insertion next to a nasal coda, especially after [m], may also apply even if the loanword is already disyllabic before vowel insertion: for example, *Gramme* can be adapted as *gé.lā.mǔ* or *gé.lán.mǔ* although sometimes simply as *gé.lán*.

11.5 Adaptation of vowels

English has more vowels than SC does, and hence many changes need to be made when English vowels are adapted to SC loanwords. It is more difficult to pinpoint the rules for the adaptation of English vowels because there is a greater range of variation and detailed studies are lacking. It may look like generalizations are hard to come by; however, the adaptation of vowels still follows the underlying principle of matching an English sound closely when possible without creating impossible SC sounds, sound sequences, and syllable types. The greater degree of variation occurs because there can be several possible close matches in term of phonetic similarities and/or there can be several potential choices of characters preferred by different creators of loanwords. The discussion in this section, therefore, cannot be comprehensive since more research is needed; instead, we look at sample examples for illustration and seek generalizations and explanations as we can.

In general, the more stable correspondences include the following: (i) an English high front vowel such as [i] and [ɪ] tends to be just high front [i] in SC; (ii) a high back vowel such as [u] and [ʊ] tends to be just high back [u] in SC; (iii) a low back vowel [ɑ] is usually matched by a low SC vowel [a]/[ɑ], a low-back diphthong [ɑu], or sometimes a glide-vowel sequence such as [ja]; and (iv) the English diphthongs [aɪ] and [aʊ] mostly correspond to [ai] and [ɑu] respectively in SC. These are expected outcomes given the close match of the vowel features. On the other hand, for English vowels/diphthongs or glide-vowel sequences that SC does not have (e.g. [æ], [ɔ], [ɔi], [ju]) and for vowels that have restricted distributions in SC (e.g. [e], [o], [ə], and rhotacized vowels), there are more variations; however, the corresponding English and SC vowels/diphthongs or glide-vowel sequences seem to always share at least some vowel features such as [high], [round], and [back]. In what follows, we go through sample examples of these more complicated cases.

11.5.1 Front low vowel

Examine first the examples in (15), where the front low vowel [æ] has several possible correspondences in SC.

(15)   ENGLISH   SC
    a. *Sam*   [sæm]   *shān.mǔ*   [ṣan.mu]
    b. *Gallup*   [gǽ.ləp]   *gài.luò.pǔ*   [kai.lwo.pʰu]
    c. *California*   [kʰǽ.lɪ.foɹ.njə]   *jiā.lì.fú.ní.yà* [tɕja.li.fu.ni.ja]
    d. *jazz*   [dʒæz]   *jué.shì*   [tɕɥe.ṣɹ]

Recall that SC has one low vowel phoneme but phonetically there are two low vowels: the back low vowel [ɑ] appears before a [+back] segment (a velar nasal or [u]) and the front low vowel [a] appears in an OPEN SYLLABLE or before a [−back] segment ([n] or [i]) (§7.2.3). In (15a–c), we see that the vowels/diphthongs or glide-vowel sequences in SC that correspond to English [æ], which is [+low, −back], all have the features [+low, −back]. In (15bc), we even see an added high front vowel or glide that can move [a] more fronted and thus emphasize the [−back] aspect of [æ]. The glide-vowel sequence in (15d) is a special case where the [+low] feature of [æ] is not retained; however, the [−back] feature is exhibited since both [ɥ] and [e] are [−back] and [e] has the [−high] feature, which is also shared by a low vowel.

What we do not see is a change of [æ] to a high vowel [i] or [u] or to a back vowel/diphthong such as [ɑu], [o], or [ɔ]. The generalization then is that [æ] is mostly adapted in SC as a low front vowel that may or may not be accompanied by a front glide/vowel or alveolar nasal. The frontness of [æ] seems to be the main feature to be preserved, since in (15bc) the presence of the high front glide/vowel can enhance the frontness characteristic. The example in (15d) shows that the [+low] feature can be lost in SC but frontness is preserved although the main vowel [e] also shares [−high] with the low vowel.

In (15bc), English vowels or glide-vowel sequences other than [æ] have also been changed in SC, but some vowel features are retained. In (15b), the mid central vowel [ə] is changed to [wo]. We will see in §11.5.5 that a central vowel can be adapted to either a front vowel or a back vowel. In (15c), English [o] becomes [u] in SC, both of which have the [+back, +round] features although the vowel height is changed. We will see more examples illustrating adaptation of mid back rounded vowels in §11.5.3. The glide-vowel sequence [jə] in English is not allowed in SC, where only [je] is possible due to mid vowel assimilation (§7.2.4). However, [jə] does not become [je] and is instead adapted into two separate syllables: [i] + [ja]. One possible reason is that the schwa in this particular context is perceived as being more like a back or mid-low vowel. Another possibility is that sometimes the spelling of a foreign word rather than the actual pronunciation of the word influences the choice of sounds in the loanword, and in this case the final vowel is spelled with *a*.

11.5.2 Front high and front mid vowels

The examples in (16) show the variation in the adaptation of high and mid front vowels in English. As mentioned earlier, in general a high front vowel is matched by [i] in SC. However, if the high vowel is preceded by [w] as in (16a), which is not possible in SC, then [ei] is used instead, as we saw earlier in (14a).

(16)   ENGLISH   SC
    a. *Wilson*   [wɪl.sən]   *wēi.er.xùn*   [wei.ɔɹ.ɕyn]
                                   wēi.er.sēn   [wei.ɔɹ.sən]
    b. *Sidney*   [sɪd.ni]   *xī.ní*   [ɕi.ni]
                                     xuě.lí   [ɕɥe.li]
    c. *Reagan*   [ɹeɪ.gən]   *léi.gēn*   [lei.kən]
                                     lǐ,gēn   [li.kən]
    d. *Blair*   [blɛɹ]   *bù.lái.ěr*   [pu.lai.ɔɹ]
                                     bù.léi.ěr   [pu.lei.ɔɹ]
    e. *Shoemaker* [ʃju.meɪ.kʰə]   *xiū.mài.kè*   [ɕjou.mai.kʰɤ]
    f. *James*   [dʒeɪmz]   *zhān.mǔ.sī*   [tʂan.mu.sɹ]
    g. *David*   [dei.vɪd]   *dà.wèi*   [ta.wei]

In (16b), there are two variants for the same word, and the second variant uses a combination of a high front glide and a mid front vowel: [ɥe]. Such a less faithful matching is often tolerated when the use of a particular character is deemed preferable: in this particular case the first syllable *xuě* is represented by a character meaning 'snow'. Note however that at least some features of [ɪ], which has [+high, −back], are still retained since [ɥ] is also [+high, −back] and [e] is [−back].

As shown in (16cd), the English mid vowels [ei] and [ε] are replaced by [ei] in SC, which is the closest match in phonetic similarities. However, a variant such as [i] in (16c), which retains the [−back] feature, is tolerated. The variant in (16d), in which [ai] is used for English [ɛ], is not uncommon either. The diphthong [ai] has a [−high] feature from [a] and [−low, −back] from [i] and these features are also shared by [ɛ], which is also [−high, −low, −back]. The close relationship between a mid vowel [e] or [ɛ] and the diphthong [ai] is also evident in the process of MONOPHTHONGIZATION (which changes a diphthong to a monophthong) in many languages where [ai] becomes [e] or [ɛ]. As we will see in §11.5.3, the same relationship also holds for the mid back vowel [o] or [ɔ] and the diphthong [au].

The example in (16e) shows that, similarly to [ɛ], [ei] can also be adapted as [ai]. The conversion of the glide-vowel sequence [ju] to [jou] will be discussed in §11.5.4 below. The reason that the schwa in the final syllable is changed to [ɤ] can be attributed to the fact that SC does not allow a short vowel such as a schwa to end a simple CV syllable, as discussed in §8.1.4.

In (16f) the correspondence between an English mid front vowel/diphthong [e] or [ei] with [an] in SC is similar in nature to the relationship between a mid front vowel and the [ai] diphthong for (16cde). Note that [a] is [−high] and so is the [e] in [ei], and in SC both [a] and [n] are considered [−back] as opposed to the [+back] [ɑ] and [ŋ] (§5.3, §7.2.3). Therefore [ei] and [an] match in terms of the [−back, −high] features. The prediction then is that a back mid diphthong [ou] could be adapted as [ɑŋ] since both share the [+back, −high] features, and indeed we will see one such example in the next subsection.

Finally, (16g) is a rare example where [ei] becomes [a]. Although [a] in a SC open syllable may be considered front, the two vowels are phonetically less similar. The choice of [a] may be influenced by the spelling of the vowel as *a*, or the word may have been borrowed through a different language. In this example, we also see that [vɪ] is changed to [wei] in SC because SC does not have [v] and does not allow the combination of *[wi]. For the vowel in the second syllable, the diphthong [ei] in SC at least retains the features [−back] and [+high] of English [ɪ].

Up to this point, we have seen that a front mid or front low vowel/diphthong in English is almost always matched with one that is also front; i.e. the feature [−back] is crucial. On the other hand, the vowel height features can sometimes deviate from the original English vowels to produce variants.

11.5.3 Back rounded vowels

The examples in (17) illustrate how the high back rounded vowels in English, [u] and [ʊ], are adapted: SC [u] is most commonly used but a back rounded diphthong [ou] or even a back unrounded vowel [ɤ] can occur as variants. Note that the second variant of (17c) needs a high front glide [j] in SC since the alveolo-palatal used to replace [dʒ] must be followed by a high vowel or glide.

🎧 (17)   Eɴɢʟɪsʜ   SC

     a. *Bruce*   [bɹus]   *bù.lǔ.sī*   [pu.lu.sɻ]

     b. *Cook*   [kʰʊk]   *kù.kè*   [kʰu.kʰɤ]

                                kòu.kè   [kʰou.kʰɤ]

     c. *Judy*   [dʒu.di]   *zhū.dì*   [tʂu.ti]

                                  qiú.dì   [tɕʰjou.ti]

As for the English back mid rounded vowel/diphthong, [o]/[oʊ], one can easily expect a SC correspondence that has the [+round, +back] features as in (18a–d). The SC match can be a diphthong [ou], a high back rounded vowel [u], or a glide-vowel sequence [wo] that retains the mid back rounded vowel [o]. Since [o] can appear only after [w] or before [u] (§7.2.4), these variations are then within the normal range of expectation.

🎧 (18)   Eɴɢʟɪsʜ   SC

     a. *Owen*   [oʊ.wən]   *ōu.wén*   [ou.wən]

     b. *Dole*   [doʊl]   *dù.ěr*   [tu.əɹ]

     c. *Stone*   [stoʊn]   *shǐ.dōng*   [ʂɻ.tuŋ]

     d. *Rose*   [ɹoʊz]   *luó.sī*   [lwo.sɻ]

     e. *Ohio*   [oʊ.haɪ.oʊ]   *ér.hài.ér*   [ɤ.xai.ɤ]

     f. *Joanna*   [dʒoʊ.æ.nə]   *qiáo.ān.nà*   [tɕʰjɑu.an.na]

     g. *Arizona*   [æ.ɹɪ.zoʊ.nə]   *yà.lì.sāng.nà*   [ja.li.sɑŋ.na]

The example in (18e) shows that an alternative is to have a mid back unrounded vowel which shares with [o] the [−high, −low, +back] features although the [+round] feature is not retained. In (18fg), English [oʊ] is adapted as either [ɑu] or [ɑŋ], which is parallel to the conversion of [eɪ] to [ai] and [an] discussed in the previous subsection. The diphthong [ɑu] shares with [oʊ] the [+back, +round] features and both segments in [ɑŋ] are [+back]. Again, as mentioned in the previous subsection, the front versus back property is faithfully retained as we do not see examples where an English back vowel/diphthong is converted to a front vowel/diphthong in SC.

The examples in (19) show that the mid back vowel [ɔ] and the diphthong [ɔɪ] follow the similar adaptation patterns as [o]/[oʊ], and you should now be able to identify by yourself which features of [ɔ] are retained through vowel adaptation.

🎧 (19)   ENGLISH   SC

   a. *Paul*   [pʰɔl]   *bǎo.luó*   [pɑu.lwo]

   b. *Gore*   [gɔɹ]   *gāo.ěr*   [kɑu.əɹ]

   c. *Austin*   [ɔs.tən]   *ào.sī.dīng*   [ɑu.sɹ.tjəŋ]

   d. *Oregon*   [ɔ.ɹɪ.gən]   *ér.lè.gāng*   [ɤ.lɤ.kɑŋ]

                                ào.ruì.gāng [ɑu.ɹwei.kɑŋ]

   e. *Longfellow* [lɔŋ.fɛ.loʊ]   *lǎng.fèi.luó* [lɑŋ.fei.lwo]

   f. *Laura*   [lɔ.ɹə]   *luó.lā*   [lwo.la]

   g. *Illinois*   [ɪ.lɪ.nɔɪ]   *yī.lì.nuò*   [ji.li.nwo]

   h. *Joyce*   [dʒɔɪs]   *qiáo.yī.sī*   [tɕʰjɑu.ji.sɹ]

The diphthong [ɔɪ], which is illicit in SC, is either treated as [ɔ] by ignoring [ɪ] as in (19g) (just like (19f)) or adapted into two different syllables, as in (19h), where the SC correspondence of [ɔ] and that of [ɪ] belong to two syllables.

The generalizations that have emerged are that: (i) a front English vowel is matched with a front vowel in SC and a back English vowel is converted to a back vowel; and (ii) rounding and height features are often but not always retained. The mid central vowel such as the schwa [ə], on the other hand, seems to be ambivalent between front and back since it can stay as a central vowel as (18a) and (19c), or be converted to a front low vowel as in (18fg) and (19f) or a back low vowel as in (19d). Mid central vowels will be discussed in §11.5.5.

11.5.4 Glide-vowel sequences

The glide-vowel sequences [ju] and [wi] in English are not possible sequences in SC because SC does not allow two high vocoids with different backness in a sequence (§5.3). Up to now, we have seen three types of strategies in dealing with non-permissible sounds or sequences for SC. The first strategy is to apply nucleus insertion (§11.3.1) to break apart non-permissible sequences in a syllable. Since schwa is the basic default vowel for insertion, as mentioned in §11.3.1, we can insert a schwa between [j] and [u] and between [w] and [i], and because of mid vowel assimilation (§7.2.4), the resulting sequences become [jou] as in (20ab) and [wei] as in (20de). Another strategy is deletion (§11.3.2), and in (20c) we see one such example where [j] is deleted and only [u] appears in the SC loanword. The third strategy is to make changes to the original offending sound(s). The example in (20f) shows that when the relevant syllable ends in a nasal, then it is possible to replace the high front vowel [ɪ] with a schwa.

🎧 (20)   ENGLISH   SC

    a. *New York*   [nju.jɔɹk]   *niǔ.yuē*   [njou.ɥe]
    b. *New Orleans*   [nju.ɔɹ.ljənz]   *niǔ.ào.liáng*   [njou.ɑu.ljɑŋ]
    c. *Duke*   [djuk]   *dù.kè*   [tu.kʰɤ]
    d. *William*   [wɪ.ljəm]   *wēi.lián*   [wei.ljɛn]
    e. *Wilkins*   [wɪl.kɪnz]   *wēi.ěr.jīn.sī* [wei.ɔɹ.tɕin.sɹ̩]
    f. *Quincy*   [kʰwɪn.si]   *kūn.cī*   [kʰwən.çi]

11.5.5 Mid central vowels

As noted in §11.5.3, a mid central vowel stays as a mid central vowel or becomes either a front or back vowel. Recall that in SC the mid central phoneme /ə/ in SC becomes [e] when next to a high front vowel/glide ([ei], [je], [ɥe]) and [o] when next to a high back rounded vowel/glide ([ou], [wo]) (§7.2.4). The only time we see a true mid central vowel [ə] is when the vowel is inserted before a nasal coda (e.g. /un/ → [wən]) (§8.1.5) or in a nasal ending rime such as [ən] and [əŋ]. In addition, in a CV or V syllable, an underlying schwa nucleus becomes a mid back tense vowel [ɤ] as discussed in §8.1.4 (e.g. /kə/ → [kɤ]).

Consider first the examples in (21), where each English word has at least a mid central vowel [ə] or [ʌ]. The correspondence in SC can be a mid central vowel [ə] before a nasal as in (21af) and a mid back unrounded [ɤ] in a CV syllable as in (21ab). These are what we would expect given the distribution patterns of mid vowels in SC.

🎧 (21)   ENGLISH   SC

    a. *Kentucky*   [kən.tʰʌ.ki]   *kěn.dé.jī*   [kʰən.tɤ.tɕi]
    b. *Connecticut* [kən.nɛ.tɪ.kət]   *kāng.nǎi.dí.kè*   [kʰɑŋ.nai.ti.kʰɤ]
    c. *Douglas*   [dʌg.ləs]   *dào.gé.lā.sī*   [tɑu.kɤ.la.sɹ̩]
    d. *Hillary*   [hɪ.lə.ɹi]   *xī.lā.ruǐ*   [çi.la.ɹwei]
                                        xǐ.lái.lì   [çi.lai.li]
    e. *Adam*   [æ.dəm]   *yà.dāng*   [ja.tɑŋ]
    f. *Hilton*   [hɪl.tən]   *xī.ěr.dùn*   [çi.ɔɹ.twən]
    g. *William*   [wɪ.ljəm]   *wēi.lián*   [wei.ljɛn]

In addition, since [e] and [o] are allophones of /ə/ in SC, and [e] and [o] in English can be adapted as [ai] and [ɑu] respectively in SC as discussed in §§11.5.2–11.5.3, it seems reasonable to match the mid central vowel with these diphthongs and indeed we see such examples in (21cd). Finally, a low vowel is often used to replace a mid central vowel. Following the rules in SC, [ɑ] is used before a velar nasal, as in (21be), and [a] is used in an open syllable, as in (21cd). In (21g), the [ɛ] vowel that corresponds to the English schwa results from the low vowel raising rule, i.e. /ian/ → [jɛn] (§7.2.3), so we can say that the English schwa is converted either to a low vowel or to a mid front vowel. It seems that if the English spelling has an *a* for the schwa, SC often matches it with a low vowel.

The rhotacized mid central vowel [ɚ] in American English also has a wide array of counterparts in SC. Other than [a] and [ɤ] in (22abcf), we also see [e] and [o] in SC. Since [e] and [o] are derived from /ə/ and only appear next to [i]/[j] and [u]/[w] respectively, we can see the expected patterns in (22c–f).

(22) | ENGLISH | | SC | |
|---|---|---|---|
| a. *Richard* | [ɹɪ.tʃɚd] | *lǐ.chá* | [li.tʂʰa] |
| b. *Hertz* | [hɚz] | *hè.zī* | [xɤ.tsɹ̩] |
| c. *Curt* | [kʰɚt] | *kē.tè* | [kʰɤ.tʰɤ] |
| | | *kòu.tè* | [kʰou.tʰɤ] |
| d. *Gilbert* | [gɪl.bɚt] | *jí.bó.tè* | [tɕi.pwo.tʰɤ] |
| *Bird* | [bɚd] | *bó.dé* | [pwo.tɤ] |
| e. *Virginia* | [vɚ.dʒi.njə] | *wéi.qín.ní.yà* | [wei.tɕʰin.ni.ja] |
| | | *wéi.jí.ní.yà* | [wei.tɕi.ni.ja] |
| f. *Wordsworth* | [wɚdz.wɚθ] | *wò.zī.huá.sī* | [wo.tsɹ̩.xwa.sɹ̩] |
| | | *huò.zī.huá.sī* | [xwo.tsɹ̩.xwa.sɹ̩] |

It is more difficult to come up with precise generalizations for the adaptation of English mid central vowels, although the sample examples we have discussed clearly follow the distributional patterns of SC mid vowels: schwa before a nasal, [ɤ] in an open syllable, [e] when adjacent to a high front vowel/glide, and [o] when next to a high back rounded vowel/glide. In addition, since a mid vowel is [−high] and [−low], the SC counterpart either contains a mid vowel or a low vowel, which also has the [−high] feature. Finally, in §§11.5.1–11.5.3, we have come up with the generalization that retention of [−back] and [+back] features is most important since the front and back vowels in English are matched respectively with front and back counterparts. On the other hand, an English mid central vowel can become either front or back in SC. It seems that SC treats an English mid central vowel as neither [−back] nor [+back], just as SC treats the underlying /ə/ (§7.1.1, §7.2.4). This treatment then explains why mid central vowels can be converted to either front or back segments in SC.

11.6 Summary

This chapter discusses how SC creates loanwords from English. Although SC tends to prefer the meaning-based method, the sound-based method used mostly for proper names illustrates how universal phonetic/phonological principles and the phonetics and phonology of SC play a crucial role in the adaptation of foreign sounds and syllables.

- When an English syllable type is not possible in SC, nucleus insertion, segment deletion, and segment change are used to bring an illicit structure to conform to an acceptable SC structure (§§11.2–11.3, §11.5.4).
- Intuitively speaking, the SC sound that is phonetically most similar to the English sound should be used. However, due to factors such as the restricted distribution of certain sounds in SC and the preferred choice of certain written characters, a limited range of variation is tolerated (§11.2).
- General phonetic/phonological principles, syllable structure constraints (chapter 5), and segmental constraints/rules (chapters 7 and 8) are involved in shaping acceptable loanwords (§§11.2–11.5).
- The general phonetic/phonological principles include: (i) matching sounds with similar phonetic/phonological features; and (ii) replacing or deleting sounds based on perceptibility of a sound in a particular context (§§11.4–11.5).
- The relevant SC constraints/rules include: (i) the non-existence of [wi] and [ju] in SC; (ii) the requirement for alveolo-palatals, but not dental/post-alveolar fricatives/affricates and velars, to be followed by high front vowels/glides; and (iii) rules such as mid vowel and low vowel assimilation, mid vowel tensing, and schwa insertion (§§11.4–11.5).
- The acceptable variants in SC for a corresponding English consonant share most phonetic/phonological features with the English sound they try to match (§11.4).
- The variations allowed in the adaptation of consonants include: (i) the choice between [w] and [f] for English [v]; (ii) the choice of different coronal fricatives/affricates for English coronal fricatives; (iii) aspirated voiceless consonants for unaspirated voiceless ones and vice versa; (iv) conversion of English onset [ɹ] to [ɹ], [l], or [ɹw]; (v) variation of either [n] or [ŋ] for an English coda nasal; and (vi) variation in retention and deletion of an English coda liquid (§11.4).
- The variations allowed in the adaptation of vowels are more complex but all corresponding vowels, diphthongs, or glide-vowel sequences between English and SC are similar in terms of some vowel feature(s) (§11.5).
- The emerging generalizations for the adaptation of vowels are: (i) the front and back English vowels are matched with front and back vowels respectively in SC, indicating that the features [−back] and [+back] are crucial for the adaptation process; (ii) although height and rounding

features may not always be faithfully retained, in most cases, the matching of height and rounding features is quite common; (iii) a mid central vowel is treated as neither [+back] nor [−back] and thus can be converted to either back or front segments/sequences, and it can also be adapted into either a mid or low vowel since both of them have the [−high] feature; and (iv) the SC variants of an English mid central vowel strictly follow the distributional patterns of SC mid and low vowels (§11.5).

EXERCISES

🎧 1   Examine the following examples and explain how and why each English word is adapted into the corresponding SC loanword. In your explanation, cite the generalizations of sound-based adaptation discussed in this chapter and the phonetic/phonological constraints/rules in SC discussed in previous chapters.

ENGLISH		SC	
Grant	[gɹænt]	gé.lán.tè	[kɤ.lan.tʰɤ]
Smith	[smɪθ]	shǐ.mì.sī	[ʂɹ.mi.sɹ]
Alan	[æ.lən]	yà.lán	[ja.lan]
		yà.lún	[ja.lwən]
Alice	[æ.lɪs]	ài.lì.sī	[ai.li.sɹ]
Amy	[eɪ.mi]	ài.mī	[ai.mi]
		ài.měi	[ai.mei]
Jackson	[dʒæk.sən]	jié.kè.shēng	[tɕje.kʰɤ.ʂən]
Wisconsin	[wɪs.kʰɑn.sɪn]	wēi.sī.kāng.xīn	[wei.sɹ.kʰaŋ.ɕin]
Victoria	[vik.tʰɔ.ɹjə]	wéiduōlìyà	[wei.two.li.ja]
Lawrence	[lɔ.ɹəns]	láo.lún.sī	[lau.lwən.sɹ]
Gillman	[gɪl.mən]	jí.ěr.màn	[tɕi.əɹ.man]
Gear	[gɪɹ]	jí.ěr	[tɕi.əɹ]
Bell	[bɛl]	bèi.ěr	[pei.əɹ]
Bayle	[beil]	bài.ěr	[pai.əɹ]
Bartlett	[bɑɹt.lɪt]	bā.tè.lì	[pa.tʰɤ.li]
Hume	[hjum]	xiū.mǔ	[ɕjou.mu]
Ferdinand	[fɚ.dɪ.nənd]	fèi.dí.nán	[fei.ti.nan]
Herbert	[hɚ.bɚt]	hè.bó.tè	[xɤ.pwo.tʰɤ]

2   Collect a list of sound-based SC loanwords from Chinese newspapers, broadcast news, magazines, or books for which you know the corresponding English words. (See Appendix C for internet resources for Chinese media.)

(i) For each loanword, provide the *pīnyīn* and phonetic transcription for each written character.

(ii) For each loanword, explain how and why it is adapted into SC.

3   Collect a list of English words or proper names that have not been adapted to SC yet or have not been in regular use. Then based on the generalizations discussed in this chapter, create an acceptable SC sound-based loanword for each word/name.

4   Collect a list of sound-based SC loanwords from Chinese newspapers, magazines, or books where you are not informed of what the corresponding English (or foreign) words are.

(i) For each loanword, provide the *pīnyīn* and phonetic transcription for each written character.

(ii) For each loanword, try to figure out what the original English (or foreign) word may be.

12 Variation in SC

As mentioned in §1.2, there exist different degrees of variation among speakers of SC and in fact many speakers do not possess the ideal textbook SC accent. Now that we have become familiar with the phonetics and phonology of SC, the question is: in what way may one SC speaker differ from another? This chapter addresses this question by introducing the types of SC varieties (§12.2) and by examining the SC varieties spoken in Taiwan as a case study (§12.3). Before the main discussion, some background regarding the different languages and dialects of the Chinese language family is provided in §12.1. The final section (§12.4) summarizes the main points of the chapter.

12.1 Chinese languages and dialects

In §1.1 I briefly introduced the diverse varieties in the Chinese language family and I also noted that many of them can be considered separate languages rather than dialects of the same language, since they are mutually unintelligible and have very different linguistic structures. If we compare the phonetic and phonological systems of Cantonese (a Yue dialect spoken in Canton and Hong Kong), Taiwanese (a southern Min dialect spoken in Taiwan), and SC, we see that they have different sets of consonants, vowels, tones, permissible syllable types, and phonological rules and constraints. For example, both Cantonese and Taiwanese have a larger number of tones than SC, seven in Taiwanese and nine in Cantonese depending on different analyses; they allow [p], [t], and [k] in syllable coda position, which is impossible for SC; and they do not have the post-alveolar consonants as in SC. For the vowel differences, Taiwanese has phonemic nasalized vowels that SC does not have, Cantonese has more than one front rounded vowel whereas SC has only one and Taiwanese has none, and neither Taiwanese nor Cantonese have the syllabic consonants (apical vowels) of SC. As for the phonological rules, the palatalization rule in SC (§7.2.1) is not present in Taiwanese and Cantonese, and Taiwanese tone sandhi changes every tone in a phrase except the phrase final one, which is not shared by SC and Cantonese. There are many other linguistic differences and I cannot mention them all here. The main point is that different subfamilies within Chinese, such as Mandarin, Yue, Wu, northern Min, southern Min, Hakka, etc. (see §1.1), are more like different languages, so let us treat them as such by calling them *Mandarin Chinese, Yue Chinese, Wu Chinese, Min Chinese*, etc.

Then within each of these Chinese languages (i.e. Chinese language subfamilies), there are many varieties, some of which are mutually intelligible but some of which are not. Should these varieties within each Chinese language be considered different languages or just dialects of the same language? There is no easy answer to this question because the degree of mutual intelligibility and linguistic differences constitute a continuum and we do not have a clear-cut point where a language versus a dialect can be definitively defined. For convenience, let us treat the different varieties within each Chinese language as dialects, although we should keep in mind that some of these dialects are so different that they might be more like different languages. With this assumption, then, the different varieties of Mandarin Chinese, for example, are referred to as *Mandarin dialects*, and the different varieties of Yue Chinese as *Yue dialects*.

Since the phonetic and phonological systems of SC are based on the Beijing dialect and since the Beijing dialect is one of the Mandarin dialects, SC belongs to the group of Mandarin dialects. Among the Mandarin dialects, linguistic differences still exist but the differences are not as dramatic as those between Mandarin Chinese and other Chinese languages such as Yue Chinese, Wu Chinese, and Min Chinese. For example, many Mandarin dialects have similar consonant and vowel systems, although some of them do not have the post-alveolar consonants of the Beijing dialect and SC. In general, Mandarin dialects have fewer tones, mostly four or five, when compared to Yue and Min Chinese; however, the tonal pitch values can vary from one Mandarin dialect to another. For example, in Xi'an, a northwestern Mandarin dialect, the pitch values for the corresponding tone 1, tone 2, tone 3, and tone 4 in SC are 31, 24, 42, and 55 respectively (Norman 1988:196). Except for tone 2, which is just a little lower than 35 in SC, the other three tones between these two Mandarin dialects are very different: 31, 42, and 55 in Xi'an correspond to 55, 213, and 51 in SC respectively. For more details about the similarities and differences among Mandarin dialects, see Norman (1988:190–7).

Since Mandarin Chinese is the largest Chinese language, spoken by more than 70 percent of Chinese speakers in the northern and southwest regions of China, it is often referred to as the *northern dialect*. The other Chinese languages, spoken mostly in the southern and southeastern parts of China, may be conveniently referred to as the *southern dialects*.

In this section, I have provided a brief introduction to the degree of diversity among Chinese languages and dialects, and with this background knowledge we now turn to different varieties of SC.

12.2 Varieties of SC

Although SC is very similar to the Beijing dialect, these two are not identical. As mentioned in §1.2, the vocabulary and the grammar of SC are based on the broader northern Mandarin dialects and there are phonetic and phonological differences between SC and the Beijing dialect. For example, some syllable types used in the Beijing dialect (e.g. *biā* 'paste') are not used in SC, [w] may be pronounced as [v] in some syllables, and NEUTRAL TONE (§4.2.2) and RHOTACIZED vowels (§3.4.5 and §8.2) are pervasive in the Beijing dialect but much more limited in SC (see Chen 1999:37–46 for more details).

What is considered to be the prescribed standard of SC is typically found in national radio and television broadcasts in China and those SC speakers from Beijing that do not exhibit special local features peculiar to the Beijing dialect. However, not many SC speakers attain this particular standard accent. Since most Chinese speak at least one local Chinese language/dialect (usually their native language/dialect) and acquire SC as a second language/dialect, a wide range of accents with various degrees of approximation to the prescribed standard is found among SC speakers. In general, those accents that are closer to the prescribed standard with minor differences are generally accepted as standard accents of SC. That is, there is an acceptable range of variation in accents that is generally considered to be standard, just as the so-called standard English in North America also tolerates a range of slightly different accents. On the other hand, those accents with a stronger influence by local languages/dialects are often considered non-standard and can be labeled as *dialect-accented SCs* or *local SCs* (cf. Chen 1999:42). The local norm of SC or the acceptable standard accents of SC in a particular region can be closer to the standard type, somewhere between the standard type and the non-standard type, or closer to the non-standard type.

The prescribed standard in Taiwan and Singapore is essentially the same as that in mainland China with some minor differences in the use of vowel rhotacization and neutral tone and in vocabulary. In everyday speech, however, the acceptable norm of SC tolerates more differences from the prescribed standard. For example, one most obvious difference is the tendency to pronounce the post-alveolars [tʂ], [tʂʰ], and [ʂ] as dentals/alveolars [ts], [tsʰ], and [s] respectively (§2.2.4). In fact, many of the divergences in SC pronunciation found in Taiwan and Singapore are also shared by the norms of SCs in many regions of mainland China, especially those areas speaking southern dialects.

Not only does a local language/dialect alter the prescribed SC features to produce a local norm of SC and the non-standard accents, but a local language/dialect can also be influenced by SC. Since the use of SC has become more and more widespread, especially among younger generations, some local languages/dialects seem to have gone through subtle or not-so-subtle changes to become more like SC with respect to certain linguistic features and structures. Exactly which languages/dialects and what linguistic aspects have been undergoing changes require more detailed research.

The next section examines the major phonetic and phonological characteristics of the SC varieties spoken in Taiwan as a case study to illustrate the different types of SC discussed in this section.

12.3 SC in Taiwan

The local languages in Taiwan include Taiwanese (a southern Min dialect very similar to Amoy or the Xiamen dialect in Fujian Province in mainland China), Hakka Chinese, and Austronesian languages spoken by the aboriginal people. Since about three quarters of the people speak Taiwanese, the SC spoken in Taiwan is mostly influenced by Taiwanese. The accents of SC range from those closer to the prescribed standard to those somewhere between the prescribed standard and the non-standard Taiwanese-accented SC and to those with heavy Taiwanese accents. It is difficult to have a clear-cut classification of different SC varieties along this continuum of differences; however, for convenience and based on the discussion in the previous section, let us set up four types of SC: (i) *the prescribed standard* (as found in national broadcasts in China and Beijing SC speakers) or the textbook standard; (ii) *the standard norm* or *the standard accent* acceptable to SC speakers in general; (iii) *the local norm* or the *local standard* in actual usage; and (iv) *the non-standard accent* heavily influenced by the local language/dialect. Since the local norm and the non-standard accents differ mainly in the degree of influence from the local language/dialect and/or the degree of divergence from the standard norm, sometimes it may not be easy to cleanly separate the last two types. For example, *Taiwan Mandarin* (*Táiwān Guóyǔ*) is a term that has been used to refer to either the local norm of SC in Taiwan or the non-standard accents heavily influenced by Taiwanese or both. To make a finer distinction between these two types, I refer to the local norm of SC in Taiwan as *Taiwan SC* (which has less divergence from the standard norm and less Taiwanese accent) and the non-standard accents as *Taiwanese-accented SC* (which has more divergence from the standard norm and a heavier Taiwanese accent). The term *Taiwanese-accented SC* was previously used more generally by Duanmu (2000:263) to cover the SC spoken by those who grew up in Taiwan and whose first language is Taiwanese, whereas our use of this term is more restricted.

As mentioned in the previous section, the prescribed standard in Taiwan is essentially the same as the one taught and promoted in China and overseas with only minor differences. However, as in most regions in China, only a few speakers in Taiwan have acquired the prescribed standard accent.

More realistically, the standard norm of SC is one that is relatively close to the prescribed standard within an acceptable range of variation. In Taiwan, there are certainly speakers with the general standard accent but most SC speakers in Taiwan either speak in accordance with the local norm of SC or have non-standard accents. This state of affairs is also present in most regions in China. What is interesting is that, based on my impressionistic observation, the smaller number of speakers with the general standard accent seems to have decreased further over the years, and Taiwan SC, i.e. the local norm of SC, seems to have been moving toward the direction of Taiwanese-accented SC in the past decade; that is, some characteristics of Taiwanese-accented SC are more tolerated as the local norm.

The following subsections examine how Taiwan SC and Taiwanese-accented SC differ from the prescribed and general standard accents with respect to consonants (§12.3.1), vowels (§12.3.2), tone and stress (§12.3.3), and some additional aspects (§12.3.4). This case study is mostly based on my own observations and unpublished research over the years but various parts of the observations/data here can also be found in Kubler (1985), Wei (1984), and Duanmu (2000:263–7).

12.3.1 Consonants

The first major characteristic of Taiwan SC is that the post-alveolars [tʂ], [tʂʰ], and [ʂ] are not distinguished from the dentals [ts], [tsʰ], and [s], as the examples in (1a) show. The post-alveolar approximant [ɹ] is pronounced as [z], as in (1b). The lack of post-alveolars is also prevalent in Singapore SC and numerous local norms of SC. One consequence of this difference in pronunciation is that some words that are distinguished in SC are pronounced the same, as the examples in (1c) show.

(1) | SC | TAIWAN SC | EXAMPLE | | SC | TAIWAN SC |
|---|---|---|---|---|---|
| a. | [tʂ] | [ts] | zhè | 'this' | [tʂɤ]₅₁ | [tsɤ]₅₁ |
| | [tʂʰ] | [tsʰ] | chē | 'car' | [tʂʰɤ]₅₅ | [tsʰɤ]₅₅ |
| | [ʂ] | [s] | shé | 'snake' | [ʂɤ]₃₅ | [sɤ]₃₅ |
| b. | [ɻ] | [z] | ràng | 'let, allow' | [ɻɑŋ]₅₁ | [zɑŋ]₅₁ |
| c. | [ʂ] | [s] | shān | 'mountain' | [ʂan]₅₅ | [san]₅₅ |
| | [s] | [s] | sān | 'three' | [san]₅₅ | [san]₅₅ |

Some Taiwan SC speakers pronounce the post-alveolars as alveolars or somewhere between the dentals and the post-alveolars. For broad phonetic transcription, the same symbols are used for both dentals and alveolars, but for
these speakers, the post-alveolars, pronounced as alveolars, are somewhat distinguishable from the dentals. There are also speakers who pronounce both the
SC dentals and post-alveolars as alveolars without distinguishing the two series
of consonants. The [z] sound that is used to replace [ɻ] is more commonly
pronounced as an alveolar.

Note, however, that post-alveolars are not completely absent in Taiwan SC.
Some educated speakers do pronounce post-alveolars sometimes, e.g. in a formal speech or in teaching, but these speakers often confuse the two sets of
consonants and can mispronounce a dental as a post-alveolar and vice versa.
For example, shísān 'thirteen', which should be [ʂɻ]₃₅ [san]₅₅, is mispronounced
as [sɻ]₃₅ [ʂan]₅₅. These speakers know that there is a distinction between post-
alveolars and dentals based on what they studied in school, but they have not
really acquired the distinction and can 'overcorrect' their pronunciation in the
wrong way. However, Taiwan SC speakers (including those who do know the
distinction) do not emphasize the correct pronunciation of the post-alveolars
and consider such emphasis unnatural (Wei 1984:32).

The second common characteristic of Taiwan SC is the variation in syllable
final nasals, especially after [i] and [ə] vowels (Lin 1988). The examples in (2)
show that the syllable-final nasal can be either [n] or [ŋ], regardless what the
original nasal is. In actual articulation, the nasal can be a nasal approximant
without a complete closure in the oral tract, which makes it sound like having no
clear place of articulation. In (2), I use [N] to indicate this nasal approximant.

(2) | SC | TAIWAN SC | EXAMPLE | | SC | TAIWAN SC |
|---|---|---|---|---|---|
| a. | [n] | [n] | gēn | 'root' | [kən]₅₅ | [kən]₅₅ |
| | | [ŋ] | | | | [kəŋ]₅₅ |
| | | [N] | | | | [kəN]₅₅ |
| b. | [n] | [n] | yín | 'silver' | [jin]₃₅ | [jin]₃₅ |
| | | [ŋ] | | | | [jiŋ]₃₅ or [jiəŋ]₃₅ |
| | | [N] | | | | [jiN]₃₅ |

c. [ŋ] [ŋ]   *děng* 'wait'   [təŋ]$_{214}$ [təŋ]$_{214}$
        [n]   [tən]$_{214}$
        [N]   [təN]$_{214}$
d. [ŋ] [ŋ]   *tīng* 'listen' [tʰiəŋ]$_{55}$ [tʰiŋ]$_{55}$ or [tʰjəŋ]$_{55}$
        [n]   [tʰin]$_{55}$
        [N]   [tʰiN]$_{55}$

Like Taiwan SC speakers, Taiwanese-accented SC speakers also confuse syllable-final nasals and the distinction between dentals and post-alveolars, but they have an accent more strongly influenced by Taiwanese. For example, [ɹ] is pronounced more commonly as Taiwanese [l], which is articulated with shorter duration than the [l] in SC, or sometimes as a voiced alveolar affricate [dz] (a consonant present in Taiwanese but not SC). Furthermore, speakers of Taiwanese-accented SC can mix up syllable initial [n] and [l] in some words, which is also common in some local SCs in China, and pronounce SC [f] as [hw] because Taiwanese does not have [f]. Examples are given in (3), in which Taiwanese-accented SC is abbreviated as TASC. You may notice that some vowels and tones are also changed in TASC, which will be discussed in §§12.3.2–12.3.3.

🎧 (3)   SC   TASC   EXAMPLE   SC   TASC
   a. [ɹ] [l]   *rúguǒ* 'if'   [ɹu]$_{35}$[kwo]$_{214}$ [lu]$_{35}$[kɔ]$_{21}$
      [dz]   [dzu]$_{35}$[kɔ]$_{21}$
   b. [n] [l]   *nǐ*   'you'   [ni]$_{214}$ [li]$_{21}$
      [l] [n]   *lěng* 'cold' [ləŋ]$_{214}$ [nəŋ]$_{21}$
   c. [f] [hw]   *fēi*   'fly'   [fei]$_{55}$ [hwe]$_{55}$

It is important to understand that what I have done here is just a rough classification and the sets of characteristics of Taiwan SC and Taiwanese-accented SC are not necessarily clearly distinguishable. For example, a Taiwan SC speaker may sometimes also mix up syllable-initial [n] and [l] and mispronounce [f]. Therefore, the difference between the two varieties is a matter of the degree and frequency of divergence from the standard norm of SC and the perception of Taiwanese accent when speaking SC, with Taiwan SC having less Taiwanese accent and less divergence from the standard norm.

12.3.2 Vowels

It is typical for a SC speaker in Taiwan to pronounce [ɔ] or [o] as the main vowel in a /əŋ/ rime preceded by a labial consonant (Lin 1989:91–2) or to replace /u/ in a /uŋ/ rime with [ɔ] or [o], as the examples in (4) show. This rule of changing the main vowel to [ɔ] between a labial and a velar nasal and to replace [u] before a velar nasal is so prevalent that it can be considered to be part of the local norm. The variation between [u] and [ɔ]/[o] as in (4b) is also common among other SC speakers (cf. §8.1.5).

(4)   EXAMPLE   SC   TAIWAN SC

   a. (i)   *fēng* 'wind'   [fəŋ]₅₅   [foŋ]₅₅ / [fɔŋ]₅₅

      (ii) *péng* 'tent'   [pʰəŋ]₃₅   [pʰoŋ]₃₅ / [pʰɔŋ]₃₅

      (iii) *wēng* 'old man'   [wəŋ]₅₅   [woŋ]₅₅ / [wɔŋ]₅₅

      (iv) *mèng* 'dream'   [məŋ]₅₁   [moŋ]₅₁ / [mɔŋ]₅₁

   b. (i)   *dōng* 'east'   [tuŋ]₅₅   [toŋ]₅₅ / [tɔŋ]₅₅

      (ii) *cóng* 'from'   [tsʰuŋ]₃₅   [tsʰoŋ]₃₅ / [tsʰɔŋ]₃₅

      (iii) *hóng* 'red'   [xuŋ]₃₅   [xoŋ]₃₅ / [xɔŋ]₃₅

SC speakers in Taiwan rarely have *r*-suffixation and the accompanying rhotacization of vowels, which we discussed in §8.2. This is also a common characteristic among many SC speakers. As for the pronunciation of the basic rime *er*, some Taiwan SC speakers and almost all Taiwanese-accented SC speakers do not rhotacize the mid central vowel.

(5) EXAMPLE SC   TAIWAN SC   TASC

   èr 'two'   [əɹ]₅₁   [əɹ]₅₁ or [ə]/[ɤ]₅₁   [ə]/[ɤ]₅₁

The vowel differences in (6a) are also characteristics that Taiwanese-accented SC and Taiwan SC speakers may exhibit, but those in (6b–f) are more commonly present in Taiwanese-accented SC. The tonal differences for tone 3 in (6a) and (6f) will be discussed in §12.3.3.

(6)

	SC	TASC	EXAMPLE		SC	TASC
a.	[ou]	[o]/[ɔ]	*dōu*	'all'	[tou]₅₅	[to]/[tɔ]₅₅
	[ei]	[e]	*gěi*	'give'	[kei]₂₁₄	[ke]₂₁
b.	[wo]	[o]/[ɔ]	*guō*	'wok'	[kwo]₅₅	[ko]/[kɔ]₅₅
	[je]	[e]	*xiè*	'thank'	[ɕje]₅₁	[se]₅₁
c.	[y]/[ɥ]	[i]/[j]	*yú*	'fish'	[ɥy]₃₅	[ji]₃₅
		[ɨ]				[ɨ]₃₅
d.	[ɻ̩]	[ɯ]/[u]	*shí*	'ten'	[ʂɻ̩]₃₅	[su]/[sɯ]₃₅
			sì	'four'	[sɻ̩]₅₁	[su]/[sɯ]₅₁
e.	[ɤ]	[o]/[ɔ]	*gē*	'song'	[kɤ]₅₅	[ko]/[kɔ]₅₅
f.	[ən]	[ɛn]	*hěn*	'very'	[xən]₂₁₄	[xɛn]₂₁
						[xjɛn]₂₁

In (6ab), the high glides and the high vowel of a diphthong are deleted. In SC [e] and [o] are possible only when next to a high vowel/glide (§7.2.4). In Taiwanese, there is no such requirement, and Taiwanese-accented SC reflects this freedom. Note that the alveolo-palatal consonant in the second example of (6b) is pronounced as an alveolar [s]. Since alveolo-palatals are present only before a high front vowel/glide (§7.2.1), the palatal feature is naturally lost when the high front glide is not pronounced.

The high front rounded vowel and glide in (6c) are absent in Taiwanese and they are replaced with an unrounded high vowel/glide. The vowel can be [i] or slightly centralized to become a high central vowel [ɨ]. Taiwanese also does not have syllabic consonants and they are replaced with a high back vowel, either the rounded [u] or the unrounded [ɯ], as shown in (6d). The mid back vowel in Taiwanese is either [o] or [ɔ], so the mid back unrounded vowel [ɤ] in SC is replaced with either of these rounded mid vowels. Finally, the lack of the [ən] rime in Taiwanese also leads to the change of the vowel to a front vowel, as in (6f), or sometimes even to a back vowel such as [xun]$_{21}$ or [xən]$_{214}$.

Compared to consonant differences, the vowel differences, especially those in (6b–f), generally give a stronger impression of a heavy Taiwanese accent and the lack of proficiency in SC. The usual complaints from learners of SC about the difficulty in understanding Taiwanese-accented SC are often caused by the changed vowels and rimes, some of which are not even possible in SC. In addition, the vowel changes can also lead to potential ambiguities: for example, the word *xūyào* [ɕy]$_{55}$ [jɑu]$_{51}$ 'need' is pronounced like *xīyào* [ɕi]$_{55}$ [jɑu]$_{51}$ 'western medicine' (Kubler 1985:103).

In addition to these more obvious vowel differences, subtle phonetic differences may also contribute to the perception of Taiwan SC and Taiwanese-accented SC as being different from the prescribed standard. For example, the high back vowel [u] may be pronounced with only slight rounding or without much rounding: *kū* 'cry' [kʰu] may sound somewhere between [kʰu] and [kʰɯ]. Exactly what the fine-grained phonetic differences are and how the vowels of SC and the vowels of Taiwan SC/Taiwanese-accented SC are located in the perceptual vowel space require detailed acoustic investigation.

12.3.3 Tone and stress

Recall that the neutral tone occurs when a phrase final syllable becomes unstressed (§9.3, §10.1.2). Stress loss and the neutral tone occur less frequently in Taiwan SC and much less frequently in Taiwanese-accented SC since Taiwanese has only a few grammatical words with a neutral tone. One often hears the comment that, compared to Beijing SC, the SC spoken in Taiwan sounds 'heavy', which presumably is due to relatively few light short unstressed syllables. In general the kinship terms such as *māma* 'mother' and *dìdi* 'younger brother' and common grammatical morphemes such as the noun suffix *zi* in *yǐzi* 'chair' and aspect marker *le* in *lái le* 'have come' still retain the neutral tone, but the duration of the neutral-toned syllable in Taiwan SC and Taiwanese-accented SC is relatively long, which is unlike the shorter duration exhibited in Beijing SC. The neutral tone in disyllabic words is usually pronounced with a full tone, as the examples of SC and TASC in (7) show.

(7) EXAMPLE   SC   TASC
  a. *dōngxi*   'thing'   [tuŋ]55 [ɕi]2   [tɔŋ]55 [ɕi]**55**
  b. *xiānsheng* 'Mr.'   [ɕjɛn]55 [ʂəŋ]2   [sɛn]55 [səŋ]**55**
  c. *dìfang*   'place'   [ti]53 [fəŋ]1   [ti]53 [hwɑŋ]**55**
  d. *shétou*   'tongue'   [ʂɤ]35 [tʰəu]3   [sɔ]35 [tʰɔ]**35**
  e. *dànshi*   'but'   [tan]53 [ʂɿ]1   [tan]53 [su]**51**

Notice that the vowel/rime under the neutral tone in SC can be reduced as in (7cd) (§7.3.2) and that some consonants and vowels in TASC are pronounced differently as discussed in the previous two subsections. Although Taiwan SC speakers do not have a neutral tone in these words, compared to TASC speakers they usually have consonants and vowels closer to the standard norm. The example in (7a) is interesting in that in SC *dōngxi* with a neutral tone means 'thing' but *dōngxī* with a full tone in the second syllable means 'east and west'. In Taiwanese-accented SC and Taiwan SC, the same pronunciation is used for both meanings.

In §4.2.3 and §9.2.1, we learned that tone 3 has the pitch value 21 before another tone but stays as 214 in phrase final position, but Taiwan SC and Taiwanese-accented SC often do not have the final rise of pitch for tone 3, as shown in (8). There is a preference for having a phrase final low tone to replace tone 2 and the phonetically high neutral tone after tone 3 (§9.3), as shown in (8bc)[1]. Sometimes even the tone 2 derived from tone 3 sandhi (§4.2.3, §9.4) becomes a low tone, as the example in (8d) illustrates (cf. Duanmu 2000:265).

(8) EXAMPLE   SC   TASC
  a. *hénhǎo* 'very good'   [xən]35 [xɑu]214   [xɛn]35 [xɑu]**21**
     xiǎogǒu 'little dog'   [ɕjɑu]35 [kou]214   [ɕjɑu]35 [kɔ]**21**
  b. *bùnéng* 'cannot'   [pu]53 [nəŋ]35   [pu]53 [nəŋ]**21**
     kěxí   'it's a pity' [kʰɤ]21 [ɕi]35   [kʰɔ]21 [ɕi]**21**

---

[1] The word *kěxí* in (8b) has tone 2 for the second syllable in Taiwan. Beijing SC has *kěxī* with tone 1 for the second syllable.

c. *hǎo le*   'it's done'   [xɑu]21 [lə]4   [xɑu]21 [lə]21

yǐzi   'chair'   [ji]21 [tsɻ]4   [ji]21 [tsu]21

d. *xiǎogǒu*   'little dog'   [ɕjɑu]35 [kou]214   [ɕjɑu]21 [kɔ]21

Other minor tonal differences include: (i) the use of a different tone from SC for a particular word, e.g. *jiàoxué* 'teaching' has tone 4 in the first syllable in SC but tone 1 for most SC speakers in Taiwan (Duanmu 2000:264); and (ii) the use of a fixed tone 3 plus tone 2 sequence for reduplicated kinship terms by some SC speakers in Taiwan, especially when talking to children, e.g. *dìdi* [ti]53 [ti]1 'younger brother' is pronounced as [ti]21 [ti]35.

12.3.4 Other differences

CONSONANT WEAKENING (§7.3.1) and SYLLABLE CONTRACTION (§8.1.6) in Taiwan SC and Taiwanese-accented SC can differ from SC because of the differences in some consonants and vowels, as the two examples in (9) show (see also Duanmu 2000:266–7).

(9)   EXAMPLE   SC   TASC

a. Consonant weakening

zuò zhe   'sitting'   [tswo]53 [tʂə]1   [tsɔ]53 [tsə]21

→ [tswo]53 [dʐə]1   [tsɔ]53 [dzə]21

b. Syllable contraction

kéyǐ   'can, may'   [kʰɤ]35 [ji]214   [kʰɔ]35 [ji]21

→ [kʰəi]52   [kʰɔi]52

Since a post-alveolar is pronounced as a dental or alveolar in Taiwanese-accented SC (§12.3.1), (9a) shows that the corresponding weakened consonant of [tʂ] is a voiced post-alveolar in SC but a voiced dental or alveolar in Taiwan SC. In (9b), the resulting vowel of syllable contraction in Taiwanese-accented SC differs from that in SC since [ɤ] in SC is pronounced as [ɔ] in Taiwanese-accented SC (§12.3.2).

The intonation of Taiwan SC and Taiwanese-accented SC sounds different from that of Beijing SC in particular. This impression is partly due to the infrequent use of the neutral tone and the general lack of unstressed syllables, partly due to the preference of using a low tone at the phrase boundary as mentioned in the previous subsection, and partly due to the extensive use of Taiwanese discourse makers such as [a]55 and [xo]21 by Taiwanese-accented SC speakers. The discourse marker [a]55 usually occurs in phrase initial position to connect to the previous phrase or discourse (similar to 'and then . . .') and/or to attract attention to what is to be said, and [xo]21 is usually used in phrase final position to solicit agreement, to check if the listener is following, and/or to show friendliness. The use of these two discourse particles is one of the most salient characteristics of Taiwanese-accented SC speakers. However, whether or not the impressionistic differences in intonation also stem from differences in relative pitch level and/or pitch pattern (cf. §10.2.2) requires more research.

Finally, there are some differences in vocabulary and sentence structure. For example, *zhìliàng* is used in China and *pǐnzhí* is used in Taiwan to refer to the 'quality' of a product, and, as discussed in §§11.1–2, different loanwords may be used in China and Taiwan. One common syntactic difference in the SC spoken in Taiwan is the use of *yǒu* 'have' as a grammatical marker to replace the aspect marker *le*, e.g. *wǒ kàndào le* 'I saw it; I have seen it' in SC becomes *wǒ yǒu kàndào*. The details of lexical and syntactic differences are beyond the scope of this book, but the general point is that the more Taiwanese-influenced characteristics a speaker exhibits (both phonetic/phonological and lexical/syntactic), the more likely his/her SC will be perceived as Taiwanese-accented SC.

12.4 Summary

There is a wide range of diversity in SC due to the influence of local languages and dialects. This chapter attempts to classify different varieties of SC, and presents a case study from Taiwan SC and Taiwanese-accented SC to illustrate how local varieties of SC can differ from the prescribed or standard norm of SC.

- The Chinese language family consists of several mutually unintelligible languages such as Mandarin, Wu, Yue, Min, etc., and each Chinese language has many dialects that may or may not be mutually intelligible (§12.1).
- The prescribed standard of SC is spoken by only a small percentage of SC speakers and the generally acceptable standard norm of SC can deviate somewhat from the prescribed standard (§12.2).
- While Beijing SC is considered to be closest to the prescribed standard, other local or regional SCs are inevitably tinted with local languages/dialects. A dialect-accented SC variety is considered non-standard, but a local standard of SC can be close to the standard norm or to the non-standard type or somewhere in between (§12.2).
- To illustrate how a local SC can differ from prescribed standard, we have examined the characteristics of two SC varieties spoken in Taiwan, Taiwan SC (the local standard) and Taiwanese-accented SC (the dialect-accented variety). Fewer occurrences of post-alveolars, rhotacized vowels, neutral

tone, and unstressed syllables, and the strong tendency to use phrase final
low tone and to remove the final rise of a phrase final tone 3, are shared by
both SC varieties (§12.3).

- Taiwan SC and Taiwanese-accented SC differ with respect to the degree to
which the divergences from the prescribed or standard norm of SC are
exhibited. Taiwanese-accented SC diverges more away from the prescribed
norm, and is particularly marked by vowel differences and the intonation
pattern with Taiwanese discourse markers (§12.3).

EXERCISES

1 Consider the following examples from Taiwanese-accented SC.

(i) Give the IPA phonetic transcription of prescribed SC based on the *pīnyīn*
provided for each example.

(ii) Based on the discussion in this chapter, identify and explain the
pronunciation differences between TASC and SC in each example.

EXAMPLE			TASC	SC
a.	*ěrduo*	'ear'	[ə]21 [tɔ]55	
b.	*xuésheng*	'students'	[ɕje]35 [səŋ]55	
c.	*xuésheng*	'students'	[se]35 [sɛn]55	
d.	*zhīdao*	'know'	[tsu]55 [tɑu]51	
e.	*hǎo le*	'it's done'	[xɑu]21 [lə]21	
f.	*fēidié*	'flying saucer'	[hwe]55 [te]21	
g.	*guònián*	'celebrate the New Year'	[ko]53 [ljɛn]21	
h.	*shūběn*	'book'	[su]55 [pɛn]21	
i.	*règǒu*	'hotdog'	[dzo]53 [ko]21	
j.	*lǜsè*	'green color'	[li]53 [so]51	

2 Whenever you have a chance, talk to a speaker from Taiwan or watch news
broadcasts or movies from Taiwan.

(i) Collect examples that show the characteristics of Taiwan SC and/or
Taiwanese-accented SC.

(ii) Provide IPA phonetic transcriptions for the examples in both the prescribed
standard and the SC spoken in Taiwan.

(iii) Identify and explain the pronunciation differences between Taiwan
SC/Taiwanese-accented SC and the prescribed standard.

3   Whenever you have a chance, talk to a SC speaker that has a non-standard accent and find out where this speaker grew up and what local language/dialect he/she speaks.

(i)   Collect examples that show the special characteristics of this local SC or dialect-accented SC.
(ii) Provide IPA phonetic transcriptions for the examples in both the prescribed standard and this local SC/dialect-accented SC.
(iii) Identify the pronunciation differences between this local SC/dialect-accented SC and the prescribed standard.

Appendices

Appendix A. The International Phonetic Alphabet

The complete set of the International Phonetic Alphabet (IPA) is provided on page 283. The International Phonetic Association is the copyright owner of the International Phonetic Alphabet and the IPA charts. For more information, go to the IPA website: http://www.arts.gla.ac.uk/IPA/ipa.html.

In addition to the IPA, another set of phonetic symbols is in common use in North America and is sometimes known as the American Phonetic Alphabet (APA). One major difference is that for the vowel height, APA makes use of labels such as high, mid, low, tense, and lax whereas the IPA uses close (= high), close-mid (= mid tense), open-mid (= mid lax), and open (= low). Other differences relevant to this book are as follows:

IPA	APA	
y	ü	high front rounded vowel
j	y	high front unrounded glide or palatal glide
ɥ	ẅ	high front rounded glide
a		low front unrounded vowel
æ		low front unrounded vowel slightly higher than [a]
ɑ		low back unrounded vowel
		low back rounded vowel
ɐ		not fully open low central unrounded vowel
	æ	low front unrounded vowel
	a	low central or back vowel

When some studies use the IPA and some others use the APA for the discussion of the same language, one confusion that may arise is that the symbol [y] is the high front rounded vowel in IPA but the high front unrounded glide in APA. Another potential confusion is that for low vowels, the APA typically only distinguishes between [æ] as front low and [a] as central or back low, but the IPA makes finer distinctions for low vowels: [a] as front low, [ɑ] as back low, [ɒ] as back low rounded, [æ] as not fully open (i.e. slightly higher) front low, and [ɐ] as not fully open (i.e. slightly higher) central low. In addition, for consonants, IPA [ʃ], [ʒ], [tʃ], and [tʒ] are represented in APA as [š], [ž], [č], and [ǰ] respectively. And, for a retroflex, APA uses a diacritic dot underneath the symbol: e.g. [ʂ] in IPA is [ṣ] in APA.

In this book, I have followed the IPA for the consonant, glide, and vowel symbols, but I have departed from the IPA usage in two respects. First, for vowel height, I have adopted the APA convention in using labels such as high, mid, low, tense, and lax. Second, for tones, instead of using the graphic symbols in the IPA, I have adopted the numerical pitch values for transcription.

THE INTERNATIONAL PHONETIC ALPHABET (revised to 2005)

CONSONANTS (PULMONIC)   © 2005 IPA

	Bilabial	Labiodental	Dental	Alveolar	Postalveolar	Retroflex	Palatal	Velar	Uvular	Pharyngeal	Glottal
Plosive	p b			t d		ʈ ɖ	c ɟ	k ɡ	q ɢ		ʔ
Nasal	m	ɱ		n		ɳ	ɲ	ŋ	ɴ		
Trill	ʙ			r					ʀ		
Tap or Flap		ⱱ		ɾ		ɽ					
Fricative	ɸ β	f v	θ ð	s z	ʃ ʒ	ʂ ʐ	ç ʝ	x ɣ	χ ʁ	ħ ʕ	h ɦ
Lateral fricative				ɬ ɮ							
Approximant		ʋ		ɹ		ɻ	j	ɰ			
Lateral approximant				l		ɭ	ʎ	ʟ			

Where symbols appear in pairs, the one to the right represents a voiced consonant. Shaded areas denote articulations judged impossible.

CONSONANTS (NON-PULMONIC)

Clicks	Voiced implosives	Ejectives
ʘ Bilabial	ɓ Bilabial	ʼ Examples:
ǀ Dental	ɗ Dental/alveolar	pʼ Bilabial
ǃ (Post)alveolar	ʄ Palatal	tʼ Dental/alveolar
ǂ Palatoalveolar	ɠ Velar	kʼ Velar
ǁ Alveolar lateral	ʛ Uvular	sʼ Alveolar fricative

VOWELS

	Front	Central	Back
Close	i • y	ɨ • ʉ	ɯ • u
	ɪ ʏ		ʊ
Close-mid	e • ø	ɘ • ɵ	ɤ • o
		ə	
Open-mid	ɛ • œ	ɜ • ɞ	ʌ • ɔ
	æ	ɐ	
Open	a • ɶ		ɑ • ɒ

Where symbols appear in pairs, the one to the right represents a rounded vowel.

SUPRASEGMENTALS

ˈ	Primary stress
ˌ	Secondary stress
	ˌfoʊnəˈtɪʃən
ː	Long eː
ˑ	Half-long eˑ
˘	Extra-short ĕ
|	Minor (foot) group
‖	Major (intonation) group
.	Syllable break ɹi.ækt
‿	Linking (absence of a break)

OTHER SYMBOLS

ʍ	Voiceless labial-velar fricative
w	Voiced labial-velar approximant
ɥ	Voiced labial-palatal approximant
ʜ	Voiceless epiglottal fricative
ʢ	Voiced epiglottal fricative
ʡ	Epiglottal plosive

ɕ ʑ Alveolo-palatal fricatives

ɺ Voiced alveolar lateral flap

ɧ Simultaneous ʃ and x

Affricates and double articulations can be represented by two symbols joined by a tie bar if necessary. k͡p t͡s

DIACRITICS   Diacritics may be placed above a symbol with a descender, e.g. ŋ̊

̥	Voiceless	n̥ d̥	̤	Breathy voiced	b̤ a̤	̪ Dental	t̪ d̪
̬	Voiced	s̬ t̬	̰	Creaky voiced	b̰ a̰	̺ Apical	t̺ d̺
ʰ	Aspirated	tʰ dʰ	̼	Linguolabial	t̼ d̼	̻ Laminal	t̻ d̻
̹	More rounded	ɔ̹	ʷ	Labialized	tʷ dʷ	̃ Nasalized	ẽ
̜	Less rounded	ɔ̜	ʲ	Palatalized	tʲ dʲ	ⁿ Nasal release	dⁿ
̟	Advanced	u̟	ˠ	Velarized	tˠ dˠ	ˡ Lateral release	dˡ
̠	Retracted	e̠	ˤ	Pharyngealized	tˤ dˤ	̚ No audible release	d̚
̈	Centralized	ë	̴	Velarized or pharyngealized	ɫ		
̽	Mid-centralized	e̽	̝	Raised	e̝	(ɹ̝ = voiced alveolar fricative)	
̩	Syllabic	n̩	̞	Lowered	e̞	(β̞ = voiced bilabial approximant)	
̯	Non-syllabic	e̯	̘	Advanced Tongue Root	e̘		
˞	Rhoticity	ɚ a˞	̙	Retracted Tongue Root	e̙		

TONES AND WORD ACCENTS

LEVEL			CONTOUR		
ế or	˥	Extra high	ě or	˄	Rising
é	˦	High	ê	˅	Falling
ē	˧	Mid	e᷄	˧˦	High rising
è	˨	Low	e᷅	˨˩	Low rising
ȅ	˩	Extra low	e᷈	˦˨˦	Rising-falling
↓		Downstep	↗		Global rise
↑		Upstep	↘		Global fall

Appendix B. Tables for SC syllables: *pīnyīn* spelling and phonetic transcriptions

In the following tables, on the first column of each table, all non-glide initial consonants (i.e. the INITIAL) are listed, and the glides and/or rimes (i.e. the FINAL) are arranged on the first row of each table. The initial consonants are grouped according to the order of: (i) labials; (ii) coronal stops and lateral; (iii) dental affricates/fricative; (iv) post-alveolars; (v) alveolo-palatals; (vi) velars; and (vii) the so-called 'zero-initial'. Those zero-initial syllables in parentheses in Tables I and II are those beginning with a glide phonetically and in *pīnyīn* (see (7) in §5.2.4, §6.1.1, §6.2, and §8.1.3) and will be shown also in Tables III–IV. Each table cell consists of the *pīnyīn* letter(s) in italic and the IPA symbol(s)/phonetic transcription below.

Table I Syllables without glides: a single segment or a diphthong in the nucleus/rime.

	a	*e*	*i*	*ü*	*u*	*i*	*i*	*ai*	*ao*	*ei*	*ou*
	a	ɤ	i	y	u	ɿ	ʅ	ai	ɑu	ei	ou
b	*ba*		*bi*		*bu*			*bai*	*bao*	*bei*	
p	pa		pi		pu			pai	pɑu	pei	
p	*pa*		*pi*		*pu*			*pai*	*pao*	*pei*	*pou*
pʰ	pʰa		pʰi		pʰu			pʰai	pʰɑu	pʰei	pʰou
m	*ma*		*mi*		*mu*			*mai*	*mao*	*mei*	*mei*
m	ma		mi		mu			mai	mɑu	mei	mou
f	*fa*				*fu*					*fei*	*fou*
f	fa				fu					fei	fou

(*cont.*)

Table I (*cont.*)

	a	e	i	ü	u	zi	ai	ao	ei	ou
d	*da*	*de*	*di*		*du*		*dai*	*dao*	*dei*	*dou*
t	ta	tɤ	ti		tu		tai	tɑu	tei	tou
t	*ta*	*te*	*ti*		*tu*		*tai*	*tao*		*tou*
tʰ	tʰa	tʰɤ	tʰi		tʰu		tʰai	tʰɑu		tʰou
n	*na*	*ne*	*ni*	*nü*	*nu*		*nai*	*nao*	*nei*	*nou*
n	na	nɤ	ni	ny	nu		nai	nɑu	nei	nou
l	*la*	*le*	*li*	*lü*	*lu*		*lai*	*lao*	*lei*	*lou*
l	la	lɤ	li	ly	lu		lai	lɑu	lei	lou
z	*za*	*ze*			*zu*	*zi*	*zai*	*zao*	*zei*	*zou*
ts	tsa	tsɤ			tsu	tsɹ̩	tsai	tsɑu	tsei	tsou
c	*ca*	*ce*			*cu*	*ci*	*cai*	*cao*		*cou*
tsʰ	tsʰa	tsʰɤ			tsʰu	tsʰɹ̩	tsʰai	tsʰɑu		tsʰou
s	*sa*	*se*			*su*	*si*	*sai*	*sao*		*sou*
s	sa	sɤ			su	sɹ̩	sai	sɑu		sou
zh	*zha*	*zhe*			*zhu*	*zhi*	*zhai*	*zhao*	*zhei*	*zhou*
tʂ	tʂa	tʂɤ			tʂu	tʂɻ̩	tʂai	tʂɑu	tʂei	tʂou
ch	*cha*	*che*			*chu*	*chi*	*chai*	*chao*		*chou*
tʂʰ	tʂʰa	tʂʰɤ			tʂʰu	tʂʰɻ̩	tʂai	tʂʰɑu		tʂʰou
sh	*sha*	*she*			*shu*	*shi*	*shai*	*shao*	*shei*	*shou*
ʂ	ʂa	ʂɤ			ʂu	ʂɻ̩	ʂai	ʂɑu	ʂei	ʂou
r		*re*			*ru*	*ri*		*rao*		*rou*
ɻ		ɻɤ			ɻu	ɻɻ̩		ɻɑu		ɻou
j			*ji*	*ju*						
tɕ			tɕi	tɕy						
q			*qi*	*qu*						
tɕʰ			tɕʰi	tɕʰy						
x			*xi*	*xu*						
ɕ			ɕi	ɕy						

(*cont.*)

Table I (*cont.*)

g	*ga*	*ge*			*gu*	*gai*	*gao*	*gei*	*gou*
k	ka	kɤ			ku	kai	kɑu	kei	kou
k	*ka*	*ke*			*ku*	*kai*	*kao*	*kei*	*kou*
kʰ	kʰa	kʰɤ			kʰu	kʰai	kʰɑu	kʰei	kʰou
h	*ha*	*he*			*hu*	*hai*	*hao*	*hei*	*hou*
x	xa	xɤ			xu	xai	xɑu	xei	xou
	a	*e*	*(yi)*	*(yu) (wu)*		*ai*	*ao*	*ei*	*ou*
	a	ɤ	(ji)	(ɥy) (wu)		ai	ɑu	ei	ou

Table II Syllables without glides: a rhotacized rime or a vowel with a nasal coda in the rime.

	o	er	an	ang	en	eng	in	ün	ong
	ɔ	ɚ	an	aŋ	ən	əŋ	in	yn	uŋ
b			ban	bang	ben	beng	bin		
p			pan	paŋ	pən	pəŋ	pin		
p			pan	pang	pen	peng	pin		
pʰ			pʰan	pʰaŋ	pʰən	pʰəŋ	pʰin		
m			man	mang	men	meng	min		
m			man	maŋ	mən	məŋ	min		
f			fan	fang	fen	feng			
f			fan	faŋ	fən	fəŋ			
d			dan	dang		deng			dong
t			tan	taŋ		təŋ			tuŋ
t			tan	tang		teng			tong
tʰ			tʰan	tʰaŋ		tʰəŋ			tʰuŋ
n			nan	nang	nen	neng	nin		nong
n			nan	naŋ	nən	nəŋ	nin		nuŋ
l			lan	lang		leng	lin		long
l			lan	laŋ		ləŋ	lin		luŋ
z			zan	zang	zen	zeng			zong
ts			tsan	tsaŋ	tsən	tsəŋ			tsuŋ
c			can	cang	cen	ceng			cong
tsʰ			tsʰan	tsʰaŋ	tsʰən	tsʰəŋ			tsʰuŋ
s			san	sang	sen	seng			song
s			san	saŋ	sən	səŋ			suŋ
zh			zhan	zhang	zhen	zheng			zhong
tʂ			tʂan	tʂaŋ	tʂən	tʂəŋ			tʂuŋ
ch			chan	chang	chen	cheng			chong
tʂʰ			tʂʰan	tʂʰaŋ	tʂʰən	tʂʰəŋ			tʂʰuŋ

(*cont.*)

Table II (*cont.*)

		shan	shang	shen	sheng				
sh		*shan*	*shang*	*shen*	*sheng*				
ʂ		ʂan	ʂɑŋ	ʂən	ʂəŋ				
r		*ran*	*rang*	*ren*	*reng*				*rong*
ɹ		ɹan	ɹɑŋ	ɹən	ɹəŋ				ɹuŋ
j							*jin*	*jun*	
tɕ							tɕin	tɕyn	
q							*qin*	*qun*	
tɕʰ							tɕʰin	tɕʰyn	
x							*xin*	*xun*	
ɕ							ɕin	ɕyn	
g		*gan*	*gang*	*gen*	*geng*				*gong*
k		kan	kɑŋ	kən	kəŋ				kuŋ
k		*kan*	*kang*	*ken*	*keng*				*kong*
kʰ		kʰan	kʰɑŋ	kʰən	kʰəŋ				kʰuŋ
h		*han*	*hang*	*hen*	*heng*				*hong*
x		xan	xɑŋ	xən	xəŋ				xuŋ
	o *er*	*an*	*ang*	*en*	*eng*		(*yin*)	(*yun*)	
	ɔ ɚ	an	ɑŋ	ən	əŋ		(jin)	(ɥyn)	

NOTE: The syllable *o* [ɔ] in the second column is used for only two or three exclamation or interjection markers like *oh* or *ah* in conversation, so I have not discussed it in chapters 5 and 6. The pronunciation is close to [ɔ] and is relatively short in duration. A discourse level exclamation or interjection marker may differ in sound and syllable structure from those in content words.

Table III Syllables with the [j] glide.

	i	ia	iao	ie	iou	ian	iang	ing	iong
	ji	ja	jɑu	je	jou	jɛn	jaŋ	jəŋ	juŋ
b			biao	bie		bian		bing	
p			pjɑu	pje		pjɛn		pjəŋ	
p			piao	pie		pian		ping	
pʰ			pʰjɑu	pʰje		pʰjɛn		pʰjəŋ	
m			miao	mie	miu	mian		ming	
m			mjɑu	mje	mjou	mjɛn		mjəŋ	
f									
f									
d			diao	die	diu	dian		ding	
t			tjɑu	tje	tjou	tjɛn		tjəŋ	
t			tiao	tie		tian		ting	
tʰ			tʰjɑu	tʰje		tʰjɛn		tʰjəŋ	
n			niao	nie	niu	nian	niang	ning	
n			njɑu	nje	njou	njɛn	njaŋ	njəŋ	
l		lia	liao	lie	liu	lian	liang	ling	
l		lja	ljɑu	lje	ljou	ljɛn	ljaŋ	ljəŋ	
z									
ts									
c									
tsʰ									
s									
s									
zh									
tʂ									
ch									
tʂʰ									

(cont.)

Table III (*cont.*)

sh								
ṣ								
r								
ɹ								
j	*jia*	*jiao*	*jie*	*jiu*	*jian*	*jiang*	*jing*	*jiong*
tɕ	tɕja	tɕjɑu	tɕje	tɕjou	tɕjɛn	tɕjaŋ	tɕjəŋ	tɕjuŋ
q	*qia*	*qiao*	*qie*	*qiu*	*qian*	*qiang*	*qing*	*qiong*
tɕʰ	tɕʰja	tɕʰjɑu	tɕʰje	tɕʰjou	tɕʰjɛn	tɕʰjaŋ	tɕʰjəŋ	tɕʰjuŋ
x	*xia*	*xiao*	*xie*	*xiu*	*xian*	*xiang*	*xing*	*xiong*
ɕ	ɕja	ɕjɑu	ɕje	ɕjou	ɕjɛn	ɕjaŋ	ɕjəŋ	ɕjuŋ
g								
k								
k								
kʰ								
h								
x								

yi	*ya*	*yao*	*ye*	*you*	*yan*	*yang*	*ying*	*yong*
ji	ja	jɑu	je	jou	jɛn	jaŋ	jəŋ	juŋ

Table IV Syllables with the [ɥ] glide.

		ü	üe	üan	ün
		ɥy	ɥe	ɥɛn	ɥyn
b	p				
p	pʰ				
m	m				
f	f				
d	t				
t	tʰ				
n			nüe		
n			nɥe		
l			lüe		
l			lɥe		
z	ts				
c	tsʰ				
s	s				
zh	tʂ				
ch	tʂʰ				
sh	ʂ				
r	ɻ				
j			jue	juan	
tɕ			tɕɥe	tɕɥɛn	
q			que	quan	
tɕʰ			tɕʰɥe	tɕʰɥɛn	
x			xue	xuan	
ç			çɥe	çɥɛn	
g	k				
k	kʰ				
h	x				
		yu	yue	yuan	yun
		ɥy	ɥe	ɥɛn	ɥyn

Table V Syllables with the [w] glide.

	u	*ua*	*uai*	*o*	*uo*	*uei*	*uan*	*uang*	*uen*	*ueng*
	wu	wa	wai	wo	wo	wei	wan	waŋ	wən	wəŋ
b				*bo*						
p				pwo						
p				*po*						
pʰ		.		pʰwo						
m				*mo*						
m				mwo						
f				*fo*						
f				fwo						
d					*duo*	*dui*	*duan*		*dun*	
t					two	twei	twan		twən	
t					*tuo*	*tui*	*tuan*		*tun*	
tʰ					tʰwo	tʰwei	tʰwan		tʰwən	
n					*nuo*		*nuan*			
n					nwo		nwan			
l					*luo*		*luan*		*lun*	
l					lwo		lwan		lwən	
z					*zuo*	*zui*	*zuan*		*zun*	
ts					tswo	tswei	tswan		tswən	
c					*cuo*	*cui*	*cuan*		*cun*	
tsʰ					tsʰwo	tsʰwei	tsʰwan		tsʰwən	
s					*suo*	*sui*	*suan*		*sun*	
s					swo	swei	swan		swən	
zh		*zhua*	*zhuai*		*zhuo*	*zhui*	*zhuan*	*zhuang*	*zhun*	
tʂ		tʂwa	tʂwai		tʂwo	tʂwei	tʂwan	tʂwaŋ	tʂwən	
ch		*chua*	*chuai*		*chuo*	*chui*	*chuan*	*chuang*	*chun*	
tʂʰ		tʂʰwa	tʂʰwai		tʂʰwo	tʂʰwei	tʂʰwan	tʂʰwaŋ	tʂʰwən	

(*cont.*)

Table V (*cont.*)

sh	*shua*	*shuai*		*shuo*	*shui*	*shuan*	*shuang*	*shun*
ʂ	ʂwa	ʂwai		ʂwo	ʂwei	ʂwan	ʂwɑŋ	ʂwən
r	*rua*			*ruo*	*rui*	*ruan*		*run*
ɹ	ɹwa			ɹwo	ɹwei	ɹwan		ɹwən
j								
tɕ								
q								
tɕʰ								
x								
ɕ								
g	*gua*	*guai*		*guo*	*gui*	*guan*	*guang*	*gun*
k	kwa	kwai		kwo	kwei	kwan	kwɑŋ	kwən
k	*kua*	*kuai*		*kuo*	*kui*	*kuan*	*kuang*	*kun*
kʰ	kʰwa	kʰwai		kʰwo	kʰwei	kʰwan	kʰwɑŋ	kʰwən
h	*hua*	*huai*		*huo*	*hui*	*huan*	*huang*	*hun*
x	xwa	xwai		xwo	xwei	xwan	xwɑŋ	xwən

wu	*wa*	*wai*		*wo*	*wei*	*wan*	*wang*	*wen*	*weng*
wu	wa	wai		wo	wei	wan	wɑŋ	wən	wəŋ

Appendix C. Internet resources

Comprehensive internet resources

http://chinalinks.osu.edu/
(This site contains hundreds of China and Chinese language and linguistics related websites.)

Chinese language and dialect maps

http://www.lib.utexas.edu/maps/middle_east_and_asia/china_ling_90.jpg
http://www.rcl.cityu.edu.hk/atlas/index.htm

Pīnyīn and romanization

http://www.loc.gov/catdir/pinyin/romcover.html
(A Library of Congress page that contains correspondences between the Wade-Giles and *pīnyīn* romanization systems.)
http://www.edepot.com/taoroman.html (a comparison of different romanization systems.)
http://www.pinyin.info/
http://www.courses.fas.harvard.edu/~pinyin/ (includes a pronunciation guide.)

Chinese newspapers/media

http://www.cuteway.net/link.html
(This site contains a comprehensive list of links to Chinese newspapers, magazines, and media, including those in the US and Europe, and also links to some museums, encyclopedias, and digital maps.)

http://news.google.com/news?ned=cn (Google news – China)
http://news.google.com/news?ned=tw (Google news – Taiwan)
http://news.google.com/news?ned=hk (Google news – Hong Kong)
http://www.xinhuanet.com/ or http://www.xinhuanet.com (China)
http://news.chinatimes.com (Taiwan)
http://www.worldjournal.com (US)

Further reading

INTRODUCTION TO LINGUISTICS

Department of Linguistics, Ohio State University. 2004. *Language Files: Materials for an Introduction to Language and Linguistics.* 9th edition. Columbus, OH: Ohio State University Press.

Fasold, Ralph, and Connor-Linton, Jeffrey. 2006. *An Introduction to Language and Linguistics.* Cambridge: Cambridge University Press.

Fromkin, Victoria, Rodman, Robert, and Hyams, Nina. 2003. *An Introduction to Language.* 7th edition. Fort Worth, TX: Harcourt Brace College Publishers.

O'Grady, William, Archibald, John, Aronoff, Mark, and Rees-Miller, Janie. 2005. *Contemporary Linguistics: An Introduction.* 5th edition. New York, NY: St Martin's Press.

Radford, Andrew, Atkinson, Martin, Britain, David, Clahsen, Harald, and Spencer, Andrew. 1999. *Linguistics: An Introduction.* Cambridge: Cambridge University Press.

INTRODUCTION TO PHONETICS

Ashby, Michael, and Maidment, John. 2005. *Introducing Phonetic Science.* Cambridge: Cambridge University Press.

Ashby, Patricia. 1995. *Speech Sounds.* London: Routledge.

Catford, J. C. 2001. *A Practical Introduction to Phonetics.* Oxford: Oxford University Press.

Davenport, Mike, and Hannahs, S. J. 2005. *Introducing Phonetics and Phonology.* Oxford: Oxford University Press.

Johnson, Keith. 2003. *Acoustic and Auditory Phonetics.* Malden, MA: Blackwell Publishers.

Ladefoged, Peter. 2001. *A Course in Phonetics.* Fort Worth, TX: Harcourt College Publishers.

Ladefoged, Peter. 2005. *Vowels and Consonants: An Introduction to the Sounds of Languages.* 2nd edition. Malden, MA: Blackwell Publishers.

Ladefoged, Peter, and Maddieson, Ian. 1996. *The Sounds of the World's Languages.* Oxford: Blackwell Publishers.

Roach, Peter. 2001. *Phonetics.* Oxford and New York: Oxford University Press.

Trask, R. L. 1996. *A Dictionary of Phonetics and Phonology.* London and New York: Routledge.

INTRODUCTION TO PHONOLOGY

Carr, Philip. 1999. *English Phonetics and Phonology*. Oxford: Blackwell Publishers.

Davenport, Mike, and Hannahs, S. J. 2005. *Introducing Phonetics and Phonology*. Oxford: Oxford University Press.

Gussenhoven, Carlos, and Jacobs, Haike. 2005. *Understanding Phonology*. 2nd edition. London: Arnold Publishers.

Gussmann, Edmund. 2002. *Phonology: Analysis and Theory*. Cambridge: Cambridge University Press.

Jensen, John. 2004. *Principles of Generative Phonology: An Introduction*. Amsterdam: John Benjamins.

McMahon, April. 2002. *An Introduction to English Phonology*. Oxford: Oxford University Press.

Odden, David. 2005. *Introducing Phonology*. Cambridge: Cambridge University Press.

Roca, Iggy, and Johnson, Wyn. 1999. *A Course in Phonology*. Oxford: Blackwell Publishers.

Trask, R. L. 1996. *A Dictionary of Phonetics and Phonology*. London and New York: Routledge.

STANDARD CHINESE PHONETICS AND PHONOLOGY

Cheng, Chin-chuan. 1973. *A Synchronic Phonology of Mandarin Chinese*. The Hague: Mouton.

Duanmu, San. 2000. *The Phonology of Standard Chinese*. Oxford: Oxford University Press.

Howie, John Marshall. 1976. *Acoustical Studies of Mandarin Vowels and Tones*. Cambridge: Cambridge University Press.

Lee, Wai-Sum, and Zee, Eric. 2003. Standard Chinese (Beijing). *Journal of the International Phonetic Association* 33:109–112.

Li, Wen-Chao. 1999. *A Diachronically-Motivated Segmental Phonology of Mandarin Chinese*. New York, NY: Peter Lang.

Lin, Hua. 2001. *A Grammar of Mandarin Chinese*, Chapter 2. Munich: Lincom Europa.

Lin, Yen-Hwei. 1989. *Autosegmental Treatment of Segmental Processes in Chinese Phonology*. University of Texas PhD dissertation.

Wang, Jenny Zhijie. 1993. *The Geometry of Segmental Features in Beijing Mandarin*. University of Delaware PhD dissertation.

Wu, Yuwen. 1994. *Mandarin Segmental Phonology*. University of Toronto PhD dissertation.

CHINESE SYLLABLE STRUCTURE

Bao, Zhiming. 1990. Fanqie languages and reduplication. *Linguistic Inquiry* 21:317–350.

Bao, Zhiming. 1996. The syllable in Chinese. *Journal of Chinese Linguistics* 24:312–353.

Chung, Raung-fu. 1989. *Aspects of Kejia Phonology*. University of Illinois PhD dissertation.

Chung, Raung-fu. 1996. *The Segmental Phonology of Southern Min in Taiwan*. Taipei: Crane Publishing Co.

Duanmu, San. 1990. *A Formal Study of Syllable, Tone, Stress and Domain in Chinese Languages*. MIT PhD dissertation.

Duanmu, San. 1993. Rime length, stress, and association domains. *Journal of East Asian Linguistics* 2:1–44.

Duanmu, San. 2000. *The Phonology of Standard Chinese*. Oxford: Oxford University Press.

Lin, Yen-Hwei. 1989. *Autosegmental Treatment of Segmental Processes in Chinese Phonology*. University of Texas PhD dissertation.

CHINESE SEGMENTAL PROCESSES

Cheng, Chin-chuan. 1973. *A Synchronic Phonology of Mandarin Chinese*. The Hague: Mouton.

Duanmu, San. 2000. *The Phonology of Standard Chinese*. Oxford: Oxford University Press.

Li, Wen-Chao. 1999. *A Diachronically-Motivated Segmental Phonology of Mandarin Chinese*. New York, NY: Peter Lang.

Lin, Yen-Hwei. 1989. *Autosegmental Treatment of Segmental Processes in Chinese Phonology*. University of Texas PhD dissertation.

Lin, Yen-Hwei. 1993. Degenerate affixes and templatic constraints: Rime change in Chinese. *Language* 69:649–682.

Lin, Yen-Hwei. 2002. Mid vowel assimilation across Mandarin dialects. *Journal of East Asian Linguistics* 11:303–347.

Wang, Jenny Zhijie. 1993. *The Geometry of Segmental Features in Beijing Mandarin*. University of Delaware PhD dissertation.

Wu, Yuwen. 1994. *Mandarin Segmental Phonology*. University of Toronto PhD dissertation.

R-SUFFIXATION

Duanmu, San. 2000. *The Phonology of Standard Chinese*, Chapter 9. Oxford: Oxford University Press.

Li, Wen-Chao. 1999. *A Diachronically-Motivated Segmental Phonology of Mandarin Chinese*, §6.6. New York, NY: Peter Lang.

Lin, Yen-Hwei. 1989. *Autosegmental Treatment of Segmental Processes in Chinese Phonology*. University of Texas PhD dissertation.

Lin, Yen-Hwei. 1993. Degenerate affixes and templatic constraints: Rime change in Chinese. *Language* 69:649–682.

Wang, Jenny Zhijie. 1993. *The Geometry of Segmental Features in Beijing Mandarin*. University of Delaware PhD dissertation.

Wu, Yuwen. 1994. *Mandarin Segmental Phonology*. University of Toronto PhD dissertation.

Yin, Yuen-mei. 1989. *Phonological Aspects of Word Formation in Mandarin Chinese*. University of Texas PhD dissertation.

CHINESE TONE AND INTONATION

Bao, Zhiming. 1999. *The Structure of Tone*. Oxford and New York: Oxford University Press.

Chao, Yuen Ren. 1930. A system of tone letters. *Le Maître Phonétique* 45:24–27.

Chao, Yuen Ren. 1933. Tone and intonation in Chinese. *Bulletin of the Institute of History and Philology, Academia Sinica* 4:121–134.

Chen, Matthew Y. 2000. *Tone Sandhi: Patterns Across Chinese Dialects.* Cambridge: Cambridge University Press. (Chapters 1–2 on Chinese tone and tonal processes in general; chapter 9 on Standard Chinese tone sandhi.)

Duanmu, San. 1996. Tone: An overview. *Glot International* 2:3–10.

Duanmu, San. 2000. *The Phonology of Standard Chinese*, Chapters 10–11. Oxford: Oxford University Press.

Myers, James, and Tsay, Jane. 2003. Investigating the phonetics of Mandarin tone sandhi. *Taiwan Journal of Linguistics* 1:29–68.

Shen, Xiao-nan. 1989. Toward a register approach in teaching Mandarin tones. *Journal of Chinese Linguistics* 24:27–47.

Shen, Xiao-nan. 1989. Interplay of the four citation tones and intonation. *Journal of Chinese Linguistics* 17:61–74.

Shen, Xiao-nan. 1989. *The Prosody of Mandarin Chinese.* Berkeley, CA: University of California Press.

Shih, Chi-lin. 1986. *The Prosodic Domain of Tone Sandhi in Chinese.* University of California, San Diego, PhD dissertation.

Shih, Chi-lin. 1988. Tone and intonation in Mandarin. *Working Papers of the Cornell Phonetics Laboratory* 3:83–109.

Shih, Chi-lin. 1997. Mandarin third tone sandhi and prosodic structure. In *Studies in Chinese Phonology*, ed. by Jialing Wang and Norval Smith, 81–124. New York: Mouton de Gruyter.

Yip, Moira. 1980. *The Tonal Phonology of Chinese.* MIT PhD dissertation. Published 1990, New York: Garland Publishing.

Yip, Moira. 2002. *Tone.* Cambridge: Cambridge University Press. (Chapters 1–5 on tone in general and chapter 7 on Asian tone languages.)

Zhang, Nina. 1997. The avoidance of the third tone sandhi in Mandarin Chinese. *Journal of East Asian Linguistics* 6:293–338.

Zhang, Zhengsheng. 1988. *Tone and Tone Sandhi in Chinese.* Ohio State University PhD dissertation.

References

Bao, Zhiming. 1990. Fanqie languages and reduplication. *Linguistic Inquiry* 21:317–350.

Bao, Zhiming. 1996. The syllable in Chinese. *Journal of Chinese Linguistics* 24:312–353.

Carr, Philip. 1999. *English Phonetics and Phonology.* Oxford: Blackwell Publishers.

Catford, J. C. 2001. *A Practical Introduction to Phonetics.* Oxford: Oxford University Press.

Chao, Yuen Ren. 1930. A system of tone Letters. *Le Maître Phonétique* 45:24–27.

Chao, Yuen Ren. 1933. Tone and intonation in Chinese. *Bulletin of the Institute of History and Philology, Academia Sinica* 4:121–134.

Chao, Yuen Ren. 1948. The voiced velar fricative as an initial in Mandarin. *Le Maître Phonétique* 89:2–3.

Chao, Yuen Ren. 1968. *A Grammar of Spoken Chinese.* Berkeley, CA: University of California Press.

Chen, Matthew Y. 2000. *Tone Sandhi: Patterns Across Chinese Dialects.* Cambridge: Cambridge University Press.

Chen, Ping. 1999. *Modern Chinese: History and Sociolinguistics.* Cambridge: Cambridge University Press.

Cheng, Chin-chuan. 1973. *A Synchronic Phonology of Mandarin Chinese.* The Hague: Mouton.

Chung, Raung-fu. 1989. *Aspects of Kejia Phonology.* University of Illinois PhD dissertation.

Chung, Raung-fu. 1996. *The Segmental Phonology of Southern Min in Taiwan.* Taipei: Crane Publishing Co.

Clements, George N., and Hume, Elizabeth V. 1995. The internal organization of speech sounds. In *The Handbook of Phonological Theory*, ed. by John A. Goldsmith, 245–306. Oxford: Blackwell.

DeFrancis, John. 1984. *The Chinese Language: Fact and Fantasy.* Honolulu: University of Hawaii Press.

Duanmu, San. 1990. *A Formal Study of Syllable, Tone, Stress and Domain in Chinese Languages.* MIT PhD dissertation.

Duanmu, San. 2000. *The Phonology of Standard Chinese.* Oxford: Oxford University Press.

Keating, Patricia A. 1988. Palatals as complex coronals: x-ray evidence. *UCLA Working Papers in Phonetics* 69:77–91.

Keating, Patricia A. 1991. Coronal places of articulation. In *The Special Status of Coronals: Internal and External Evidence*, ed. by Carole Paradis and Jean-Francois Prunet, 29–48. San Diego, CA: Academic Press.

Kubler, Cornelius C. 1985. *The Development of Mandarin in Taiwan: A Case Study of Language Contact*. Taipei: Taiwan Xuesheng Shuju [Student Book Co., Ltd.].

Ladefoged, Peter. 2001. *A Course in Phonetics*. Fort Worth, TX: Harcourt College Publishers.

Ladefoged, Peter, and Maddieson, Ian. 1996. *The Sounds of the World's Languages*. Oxford: Blackwell Publishers.

Lee, Wai-Sum, and Zee, Eric. 2003. Standard Chinese (Beijing). *Journal of the International Phonetic Association* 33:109–112.

Li, Charles N., and Thompson, Sandra A. 1981. *Mandarin Chinese: A Functional Reference Grammar*. Berkeley, CA: University of California Press.

Li, Fang-Kui. 1966. The zero initial and the zero syllabic. *Language* 42:300–302.

Liberman, Mark. 1975. *The Intonational System of English*. MIT PhD dissertation.

Lin, Yen-Hwei. 1988. Consonant variation in Taiwan Mandarin. *Linguistic change and contact, Proceedings of NWAV-XVL, Texas Linguistic Forum* 30:200–208. Austin: University of Texas.

Lin, Yen-Hwei. 1989. *Autosegmental Treatment of Segmental Processes in Chinese Phonology*. University of Texas PhD dissertation.

Lin, Yen-Hwei. 2002. Mid vowel assimilation across Mandarin dialects. *Journal of East Asian Linguistics* 11:303–347.

Lyovin, Anatole. 1997. *An Introduction to the Languages of the World*. Oxford: Oxford University Press.

Norman, Jerry. 1988. *Chinese*. New York: Cambridge University Press.

Packard, Jerome L. 1990. A lexical morphology approach to word formation in Mandarin. In *Yearbook of Morphology 1990*, ed. by Geert Booij and Jaap van Marle, 21–37. Dordrecht: Foris.

Packard, Jerome L. 2000. *The Morphology of Chinese: A Linguistic and Cognitive Approach*. Cambridge: Cambridge University Press.

Peng, Shu-Hui. 2000. Lexical versus 'phonological' representation of Mandarin sandhi tones. In *Laboratory Phonology V: Acquisition and the Lexicon*, ed. by Michael B. Broe and Janet B. Pierrehumbert, 152–167. Cambridge: Cambridge University Press.

Pierrehumbert, Janet B. 1980. *The Phonology and Phonetics of English Intonation*. MIT PhD dissertation.

Ramsey, S. Robert. 1989. *The Languages of China*. Princeton, NJ: Princeton University Press.

Selkirk, Elisabeth O. 1982. The syllable. In *The Structure of Phonological Representation*, ed. by Harry van der Hulst and Norval Smith, 337–383. Dordrecht: Foris.

Shen, Jong. 1994. Beijinghua Shengdiao de yinyu he yudiao [Pitch range of tone and intonation in Beijing dialect]. In *Beijing Yuyan Shiyanlu* [*Working papers in experimental phonetics*], ed. by Tao Li and Wang Lijia, 73–130. Beijing: Beijing University Press.

Shen, Xiao-nan. 1989a. Interplay of the four citation tones and intonation. *Journal of Chinese Linguistics* 17:61–74.

Shen, Xiao-nan. 1989b. *The Prosody of Mandarin Chinese*. Berkeley, CA: University of California Press.

Shih, Chi-lin. 1986. *The Prosodic Domain of Tone Sandhi in Chinese*. University of California, San Diego, PhD dissertation.

Shih, Chi-lin. 1987. *The Phonetics of the Chinese Tonal System*. AT&T Bell Laboratories Technical Memorandum, MH 11255.

Shih, Chi-lin. 1988. Tone and intonation in Mandarin. *Working Papers of the Cornell Phonetics Laboratory* 3:83–109.

Shih, Chi-lin. 1997. Mandarin third tone sandhi and prosodic structure. In *Studies in Chinese Phonology*, ed. by Jialing Wang and Norval Smith, 81–124. New York: Mouton de Gruyter.

Shih, Chi-lin, and Sproat, Richard. 1992. Variations of the Mandarin rising tone. *Proceedings of the IRCS Workshop on Prosody in Natural Speech*.

Shih, Li-Jen. 2004. *Consonantal and Syllabic Adaptations in English Loanwords in Mandarin*. Michigan State University MA thesis.

Tseng, Shu-Chuan. 2005. Contracted syllables in Mandarin: Evidence from spontaneous conversations. *Language and Linguistics* 6:153–180.

Wang, William S-Y., and Li, Kung-pu. 1967. Tone 3 in Pekingese. *Journal of Speech and Hearing Research* 4:130–136.

Wei (魏), Hsiu-Ming (岫明). 1984. *Guoyu Yanbian zhi Yanjiu [Changes in the Mandarin Language in Taiwan]*. History and Chinese Literature Series No. 67. Taipei: National Taiwan University.

Xu, Yi. 1999. F0 peak delay: When, where and why it occurs. In *International Congress of Phonetic Sciences 1999*, ed. by John Ohala, 1881–1884. San Francisco.

Yip, Moira. 1980. *The Tonal Phonology of Chinese*. MIT PhD dissertation. Published 1990, New York: Garland Publishing.

Yip, Moira. 2002. *Tone*. Cambridge: Cambridge University Press.

Zee, Eric. 1980. A spectrographic investigation of Mandarin tone sandhi. *UCLA Working Papers in Phonetics* 49:98–116.

Zee, Eric. 2003a. The phonetic characteristics of the sounds in Standard Chinese (Beijing). Paper presented at *NACCL-15 (The Fifteenth North America Conference on Chinese Linguistics)*, Michigan State University.

Zee, Eric. 2003b. Vowel devoicing in Chinese. Class handouts at *Linguistics Society of America Summer Institute*, Michigan State University.

Zhang, Jie. 2000. Non-contrastive features and categorical patterning in Chinese diminutive suffixation – Max[F] or Ident[F]. *Phonology* 17:427–478.

Zhang, Nina. 1997. The avoidance of the third tone sandhi in Mandarin Chinese. *Journal of East Asian Linguistics* 6:293–338.

Zhang, Zhengsheng. 1988. *Tone and Tone Sandhi in Chinese*. Ohio State University PhD dissertation.

Glossary

ACCIDENTAL GAP A phonologically well-formed syllable or word which happens not to exist, such as [blɪk] in English and *[nje]₂₁₄ in SC. See also SYSTEMATIC GAP.

ACOUSTIC PHONETICS The branch of phonetics which studies the physical characteristics of the sound waves produced in speech.

AFFIX A morpheme that can only occur by attaching to a word or stem. An affix attached to the beginning of a word/stem is a prefix, such as *un* in *unhappy*, and an affix attached to the end of a word/stem is a suffix, such as *ness* in *happiness.*

AFFIXATION A word formation process of attaching an affix to a word/stem, e.g. the creation of *unhappiness* through attaching *un* and *ness* to *happy*. Affixation by adding a suffix is called suffixation and affixation by adding a prefix is called prefixation.

AFFRICATE A consonant produced with complete closure followed by slow release with fricative noise, e.g. [tʃ] in *church* and [ts] in SC *zuò* 'sit'.

ALLOMORPH A variant of a morpheme that occurs in a particular context: e.g. the English plural suffix *s* has three allomorphs: [z] after a voiced sound as in *dogs*, [s] after a voiceless consonant as in *cats*, and [əz] after a sibilant as in *kisses.*

ALLOPHONE A variant of a phoneme that occurs in a particular context: e.g. in English, [p] in *spot* is an allophone occurring after [s] and [pʰ] in *pot* is an allophone occurring syllable initially; in SC, [e] is an allophone of /ə/ occurring next to [i]/[j] as in *běi* 'north' and *yè* 'leaf' and [o] is another allophone of the same phoneme occurring next to [u]/[w] as in *gǒu* 'dog' and *wǒ* 'I'.

ALLOPHONIC RULE A rule that produces an allophone.

ALVEOLAR A consonant that makes use of the alveolar ridge in articulation.

ALVEOLAR RIDGE The bony area behind the upper teeth.

ALVEOLO-PALATAL A consonant that makes use of the alveolar ridge, the front part of the tongue, and the hard palate in articulation.

APICAL Articulated with the tip of the tongue.

APPROXIMANT A consonant produced with articulators approaching each other without enough constriction to cause friction.

ARTICULATOR Any specific part or organ of the vocal tract for speech production.

ARTICULATORY Pertaining to the articulation of sounds.

ARTICULATORY PHONETICS The branch of phonetics which studies the articulatory mechanisms of speech production.

ASPIRATED Produced with aspiration.

ASPIRATION Voiceless breathing that occurs after a consonant before voicing starts for the following vowel.

ASSIMILATION A phonological process by which a sound becomes more similar to an adjacent sound. If the sound becomes totally identical to an adjacent sound, the process is total assimilation. If a sound takes on only some features of an adjacent sound, the process is partial assimilation (see also TONE SPREAD).

ASSIMILATORY Pertaining to assimilation.

AUDITORY Relating to the sense of hearing or perception of speech.

BILABIAL A consonant produced with both upper and lower lips.

BROAD PHONETIC TRANSCRIPTION Phonetic transcription that does not include all the phonetic details.

CATEGORICAL Having discrete absolute distinctions between sounds or suprasegmentals (cf. GRADIENT).

CENTRAL For vowels, neither front for back, and for consonants, articulated with airflow along the medial line of the vocal tract (cf. LATERAL).

CLOSED SYLLABLE see SYLLABLE

CLOSURE The period of time the constriction of a consonant is made (cf. RELEASE).

COARTICULATION An articulation with overlapping of adjacent segments or tones when a segment or tone is influenced by adjacent segment or tone. Assimilation is a phonological process that has its origin in phonetic coarticulation.

CODA see SYLLABLE

COMPLEMENTARY DISTRIBUTION The allophones of a phoneme are said to be in complementary distribution when they occur in different and mutually exclusive contexts. See ALLOPHONE for examples.

COMPOUND A complex word formed by combining two words: e.g. in English, *hotdog* and *classroom*, and in SC, *jiēdēng* 'street light'.

CONSONANT INSERTION A phonological process that inserts a consonant in a particular context, usually between vowels or filling in the onset in an onsetless syllable.

CONSONANT WEAKENING A phonological process by which a voiceless stop becomes a voiced stop or fricative, a fricative becomes an approximant, or a long consonant become short. In general, the process reduces the degree of constriction and duration of the consonant.

CONSTRAINT A restriction on possible and impossible linguistic structures, representation, organization, or processes that applies either cross-linguistically or in a particular language (cf. RULE).

CONSTRAINT-BASED APPROACH An analytical approach in phonological theory in which constraints play the crucial role in accounting for phonological phenomena.

CONSTRICTION A narrowing or closure of articulators within the vocal tract at some particular point during an articulation.

CONTENT WORD A word with lexical content/meaning such as a noun, a verb, an adjective, or an adverb.

CONTOUR TONE see TONE

CONTRASTIVE see DISTINCTIVE

CORONAL A phonological feature for articulation made with the tip or blade of the tongue such as in dentals, alveolars, and post-alveolars.

DECLINATION A gradual general downward trend in pitch in a phrase or sentence.

DENTAL A consonant produced with constriction involving teeth.

DERIVATION The procedure by which an underlying representation is converted to surface representation through rule application.

DEVOICED When an original voiced sound becomes voiceless.

DIACRITIC A small mark added to an IPA symbol to reveal more details that distinguish different phonetic properties a symbol may exhibit; e.g. a dental nasal can be transcribed as [n̪] with a diacritic beneath the symbol as opposed to alveolar nasal [n]. See also Appendix A.

DIPHTHONG A complex vowel that changes the vowel quality during a syllable or the combination of two vowels in the nucleus, e.g. [ai] in SC (cf. MONOPHTHONG).

DISSIMILATION A phonological process by which a sound becomes less similar to an adjacent sound.

DISSIMILATORY Pertaining to dissimilation.

DISTINCTIVE Two sounds are said to be distinctive or contrastive when they can distinguish word meaning, i.e. when they are separate phonemes; e.g. /s/ and /z/ are distinctive in English since *sap* and *zap* have different meanings but differ only in the initial consonant (cf. MINIMAL PAIR). We can also say that /s/ and /z/ are phonemic consonants in English. A feature is said to be distinctive when it can differentiate two phonemes; e.g. the feature [voice] is distinctive since it differentiates /s/ from /z/ in English.

DISTINCTIVE FEATURES see PHONOLOGICAL FEATURES

DISYLLABIC Having two syllables.

DORSAL A phonological feature for articulation made with the back of the tongue or the body (both front and back) of the tongue.

F0 see FUNDAMENTAL FREQUENCY

FINAL In Chinese, the part of the syllable without the initial consonant (cf. INITIAL).

FOOT A fundamental unit of rhythm usually consisting of two or more syllables with one syllable bearing the stress or prominence.

FOOT BUILDING The process by which a sequence of syllables is parsed into feet.

FRICATIVE Consonant produced with a high degree of constriction but short of complete closure so that turbulent airflow with friction noise is created.

FUNCTION WORD A word with less lexical content or meaning and which has a grammatical function, such as a preposition (e.g. *to, for* in English), an article (e.g. *a, the* in English), a particle (e.g. the question marker *ma* in SC), or a conjunction (e.g. *and, or* in English).

FUNDAMENTAL FREQUENCY (F0) The rate of vibration of the vocal folds in speech production. If the vocal folds open and close (i.e. vibrate) 100 times per second, then the fundamental frequency (F0) is 100 Hz.

GEMINATION A phonological process by which a short segment becomes long; e.g. [n] becomes [nn].

GLIDE A vowel-like consonant produced with minimal constriction such as [j] and [w]. It is also called semi-vowel and is grouped with vowels as vocoids. A glide occupies the onset or coda position. Under some analyses, it can be part of a diphthong such as [aw] for [au].

GLOTTAL Articulated with constriction at the glottis.

GLOTTIS The opening between the vocal folds in the larynx through which airstream flows.

GRADIENT Distinctions of sounds or suprasegmentals varying along a continuum of some phonetic dimension without discrete categories (cf. CATEGORICAL).

HARD PALATE The hard bony structure at the roof of the mouth behind the alveolar ridge.

HEAVY SYLLABLE A syllable that has a long vowel and a diphthong in the rime. For some languages, a syllable with a single short vowel plus coda consonant(s) in the rime is also heavy. A heavy syllable is analyzed as having two moras.

HOMORGANIC Having the same place of articulation.

INITIAL In Chinese, the initial consonant of a syllable (cf. FINAL).

INTERDENTAL A consonant produced with the tip of the tongue slightly between the upper and lower teeth.

INTERNATIONAL PHONETIC ALPHABET see IPA

INTONATION Variation in pitch stretched over a phrase or sentence to convey syntactic and/or contextual meaning.

IPA A unified set of phonetic symbols used to transcribe possible sounds in all languages. It is designed to have a unique one-to-one correspondence between a sound and a symbol. See also Appendix A.

LABIAL A consonant whose articulation involves one or both lips.

LABIALIZED A consonant is labialized if it exhibits some degree of lip-rounding as its secondary articulation.

LABIODENTAL A consonant produced with constriction involving the upper lip and the lower teeth, such as [f] in English and SC.

LABIOVELAR A sound whose articulation involves both the lips and the velum.

LAMINAL Articulated with the blade of the tongue.

LATERAL A consonant articulated with constriction along the median line of the vocal tract while allowing airstream to flow over one or both sides of the tongue (cf. CENTRAL).

LEVEL TONE see TONE

LIGHT SYLLABLE A syllable that has a single short vowel in the rime. For some languages, a syllable with a single vowel plus coda consonant(s) in the rime is also light. A light syllable is analyzed as having one mora.

LIQUID The label for the class of consonants consisting of laterals and rhotics.

MANNER OF ARTICULATION A parameter in consonant classification based on the degree of constriction of the consonants; e.g. stops, fricatives, nasals, and approximants.

MARGIN The onset and coda of a syllable.

MAXIMAL ONSET PRINCIPLE The phonological principle that requires that a word medial consonant be syllabified as part of the onset before it is syllabified as part of the coda.

MINIMAL PAIR Two words that differ in a single consonant, a vowel, or a tone and that have different meanings. The different consonants, vowels, or tones in a minimal pair are separate phonemes and are distinctive.

MODIFIER A grammatical element that describes a property of a noun, a verb, or a phrase; e.g. *quickly* in *run quickly* and *blue* in *blue sky*.

MONOPHTHONG A vowel that has no change of vowel quality during a syllable, e.g. [a] in SC (cf. DIPHTHONG).

MONOPHTHONGIZATION A phonological process that changes a diphthong to a monophthong, e.g. from [ai] to [e].

MONOSYLLABIC Having one syllable.

MORA A phonological weight unit larger than a segment but smaller than a syllable. A syllable with one mora is a light syllable and a syllable with two moras is a heavy syllable. A short vowel has one mora, a long vowel or a diphthong has two moras, and a coda consonant may or may not have a mora depending on languages.

MORPHEME The smallest unit of language that carries information about meaning or function; e.g. the word *cats* consists of two morphemes *cat* + *s*.

MORPHOLOGY The branch of linguistics that studies the structure of word and word formation processes.

MORPHO-SYNTACTIC Pertaining to morphology and syntax.

NARROW PHONETIC TRANSCRIPTION Phonetic transcription that encodes detailed phonetic information.

NASAL A sound made with the airstream flowing through the nose. See VELUM.

NASALIZED VOWEL A vowel made with the airstream flowing through both the oral and nasal cavities.

NATURAL CLASS A group of sounds that share the same phonetic properties and pattern as a group in phonological processes.

NEUTRAL TONE A tone that occurs in a short unstressed syllable with variable phonetic realizations depending on contexts.

NON-SYLLABIC In syllable onset or coda position, i.e. not in nucleus position.

NUCLEUS see SYLLABLE

OBJECT In a sentence, a grammatical element that receives the action or denotation of the verb; e.g. in the sentence *I like dogs*, *dogs* is the object.

OBLIGATORY RULE see RULE

OBSTRUENT The class of consonants with complete closure or high degree of constriction such as stops, affricates, and fricatives (cf. SONORANT).

ONSET see SYLLABLE

OPEN SYLLABLE see SYLLABLE

OPTIONAL RULE see RULE

ORAL An articulation made with the soft palate (velum) raised to block the air passage leading to the nose (see VELUM).

PALATAL A consonant produced with the front of the tongue and the hard palate.

PALATALIZATION A phonological process by which a coronal or velar consonant becomes a palatal, palato-alveolar, or alveolo-palatal consonant, usually next to a high front vowel. The term can also be used to make a consonant palatalized.

PALATALIZED A consonant is palatalized if it involves the front of the tongue approaching the hard palate as its secondary articulation.

PALATO-ALVEOLAR A consonant made at the post-alveolar region by using the blade of tongue.

PARTIAL ASSIMILATION see ASSIMILATION

PARTICLE A grammatical element used to convey syntactic or contextual meaning; e.g. the question marker *ma* in SC as in *nǐ lái ma* 'you-come-*ma*; are you coming?'

PERCEPTUAL PHONETICS The branch of phonetics studying the perception of speech sounds.

PHONEME A distinctive (or contrastive) sound of a language that can differentiate word meaning and is also an abstract segment with predictable phonetic variants (i.e. allophones). For example, /p/ and /b/ are phonemes in English because the minimal pair *pan* and *ban* differ only in /p/ versus /b/ and have different meanings, and the phoneme /p/ has phonetic variants or allophones [pʰ] as in *pot* and [p] as in *spot*.

PHONEMIC see DISTINCTIVE

PHONEMIC TONE A tone that is distinctive and can differentiate word meaning.

PHONETIC FEATURE SEE PHONETIC PROPERTY

PHONETIC PROPERTY The component that can be independently controlled in speech production or the smallest unit that makes up segments (i.e. phonetic features) such as nasal, labial, aspiration, etc.

PHONETIC REALIZATION The actual phonetic production or phonetic variant of a phoneme, a word, an underlying representation, or any phonological form (see SURFACE REPRESENTATION).

PHONETIC RULE see RULE

PHONETICS The branch of linguistics that studies how speech is produced and perceived and what the physical properties or sound waves of the speech are.

PHONOLOGICAL FEATURES A set of phonological features or distinctive features is a set of phonetically derived properties used to distinguish all possible phonemes in languages, to uniquely characterize individual sounds, to define natural classes of sounds, and to describe phonological processes and rules.

PHONOLOGICAL PROCESS A process by which a phonological entity, such as a segment or a tone, is modified in a particular way; e.g. when a oral sound becomes a nasal sound, the process is called nasalization.

PHONOLOGICAL RULE see RULE

PHONOLOGY The branch of linguistics that studies how sounds and suprasegmentals are organized and represented, and how they vary phonetically in different contexts.

PHONOTACTIC CONSTRAINTS The set of constraints on possible and impossible sequences of segments within a syllable, a morpheme, or a word.

PHONOTACTICS see PHONOTACTIC CONSTRAINTS

PITCH The percept of rate of vibration, the frequency of a sound, or simply the auditory property of a sound that a listener can place on a scale from low to high.

PITCH CONTOUR The pattern of pitch movement; e.g. a level tone (such as the high level tone HH or 55) has no pitch movement and maintains the same pitch level (pitch height) within a syllable, whereas a contour tone (such as the falling tone HL or 51) exhibits pitch movement from one pitch level to another.

PITCH LEVEL The pitch height or scale of a pitch, e.g. high, mid, or low.

PITCH VALUE The numbers assigned to a tone to indicate its pitch level and pitch contour; e.g. the falling tone in SC starts with a high pitch level and ends with a low pitch level to form a falling pitch contour and is assigned the pitch value 51, with 5 indicating the highest pitch level and 1 the lowest.

PLACE OF ARTICULATION A parameter of sound classification based on the location where a sound is made within the vocal tract.

PLOSIVE A stop made with the airstream flowing outward from the lungs and the vocal tract.

POLYSYLLABIC Having more than one syllable or having multiple syllables.

POST-ALVEOLAR A consonant made with the tip or blade of the tongue and the region behind the alveolar ridge.

PREDICATE In a sentence, the part that excludes the subject. For example, in sentences like *I like dogs* and *I am a teacher*, *like dogs* and *am a teacher* are the predicates and *I* is the subject.

PREFIX see AFFIX

PREFIXATION see AFFIXATION

PRIMARY STRESS see STRESS

PROSODIC Pertaining to prosodic units and suprasegmentals.

PROSODIC DOMAIN Any phonological unit larger than a segment, such as a syllable, foot, phonological word, or phonological phrase, that is relevant to some phonological processes.

PROSODIC STRUCTURE Linguistic structure consisting of organized prosodic units. For example, in a word like *magazine* the prosodic structure consists of three syllables, *ma.ga.zine*, and two feet, (*maga*)(*zine*), with the first two syllables dominated by the first foot and the third syllable by the second foot.

PROSODIC UNIT A unit that is used in prosodic structure and organization and forms a prosodic domain for the application of phonological processes, e.g. syllable and foot.

REDUCTION A phonological process by which a segment or a sequence of segments is shortened or 'weakened' in some way. For example, a vowel becomes a short central vowel in an unstressed syllable or two segments within a rime are shortened into one.

REDUPLICATION A morphological (or word formation) process by which some phonological elements are repeated for lexical or grammatical purposes; e.g. *mā* 'mother' → *māma* 'mother' in SC.

REGISTER The pitch range available to a speaker. Technically, this term is used in the classification of tone in some tone languages. The pitch range is divided into high register, the higher half of the pitch range, and low register, the lower half of the pitch range. A high register tone has its pitch level and movement mostly within the higher half of the pitch range.

RELEASE The period of time or the point of time when the closure or constriction of a consonant is removed (i.e. is released) (cf. CLOSURE).

RESYLLABIFICATION A process by which a segment is reassigned from one syllable to another. For example, an original coda consonant is syllabified as an onset consonant, usually when a vowel-initial morpheme or word is added: the coda consonant [n] in the third syllable of *o.ri.gin* is resyllabified as the onset of the last syllable in *o.ri.gi.nal* when the suffix *al* is added.

RETROFLEX A post-alveolar sound made with the underside of the tip of the tongue (by curling the tongue backward) and the area between the alveolar ridge and the hard palate (i.e. the post-alveolar region).

RHOTACIZED Having the auditory quality of an *r*-like sound, e.g. the vowel before *r* (as in *far, bear*) in American English is rhotacized and the vowel in the SC syllable *er* is also a rhotacized vowel.

RHOTIC An '*r*-like' sound that may have somewhat different phonetic properties in articulation among different languages but share some similar auditory properties.

RIME see SYLLABLE

RIME REDUCTION A process by which the vowel in the rime becomes shorter or centralized or the segments within a rime are merged into one segment.

RULE A specific way of modifying a linguistic form used by a language. For example, a phonological process of nasalization that changes an oral sound to a nasal vowel can be manifested by a rule that changes an oral vowel to a nasalized vowel before a nasal consonant in one language but by a rule making the same change after a nasal consonant in another language. A rule that must apply whenever the condition is met is an obligatory rule and a rule that may or may not apply is an optional rule. Phonological rules derive surface representation (phonetic realization) from underlying representation and produce categorical outputs. A phonetic rule modifies a segment or suprasegmental in terms of phonetic properties that are not distinctive and produces gradient outputs (cf. CONSTRAINT).

SECONDARY ARTICULATION An articulation with a lesser degree of constriction simultaneously added to the primary articulation; e.g. a labialized [k], transcribed as [kʷ], has velar as the primary articulation and a lip-rounding property as the secondary articulation.

SECONDARY STRESS see STRESS

SEGMENT A speech sound such as a consonant or a vowel.

SEGMENTAL PROCESS A phonological process that modifies a segment.

SEMI-VOWEL see GLIDE

SIBILANT A fricative or affricate with high-pitched hissing sound; e.g. [s], [z], [ts], [ʃ].

SOFT PALATE see VELUM

SONORANT The class of sounds consisting of nasals, liquids, and approximants (i.e. non-obstruent consonants), which have the characteristic of allowing the airstream to flow out of the vocal tract with a lesser degree of obstruction (cf. OBSTRUENT).

SONORITY The openness and loudness (i.e. a type of prominence) of a sound (cf. SONORITY HIERARCHY).

SONORITY HIERARCHY The scale on which sounds are ranked based on the degree of sonority: e.g. vowels are more sonorous (have a higher degree of sonority) than consonants and a low vowel is ranked highest on the hierarchy/scale and a stop is placed lowest.

SONORITY SEQUENCING PRINCIPLE (SSP) A universal phonological constraint on syllable structure, which claims that the segments before and after the nucleus should have descending sonority.

STEM A morphological unit to which an affix can be attached.

STOP A consonant produced with complete closure within the oral tract.

STRESS A type of prosodic prominence typically resulting in longer duration, higher pitch, and/or greater degree of loudness within a syllable. A syllable with stress is a stressed syllable and a syllable without a stress is an unstressed syllable. When a word has more than one stress, only one stress is the primary stress and the other stress(es) have a secondary stress. For example, in a word like *o.ri.gi.na.li.ty*, the primary stress is on the fourth syllable *na* and the secondary stress is on the first syllable *o*. The primary stress has a greater degree of prominence than a secondary stress.

STRESSED SYLLABLE see STRESS

SUBJECT In a sentence, the part that indicates the doer of an action or entity to be described in the predicate; e.g. *That picture* in *That picture is pretty* and *I* in *I washed the car* are subjects.

SUFFIX see AFFIX

SUFFIXATION see AFFIXATION

SUPRASEGMENTAL A phonological element such as stress and tone that has a span larger than a single segment and is considered to be separable from segments.

SUPRASEGMENTAL PROPERTY A property or feature exhibited in a suprasegmental.

SURFACE REPRESENTATION (SR) The output of a sequence of rule applications which is considered to be the phonetic realization or phonetic representation of an underlying representation (phonological representation).

SYLLABIC In nucleus position.

SYLLABIC CONSONANT A consonant in nucleus position.

SYLLABIFICATION The procedure or rule of grouping segments into syllables.

SYLLABLE A phonological prosodic unit with a short sequence of segments that serves for the organization of words and utterances. A syllable can be divided into onset and rime, and the rime further divided into nucleus and coda. The onset and the coda contain one or more consonants or glides, whereas the nucleus usually contains a vowel or a diphthong, and less commonly a syllabic consonant. For example, for the syllable *strict*, the onset is *str*, the rime is *ict*, the nucleus is *i*, and the coda is *ct*. A syllable that ends in a consonant is a closed syllable (e.g. *pán* 'dish, plate' in SC) and one that ends in a vowel is an open syllable (*nǐ* 'you' in SC).

SYLLABLE CONTRACTION A phonological process by which segments in two or three syllables are reorganized into one single syllable.

SYNTACTIC Pertaining to syntax.

SYNTAX The branch of linguistics that studies sentence structure.

SYSTEMATIC GAP The absence of a group of phonological forms in a language as a consequence of some constraint.

TONAL COARTICULATION see COARTICULATION

TONAL PROCESS A phonological process that modifies a tone.

TONE A pitch difference or contrast that can distinguish word meaning. A tone that has similar pitch level or pitch height throughout the syllable is a level tone: e.g. tone 1 in SC as in *mā* 'mother' is a high level tone that sustains the high pitch through the syllable. A tone that changes the pitch level within the syllable is a contour tone: e.g. tone 4 in SC as in *dà* 'big' is a falling contour tone that starts with a high pitch but ends with a low pitch.

TONE 2 SANDHI The tone sandhi rule that changes tone 2 to tone 1 in SC when it is preceded by tone 1 or tone 2 and followed by any phonemic tone.

TONE 3 SANDHI The tone sandhi rule that changes tone 3 to tone 2 in SC before another tone 3.

TONE BEARING UNIT (TBU) The phonological element capable of bearing a tone, such as mora, nucleus, rime, or syllable.

TONE DELETION A tonal process that removes a tone.

TONE FEATURE A phonological feature, such as H (high) and L (low), that is used to distinguish and characterize different tones.

TONE INSERTION A tonal process that inserts a tone.

TONE LANGUAGE A language that uses tone, in addition to consonant and vowel phonemes, to distinguish word meaning.

TONE REDUCTION A tonal process by which a tone is simplified, e.g. from a complex tone such as a falling contour tone HL (high-low) to a simple H tone.

TONE SANDHI Variation in the phonetic realization of a tone under the influence of neighboring tones.

TONE SPREAD A tonal assimilation rule that expands a tone to a neighboring tone bearing unit; e.g. when a high tone in a syllable is spread to the next syllable with a low tone, the second syllable becomes a high-low falling tone.

TOTAL ASSIMILATION see ASSIMILATION.

UNDERLYING REPRESENTATION (UR) The phonological representation of sound structure in a morpheme or word that excludes phonetic information predictable by rules.

UNSTRESSED SYLLABLE see STRESS

VELAR A consonant that makes use of velum and the back of the tongue in articulation.

VELARIZATION A phonological process that adds a secondary articulation to a consonant by moving the back of the tongue toward the velum; e.g. the coda lateral in a word like *fill* is typically velarized (i.e. has undergone velarization) in American English.

VELUM The soft muscular tissue after the hard palate on the upper surface of the mouth, also called soft palate. The velum can be raised to block the air passage leading to the nose, producing an oral sound. When the velum is lowered to allow the airstream to flow through the nose, a nasal sound is produced.

VOCAL FOLDS A set of muscles located inside the larynx that can be moved together in vibration to produce a voiced sound or pulled apart to allow the airstream to flow through the glottis to produce a voiceless sound.

VOCAL TRACT The air passages through which speech sounds are produced.

VOCOID A sound with little obstruction of the airflow: vowels and glides.

VOICED Articulated with vibration of the vocal folds.

VOICELESS Articulated without vibration of the vocal folds.

VOICE ONSET TIME (VOT) The period of time lapse between the release of a consonant closure and the point at which the vocal folds start vibrating.

VOICING ASSIMILATION A phonological process by which neighboring segments share the same voice feature; that is, they are either all voiced or all voiceless.

VOWEL DEVOICING A process by which a vowel becomes voiceless.

VOWEL INSERTION A phonological process by which a vowel is inserted typically in a sequence of consonants.

VOWEL NASALIZATION A phonological process by which an oral vowel becomes a nasalized vowel.

VOWEL REDUCTION A process by which a vowel becomes shortened and centralized (closer to a central vowel).

WEAKENING A phonological process by which a segment becomes less constricted or shortened.

Index

Words in small capitals are included in the Glossary.